Aboriginal Policy Research

Moving Forward, Making a Difference

Volume III

Aboriginal Policy Research

Moving Forward, Making a Difference
Volume III

Edited by

Jerry P. White, Susan Wingert, Dan Beavon, and Paul Maxim

THOMPSON EDUCATIONAL PUBLISHING, INC.
Toronto, Ontario

Information on how to obtain copies of this book is available at:

Website: http://www.thompsonbooks.com
E-mail: publisher@thompsonbooks.com
Telephone: (416) 766–2763
Fax: (416) 766–0398

Library and Archives Canada Cataloguing in Publication

Aboriginal Policy Research Conference (2nd : 2006 : Ottawa, Ont.)
Aboriginal policy research : moving forward, making a difference /
Jerry P. White ... [et al.], editors.

Papers presented at the 2nd Aboriginal Policy Research Conference, held in Ottawa, Mar. 3, 2006.
"Volume III".
ISBN-13: 978-1-55077-162-6
ISBN-10: 1-55077-162-6

1. Native peoples--Canada--Social conditions--Congresses. 2. Native peoples--Canada--Government relations--Congresses. 3. Native peoples--Canada--Congresses. I. White, Jerry Patrick, 1951- II. Title.

E78.C2A1495 2006   305.897'071   C2006-906523-3

Managing Editor: Jennie Worden
Copy Editor: Katy Harrison
Cover/Interior Design: Tibor Choleva
Editorial Assistants: Megan Burns and Crystal Hall
Proofreader: Rachel Stuckey
Cover Illustration: Daphne Odjig, *Bundled and Ready*, 1982
                         serigraph, edition of 125, 21½" × 17½"
                         Reproduced by permission of Daphne Odjig.
                         Courtesy of Gallery Gevik, Inc. (Toronto).

Every reasonable effort has been made to acquire permission for copyrighted materials used in this book and to acknowledge such permissions accurately. Any errors or omissions called to the publisher's attention will be corrected in future printings.

Statistics Canada information is used with the permission of Statistics Canada. Users are forbidden to copy the data and redisseminate them, in an original or modified form, for commercial purposes, without permission from Statistics Canada. Information on the availability of the wide range of data from Statistics Canada can be obtained from Statistics Canada's Regional Offices, its World Wide Web site at www.statcan.ca, and its toll-free access number 1-800-263-1136.

We acknowledge the support of the Government of Canada through the Book Publishing Industry Development Program for our publishing activities.

Printed in Canada. 1 2 3 4 5 6 09 08 07 06

Table of Contents

Part Three: International Research

Acknowledgements

We would like to thank some of the many people who poured so much energy into this conference and helped make it a great success. First, we want to acknowledge the tireless efforts put forward by the coordinator, Sylvain Ouelette. This could not have been done without his amazing energy and commitment. At the National Association of Friendship Centres, President Peter Dinsdale, co-chair of the conference, was a central leader as was Alfred Gay. Many others contributed, but we wanted to specially note the work of Sandra Commanda. At Indian and Northern Affairs Canada in Strategic Research and Analysis, we would like to thank Éric Guimond, Erik Anderson, Patricia Millar, Bob Kingsbury, Norma Lewis, and Norma Chamberlain. At the University of Western Ontario we want to thank President Paul Davenport, Vice President (Research and International Relations) Ted Hewitt, and all the people in accounting and purchasing that played a role. From the Aboriginal Policy Research Consortium at Western, we want to acknowledge Susan Wingert and Nicholas Spence.

For those we have not named directly, we know how much you too have given. For our families, thanks for giving us the chance to do this project, we know you have picked up the extra. Thank you.

Jerry P. White
Dan Beavon
Susan Wingert

Introduction

Jerry White, Dan Beavon, and Susan Wingert

Introduction

In March, 2006, the second triennial Aboriginal Policy Research Conference (APRC) was held in Ottawa, Canada. This conference brought together over 1,200 researchers and policy-makers from across Canada and around the world. Aboriginal and non-Aboriginal delegates (representing government, Aboriginal organizations, universities, non-governmental organizations, and think tanks) came together to disseminate, assess, learn, and push forward evidence-based research in order to advance policy and program development. The conference was a continuation of the work begun at the first APRC held in November, 2002. The 2002 conference was co-hosted by Indian and Northern Affairs Canada (INAC) and the University of Western Ontario (UWO),[1] with the participation of nearly 20 federal departments and agencies, and four national, non-political Aboriginal organizations. By promoting interaction between researchers, policy-makers, and Aboriginal people, the conference was intended to: expand our knowledge of the social, economic, and demographic determinants of Aboriginal well-being; identify and facilitate the means by which this knowledge may be translated into effective policies; and allow outstanding policy needs to shape the research agenda within government, academia, and Aboriginal communities.

The 2002 Aboriginal Policy Research Conference was the largest of its kind ever held in Canada, with about 700 policy-makers, researchers, scientists, academics, and Aboriginal community leaders coming together to examine and discuss cutting-edge research on Aboriginal issues. The main portion of the conference spanned several days, and included over fifty workshops. In addition to and separate from the conference itself, several federal departments and agencies independently organized pre- and post-conference meetings and events related to Aboriginal research in order to capitalize on the confluence of participants. Most notably, the Social Sciences and Humanities Research Council (SSHRC) held its first major consultation on Aboriginal research the day after the conference ended. These consultations led to the creation of SSHRC's Aboriginal Research Grant Program which supports university-based researchers and Aboriginal community organizations in conducting research on issues of concern to Aboriginal peoples.[2]

The Impetus for the First Aboriginal Policy Research Conference

The idea for holding a national conference dedicated to Aboriginal issues grew from simple frustration. While there are many large conferences held in Canada every year, Aboriginal issues are often at best only an afterthought or sub-theme. More frequently, Aboriginal issues are as marginalized as the people themselves, and are either omitted from the planning agenda or are begrudgingly given the odd token workshop at other national fora. While Aboriginal peoples account for only about 3% of the Canadian population, issues pertaining to them occupy a dispro-portionate amount of public discourse. In fact, in any given year, the Aboriginal policy agenda accounts for anywhere from 10–30% of Parliament's time, and liti-gation cases pertaining to Aboriginal issues have no rival in terms of the hundreds of billions of dollars in contingent liability that are at risk to the Crown. Given these and other policy needs, such as those posed by the dire socio-economic conditions in which many Aboriginal people live, it seems almost bizarre that there are so few opportunities to promote evidence-based decision-making and timely, high-quality research on Aboriginal issues. Hence, the 2002 Aboriginal Policy Research Conference was born.

In order to address the shortcomings of other conferences, the APRC was designed and dedicated first to crosscutting Aboriginal policy research covering issues of interest to all Aboriginal peoples regardless of status, membership, or place of residence. Second, the conference was designed to be national in scope, bringing together stakeholders from across Canada, in order to provide a forum for discussing a variety of issues related to Aboriginal policy research. Finally, in designing the conference, we specifically sought to promote structured dialogue among researchers, policy-makers and Aboriginal community representatives.

The first conference was seen, worldwide, as an important and successful event.[3] The feedback that we received from participants indicated that the confer-ence provided excellent value and should be held at regular intervals. It was decided, given the wide scope and effort needed to organize a conference of this magnitude, that it should be held every three years. In March, 2006, the second APRC was held.

Aboriginal Policy Research Conference 2006

The 2006 APRC was jointly organized by Indian and Northern Affairs Canada, the University of Western Ontario, and the National Association of Friendship Centres (NAFC).[4] The 2006 APRC was intended to: (1) expand our knowledge of Aboriginal issues; (2) provide an important forum where these ideas and beliefs could be openly discussed and debated; (3) integrate research from diverse themes; (4) highlight research on Aboriginal women's issues; (5) highlight research on urban Aboriginal issues; and (6) allow outstanding policy needs to shape the future research agenda.

Although the 2002 APRC was quite successful, we wanted to raise the bar for the 2006 event. During and after the 2002 conference, we elicited feedback, both formally and informally, from delegates, researchers, sponsors, and participating organizations. We acted on three suggestions from these groups for improving the 2006 conference.

First, we made a concerted effort to ensure that Aboriginal youth participated in the 2006 conference, because today's youth will be tomorrow's leaders. The NAFC organized a special selection process that allowed us to sponsor and bring over 30 Aboriginal youth delegates from across Canada to the conference. The NAFC solicited the participation of Aboriginal youth with a focus on university students or recent university graduates. A call letter was sent to more than 100 of the NAFC centres across Canada. Potential youth delegates were required to fill out an application form, and write a letter outlining why they should be selected. The NAFC set up an adjudication body that ensured the best candidates were selected, and that these youth represented all the regions of Canada. The travel and accommodation expenses of these Aboriginal youth delegates were covered by the conference.

A parallel track was also put in place in order to encourage young researchers to participate at the conference. A graduate-student research competition was organized and advertised across Canada. Aboriginal and non-Aboriginal graduate students were invited to submit an abstract of their research. Nearly 40 submissions were received, and a blue ribbon panel selected 12 graduate students to present their research at the conference. The travel and accommodation costs of these graduate students were also covered by the conference. The research papers of the 12 graduate students were judged by a blue ribbon panel and the top five students were awarded financial scholarships of $1,000 to help with their studies.

Second, at the 2002 conference, research sessions and workshops were organized by the sponsors. The sponsors (government departments and Aboriginal organizations) showcased their own research, or research that they found interesting or important. At the 2002 conference, there was no venue for accepting research that was not sponsored. For the 2006 conference, we wanted to attract a broader range of research, so a call for papers was organized and advertised across Canada. Over 70 submissions were received from academics and community-based researchers. About half of these submissions were selected for inclusion in the conference program.

Third, the 2002 conference focused solely on Canadian research on Aboriginal issues. For the 2006 conference, we accepted research on international Indigenous issues, and many foreign scholars participated. In fact, the United Nations Permanent Forum on Indigenous Issues held one of its five world consultations at the conference. This consultation brought experts on well-being from around the globe, and greatly enhanced the depth of international involvement at the 2006 APRC.

The APRC is a vehicle for knowledge dissemination. Its primary goal is to showcase the wide body of high-quality research that has recently been conducted on Aboriginal issues in order to promote evidence-based policy making. This conference is dedicated solely to Aboriginal policy research in order to promote interaction between researchers, policy-makers, and Aboriginal peoples. It is hoped that this interaction will continue to facilitate the means by which research or knowledge can be translated into effective policies.

Of course, many different groups have vested interests in conducting research, and in the production of knowledge and its dissemination. Some battle lines have already been drawn over a wide variety of controversial issues pertaining to Aboriginal research. For example, can the research enterprise coexist with the principles of "ownership, control, access, and possession (OCAP)?" Are different ethical standards required for doing research on Aboriginal issues? Does Indigenous traditional knowledge (ITK) compete with, or compliment Western-based scientific approaches? Does one size fit all, or do we need separate research, policies, and programs for First Nations, Métis, and Inuit? Many of these issues are both emotionally and politically charged. These issues, and the passion that they evoke, render Aboriginal research a fascinating and exciting field of endeavour. The APRC provides an important forum where these ideas and beliefs can be openly discussed and debated, while respecting the diversity of opinions which exist.

The APRC was designed to examine themes horizontally. Rather than looking at research themes (e.g., justice, social welfare, economics, health, governance, demographics) in isolation from one another, an attempt was made to integrate these themes together in the more holistic fashion that figures so prominently in Aboriginal cultures. By bringing together diverse research themes, we hoped that more informed policies would be developed that better represent the realities faced by Aboriginal peoples.

This conference was also designed to ensure that gender-based issues were prominent. In addition to integrating gender-based issues with the many topics of the conference, specific sessions were designated to address issues of particular importance to policies affecting Aboriginal women. This included, for instance, a one-day pre-conference workshop on gender issues related to defining identity and Indian status (often referred to as Bill C-31). This pre-conference workshop will have its own book that will be published as a third volume of the 2006 proceedings, and the fifth volume in the *Aboriginal Policy Research* series.

The conference also gave considerable attention to the geographic divide that exists between rural and urban environments. Nearly half of the Aboriginal population lives in urban environments, yet little research or policy attention is devoted to this fact. Specific sessions were designated to address research that has been undertaken with respect to Aboriginal urban issues.

The conference engaged policy-makers and Aboriginal people as active partici-pants, rather than as passive spectators. By engaging these two groups, research gaps can be more easily identified, and researchers can be more easily apprised of how to make their work more relevant to policy-makers. In addition, the confer-ence promoted the establishment of networks among the various stakeholders in Aboriginal research. These relationships will provide continuous feedback, ensuring that policy needs continue to direct research agendas long after the conference has ended.

In the end, 1,200 delegates participated at the conference from Canada and numerous countries in Europe, Asia, Latin America, North America, and the South Pacific. The conference planning included 20 federal government departments and organizations,[5] seven Aboriginal organizations,[6] four private corporations,[7] and the University of Western Ontario. Feedback from participants and sponsors indicates that the 2006 conference was even more successful than the previous one. This was not too surprising given that there were over 90 research workshops, in addition to the plenary sessions, where delegates met to hear presentations and discuss research and policy issues.[8]

Breaking New Ground

While the APRC brought people from many nationalities and ethnicities together, it also provided a forum for showcasing Inuit, Métis and First Nations perform-ing arts. The conference delegates were exposed to a wide variety of cultural presentations and entertainment. Métis fiddling sensation Sierra Nobel energized delegates with her youthful passion and the virtuosity of her music. Different First Nations drum groups energized the audience. Juno and Academy Award–winner Buffy Sainte-Marie entertained and mesmerized everyone. We saw demonstra-tions of Métis fancy dancing, and the skill and artistic splendour of two-time world champion hoop dancer, Lisa Odjig. We heard the rhythmic and haunting sounds of Inuit throat singers, Karin and Kathy Kettler (sisters and members of the Nukariik First Nation), and we laughed uproariously at the humour of Drew Haydon Taylor (the ongoing adventures of the blue-eyed Ojibway). The confer-ence was indeed a place where diverse Aboriginal cultures met, and the artistic talents of the aforementioned performers were shared with delegates from across Canada and around the world.

Research, Policy, and Evidence-based Decisions

It was Lewis Carroll who said, "If you don't know where you are going, any road will get you there."[9] Knowing where you are going requires a plan, and that can only be based on understanding the current and past conditions. The first APRC, and the 2006 conference, was centred on promoting evidence-based policy making. We stated previously that, in part, our conference was designed to deal with the communication challenges that face social scientists, both inside and outside of government, policy-makers, and the Aboriginal community. Could we bring these different communities of interest together to develop a better understanding of the problems and processes that create the poor socio-economic conditions facing Aboriginal people in Canada? And equally, can we find the basis that has created the many successes in the Aboriginal community? Could we develop the co-operative relations that would foster evidence-based policy making and thereby make improvements in those conditions? And equally, can we develop those relations in order to promote the "best practices" in terms of the successes? We are acutely aware that policy-makers and researchers, both those in and out of government, too often live and work in isolation from each other. This means that the prerequisite linkages between research and policy are not always present. This linkage is something we referred to in earlier volumes as the research-policy nexus.[10]

Our aim has been to strengthen that research-policy nexus. The APRC is first and foremost a vehicle for knowledge dissemination, and with a "captive" audience of many senior federal policy-makers,[11] the conference was able to enhance dialogue between researchers and decision-makers and, ultimately, promote evidence-based decision making. More broadly, both the 2002 and 2006 conferences succeeded in helping to raise the profile of Aboriginal policy research issues, including research gaps, promoting horizontality, and enhancing dialogue with Aboriginal peoples.

Moreover, in order to produce superior quality research, there is much to be gained when researchers, both in and out of government, work in co-operation on problems and issues together. Beyond just disseminating the results of research, the APRC was also about the discussion and sharing of research agendas, facilitating data access, and assisting in analysis through mutual critique and review.

We feel strongly that the highest quality research must be produced, and in turn that research must be communicated to policy-makers for consideration in formulating agendas for the future. If you wish to make policy on more than ideological and subjective grounds, then you need to help produce and use high calibre research understandings. It is simply not enough to delve superficially into issues, nor be driven by political agendas that have little grounding in the current situation. The APRC is designed to challenge ideologically driven thinking and push people past prejudice, superficiality, and subjectivity.

Policy that affects Aboriginal people is made by Aboriginal organizations, Aboriginal governments, and Aboriginal communities. It is also made by national and provincial governments and the civil service and civil society that attaches to those systems. We encourage all these peoples and bodies to embrace the realities they face with the best understandings of the world that evidence can give them.

Volume Three—The Contents of the Proceedings

Our set of research and policy discussions presented here is simply an attempt to bring forward some of the vast quantity of first-class research presented at the conference. This set of papers represent a small sample of the contributions made at the conference.

This volume of selected proceedings from 2006[12] are divided into themes. Our purpose was to group research into sets of ideas where the reader might find the content complementary. In this volume (number 3 in our series) we have three sections: (1) Education and Employment Transitions, (2) Dimensions of Socio-economic Well-being and, (3) International Research.

In section one, we have a range of interesting issues related to education and transitions to employment. Ciceri and Scott (Chapter 1) note that economic security is a central issue facing Aboriginal people today. Employment represents a key source of income, provides access to income support programs (such as employment insurance and pension benefits), facilitates self-development, and enables individuals to contribute to the collective and develop social networks. Aboriginal people continue to be disadvantaged in the labour market compared to other Canadians. Using data from the 2001 census, Ciceri and Scott examine the determinants of employment among Aboriginal people in Canada in order to inform policy. They emphasize that "policies and programs must embody an understanding of the 'network of circumstances' surrounding an individual."

We chose one paper that looks at the teaching level itself. Anthony N. Ezeife (Chapter 3) draws our attention to the low representation and relative poor performance of students from Indigenous cultural backgrounds in math and science courses. He examines a case study on Walpole Island, and weaves in the general problems seen across Canada, where it has been observed that Aboriginal students shy away from these courses and that a high percentage of those who do enrol often drop out, not just from math and science, but eventually out of school itself. Ezeife argues that a good way to address this problem is to adopt culture-sensitive and holistic curricula in teaching these students—an approach that was initiated in the pilot study on Walpole Island. He argues that it is both the content and the form of the teaching that is important.

White, Spence, and Maxim (Chapter 4) look at the role of social capital in determining Aboriginal educational outcomes. Social capital is defined as the networks of social relations within the milieu, characterized by specific norms and attitudes that serve the purpose of potentially enabling individuals or groups access to a pool of resources and supports. Their paper examines the impacts of social capital on Aboriginal educational attainment in Canada, Australia, and New Zealand. It is innovative analysis that has raised a lot of interest as they create a new schema for evaluating this trendy theory. They find that social capital has a moderate influence and rarely acts alone. It influences outcomes for Aboriginal educational attainment in conjunction with other resources (human and economic/physical capital). It is contingent on the context, and this can be assessed by using their four new elements/dimension schema.

On the issue of transitions we have two papers. Maxim and White (Chapter 2), using cycle II of the Youth in Transition Survey (YITS), explore differential patterns of school completion and transition to the workforce between predominately urban Aboriginal and non-Aboriginal youth. They examine the role of students' families' values toward education, and students' levels of connectedness or engagement with schools as contributing factors to the likelihood of school completion. Of the 22,378 completed interviews, 782 individuals identified themselves as having an Aboriginal cultural or racial background. This small number made it difficult to look at all the key questions the researchers pose. The findings from this study suggest that not only are patterns of school completion different for Aboriginal and non-Aboriginal students, but that employment patterns also differ. In particular, Aboriginal students who drop out of school often have higher relative levels of employment than their non-Aboriginal counterparts. The authors are cautious, but feel they can conclude there may be some correlation between how well students do and how much support for education is expressed by parents.

Finally, Costa Kapsalis' study (Chapter 5) attempts to determine to what extent the weaker labour market performance of Aboriginal Canadians is a result of the types of occupations they have, and why their occupations differ from other Canadians. In particular, the study examines: (1) What kind of jobs do Aboriginal workers have compared to non-Aboriginal workers? (2) What is the impact of occupational differences between the two groups of workers on wage differences? and (3) What are the main factors behind their occupational and wage differences? He finds that there are significant occupational differences between Aboriginal and non-Aboriginal workers with Aboriginal workers under-represented in managerial and professional occupations, particularly in the private sector. He also finds that educational differences explain most of the occupational differences between Aboriginal and non-Aboriginal workers. He looks at the policy implications and identifies some promising policy directions for changing this situation.

Section Two of the proceedings looks at socio-economic well-being. Two of the papers deal with the centrally important issue of clean potable water. Sarah Morales, one of the graduate scholarship winners, wrote a paper (Chapter 9) that begins with the understanding that the objective of the government's policy is to ensure that people living on reserves attain a level of health, and have access to water facilities, comparable with other Canadians living in communities of a similar size and location. However, Morales argues, it is these very government policies that often prevent this objective from being attained. This is mainly because these policies lack input from Aboriginal communities, and fail to take into consideration the unique circumstances and issues that these communities face. First she explores the current federal policy adopted by government to deal with the issue of safe drinking water in First Nations communities and the inadequacies of this policy. Secondly, she suggests two working approaches to water quality in these communities. The first is the creation of a co-management regime between the federal government and First Nations governments. The second is a recognition of an Aboriginal right to govern the water resources within their traditional territory.

Graham and Fortier (Chapter 8) also attack the water issue but from a different perspective. In their paper, "Building Governance Capacity: The Case of Potable Water in First Nations Communities," they look at potable water from a community capacity-building perspective. They present a model for capacity development that outlines the various approaches, goals, and considerations for strategies to develop capacity. They examine the advantages and disadvantages of each of the possible approaches, then apply that discussion to potable water in First Nations communities. They draw lessons from the case study. The key one is that communities in the greatest need of reform for their water systems are often the least likely to be equipped to lead such reforms.

James Ford and Johanna Wandel's paper "Responding to Climate Change in Nunavut: Policy Recommendations," (Chapter 6) examines the possibilities around using policy to reduce and moderate the potential impacts of climate change in Inuit communities in Nunavut, Canada. Their focus is on hunting, and they argue that if policy is to be successful, it has to address the non-climatic determinants of vulnerability, which are of social, cultural, and economic importance to communities. If we address these areas of vulnerability, it will give communities more capacity to cope with the coming change. Ford and Wandel discuss areas where the government can have an impact on vulnerability: expansion of cultural preservation programs, strengthening of wildlife co-management arrangements, and community involvement in shaping the nature of future economic development.

Robert M. Bone (Chapter 10) uses data from the newly created Inuit database, which was created to provide previously unavailable census data about (1) Inuit identity population, (2) Canada and the four land claim regions, and (3) those residing outside of the four Inuit land claim regions. Bone uses this data to describe the Inuit identity population by population size, age, and sex for the five Inuit regions and the urban Inuit population. This more accurate and detailed data on the Inuit population is intended to inform policies affecting the Inuit in Canada.

Another paper in this section is by Jessica Ball and Ron George, "Policies and Practices Affecting Aboriginal Fathers' Involvement with Their Children." This paper offers Aboriginal fathers' perspectives on how policies and practices of federal and provincial agencies in community programs affect their involvement with their children. They argue that Aboriginal fathers have been especially excluded, both as a stakeholder group and as a resource for their children. The authors explore fathers' stories utilizing qualitative methods. They conclude that the Aboriginal fathers' stories suggest the potential for a new generation of positively involved Aboriginal fathers that urgently needs to be recognized and supported through policy reforms and resources to put policies into practice.

Mary-Jane Norris, in her "Aboriginal Languages in Canada" paper (Chapter 11) discusses the current state of First Nations, Inuit and Métis languages. She explores recent trends focusing on community-level indicators in relation to the need for community-driven language planning and strategies. Norris assesses the long-term trends over the past twenty years, and future prospects for both maintaining and revitalizing languages. Lastly, the chapter outlines policy issues that address the challenges of protecting and promoting Aboriginal languages.

The third section is a sample of the international papers that were delivered at the conference. The section begins with the remarks from Ms. Elsa Stamatopoulou, Chief, Secretariat of the UN Permanent Forum on Indigenous Issues, followed by the remarks of Eric Guimond, Acting Director of the Strategic Research and Analysis Directorate, Indian and Northern Affairs Canada (Chapter 12). They situate the current important investigation and dialogue around creating indicators of well-being that could be used worldwide to assess our human condition.

Ms. Stamatopoulou states that

> the Permanent Forum strongly believes that indicators and disaggregated data are important, not just as a measure of the situation of Indigenous peoples, but as a vital strategy in improving their lives by capturing their aspirations and world views, promoting development with identity, protecting and promoting their cultures and integrity as Indigenous peoples and empowering them to utilize such information to their benefit. I am confident to state today that what we heard with the most clarity in the discussions we held is that unless Indigenous peoples themselves participate fully and effectively in data collection and the establishment of indicators, efforts will likely be incomplete, baseless, or irrelevant, and essentially provide too fragile a foundation for wise policies, including public resource allocations.

Mr. Guimond develops the case for concluding that "developing indicators is an important task for Canada and for all of us around the world. We have to base these indicators on sound research, careful assessment, and analysis. When we develop these indicators, we have to use them in the process of understanding the realities facing peoples around the world, and to make worthwhile effective policy."

Brenda Dyack of Commonwealth Scientific and Industrial Research Organization (CSIRO) and Romy Grenier of River Consulting in Australia present their work, "Natural Resource Management and Indigenous Well-being." (Chapter 13) In that paper, they review six research case studies in Australia, New Zealand, and Canada, which seek to quantify the benefits that Indigenous people derive from natural resource management. While each project involves collaborative work among researchers and Indigenous people and groups, they have taken different routes to providing evidence of the benefits that are generated by natural resources. They look at six different approaches, and do a critique of the methodological and analytical approaches used in the six studies surveyed. The objective is to demonstrate that a diversity of valuation methods exist that can support research, and that can in turn support evidence-based policy development. They make some specific policy observations.

Whetu Wereta and Darin Bishop of Statistics New Zealand present the work to date on a draft framework for statistics that apply to the Maori people (Chapter 14). Work began in 1995 when the Maori Statistics Forum set up a working party to formulate terms of reference for the development of a Maori Statistics Framework. The terms of reference made it clear that the framework had to be "centred on Maori people and their collective aspirations" and further, that it should be "linked to Maori development." This paper traces some of the problems and solutions they have encountered.

John Taylor, Director of the Centre for Aboriginal Economic Policy Research at The Australian National University, Canberra, shares his work on "The Impact of Australian Policy Regimes on Indigenous Population Movement: Evidence from the 2001 Census" (Chapter 15). The aim of this paper is to examine recent patterns and trends in Indigenous population movement against this background of policy shift to see if there are any discernible impacts on mobility behaviour. If so (or if not), what does this mean for the likely future distribution of the Indigenous population? In short, has the new policy regime in Australia achieved a mobilization (literally) of the Indigenous population? He concludes that "although a significant shift in the Indigenous policy environment commenced in the mid-1990s, this appears not to have impacted on Indigenous mobility behaviour, at least not up to 2001. Thus, while the intent of government policy is to move towards a convergence in socio-demographic trends, there appears little evidence of this so far in Australia."

In the last paper in this book, Kalugina, Soboleva, and Tapilina (Chapter 16) share results of a pilot project, Optimizing Social Policy in the Siberian Federal District (SFD), conducted in partnership with Indian and Northern Affairs Canada, Carleton University, and the Institute of Economics and Industrial Engineering at the Siberian Branch of the Russian Academy of Sciences. This project is an attempt to develop an effective system to coordinate the activities of all levels of government in order to improve labour market participation and quality of life among Indigenous peoples of Siberia. The target region is Tomsk Oblast, or province, where the Indigenous people called the Selkup reside. They provide general guidelines for policy makers.

Endnotes

1 More specifically, the conference was organized by the Strategic Research and Analysis Director-ate, INAC and the First Nations Cohesion Project, the Department of Sociology at UWO. Dan Beavon and Jerry White acted as conference co-chairs from their respective organizations.

2 One of the other funding bodies for academic research, the Canadian Institute of Health Research, also has a program (the Institute of Aboriginal Peoples' Health) that supports research to address the special health needs of Canada's Aboriginal peoples.

3 The Canadian government commented on the importance of the APRC in a speech to the United Nations in Geneva on July 22, 2003. More specifically, see the statement by the observer delega-tion of Canada to the United Nations Working Group on Indigenous Populations, Twenty-First Session, July 21–25, 2003.

4 Consequently, there were three conference co-chairs: Dan Beavon, Director of the Strategic Research and Analysis Directorate, INAC; Jerry White, Professor of Sociology and Senior Advisor to the Vice President at the University of Western Ontario; and, Peter Dinsdale, Executive Director of the National Association of Friendship Centres.

5 The federal departments and organizations provided funding support at three different levels. Gold: Indian and Northern Affairs Canada, Human Resources and Skills Development Canada, Department of Justice Canada, Status of Women Canada, Health Canada, Veterans Affairs Canada, Fisheries and Oceans Canada, Canada Housing and Mortgage Corporation, Correc-tional Service Canada, Atlantic Canada Opportunities Agency, Canadian Council On Learning, Canadian International Development Agency, Public Safety and Emergency Preparedness, Social Sciences and Humanities Research Council of Canada, Canadian Institutes of Health Research. Silver: Canada Economic Development, Policy Research Initiative, Canadian Heritage. Bronze: Natural Resources Canada, Statistics Canada.

6 National Association of Friendship Centres, Aboriginal Healing Foundation, First Nations Statistical Institute, National Aboriginal Housing Association, Indian Taxation Advisory Board, National Aboriginal Forestry Association, National Aboriginal Health Organization.

7 Public History, Canadian North, VIA Rail Canada, and Canada Post.

8 There were also four all-day pre-conference workshops organized, which attracted nearly 300 delegates. These four pre-conference workshops included: Harvard University's research model on Aboriginal governance; Aboriginal demographics and well-being; Bill C-31 and First Nation membership; and records management for First Nations.

9 This famous quote is actually a paraphrase of what the Cheshire cat said to Alice in Carroll's book, *Alice's Adventures in Wonderland*, Chapter 6, Pig and Pepper, 1865.

10 The research-policy nexus is built on the foundation of dialogue and discourse between those making policy and those discovering and interpreting the evidence that should underscore it. When superior quality research is produced and used in making policy, this completes the structure.

11 While there are many Canadian cities with larger Aboriginal populations, in terms of both propor-tions and absolute numbers, Ottawa was selected as the most logical conference site because it would have otherwise been difficult to engage the participation of such a large number of senior federal policy-makers. In many ways, the conference was about educating and exposing this group to the vast array of research that has been done on Aboriginal issues.

12 We are also publishing a third volume from the 2006 conference (number 5 in our series) which will deal with the issues arising from the legislation known as Bill C-31. These are issues related to identity, membership, and defining populations.

Part One:
Education and Employment Transitions

1

The Determinants of Employment Among Aboriginal Peoples

Coryse Ciceri and Katherine Scott

Introduction

The knowledge economy is raising the ante—the basic requirements for securing a good job and a good income have increased. Gaps in education and skills are major reasons underlying the income and job quality polarization of many post-industrial economies. Given the prevalence of low-wage and precarious employment in Canada, the consequences of this pattern of employment are significant and long-term in nature, particularly for Aboriginal Canadians—and other historically disadvantaged groups—who now struggle first to gain access to paid employment and then to climb the earnings ladder. Economic security—and employment in particular—is a central issue for Aboriginal communities across Canada. Employment remains the key source of welfare for the majority of Canadians of all ages—as the source of direct household earnings and the basis of entitlement to key income support programs such as employment insurance and pensions, and other related benefits. Moreover, employment is an important venue of self-development; it can provide a sense of participation in a collective purpose. People also derive enormous benefits from the social networks established through work (Gallie, et al. 1998). As such, securing and sustaining employment is important to numerous social and economic goals.

Yet Aboriginal people experience significant labour market disadvantages compared to other Canadians. In general, they have lower labour force participation and employment rates, higher unemployment levels (Drost and Eryou 1991; Peters and Rosenberg 1995; Mendelson and Battle 1999; Mendelson 2004), lower levels of representation in well-paid employment and consequently, lower average wages and earnings compared to other workers (De Silva 1999; Maxim et al. 2001). Poor employment outcomes are linked to high levels of economic insecurity among Aboriginal peoples, including persistent poverty, which in turn continues to profoundly influence the life chances and aspirations of Aboriginal people, their families and their communities (Brunnen 2003). The gap in employment outcomes poses a formidable challenge for both Aboriginal people and all levels of government in Canada. Understanding what factors influence labour market outcomes is important in identifying relevant programs and policies that facilitate access to meaningful, well-paid employment and the benefits that flow from employment for Aboriginal peoples.

Figure 1.1: Working-age Population by Aboriginal Status, Canada 2001

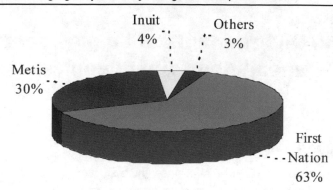

$$N = 417,725$$

Note: Category "others" includes people who declared multiple Aboriginal identities and those who declared themselves as Registered Indian and/or Band members without Aboriginal identites response.

Source: CCSD calculations based on 2001 Census Public Use Microdata Files

Demographic Profile of Aboriginal Peoples

The following is an overview of demographic and economic realities of Aboriginal peoples in Canada. It describes persistent disparities in the circumstances of Aboriginal peoples that set the context for the following analysis of employment and discussion of program and policy:

1. The Aboriginal population is growing. In 2001, there were nearly one million Aboriginal people living in Canada, an increase of over 20% from 1996. In the same period, there was an even larger increase in the numbers of working-age Aboriginal peoples, aged 25 to 64 years. In 1996, 335,450 individuals identified as Aboriginal; in 2001, 417,725 claimed Aboriginal ancestry.[1] The growth in the Aboriginal population is one of the most significant demographic trends in Canada today, and most decidedly, an important consideration in the development of future employment policies and programs.

2. There has been significant growth among the Métis and Inuit populations. According to the 2001 Census, over six in 10 Aboriginal peoples (62.3%) identified as North American Indian,[2] while three in ten (30.0%) identified as Métis, and one in twenty (4.4%) indicated that they were Inuit as shown in **Figure 1.1**.[3] Between 1996 and 2001, the percentage of North American Indians dropped slightly (-1.9%) while the proportion of Métis grew slightly (1.7%). The share of the Inuit population was stable over this five year period (0.2% change). However, as noted above, the overall

Figure 1.2: Working-age Population by Household Type and Aboriginal Status, Canada 2001

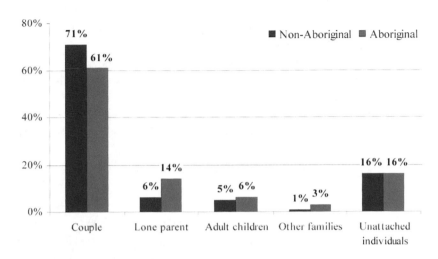

Source: CCSD calculations based on 2001 Census Public Use Microdata Files

numbers of each group grew between 1996 and 2001, most notably among the Métis (32.1%) and the Inuit (29.9%). Over half of Aboriginal people aged 25 to 64 years (57%) reported that they were registered Indians under the *Indian Act*; 56% indicated that they were members of an Indian Band or First Nation.

3. The age profile of this group among Aboriginal people is quite distinct from the non-Aboriginal population. Aboriginal peoples tend to be younger than non-Aboriginal peoples. Indeed, the Aboriginal population is growing at a much faster rate than the total population—a trend noted above.[4] As a result, a large number of Aboriginal young adults will be entering the labour market over the next ten years, particularly in Western Canada. In 2000, over one-third of working-age Aboriginal people were between 25 and 34 years old compared to one quarter of their non-Aboriginal counterparts. By contrast, 55 to 64 year olds made up only 12% of the working-age Aboriginal population compared to 17% among non-Aboriginals. The Inuit have the youngest working-age population compared to First Nations peoples and the Métis.

4. The Aboriginal population has comparatively high rates of mobility (Norris and Clatworthy 2003). In the year before the 2001 Census, 21% of Aboriginal working-age people had moved whereas this was the case among only 13% of non-Aboriginal respondents. However, in his analysis of 2001 Census data, Michael Mendelson points out that there has not been a "massive migration off the reserves and into the cities" (Mendelson 2004, 7).

Rather, the proportion of Aboriginal people living on-reserve and in other rural and urban areas has stayed roughly the same as the number of Aboriginal people has grown. Aboriginal peoples are moving back and forth between reserves and other communities. This is an important point to keep in mind in the design of employment programs.

5. There are slightly more women of working age within the Aboriginal population than the non-Aboriginal population. This is an important factor to take into account in order to understand the employment dynamics within the Aboriginal community, given the historic position of women vis-à-vis the paid labour market, and the share of caring responsibilities that women continue to shoulder.

6. The proportion of lone-parent households is higher for Aboriginal working-age adults for among non-Aboriginal working age adults (see **Figure 1.2** – page 5). The proportion of Aboriginal lone-parent families headed by women is more than twice that among the non-Aboriginal population.[5] Inuit peoples are more slightly more likely to live in couple families (in which a member of either a married or common-law couple is the economic family reference person) and somewhat less likely to be unattached individuals compared to First Nations people and the Métis. Approximately one in seven First Nations, Métis, and Inuit families are headed by a lone parent compared to one in 17 non-Aboriginal families.

7. Aboriginal people commit more hours per week to household and caring tasks than do non-Aboriginal Canadians. For example, in 2001, 25% of working-age Aboriginal respondents spent more than 30 hours per week involved in housework, compared to 16% of non-Aboriginal respondents. The percentage of Aboriginal women working more than 30 hours a week on household tasks was higher than the percentage of Aboriginal men (33% compared to 16%). Even so, Aboriginal men were twice as likely as non-Aboriginal men to be in this group.[6] Similarly, Aboriginal people were almost twice as likely as non-Aboriginals to report that they spent more than 30 hours per week caring for children (28% compared to 16%). And again, this was true for both Aboriginal men and women. By contrast, over half of the non-Aboriginal working-age population (53%) reported that they did not spend any time caring for children, compared to 43% of the Aboriginal population. This may be linked to the higher birth rate, as noted, as well as the higher proportion of lone-parent families within the Aboriginal community. Working-age adults in the Aboriginal community are more likely to provide more than 10 hours per week of elder care, but the difference with the non-Aboriginal population is not large.

8. Aboriginal young people will be more highly educated than any previous group in the past. Between 1996 and 2001, the education profile of Aboriginal peoples improved noticeably (Statistics Canada 2003a). Nonetheless,

there remains a significant gap in educational attainment between Aboriginal and non-Aboriginal people. Almost half of Aboriginal people aged 25 to 64 do not have an educational degree, certificate, or diploma compared to one-quarter of the non-Aboriginal population aged 25 to 64 years. There are gaps as well in the proportion of Aboriginal and non-Aboriginals who hold a high-school diploma, a trade certificate, or a college degree, and especially those who hold university degrees. Non-Aboriginals are more than twice as likely to have completed university. Despite notable progress, the education gap has been slow to narrow—in part because non-Aboriginals have been increasing their levels of educational attainment as well. The emphasis in policy on attaining educational qualifications is an important one though. Generally, those with a trade certificate have substantially improved employment and income characteristics compared to those without a certificate. Indeed, there is some evidence that certification is of greater importance to Aboriginal peoples than to others (Indian and Northern Affairs Canada 2005). By and large, Inuit people have the greatest educational challenges. Fewer Inuit people hold educational degrees than the Métis or First Nations peoples. The Métis are most likely to hold an educational degree or diploma.

9. The proportion of Aboriginal people who are full-time students is notably larger than among non-Aboriginals,[7] while the proportion of part-time students is the same. Greater numbers of students is certainly one factor behind the lower rates of employment among Aboriginal peoples.

10. The average income of non-Aboriginals was 1.5 times higher than the average income of Aboriginal people. In 2000, the average total income of Aboriginal peoples was $22,190, while the average among non-Aboriginals was much higher at $34,140. Aboriginal people have been making some economic progress, but compared to the growth in labour market participation, the gap in income between Aboriginals and non-Aboriginals is cause for concern. Between 1995 and 2000, the average total income increased by $2,980 (constant dollars). But the income gap only narrowed slightly as average income among non-Aboriginals improved at the same time.[8] The discrepancies between average Aboriginal and average non-Aboriginal wages and salaries are even greater. The average wage and salaries of the non-Aboriginal working population was almost two times higher than that of the Aboriginal population in both 1995 and 2000. In 1995, the average salary of Aboriginal people reporting employment income was $13,780 (constant dollars), compared to an average of $24,210 (constant dollars) for the non-Aboriginal working-age population. In 2000, average salaries had increased among Aboriginal people but they were still significantly lower than their non-Aboriginal counterparts ($16,890 and $27,600, respectively). In 2000, one-third of Aboriginal people aged 25 to 64 years (33.0%) did not have any employment income, compared to roughly one

quarter of non-Aboriginals (23.9%). The proportion of Aboriginals in this group, however, fell between 1995 and 2000 (as it did among non-Aboriginals as well). Lastly, average government transfer received by the Aboriginal population is almost two times greater than that received by the non-Aboriginal population. There was a decrease, however, between 1995 and 2000 in the average amount received by Aboriginal people in receipt of transfers ($4,210 (2000 dollars) in 1995 compared to $3,720 in 2000).

This portrait highlights a number of facts important to the following discussion of employment. Chief among them is the fact that the Aboriginal population in Canada is growing, a result of both higher rates of fertility and the fact that more individuals are identifying as Aboriginal. The Aboriginal population is younger than the non-Aboriginal population and over time will make up an increasing percentage of Canada's labour force, particularly in the west. Over half of Aboriginal people live in urban areas and 80% of working-age Aboriginal people do so. The proportion of Aboriginals living on reserve stayed roughly the same between 1996 and 2001 in the face of population growth and comparatively high rates of mobility. The education gap remains significant. Almost half of Aboriginal people have less than a high school education, while twice as many non-Aboriginals (when compared to Aboriginals) are university graduates. Improvements in educational attainment notwithstanding, little progress has been made reducing the income disparities between Aboriginal peoples and non-Aboriginals: In 2000, average total incomes of non-Aboriginals were one-and-a-half times higher than the total incomes of Aboriginal peoples, and average earnings and wages were two times higher.

Goals and Guiding Questions

There is a significant body of existing research on the socio-economic status of Aboriginal peoples in Canada. There are basic demographic profiles of the Aboriginal population which provide important information on a range of subjects relevant to the study of determinants of employment (Conference Board of Canada 2003; Statistics Canada 2003; Mendelson and Battle 1999; Mendelson 2004). Other studies have attempted to explore the factors associated with wage inequalities (Banerjee et al. 1991; George and Kuhn 1994; Pendakur et al. 1998, 2002; De Silva 1999; Maxim et al. 2001). These studies have identified low levels of educational attainment; a comparatively young population; the location/residence of many Aboriginal people in remote communities and on reserves; lack of training and of language proficiency; gender; and discrimination in the labour market as key factors behind poor labour market outcomes, specifically low wages, among Aboriginal peoples (See Clatworthy et al. 1995; Drost 1995; George et al. 1995; RCAP 1996a; Hull 2000). To date, however, very little work has been completed examining the determinants of Aboriginal employment in Canada.[9]

The broad goal of this research project is to explore the determinants of employment among Aboriginal people living in Canada, using 2001 Census data, and to discuss the policy implications of these findings for improving employment prospects for Aboriginal people.[10] Specifically, this project will identify and examine the key factors associated with employment, and compare and contrast the major determinants of employment for Aboriginal Canadians and non-Aboriginal Canadians. In addition, the project will look at the likelihood of Aboriginal people—here including First Nations, Métis, and Inuit—to hold full-time jobs and employment that matches their education and skills.

The following questions will guide the study:

1. What is the current employment situation of Aboriginal people? Is it the same for the different groups (First Nations, Métis, and Inuit)? How does their employment standing compare and contrast with the situation of non-Aboriginal Canadians?

2. What is the probability of Aboriginal people being employed? Is the probability the same for the different Aboriginal groups (First Nations, Métis and Inuit)? What is the probability of holding employment that matches one's level of education?

3. What are the reasons behind the poorer employment outcomes among Aboriginal peoples compared to non-Aboriginal peoples?

4. What key issues need to be taken into consideration in the design of policies and programs to improve the labour market outcomes for Aboriginal peoples?

Methodology

Data

The major goal of this study is to identify the factors related to the probability of employment and participation in the labour force for Aboriginal people, and how these factors are similar to or different from those of non-Aboriginal people. To answer these questions, this study used the individuals file of the 2001 Census Public Use Microdata Files (PUMF). The PUMF are based on a 2.7% sample of unaggregated, anonymous records from the 2001 Census database. The individuals file contains 138 variables, and provides data on the characteristics of the population such as demographic information, education history of individuals, labour market activity, and income levels. Data are provided for Canada as a whole, provinces and territories, and for 19 selected Census Metropolitan Areas (CMAs).

The PUMF have several limitations that will impact the study. For instance, these files do not include variables such as work experience, training, or hourly wage. In addition, some information is aggregated. For example, the variable "years of schooling" is not continuous but aggregated. Moreover, data are only data available for 19 of 27 CMAs. With regard to Aboriginal peoples, the PUMF do not include a flag to differentiate between those living on-reserve and off-reserve, despite the fact that this information was gathered in the Census. As well, under-coverage in the Census was higher among Aboriginal people than other segments of population. Enumeration was not permitted or was interrupted before it could be completed on 30 Indian reserves and settlements. As a result, 30,000 to 35,000 people living on reserves and in settlements were incompletely enumerated. This incomplete enumeration has the greatest impact with respect to data on North American Indians, and for persons registered under the *Indian Act* (Statistics Canada 2003b). However, in spite of some shortcomings, the Census remains the most comprehensive source of information on various socio-economic, demographic, and labour market characteristics of Canada's Aboriginal population.

The following definitions have been used to identify Aboriginal peoples in the 2001 Census of Canada and will be used in this study.

- **Aboriginal Identity** refers to those persons who reported identifying with at least one Aboriginal identity group, e.g., North American Indian, Métis or Inuit, and/or those who reported being a Treaty Indian or a Registered Indian as defined by the *Indian Act of Canada*, and/or those who were members of an Indian Band or First Nation. As well, those who report multiple Aboriginal identities are included.[11]

- **Non-Aboriginal** refers to all those who did not respond in the positive to the Aboriginal question. For the purposes of this study, we have excluded immigrants, non-permanent residents and non-Aboriginal individuals who identify as members of a visible minority. This was done in order to remove the potential effect of the presence of other historically disadvantaged groups such as new immigrants and visible minorities in the non-Aboriginal category on our comparative analysis.

- **Working-age Population** includes all those aged 25–64 years in the labour force. We have chosen this age group in order to base the analysis on the working-age population, and avoid confounding the effects of transition from school to work for the younger age groups, and from work to retirement for the older age groups.

Data Analysis

Our primary objective is to estimate the effects of several determinants on the probability of accessing the labour market (having a job), of accessing a good job (having a full-time job), and of accessing an appropriate job for one's level of education and skill. Specifically, logistic regression analysis will be used to determine the influence of various factors on Aboriginal people's probability of:

- Being employed (dependent variable no. 1);
- Being employed full time, that is being employed for at least 30 hours per week[12] (dependent variable no. 2); and
- Occupying a job that matches one's skill level (dependent variable no. 3).

The third dependent variable is based on the 2001 National Occupational Classification (NOC) that includes skill/education characteristics for each occupation. As such, it is possible to determine if the individual occupies a job that corresponds to his/her level of skill/education.

Three different logistic regression models are presented below, one for each research question. Each model explores the determinants of employment for three working-age population groups: the total working-age population, the Aboriginal working-age population, and the non-Aboriginal working-age population. We have devised this methodology in order to test for the effect of two main independent variables—Aboriginal status and Aboriginal identity group (First Nations, Métis, Inuit)—controlling for the effect of known individual-level predictors of employment. These include demographic factors (e.g., gender, age, and family status), educational attainment (e.g., highest degree attained, and student status), and mobility. We also look at whether or not an individual lives within a Census Metropolitan Area (CMA). There are a host of other structural factors that come into play in an individual's decision to seek out employment, such as the presence of support networks, the vitality of local economies, and systemic discrimination. However, given the limits of existing data sets and quantitative methodologies, the paper concentrates on human capital variables.

Results—Descriptives

Being Employed

In 2001, there were large discrepancies in the labour market experiences of Aboriginal and non-Aboriginal working-age people, despite overall employment gains between 1996 and 2001. In 1996, just over half of Aboriginal people (53%) were employed in the paid labour market.[13] By 2001, the proportion of the Aboriginal working-age population engaged in the paid-labour market had climbed five percentage points, reflecting in part improved economic conditions through the last half of the 1990s. The gap in employment rates between Aboriginals and non-Aboriginals narrowed slightly over this period, but remained significant. In 2001, over three quarters of non-Aboriginals were employed, a difference of 18 percentage points over Aboriginals.

Men were more likely to be employed than women, although the gap in employment is slightly narrower among Aboriginal men and women. In 2001, 62% of Aboriginal men were engaged in the paid-labour market compared to 54% of Aboriginal women. Among non-Aboriginals, the respective employment rates were 82% and 71%.

Figure 1.3: Unemployment Rates of Working-age Population by Aboriginal Status, Provinces and territories, 2001

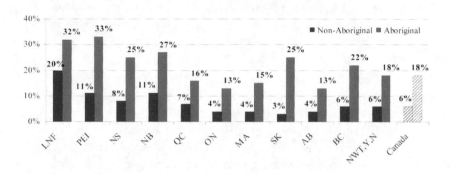

Source: CCSD calculations based on 2001 Census Public Use Microdata Files

Figure 1.4: Working-age Population by Occupation by Required Level of Education and Aboriginal Status, Canada, 2001

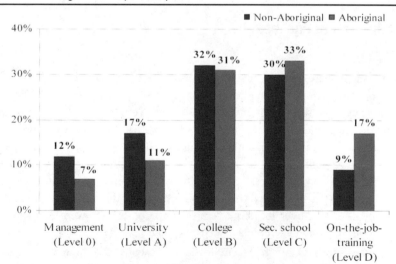

Source: CCSD calculations based on 2001 Census Public Use Microdata Files

Within the Aboriginal population, the Métis had a higher rate of employment in 2001 than the Inuit or First Nations : 67.8% compared to 63.1% and 53.2% respectively. However, the Inuit working-age population experienced the largest increase in employment between 1996 and 2001, almost ten percentage points. The employment rate among the Métis increased by approximately eight percentage points, while the employment rate among First Nations people increased by a modest three percentage points.

Aboriginal people also experienced higher rates of unemployment compared to non-Aboriginal people.[14] In 2001, Aboriginal people were three times more likely to be unemployed than non-Aboriginals: 17.5% of working-age Aboriginal adults compared to 5.6% of non-Aboriginals. Again, there was improvement from 1996 when 22.3% of working-age Aboriginal adults were unemployed. However, this gap remains a significant barrier to economic security among Aboriginal people.

The discrepancies in the rate of unemployment by province and territory are even more pronounced (**Figure 1.3**). The highest rates of unemployment are found in Eastern Canada, particularly among Aboriginal peoples. Yet the discrepancies are large in the West—particularly Saskatchewan and British Columbia—where large numbers of Aboriginal people live.

Over one in five First Nations people were unemployed in both 1996 and 2001. The Métis experienced the largest decrease in unemployment over this period, falling from 18.8% in 1996 to 12.4% in 2001. The rate of unemployment among the Inuit in 2001 was 16%. These data show that the labour market challenges facing Aboriginal people do not stem from an unwillingness to participate in the labour market, but rather from a lack of success in securing and retaining employment. This raises important questions about the reasons behind such high levels of unemployment.

The proportion of Aboriginal people aged 25 to 64 years "not in the labour force" (NILF) is notably higher than among non-Aboriginal people. In 2001, 124,110 Aboriginal persons (or 29.7%) were in this situation, compared to only 19.2% of non-Aboriginal people. People not in the labour force may include students, homemakers, retired workers, seasonal workers in an "off" season who were not looking for work at the time of the Census, and persons who could not work because of a long-term illness or disability. Over one third of working-age Aboriginal women (36%) and almost one quarter of Aboriginal men (23%) were "not in the labour force" in 2001 compared to 25% of non-Aboriginal women and 13% of non-Aboriginal men.

Having a Full-Time Job

In 2001, among Aboriginal and non-Aboriginal working-age people employed in the week prior to the Census, for whom we have complete information, the likelihood of having a full-time job was roughly the same. Both groups experienced an increase in the proportion of workers engaged in full-time employment between

Figure 1.5: Working age Population by Education and Skill required by main Occupation, by Aboriginal Status, Canada, 2001

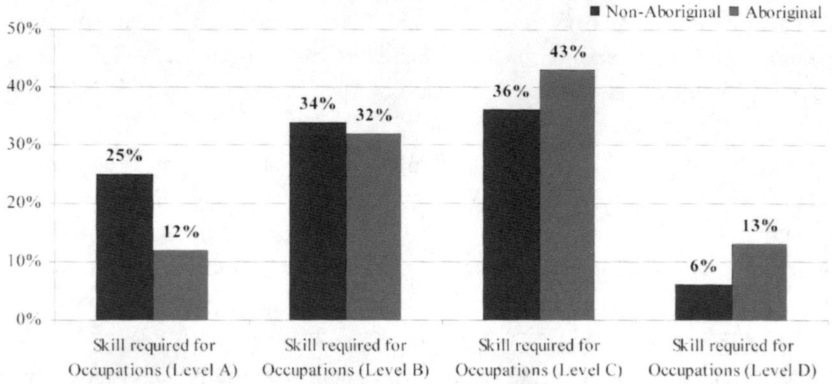

Source: CCSD calculations based on 2001 Census Public Use Microdata Files

1996 and 2001, and conversely, a decrease in the proportion of workers employed on a part-time basis. The proportion of Inuit working full-time is slightly lower than among First Nations people and Métis, 81% compared to 85% and 86% respectively. Overall, Aboriginal workers represented 2.5% of the full-time working population, and 2.9% of the part-time working population.

Having an "Appropriate" Job

Economic well-being does not exclusively hinge on having a job. The quality of employment is clearly important, particularly in the Canadian labour market that is characterized by a pool of low-wage, precarious employment (Jackson 2005).

Figure 1.4 (page 12) presents the distribution of occupations held by Aboriginals and non-Aboriginals aged 25 to 64 years, organized by the level of education and skill deemed necessary to access each occupation. The occupation skill levels in this figure refer to the highest level of education and/or training required for each occupational group. It is based on the National Occupational Classification (2001).[15] As we see, Aboriginal people are more likely to hold medium-skilled and low-skilled occupations, that is, occupations for which college education, high-school, or on-the-job-training are required. For instance, they are over-represented in occupations that are characterized by the on-the-job-training compared to the experience of non-Aboriginals. And they are under represented in managerial occupations or occupations for which a university degree is needed, compared to non-Aboriginals.

Figure 1.5[16] looks at the distribution of education and skill among Aboriginal and non-Aboriginal people. Non-Aboriginals are more than twice as likely to have the education and skills required for Level A occupations—those that require a university degree. By contrast, Aboriginal people are more likely to have the education and skills

Table 1.1: Occupation / Skill Match Summary

	Total	Non-Aboriginal	Aboriginal
Qualified for the job	4,366,925	48%	42%
Overqualified for the job	2,943,405	32%	35%
Overqualified – by 1 level	2,257,485	25%	27%
Overqualified – by 2 levels	628,475	7%	7%
Overqualified – by 3 levels	57,450	1%	1%
Underqualified for the job	1,876,695	20%	24%
Underqualified – by 1 level	1,660,270	18%	19%
Underqualified – by 2 levels	213,095	2%	4%
Underqualified – by 3 levels	3,330	0%	0%
Sub-Total	9,187,025	100%	100%
Those in managerial occupations	1,208,160	12%	7%
Total	10395,185		

Source: CCSD calculations based on 2001 Census Public Use Microdata Files

required for Level C and Level D occupations. Indeed, they are more than twice as likely compared to non-Aboriginals to have the skills required for Level D occupations—that is less than eight years of schooling and no formal employment training. Overall, as shown in **Table 1.1**, we see that roughly four out of ten Aboriginal people (42%) hold a job commensurate with their skills and training compared to just under half of non-Aboriginals (48%). One quarter (24%) hold jobs for which they do not technically have the qualifications required, and 35% hold jobs for which they are overqualified. The respective figures for non-Aboriginals are 20% and 32%. Generally speaking, there is not a large gap between the experience of Aboriginal people and non-Aboriginals in this regard. Roughly one third of working-age adults in Canada are formally overqualified for the jobs that they hold. This speaks to the stock of employment that is currently available in Canada; underemployment is a significant problem.

However, there remain significant challenges for Aboriginal people when we probe these data further. **Table 1.2** (page 16) presents a more detailed breakdown of our findings. It shows that even when Aboriginal people acquire higher levels of education, they are still more likely than non-Aboriginals to be employed in a job that does not match their skill set. This is true for Aboriginal people with the credentials and training for Level A, Level B, and Level C occupations. By contrast, Aboriginal people with low levels of education (skills required for Level D occupations) are more likely than non-Aboriginals to have a job that matches their skill set. This is not surprising given the comparatively larger number of Aboriginal people with low levels of education (individuals with less than eight years of schooling). But again, we see that this group of Aboriginal people is

Table 1.2: Occupation / Skill Match among Working-age Population, by Aboriginal Status, Canada, 2001

	Skill required for occupations (Level A)	Skill required for occupations (Level B)	Skill required for occupations (Level C)	Skill required for occupations (Level D)
Non-Aboriginal				
Good skill set match	56%	47%	45%	25%
Bad skill set match	44%	53%	55%	75%
Aboriginal				
Good skill set match	47%	42%	41%	32%
Bad skill set match	53%	58%	59%	68%

Source: CCSD calculations based on 2001 Census Public Use Microdata Files

generally less likely to hold occupations that require higher levels of education compared to non-Aboriginals. This table highlights clearly the education and training gap that continues to delimit the employment and income prospects of Aboriginal people at present—and potentially in the future.

Results—Logistic Regression

The previous section paints a picture of the employment gap between Aboriginal and non-Aboriginal Canadians. What then are some of the potential reasons behind these persistent disparities in the employment prospects of Aboriginal people? And what are their policy implications?

We know from available evidence that Aboriginal people have lower rates of employment and higher rates of unemployment compared to non-Aboriginal people. The following analysis shows that they have a lower likelihood or lower odds of being employed as well. Indeed, Aboriginal people aged 25 to 64 years are 43% as likely to be employed, according to findings from the 2001 Census. Aboriginal identity does have an impact on the likelihood of employment. While all Aboriginal people are less likely to be employed than non-Aboriginals, people who identify as Inuit are slightly more likely to be employed than Métis people who are more likely to be employed than First Nations people after controlling for socio-demographic factors.

Looking at both the Aboriginal and non-Aboriginal populations, we find that several factors are influential in predicting the likelihood of employment, in addition to Aboriginal identity. Moreover, the factors that positively and negatively influence the likelihood of employment are the same for Aboriginal people and non-Aboriginals.[17]

Educational attainment is the key determinant of employment for Aboriginal people (see Drost and Eryou 1991; Drost 1995; White et al. 2003). Controlling for other known predictors of employment, including Aboriginal status, the impact of education on employment is clear. Aboriginal university graduates, for example, are five times more likely to be employed than Aboriginal people without an educational degree or diploma. With each higher degree earned, the likelihood of employment increases significantly. Education is also important for non-Aboriginals but to a lesser degree. Certainly, non-Aboriginal university graduates are three and a half times more likely to be employed than those without any formal education qualifications, but the impact is less pronounced. Our findings clearly show that the rate of return of higher levels of education is higher for Aboriginal people.

Our findings also confirm that men are more likely to be employed than women, but gender appears to have a larger impact on the likelihood of employment among non-Aboriginals. Among non-Aboriginals aged 25 to 64 years, men are twice as likely to be employed than women. The gap between Aboriginal women and Aboriginal men is slightly narrower. Aboriginal women are 69% as likely as Aboriginal men to be employed, holding other factors such as age and family status (being a lone parent or an unattached individual) constant. This is not to say that Aboriginal women are more likely to be employed than non-Aboriginal women as we note above, but that the gender gap in employment is slightly narrower within the Aboriginal community.

Being a lone parent is also linked to lower rates of employment when compared to those living in families, controlling for factors such as education and Aboriginal identity. However this trend is much less pronounced among non-Aboriginals—an interesting finding. While non-Aboriginal women are 48% as likely to be employed as non-Aboriginal men, non-Aboriginal lone parents are 89% as likely as those who are not lone parents to be employed. This suggests that there are other factors that reduce the likelihood of women being employed compared to men. By contrast, the odds of employment among Aboriginal women and among Aboriginal lone parents are virtually the same at 0.69 and 0.70 respectively.

In their comparative study of Aboriginal and non-Aboriginal women, White et al. find that lone parents are less likely to be employed than those who are married or living alone. Moreover, the presence of young children has an important influence on the likelihood of employment: In 1996, among all Canadian women, about 61% of those with no children under 15 years, and one or more 15 years and older, were employed, compared with only 45% of those with one or more children under two years and none under five years (White et al. 2003, 399, 402). However, among Registered Indians, the impact of having small children appears to be less compared to other Aboriginal women and non-Aboriginal women. They suggest that there might be "a special set of circumstances operating in First Nations communities, such as the extended family network that somehow

Figure 1.6: Proportion of Full-time/Part-time Workers by Aboriginal Status, Canada 2001

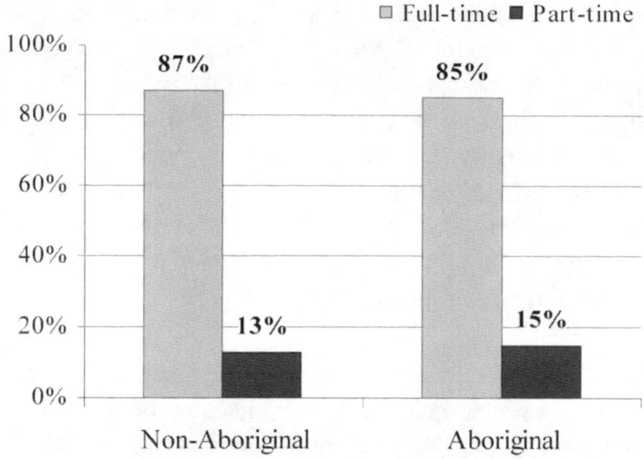

Source: CCSD calculations based on 2001 Census Public Use Microdata Files

moderates the negative effects of minor children on labour force participation in such communities" (*ibid.*, 406). The question of lone parent status bears further exploration.

Migration within the last year is also linked with decreased odds of employment. Whereas one might have expected individuals that have recently moved to have higher rates of employment, this does not appear to be the case. Migration within the last year negatively influences the prospect of employment (compared to those who did not move). The impact is slightly greater among Aboriginal peoples than non-Aboriginals. This is important to keep in mind given the high rate of mobility within the Aboriginal population.

Other factors are linked with a higher likelihood of employment, including age, working part-time, and living in an urban area. For both Aboriginal people and non-Aboriginals, the relationship between age and the likelihood of employment is curvilinear: The likelihood of employment tends to increase with age overall. However, the rate of increase begins to diminish among older individuals, and at some point, (as individuals near retirement), increased age actually begins to decrease the likelihood of employment. In our study, for all models, we find that years of age increase the odds of employment. At younger ages, the impact of the decay term is small; however, at older ages the impact of the decay term becomes quite noticeable—for both Aboriginal peoples and non-Aboriginals. However, increased age has a greater positive impact on the likelihood of employment among non-Aboriginals (looking at the impact of age alone).[18]

Part-time students also have a higher likelihood of being employed compared to non-students.[19] And, living in a Census Metropolitan Area (a proxy for an urban centre) is linked to higher rates of employment, slightly more so among Aboriginal peoples than non-Aboriginals (1.40 compared to 1.26) after holding our co-variates constant. This finding, at least in part, reflects the higher rate of employment growth in urban centres over this period compared to non CMAs (Heisz et al. 2005).

What is the impact of Aboriginal status on the likelihood of employment after taking other socio-demographic factors into account? Succinctly stated, Aboriginal status matters. Aboriginal identity remains an important determinant of employment. Factors such as comparatively low levels of education clearly account for some of the difference in the employment prospects of Aboriginals and non-Aboriginals. Yet, holding constant the co-variates in our model, Aboriginal people as a group are still 48% as likely to be employed as non-Aboriginal people. Looking specifically at each group, First Nations people are 41% as likely to be employed, the Inuit are 64% as likely to be employed, and the Métis are 71% as likely to be employed compared to non-Aboriginals after controlling for the effects of a number of socio-demographic factors.[20] This does not mean that education is not important, as we have argued above. Education is key to improving employment prospects, particularly for Aboriginal people. But, the disproportionately large population of Aboriginal people with low levels of education continues to influence the overall likelihood of employment. Certainly, there are other factors that influence the likelihood of employment, factors that have not been included in our model. For instance, the health status of workers has emerged as an important determinant of employment in the Australian literature. We also know that having a disability reduces the likelihood of being employed and Aboriginal persons have a much higher rate of disability than non-Aboriginals. Local economic conditions such as the stock of employment opportunities, and level of unemployment are important to consider. And finally, other structural issues such as culture and discrimination may well influence employment outcomes. Certainly, the need to look for explanations apart from variations in individual characteristics is revealed in the size of the gap in employment opportunities reported here.

What factors influence the likelihood of being employed full-time among Aboriginal people? Are the odds of full-time employment the same for Aboriginal people and non-Aboriginals? **Figure 1.6** shows that that proportion of full-time and part-time workers among Aboriginal and non-Aboriginal workers is roughly similar. However, overall, Aboriginal people are 50% less likely to be employed on a full-time basis than non-Aboriginals—that is, they have a smaller chance of securing full-time employment. This is true for First Nations people, the Métis and Inuit. The odds of full-time employment, however, are higher among the Métis and Inuit compared to First Nations people (1.64 and 1.27 times higher respectively). This holds true when we hold constant factors such as education, age, and gender as well.

What factors influence full-time employment among Aboriginal people? The same factors that influence access to employment appear to influence access to full-time employment. As the level of education increases, the odds of being employed full-time increase as well. Individuals without any educational credentials are

Table 1.3: Likelihood of Employment among Aboriginal People compared to Non-Aboriginal People, Canada, 2001

	Likelihood of being employed				Likelihood of being employed full-time			
	FN	Métis	Inuit	Total	FN	Métis	Inuit	Total
Impact of Aboriginal identity alone	0.35	0.66	0.53	0.43	0.43	0.70	0.55	0.50
Impact of Aboriginal identity taking other social and demographic factors into account	0.41	0.71	0.64	0.48	0.48	0.74	0.64	0.56
Difference	0.06	0.05	0.11	0.05	0.05	0.04	0.09	0.06

hugely disadvantaged compared to those with higher levels of education, particularly university graduates. The gap in employment prospects among Aboriginal peoples between those with an educational credential and those without is very pronounced. Again, the returns of education as measured by access to full-time employment are higher among Aboriginal peoples than non-Aboriginals.

Being at school full-time decreases the likelihood of having full-time employment (as it decreases the likelihood of being employed). Being a part-time student is not a significant predictor of full-time employment among Aboriginal people aged 25 to 64 years.

Women are much less likely than men to be employed full time. This is not surprising as women tend to have higher rates of part-time employment. And we see that Aboriginal women are less likely to be employed full-time than to be employed on either a full-time or part-time basis (54% as likely to be employed full-time compared to 69% as likely to be employed compared to men). However, again, there is a significant difference in the likelihood of full-time employment between Aboriginal and non-Aboriginal women. Aboriginal women are 1.5 times more likely than non-Aboriginal women to be employed full time.

Aboriginal lone parents—the majority of whom are women—are less likely to be employed than non-lone parents as one might expect, but not to a large degree. Indeed, the odds of full-time employment among Aboriginal lone parents are generally greater than the odds of employment (0.84 compared to 0.70). And among non-Aboriginals, lone parents are more likely to be employed full-time than non-lone parents—an interesting point to explore further.

Living in a Census Metropolitan Area is also linked to higher odds of full-time employment for both Aboriginals and non-Aboriginals, more so among Aboriginals. And as working-age adults age, their full-time employment prospects improve.

What is the impact of Aboriginal status on the likelihood of full-time employment after taking factors such as education and place of residence into account? The impact of Aboriginal status is still an important determinant of full-time employment even after controlling for a number of other factors (See **Table 1.3**). While the overall likelihood of full-time employment is higher than the likelihood of employment (full-time and part-time), a significant difference remains compared with the non-Aboriginal population, particularly for First Nations people. Again, these findings point to the impact of other individual and structural factors in explaining the differential in employment opportunities between Aboriginal and non-Aboriginal people.

What factors influence the likelihood of being employed in a job that matches one's level of education among Aboriginal people? Are the odds of holding an appropriate job where there is a match between skills and employment the same for Aboriginal people and non-Aboriginals? The likelihood of having a job where skill and job content match is lower among Aboriginal peoples compared to non-Aboriginal people. However, the difference is smaller than the difference in the odds of holding a job or holding a full-time job. Aboriginal people are 27% less likely than non-Aboriginals to hold "appropriate" employment, and 20% less likely after holding constant level of education, gender, place of residence, etc. Stated another way, the odds of a person getting a job that matches his or her skill set—regardless of level of education—is slightly better than the odds of securing employment in the first place.

Again, Métis people have a greater chance of obtaining employment that corresponds with their skills than First Nations people. However, the odds of an Inuit person having a "job/education match" are lower than that of First Nations people.

What factors influence the likelihood of securing employment that corresponds to an individual's education and training? The same types of factors influence the likelihood of having a "job/education match" among Aboriginal peoples and non-Aboriginals. However, there are notable differences. For example, education is predictably an important determinant of the education/job match, after controlling for a variety of other factors. Aboriginal university graduates are three times as likely as those without any educational qualifications to have a job/education match, indeed, they are more likely to have a job/education match than non-Aboriginals. However, the odds of securing a job that matches one's education are lower for college degree holders than for trade school graduates, for both Aboriginals and non-Aboriginals. Indeed among Aboriginal peoples, the value of a college degree and high school diploma is effectively the same with respect to enhancing one's odds of securing an "appropriate" job. This raises important questions about the job market for college degree holders. It may also reflect the relatively high numbers of Aboriginal people in trade school and the sectors of the economy within which they work.

Men are more likely to hold "appropriate" employment compared to women, however, among Aboriginal women, the gap is less than the gender gap in employment prospects (0.77 compared to 0.69). Indeed, while non-Aboriginal women were 33% as likely to be employed full-time compared to non-Aboriginal men, they are 82% as likely to be employed in jobs that correspond to their education and training. There is not a large difference in this regard between Aboriginal and non-Aboriginal women. However, it is worth noting that non-Aboriginal women have better odds than Aboriginal women in contrast to our findings for question 1 and question 2 (page 9). Again, this is not an indicator of access to "good employment" per se; rather, women, regardless of education, have a good—although not equal—chance of obtaining a job that matches their skills. The odds of having a job/skill match are lower for lone parents (compared to non-lone parents) and for unattached individuals (compared to those in economic families). However, the gaps are not large.

While urban living or a recent move appears to have little influence (indeed, the differences are not significant among Aboriginal peoples), additional years of age do affect the likelihood of securing appropriate employment somewhat.

Aboriginal people are less likely to be employed, are more likely to be unemployed, and more likely to be outside of the labour force all together compared to non-Aboriginals. Aboriginals are somewhat more likely to be under-qualified and overqualified for their jobs. Statistical analysis confirms that lower educational attainment is a significant factor underlying Aboriginal labour force status. However, known predictors of employment such as age, gender, family status, mobility, and place of residence only explain a portion of the difference in the odds of employment between Aboriginal peoples and non-Aboriginals. Clearly Aboriginal status and other individual and structural factors play a role in circumscribing the employment prospects of Aboriginal Canadians.

Policy Implications

High levels of participation in the labour market reveal that the problem is not exclusively about employment incentives. Rather, the problem is jobs. The problem is unsupportive learning environments. The problem is the health and sustainability of Aboriginal communities. The problem is the historic legacy of colonialism and racism. Part of the answer strongly suggested by our study is the critical need to increase the educational attainment of Aboriginal people. There is a pressing need to encourage young people to complete high school, at a minimum, particularly First Nations youth on reserves. Resources are also needed to encourage Aboriginal people to pursue post-secondary training, and to support other working-age adults via continuing education and skills upgrading, literacy and basic skills development, apprenticeships and employment training, and job preparation and mentoring—with programs that are both culturally sensitive and inclusive. At the same time, investment in child care, transportation, assistance with other work-related expenses, as well as secure housing, is a prerequisite for any successful initiative. Employment programs that focus only on skills upgrading or job preparation will have limited success. As evidence from the review of the AHRDS reveals, systems of learning and support need to be fundamentally rethought for children, youth and adults. Similarly, initiatives that focus exclusively on the individual, and fail to take into account the family and/or community will not achieve lasting outcomes. In this regard, the nature of women's roles in the productive and caring activities of their communities demands particular attention.

Education is only part of the answer. Despite the significant return to education, the very size of the employment gap reveals the entrenched character of the structural problems facing Aboriginal communities across Canada. The socio-spatial isolation of Aboriginal people on reserves, in remote communities, in the North, and in our urban centres is a particularly difficult policy problem. What can be done, for instance, to improve the labour market on and around reserves. Canada's sizeable pool of low-wage employment—characterized by high turnover, poor working conditions, and limited earning or occupation mobility—is another significant policy challenge. Workers, particularly those with low levels of education as is common in the Aboriginal community, are effectively trapped at the bottom of the labour market. Over time, many are being pushed out of the labour market all together.

The Canada West Foundation makes the point that there is an opportunity to address Aboriginal labour market disparities to benefit Aboriginal people and non-Aboriginal people alike. In order to realize this potential however, policies and programs cannot be limited to communicating the benefits of educational attainment and labour market participation to Aboriginal people. Rather, policies and programs must embody an understanding of the "network of circumstances" surrounding an individual. "Factors such as social conditions, family and community influences, workplace alienation, individuals' aspirations, transition adjustments, access to financial and social support structures, and sense of identity all influence decisions and outcomes. These factors must be taken into consideration if policies and programs designed to improve labour market outcomes for Aboriginal people are to be successful (Brunnen 2003a, 22).

Our study has clearly only scratched the surface. A diverse range of factors—both individual and structural—influence the prospects of employment among Aboriginal peoples. Improving educational attainment and addressing gender inequities are clearly important in this regard. However, much remains to be done to create the conditions for greater economic security and well-being among Aboriginal peoples.

Acknowledgements

We would like to acknowledge the assistance of several colleagues at the Canadian Council on Social Development. Rebecca Gowan, Spyridoula Tsoukalas, Paul Roberts and Gail Fawcett provided invaluable assistance and advice. Thanks also to Alfred Gay from the National Association of Friendship Centres. The authors would like to acknowledge the support provided by the Policy and Research Coordination Directorate at Human Resources and Social Development Canada.

Research assistance was provided by Rebecca Gowan on behalf of the Canadian Council on Social Development and the National Association of Friendship Centres.

Endnotes

1 There are several reasons behind this significant increase in population. The birth rate among Aboriginal peoples is comparatively higher than the birth rate among non-Aboriginals. However, at least half of the increase has been linked to the growing number of Canadians choosing to identify as Aboriginal. Statistics Canada has also noted that some of the increase is likely due to more complete enumeration of reserves in the 2001 Census. See Statistics Canada (2003b). Aboriginal Peoples in Canada: A Demographic Portrait, Catalogue No. 96F0030XIE2001007. Ottawa: Industry Canada.

2 The term "North American Indian" is used in the Census. In this report, we have elected to use the term First Nations people to describe this group.

3 In the following calculations, we have combined the "other Aboriginal" category (here including Aboriginal people of multiple Aboriginal ancestry and those who identified themselves as Registered Indians and/or Band members but not Aboriginal) with the First Nations category. This group represents less than 1% of the unweighted observations.

4 The Aboriginal population is expected to grow at an average annual rate of 1.8%, more than twice the rate of 0.7% for the general population. The Inuit population will have the fastest rate of growth (about 2.3%) compared with 1.9% for the North American Indian population and 1.4% for the Métis (these figures are based on medium growth scenarios) (Statistics Canada, 2005a).

5 As well, a larger proportion of Aboriginal adults live in common-law households compared to non-Aboriginal adults, 20% compared to 14%. These individuals are included under couple households in **Figure 1.1** (page 4).

6 Aboriginal people were also more likely to report that they did no housework at all compared to non Aboriginals (9% compared to 6%).

7 This may well reflect the younger age profile of the Aboriginal working age population.

8 The median income is the income which falls in the middle of the distribution of incomes for that year (ordered by size). The median represents the middle of the distribution of incomes and 50% of the incomes are below this income and 50% are above. In 2000, the median income for the Aboriginal population was $17,140; in 1995, median income was $14,190 (constant dollars). Among non-Aboriginals, median income was $26,700 (constant dollars) in 1995 and $29,780 in 2000.

9 The exception is Jerry White, Paul White and Stephen Obeng Gyimah (2003), "Labour Force Activity of Women in Canada: A Comparative Analysis of Aboriginal and Non-Aboriginal Women," Canadian Review of Sociology and Anthropology, Vol. 40, No. 4.

10 For the purposes of this study, Aboriginal Identity refers to those persons who reported identifying with at least one Aboriginal group in the Census, i.e. North American Indian, Métis or Inuit, and/or those who reported being a Treaty Indian or a Registered Indian as defined by the *Indian Act* of Canada and/or who were members of an Indian Band or First Nation. Those who report multiple Aboriginal identities are included as well. Please see the Methodology section.

11 For the purposes of this study, the analysis includes those who were born in Canada, and do not identify as an immigrant or a member of a visible minority. In instances where individuals identify as Aboriginal and an immigrant or visible minority, these cases have been excluded from the analysis.

12 This information is based on the variable "hours worked for pay or in self-employment in reference week." If the number of hours worked is greater or equal to 30, the employment is considered full-time. However, this variable is not perfectly related to the job held by individual at time of the Census; rather it refers to the number of hours that a person worked at all jobs held in the week prior to the Census day. Thus, the number of hours may correspond to one main job or to several jobs. In addition, if a person was absent, with or without pay, for part of the week because of illness, vacation, or some other reason at time of the Census, the information was not gathered. In this case, when it was possible, we have imputed the information on the number of hours worked.

13   The employment rate refers to the number of persons employed in the week prior to Census day, expressed as a percentage of the total population aged 25 to 64 years.

14   The unemployment rate refers to the number of persons who are unemployed during the reference week prior to Census day, expressed as a percentage of the labour force.

15   There is ongoing debate about the National Occupational Classification and its definition of skill levels. These levels are based largely on educational requirements for particular occupations and not a detailed assessment of the required skills. That said, we are using the NOC classification system as the one available to us. It provides a useful tool to assess the match of employment and education/skill within the working age population.

16   Please note that management occupations have been excluded from the following analysis because there are no set skill requirements for a management job.

17   Please note that there are many factors that influence the likelihood of employment. We have included six important factors in our analysis.

18   Our age squared (age^2) variable is significant and decreases the likelihood of employment in the three models.

19   This finding is not surprising as the respondents are over age 25 and are thus more likely to be pursuing education on a part-time basis.

20   After controlling for the covariates in our model, both the Inuit and Métis are still more likely to be employed than First Nations people. However, the Inuit have higher odds of employment than the Métis, both compared to First Nations people: 1.76 to 1 and 1.67 to 1 respectively.

References

Anderson, John et al. (2003). *Expanding the Federal Pay Equity Policy Beyond Gender*. Ottawa: Canadian Council on Social Development.

Arthur, W.S. et al. (2004). Careers and Aspirations: Young Torres Strait Islanders, 1999–2003. Discussion Paper No. 259/2004. Canberra: Centre for Aboriginal Economic Policy Research, The Australian National University.

Banerjee, A.K.P., J. Alam and P. De Civita, (1991). "Wage Gap Between Aboriginals and Non-Aboriginals in Canada: An Empirical Analysis." Paper presented at the Annual Meeting of the Canadian Economic Association. Kingston, June 2–4. Cited in White, Maxim and Gyimah (2003).

Brunnen, Ben (2003a). "Achieving Potential: Towards Improved Labour Market Outcomes for Aboriginal People." *Building the New West Project Report #19*. Calgary: Canada West Foundation.

Brunnen, Ben (2003b). "Encouraging Success: Ensuring Aboriginal Youth Stay in School." *Building the New West Project Report #22*. Calgary: Canada West Foundation.

Brunnen, Ben (2004). "Working Towards Parity: Recommendations of the Aboriginal Human Capital Strategies Initiative." *Building the New West Project Report #24*. Calgary: Canada West Foundation.

Carter, Tom and Chesay Polevychok (2004). Literature Review on Issues and Needs of Aboriginal People. Federation of Canadian Municipalities.

Clatworthy, S., J. Hall and N. Loughran (1995). *Public Policy and Aboriginal Peoples, Project Area 3: Employment of the Aboriginal Labour Force*. Ottawa: Royal Commission on Aboriginal Peoples.

Conference Board of Canada, Loizides, Stelios and Janusz Zieminski (1998). "Member's Briefing. Employment Prospects for Aboriginal People." Ottawa: November 1998.

Conference Board of Canada (2003). "Insights on Western Canada: A Socio-economic Report." Ottawa: August 2003.

DeSilva, A. (1999). "Wage Discrimination against Natives." Canadian Public Policy, vol. 25, no 1: 65–85.

Dion Stout, Madeleine and Gregory D. Kipling (1998). "Aboriginal Women in Canada: Strategic Research Directions for Policy Development." Ottawa: Status of Women Canada.

Drost, H. and T. Eryou (1991). "Education/Training and Labour Force Status: A Cross-section Study of Canadian Natives." Paper presented at the Annual Meeting of the Canadian Economic Association, Kingston, June 2–4. Cited in White, Maxim and Gyimah (2003).

Drost, Helmar (1994). "Schooling, Vocational Training and Unemployment: The Case of Canadian Aboriginals." *Canadian Public Policy—Analyse de Politiques*, Vol. 20, No. 1.

Drost, Helmar (1995). "The Aboriginal-white Unemployment Gap in Canada's Urban Labour Markets." In *Market Solutions for Native Poverty: Social Policy for the Third Solitude*. H. Drost, B.L. Crowley and R. Schwindt (eds.). Toronto: C.D. Howe Institute.

Gallie, Duncan (2002). "The Quality of Working Life in Welfare Strategy." In *Why We Need a New Welfare State*. Gosta Esping-Andersen (ed.). New York: Oxford University Press.

George, P. and P. Kuhn (1994). "The Size and Structure of Native-white Wage Differentials in Canada," *Canadian Journal of Economics*, Vol. 27, No. 1.

George, P., P. Kuhn and A. Sweetman (1995). *Patterns of Employment, Unemployment and Poverty: A Comparative Analysis of Several Aspects of the Employment Experience of Aboriginal and Non-Aboriginal Canadians Using 1991 Census Public Use Microdata*. Ottawa: Royal Commission on Aboriginal Peoples.

Gray, M.C, and B. Hunter (2005). "Indigenous Job Search Success." Discussion Paper No. 274/2005. Canberra: Centre for Aboriginal Economic Policy Research, The Australian National University.

Heisz, Andrew, Sébastien LaRochelle-Côté, Michael Bordt and Sudip Das (2005). "Trends and Conditions in Census Metropolitan Areas: Labour Markets, Business Activity, and Population Growth and Mobility in Canadian CMAs." Statistics Canada. Ottawa: Ministry of Industry. Catalogue No. 89-613-MIE, No. 006

Hunter, B (1996). "The Importance of Education in Improving the Indigenous Employment Outcomes." Issue Brief November 12 1996. The Centre for Aboriginal Economic Policy Research. The Australian National University.

Hunter, B. (2004). "Indigenous Australians in the Contemporary Labour Market: 2001." The Centre for Aboriginal Economic Policy Research. Canberra: Australian Bureau of Statistics.

Hull, J. (2000). "Aboriginal Post-secondary Education and Labour Market Outcomes in Canada, 1996." Ottawa: Indian and Northern Affairs Canada.

Indian and Northern Affairs Canada (1997). "Gathering Strength: Canada's Aboriginal Action Plan." Ottawa. Indian and Northern Affairs Canada. <**www.ainc-inac.gc.ca/gs/chg_e.html**>.

Indian and Northern Affairs Canada (2005). "Post Secondary Education and Labour Market Outcomes Canada, 2001." Ottawa: Indian and Northern Affairs Canada. < **www.ainc.inac.gc.ca/pr/ra/pse/01/ index_e.html** >.

Jackson, Andrew (2005). *Work and Labour in Canada*. Toronto: Canadian Scholars' Press.

Kenny, Carolyn (2002). "North American Indian, Métis and Inuit Women Speak about Culture, Education and Work." Ottawa: Status of Women Canada.

Lamontagne, Francois (2004). "The Aboriginal Workforce: What Lies Ahead." CLBC Commentary. Ottawa: Canadian Labour and Business Centre.

Levesque, Carole et al. (2001). "Aboriginal Women and Jobs: Challenges and Issues for Employability Programs in Quebec." Ottawa: Status of Women Canada.

Maxim, P., J. White and D. Beavon (2001). "Dispersion and Polarization of Income among Aboriginal and non-Aboriginal Canadians." *Canadian Review of Sociology and Anthropology*, Vol. 38, No. 4.

Mendelson, M. and K. Battle (1999). "Aboriginal People in Canada's Labour Market." Ottawa: Caledon Institute of Public Policy. Ottawa.

Mendelson, M. (2004). "Aboriginal People in Canada's Labour Market: Work and Unemployment, Today and Tomorrow." Ottawa: Caledon Institute of Public Policy. Ottawa.

Newhouse, David and Evelyn Peters (eds.) (2003). *Not Strangers in these Parts: Urban Aboriginal Peoples*. Ottawa: Policy Research Initiative.

Norris, Mary Jane and Stewart Clatworthy (2003) "Aboriginal Mobility and Migration within Urban Canada: Outcomes, Factors and Implications." In *Not Strangers in these Parts: Urban Aboriginal Peoples*. David Newhouse and Evelyn Peters (eds.). Ottawa: Policy Research Initiative.

Pendakur, K. et al. (1998). "The Colour of Money: Earnings Differentials among Ethnic Groups in Canada." *Canadian Journal of Economics*, Vol. 31, No 3.

Pendakur, K. et al. (2002). "Colour my World: Have Earnings Gaps for Canadian-born Ethnic Minorities Changed over Time?" *Canadian Public Policy*, Vol. 28, No 4.

Peters, E. and M.W. Rosenberg (1995). "Labour Force Attachment and Regional Development for Native Peoples: Theoretical and Methodological Issues," *Canadian Journal of Regional Studies*, Vol. 18, No. 1.

Royal Commission on Aboriginal Peoples (1996a). Report of the Royal Commission on Aboriginal Peoples, Volume 4, Perspectives and Realities. Ottawa: Minister of Supply and Services.

Royal Commission on Aboriginal Peoples (1996b). Report of the Royal Commission on Aboriginal Peoples, Volume 5, Renewal: A Twenty-year Commitment. Ottawa: Minister of Supply and Services.

Saskatchewan Women's Secretariat (1999). "Profile of Aboriginal Women in Saskatchewan." Regina: Queen's Printer.

Scott, Katherine (1997). "Are Women Catching Up in the Earnings Race?" Social Research Series, Working Paper No. 3. Ottawa: Canadian Council on Social Development.

Statistics Canada (2003a). "Education in Canada: Raising the Standard." Ottawa: Statistics Canada. Catalogue no. 96F0030XIE2001012.

Statistics Canada (2003b). Aboriginal Peoples of Canada: A Demographic Profile. Ottawa: Ministry of Industry. Catalogue No. 96F0030XIE2001007.

Statistics Canada, Demography Division (2005a). "Projections of the Aboriginal populations: Canada, Provinces and Territories, 2001 to 2017." Ottawa: Minister of Industry. Catalogue no. 91-547-XIE.

Statistics Canada (2005b). "Aboriginal peoples living off-reserve in Western Canada: Estimates from the Labour Force Survey," April 2004–March 2005. Ottawa: Labour Statistics Division.

Tabachnik, B. G., and Fidell, L. S. (1996). *Using Multivariate Statistics* (3rd ed.). New York: Harper-Collins College Publishers.

Vosko, L., N. Zukewich, and C. Cranford (2003). "Non-standard Work and Precariousness in the Canadian Labour Market," Perspectives on Labour and Income. Ottawa: Statistics Canada.

White, J., P. Maxim and D. Beavon (eds.) (2003a). *Aboriginal Conditions: Research Foundations for Public Policy*. Vancouver: UBC Press.

White, J., P. Maxim and D. Beavon (eds.) (2003b). "Labour Force Activity of Women in Canada: A Comparative Analysis of Aboriginal and non-Aboriginal Women," *Canadian Review of Sociology and Anthropology*, Vol. 40, No. 4.

Appendices

Appendix 1.1 Logistic Regression Output: Summary

	Be employed		Be employed full time		Be employed in a job that matches one's qualification and skills	
	Logit	Odds	Logit	Odds	Logit	Odds
With no covariates						
Be an aboriginal person	-0.84**	0.43	-0.68**	0.50	-0.32**	0.73
Constant	1.17**		0.60**		-0.60**	
Model information						
Log likelihood	369,502.54		436,614.25		434,021.65	
Chi Square	1,762.10		1,256.19		234.381	
Level of signification	< 0.001		< 0.001		< 0.001	
With covariates (full model)						
Be an aboriginal person	-0.73**	0.48	-0.60**	0.56	-0.22**	0.80
Constant	-3.45**		-3.50**		-2.68**	
Model information						
Log likelihood	320,147.63		383,482.32		420,876.69	
Chi Square	51,117.00		54,388.11		13,379.35	
Level of signification	< 0.001		< 0.001		< 0.001	

* p<.05 ** p<.01 Odds=e^{logit}

Appendix 1.2 Likelihood of Being Employed

Odds of being employed	Model 1 Total (25-64 yrs)		Model 2 Aboriginal		Model 3 Non-Aboriginal	
	Logit	Odds	Logit	Odds	Logit	Odds
Aboriginal identities[a]						
First Nation	-0.91**	0.41	--	--	--	--
Métis	-0.35**	0.71	0.51**	1.67	--	--
Inuit	-0.44**	0.64	0.57**	1.76	--	--
[Non Aboriginal]	--	--	--	--	--	--
Education						
[Less than high school]	--	--	--	--	--	--
Secondary graduation diploma	0.62**	1.86	0.86**	2.38	0.61**	1.83
Trade certificate	0.76**	2.14	0.96**	2.61	0.74**	2.10
College certificate/diploma	1.02**	2.84	1.38**	4.00	1.02**	2.78
University diploma	1.26**	3.55	1.61**	5.00	1.25**	3.50
Student						
Full time	-1.47**	0.23	-1.23**	0.29	-1.50**	0.22
Part time	0.26**	1.30	0.35**	1.41	0.25**	1.29
[not at school]	--	--	--	--	--	--
Gender						
Female [male]	-0.71**	0.49	-0.37**	0.69	-0.73**	0.48
Age						
Age	0.27**	1.30	0.19**	1.21	0.26**	1.30
Age2	-0.004**	0.99	-0.003**	0.99	-0.004**	0.99
Family situation						
Be an unattached individual	-0.21**	0.81	-0.18**	0.83	-0.21**	0.81
[Be in an economic family]	--	--	--	--	--	--
Be a lone parent	-0.14**	0.87	-0.35**	0.70	-0.13**	0.89
[Not a lone parent]	--	--	--	--	--	--
Geographies						
CMA [non CMA]	0.24**	1.27	0.33**	1.40	0.23**	1.26
Movers [non-movers]	-0.17**	0.84	-0.24**	0.78	-0.17**	0.85
Constant	-3.44**		-3.70**		-3.40**	
Model information						
Log likelihood	319989.81		13653.35		306047.45	
Chi square	51274.83		1708.68		48093.07	
Level of signification	<0.001		<0.001		< 0.001	

[a] Categories of reference are in [ ]; Non-Aboriginal is the category of reference only in model 1; First Nation is the category of reference only in model 2

* p<.05 ** p<.01

Odds=elogit

Appendix 1.3 Likelihood of Being Employed Full-time

Odds of being employed full-time	Model 1 Total (25-64 yrs)		Model 2 Aboriginal		Model 3 Non-Aboriginal	
	Logit	Odds	Logit	Odds	Logit	Odds
Aboriginal identities[a]						
First Nation	-0.73**	0.48	--	--	--	--
Métis	-0.30**	0.74	0.38**	1.46	--	--
Inuit	-0.45**	0.64	0.36**	1.44	--	--
Non-Aboriginal	--	--	--	--	--	--
Education						
[Less than high school]	--	--	--	--	--	--
Secondary graduation diploma	0.51**	1.67	0.81**	2.24	0.50**	1.65
Trade certificate	0.61**	1.85	0.84**	2.31	0.60**	1.82
College certificate/diploma	0.76**	2.15	1.20**	3.33	0.74**	2.10
University diploma	0.95**	2.58	1.52**	4.58	0.93**	2.53
Student						
Full time	-1.55**	0.21	-1.31*	0.27	-1.57**	0.20
Part time	0.19**	1.21	0.16		0.19**	1.21
[Not at school]	--	--	--	--	--	--
Gender						
Female [male]	-1.07**	0.34	-0.61*	0.54	-1.09**	0.33
Age						
Age	0.24**	1.27	0.17**	1.19	0.24**	1.27
Age2	-0.003**	0.99	-0.002**	0.99	-0.003**	0.99
Family situation						
Be an unattached individual	-0.05**	0.94	-0.11*	0.89	-0.05**	0.95
[Be in an economic family]	--	--	--	--	--	--
Be a lone parent	0.06**	1.06	-0.17**	0.84	0.07**	1.10
[Not a lone parent]	--	--	--	--	--	--
Geographies						
CMA [non CMA]	0.23**	1.26	0.30**	1.36	0.23**	1.26
Movers [non-movers]	-0.11**	0.89	-0.25**	0.78	-0.10**	0.90
Constant	-3.49**		-3.61**		-3.47**	
Model information						
Log-Likelihood	383,389.30		14,075.21		368,943.51	
Chi-square	54,481.14		1,551.58		52,043.95	
Level of signification	<0.001		<0.001		<0.001	

[a] Categories of reference are in [ ]; Non-Aboriginal is the category of reference only in model 1; First Nation is the category of reference only in model 2

* p<.05 ** p<.01

Odds=elogit

Appendix 1.4 Likelihood of Having an "Appropriate" Job

Odds of having appropriate employment	Model 1 Total (24-65yrs)		Model 2 Aboriginal		Model 3 Non-Aboriginal	
	Logit	Odds	Logit	Odds	Logit	Odds
Aboriginal identities						
[First Nation]	-0.31**	0.73	--	--	--	--
Métis	0.010		0.28**	1.32	--	--
Inuit	-0.52**	0.60	-0.19		--	--
[Non-Aboriginal]	--	--	--	--	--	--
Education						
[Less than high school]	--	--	--	--	--	--
Secondary grad. diploma	0.14**	1.15	0.33**	1.39	0.14**	1.14
Trade certificate	0.51**	1.66	0.54**	1.71	0.51**	1.66
College certificate/ diploma	0.20**	1.22	0.33**	1.40	0.20**	1.22
University diploma	0.82**	2.27	1.10**	3.00	0.81**	2.26
Student						
Full time	-0.32**	0.72	-0.42**	0.66	-0.32**	0.73
Part time	-0.002		0.020		0.003	
[not at school]	--	--	--	--	--	--
Gender						
Female [male]	-0.19**	0.82	-0.25**	0.77	-0.19**	0.82
Age						
Age	0.11**	1.12	0.08**	1.09	0.11**	1.12
Age^2	-0.001**	0.99	-0.001**	0.99	-0.001**	0.99
Family situation						
Be an unattached individual	-0.07**	0.92	-0.17**	0.84	-0.07**	0.93
[Be in an economic family]	--	--	--	--	--	--
Be a lone parent	-0.07**	0.93	-0.19**	0.82	-0.07**	0.94
[Not a lone parent]	--	--	--	--	--	--
Geographies						
CMA [non-CMA]	0.02*	1.02	0.07		0.02**	1.02
Movers [non-movers]	-0.03**	0.97	0.02		-0.03**	0.97
Constant	-2.67**		-2.46**		-2.69**	
Model information						
Log likelihood	420824.74		13,060.07		407731.49	
Chi Square	13431.30		460.15		12769.95	
Level of signification	<0.001		<0.001		<0.001	

[a] Categories of reference are in [ ]; Non-Aboriginal is the category of reference only in model 1; First Nation is the category of reference only in model 2

* p<.05 ** p<.01

Odds=e^{logit}

2

School Completion and Workforce Transitions among Urban Aboriginal Youth

Paul Maxim and Jerry White

Introduction

Across Canada, young people of Aboriginal origin have lower levels of post secondary education than the national average. In the general population, we know that young people who do not complete high school also have greater difficulties making the transition to the labour force than those who complete high school. Using Cycle II of the Youth in Transition Survey (YITS), this study explores differential patterns of school completion and transition to the workforce between predominately urban Aboriginal and non-Aboriginal youth. We also examine the role of students' families' values toward education, and students' levels of connectedness or engagement with schools as contributing factors to the likelihood of school completion.

First Nations Educational Attainment

The gap in levels of formal educational achievement between Canadians of Aboriginal and non-Aboriginal origin is well documented. Essentially, the research shows that First Nations students have consistently lower average educational achievement than the student population at large (King 1993; Hull 2000; 2005; White and Maxim 2002b). This lower attainment appears to be correlated with several life outcomes, including lower income (Maxim, White and Beavon 2003), reduced well-being (Beavon and Cook 2003; Wilkinson 1997), and lower rates of labour force participation (White and Maxim 2002a; White, Maxim and Gyimah 2003; Hull 2005).

In its April 2000 report, the Auditor General of Canada identified this discrepancy in educational attainment as unacceptable. Targeting education as a policy priority is predicated on the research that suggests there are real and substantial social and economic returns to improvements in human capital (Jankowski and Moazzami 1995; White, Maxim and Beavon 2003). This return is particularly dramatic for Aboriginal persons who increase their educational attainment (see also MacPherson 1991).

While across the board progress in the level of education among Aboriginal youth has been made over the past few decades, the available literature points out certain consistent patterns of under achievement. One observation, for example, is that First Nations people residing off-reserve have a greater educational attainment than those living on-reserve (McDonald 1991; Canada 1991). Armstrong, Kennedy and Oberle (1990) find, using 1986 data, that only 25% of those identifying themselves as "North American Indian" in the census completed high school as compared with one-half of the non-Indian population. Siggner (1986) found that in 1971 less than 3% of the First Nations out-of-school population had attained any post secondary education. Encouragingly, by 1981 that proportion had risen to 19%, but this was still less than half the national average. By the early 1990s, only 2.3% of Aboriginal high school completers were going on to university (King 1993).

In a study of First Nations high school dropouts from Ontario schools, MacKay and Myles (1989) report that while the enrolment of students increased throughout the 1980s, the overall graduation rate from high school for registered Indians varied between 33% and 55% of the grade nine cohorts they studied. This is much lower than for the non-Aboriginal population where completion rates of more than 70% were reported in all of the districts that MacKay and Myles studied. Tait (1999) reports that nationally, in 1986, Aboriginal people were 2.2 times more likely not to complete high school than non-Aboriginal people. Disconcertingly, by 1996 that relationship for Aboriginal people was measured at 2.6 times more likely not to have completed high school (for further discussions, see Urion, 1993).

The picture is not completely gloomy since some signs of improvement appeared between 1986 and 1996. The percentage of young Aboriginal adults with less than a high school diploma dropped from 60% to less than 45%. Those completing any form of post-secondary education increased from 15% to 20%, while the number of Aboriginal persons holding a university degree doubled from 2% to 4%.[1] However, even more gains appeared in the non-Aboriginal population, and this meant that the differences between the two populations generally widened. In the same decade, the largest increase in the gap between non-Aboriginal and Aboriginal educational attainment was for persons 20–29 years of age (Urion 1993).

More recent studies in British Columbia (2000a, 2000b) indicate that 61% of Aboriginal students compared with 23% of non-Aboriginal students do not complete high school in six years; 14% of Aboriginal students do not progress to grade nine compared with 4% of non-Aboriginal students; and Aboriginal students are behind age-grade level norms in every grade in every district examined.

Nationally, White and Maxim (2002b) looked at three measures of educational attainment: age appropriateness for the grade the students were in, graduation rates, and dropout rates. The average age-appropriate rate of First Nations students lagged behind the general population by approximately 78%. The age-appropriate rate was much higher among younger students, however, with the rate among students in grades nine or lower being 90.8%, but this dropped significantly to 55.4% among the high school grades. White and Maxim calculated the graduation rate from a sample of those students who were included on the nominal rolls, and who graduated or withdrew from grades 12 or 13 only. The First Nations' graduation rate among this sample averaged 19.8%. The third measure of educational attainment used in the study was the withdrawal rate. The sample used for this measure included Band-resident registered Indian students who were 16 years of age, actively registered at the schools, and who graduated or withdrew in 1995–1996. Among those, the withdrawal rate is 17.8% (see Reyhner 1991; 2001; and Ward 1995 for similar US studies).

White and Maxim also found that Band students who chose to go to provincially operated schools had a higher age-appropriate rate than those in the Band-operated schools, but that students tended to withdraw in larger numbers. Before grade nine, the age-appropriate rate for students in provincial schools was 92.8% while in Band schools it was 86%. After grade nine, the age-appropriate rate dropped to 62% for provincial schools, and 43.8% for Band schools. The withdrawal rate for provincial schools was 18.2% as compared with 11.8% for Band schools (see also Kirkness and Bowman 1992). White and Maxim (2002b) noted, however, that provincial schools do not differ significantly on graduation rates or withdrawal rates compared with Band schools.

Overwhelmingly, the research shows that the returns of education are dramatic. Maxim, White and Beavon (2003) suggest that although levels of educational attainment among First Nations people continue to be lower than among non-Aboriginals, the economic rate of return of higher education is much higher for First Nations people. This suggests that formal education is a major factor in allowing the First Nations population to achieve economic parity with the rest of the country. One of the brightest rays of hope lies in the finding that there are community correlates with educational achievement. The most promising is that as the average level of education increases in the parental population, there are incremental gains in students' levels of achievement. This indicates that as we make improvements in the achievement of this cohort and the next generation of students, these improvements will trigger even greater positive consequences in later generations.

We noted above that the recent studies suggest that students at the primary level show better achievement than students at the high school level. This may indicate that primary students are adequately prepared and that there are structural impediments to the success of these Aboriginal students in the high school system itself.[2] Conversely, it could also suggest that students' preparation at the primary level is inadequate. That inadequacy may be a result of curriculum, instruction quality, social or early promotion, a combination of these, or a range of other issues. It may also be the case that both problems exist, but are masked at the primary levels because the students are at or closer to home; laws force students to remain in school until age sixteen; parents play a greater positive role of encouragement at the elementary level; or, the lack of skills matches due to a deficiently integrative curriculum is less pronounced.

In a recent study, Spence, White and Maxim (2006) looked at five categories of community level explanatory variables: isolation, school type (Band versus provincial school), demographic factors (such as age and sex distribution), economic indicators (such as labour force participation and per capita average income), and human capital. They attempt to see how these influence three measures of school attainment: age appropriateness by grade level, drop-out rates, and graduation rates. The preliminary results indicate that isolation is not a powerful explanation for educational attainment, while demographic factors do play a role. They found the age dependency ratio has a strong negative effect on the graduate rate. This is no surprise, as we would expect a dilution effect of resources at the community level; that is, there would collectively be less financial, emotional, and time resources available as the proportion of children to adults increases. Other important factors they identified include the proportion of single adults (which decreases the age appropriate rate and graduate rate, and increases the withdrawal rate), and the community's educational levels were very positively associated with educational achievement in the younger generation. More research has to be done, however, to determine the relative influence of these many competing issues.

The Youth in Transition Survey

The Youth in Transition Survey (YITS) is a longitudinal survey conducted by Human Resources and Skills Development Canada and Statistics Canada to provide information about school achievement and school-to-work transitions among young people. The survey focuses on several factors influencing education, training, and work, while capturing data about the levels of educational attainment. The data set can be used to detect some of the explanatory factors for these outcomes. A major strength of the YITS is that it looks at several influential factors relating to school completion, including demographic factors such as family background, as well as personal aspirations and expectations, school experiences, academic achievement and employment experiences.

The original plan for Cycle 1 of the YITS was to conduct a longitudinal survey for each of two cohorts, one aged 15, and one aged 18–20. The age 15 cohort in Cycle 1 of YITS focussed on reading and mathematics skills, and included students who had also been participants in the Programme for International Student Assessment (PISA). This study focuses on the second cohort, or Cycle 2, which Statistics Canada identifies as the "18–20 year-old YITS Cohort." These young people were born in the years 1979 to 1981 inclusive.

The sample design for the 18–20 year old group is similar to that of the Labour Force Survey conducted monthly by Statistics Canada (see Statistics Canada 2003 for survey details). The initial target sample consisted of 29,000 persons. The sample frame *excluded* those living in some remote areas, including the northern territories, communities identified as "Indian reserves," and Canadian Forces bases. The survey was conducted during January and February 2000, with approximately 22,000 youth participating in the first survey cycle.[3] The survey was conducted over the telephone using computer-aided telephone interviewing (CATI) software. Of the 22,378 completed interviews, 782 individuals identified themselves as having an "Aboriginal" cultural or racial background. This category includes many different Aboriginal groups. Specifically, the question the survey participants were asked was:

> People in this country come from many different cultural or racial backgrounds. I'm going to read you a list. Are you ... Aboriginal, that is North American Indian, Métis, or Inuit?

Access to the survey data is restricted by Statistics Canada to pre-qualified researchers who must conduct the analysis through an RDC.[4]

A Note on Problems and Caveats

While allowing us to tap into the wide diversity of urban Aboriginal youth, the ethnicity identifier we note above poses substantial limitations upon our analysis. First, it relies on the young person to self-identify. That is to say, the definition appears more closely related to the identity question asked in the census than the origins question. Thus, there are the potential problems of false positives— those who indicated being Aboriginal but who are not—and more likely, false negatives—those who are Aboriginal but fail to identify themselves as such— within the sample. Fundamentally, the question casts a broad net and does not allow us to clearly distinguish between those who actively identify as Aboriginal and those who do not, and between those who might be "visibly" Aboriginal and those who are not.

The underlying homogeneity imposed by the question also prevents us from distinguishing between registered Indians and other Aboriginal peoples. This is problematic because previous research has shown that many registered Indian families move regularly between reserves and urban residences (Norris, Cooke and Clatworthy, 2003). Non-registered Indian Aboriginals, on the other hand, are probably more likely to have greater residential stability. Even those who change accommodations frequently among this latter group, are more likely to remain in the same school district that those who move between different communities.

The sample size also posed a substantial limitation on the range of analyses that we could conduct and on the results we can report. On the grounds of confiden-tiality, the RDC (Statistics Canada) does not allow the reporting of results that have used variables with five or fewer unweighted cases. This precludes the construction of some tables. For example, the numbers in the Aboriginal subpor-tion of the sample are too small to permit a reliable analysis of gender-specific reasons for leaving school. Of course, these issues of definition, and the relatively small sample size, impose substantial caveats on our conclusions.

The Results

Given our review of the YITS data, we have concluded that the study can focus on three statuses: non-high-school graduates (those still in high school and those who left), high-school graduates (those seeking employment and those who continued to further schooling), and post-secondary students. We then can examine some correlates of school continuance, such as parental attitudes and student perceptions of treatment in the institution. We report the findings in two sections of this report. The first, as illustrated by **Figure 2.1** (page 49), is a graphic presentation that uses labelled paths to illustrate the comparison between Aboriginal respondents and non-Aboriginal respondents.

Figure 2.1 shows the students' education/employment status. The left-hand side of the figure provides estimates for non-Aboriginal youth, while the right-hand side provides estimates for Aboriginal youth. The percentages on the outside of the diagram indicate the distribution of young people by level of schooling.

The major difference between the Aboriginal and non-Aboriginal samples stems from the differences in the proportions who do not acquire a secondary school diploma, and in the proportions who go on to some type of post-secondary education. Almost 43% of the Aboriginal sample does not have a secondary school diploma. This figure is only slightly less than twice the 23.5% estimated for the non-Aboriginal sample. Interestingly, similar proportions of Aboriginal and non-Aboriginal students report having a high-school diploma. On the other hand, about 54% of the non-Aboriginal students participate in some form of post-secondary education, while only 35.5% of the Aboriginal students are exposed to education or training beyond high school.

Among those students with less than a high-school diploma, about 12% of the non-Aboriginal and 21% or the Aboriginal samples are continuing in school. Similar percentages of non-Aboriginal and Aboriginal youth (11% and 22% respectively) are "leavers" or "dropouts." In summary, about twice as many Aboriginal as non-Aboriginal youth do not complete high school, but the split between proportions of leavers and continuers is similar for both groups. One major difference between the two groups without high school completion is in the relative proportions of leavers who are employed. About 75% of the Aboriginal youth who leave school before completing high school are employed within a year while only about 48% of the non-Aboriginal school leavers are employed.

This disparity raises an interesting issue. While it is common to focus on the relative "push" factors for leaving school early, the higher rate of employment among Aboriginal students could suggest that employment might be a bigger draw than school for Aboriginal students. That is to say, it is possible that the attractiveness of employment might be drawing proportionately more talented Aboriginal students away from the school system than non-Aboriginal students. We present this possibility since it is difficult to believe that there are more employment opportunities for urban Aboriginal youth than non-Aboriginal youth with less than high school education. Other research, plus some limited analysis of the YITS survey, also suggests that Aboriginal youth tend to live in families that are disproportionately single parent, and with fewer economic resources than their non-Aboriginal counterparts. Consequently, even marginal jobs can provide a substantial improvement in a family's standard of living.

Under these circumstances, the job market serves as more of a pull factor for Aboriginal than for non-Aboriginal students. If this pattern holds up, then the policy implications for keeping Aboriginal youth in school are quite different than if we focus on push factors alone. If we view school dropping out as primarily a function of the school environment, then ameliorative policies should clearly be directed toward schools. On the other hand, if there are substantial pull factors relating to families' socioeconomic circumstances, then changing the school environment only will not address a large portion of the problem. Under these circumstances, we require policies that negate the economic attractiveness of leaving school early. While many options are conceivable, linking increased family welfare and other support payments to students remaining in school could offset the advantages of employment income for young people. We also suspect that significant gender differences exist, but the numbers in the Aboriginal sample are too small to permit a reliable analysis of gender-specific reasons for leaving.

Among those who complete high school, but do not go on to some form of post-secondary education, rates of employment are reasonably high but not exceptional. About 72% of the non-Aboriginal high school graduates are employed while about 78% of the Aboriginal students are employed. The higher employment rates for Aboriginal young people at both the non-high-school graduate and high-school graduate level suggests that the less well-educated Aboriginal students are of better "quality" than their non-Aboriginal counterparts. This reasoning is also consistent with the fact that proportionately more non-Aboriginal youth continue to post-secondary education than Aboriginal youth. If we assume that underlying intellectual and other performance abilities are similarly distributed among the two samples of young people, then it is reasonable for us to conclude that proportionately more of the "capable" non-Aboriginal than Aboriginal youth continue to post-secondary education. Relatively more "capable" Aboriginal youth, however, may seek employment prior to post-secondary education.

While one might take a positive view of the fact that 72% of the non-Aboriginal and 78% of the Aboriginal high-school graduates are employed, we should also remember that 28% of the non-Aboriginal and 22% of the Aboriginal students are unemployed. From census data, we know that these rates of unemployment will drop as the young people age. Still, the employment picture for young people who complete high school, but do not pursue post-secondary education is not all rosy. Among those students who seek post-secondary education, the relative proportions of leavers, continuers, and graduates are not too different across the two groups of young people. There is, however, a higher propensity for

Aboriginal youth to be post-secondary school leavers than non-Aboriginal youth (14% vs. 9%).

Although it is not shown in the diagram, we should also point out that the type of post-secondary education in which Aboriginal students participate is different from that of their non-Aboriginal counterparts. Far more non-Aboriginal youth go on to university than Aboriginal youth, while Aboriginal youth are more likely to be engaged in trades, certificate, or diploma programs offered through non-university venues such as community colleges.

While Figure 2.1 provides some relevant descriptive material, the distribution of students across the two groups begs a series of interesting questions. First, what is the relative impact of school push factors in comparison to employment pull factors for those students who have less than high school completion? We generally assume that students—particularly Aboriginal students—who leave school early are "turned off" the formal education system. While this position undoubtedly has merit, it may also be the case that employment opportunities, as remuneratively limited as they may be, might be more attractive to Aboriginal than non-Aboriginal students. We could easily see this being the case if proportionately more Aboriginal students are living in dire economic circumstances than non-Aboriginal students.

We also know little about those students (in either group) who chose to return to school to continue their education. Ironically, the ratio of leavers to continuers among those with less than high school is similar for Aboriginal and non-Aboriginal students, although the absolute rate for Aboriginal students is twice that of their non-Aboriginal counterparts. Yet another factor that needs further exploration is the degree to which those Aboriginal students who go into post-secondary education, in comparison to those who do not, reflect a similar pattern to non-Aboriginal post-secondary participants. Unfortunately, the small sample of Aboriginal students in the YITS survey precludes any detailed analysis.

Some initial analysis also suggests that there are gender differences in the patterns of school participation across the two groups. Unfortunately, the numbers are too small to conduct detailed analysis for some categories. And, of course, there is the big issue of "aboriginality" itself. The YITS survey treats Aboriginal young people as a homogenous entity. Previous research by Indian and Northern Affairs Canada suggests that residential patterns and other characteristics of registered Indian children are quite different from the Inuit, Métis, and other non-registered Aboriginal youth.

Correlates of School Continuance—Results and Discussion

Several factors are known to be related to students' tendencies to leave school early. Within this study, we will examine five dimensions for which data are available within the YITS survey. Those dimensions include parental attitudes

Table 2.1: Sample Sizes for All Tables.

	Non-Aboriginal		Aboriginal	
	Female	Male	Female	Male
Below High School Completion	1,889	3,041	172	201
High School Graduation	2,461	2,889	102	86
At Least Some Post-Secondary	6,293	4,985	137	83

toward schooling; students' attitudes toward schooling; students' social experience (acceptance); students' levels of school engagement; and the stability of the learning environment.

Typical of the correlates we examined, is the question: How important was/is it to your parent(s) or guardian(s) that you graduate from high school? Was/is it:

1. Not important at all

2. Slightly important

3. Fairly important

4. Very important

We retained this four-point rating scale for our analysis. Individuals who reported that they didn't know, refused to answer, or were part of a valid skip, were excluded from the analysis. This resulted in 781 of the 782 young people in the Aboriginal sample being retained, and less than 200 of the 22,000 others being excluded. The overall sample size for each category analyzed is presented in **Table 2.1**. Weighted Ns were used for all of the analyses conducted in this study.

Parallel figures for the data presented in the tables are provided in the appendix (pages 46–48). Those figures also provide 95% confidence intervals about the point estimates. All of the differences identified in the following discussion are based on findings of statistically significant differences. We should note that the very large sample size among the non-Aboriginal sample often results in statistically significant differences by gender within that sample, even when the differences are substantively very small. Thus, care should be taken when interpreting those differences. This comment is not as applicable to the Aboriginal sample, however, since the unweighted cell sizes are much smaller.

Parents' Attitudes Toward Education

The survey raised two questions regarding parents' attitudes toward education. These were: "How important was/is it to your parent(s) or guardian(s) that you graduate from high school?" and "How important was/is it to your parent(s) or guardian(s) that you get more education after high school?" Responses to both of those questions are listed in **Table 2.2** and **Table 2.3** (page 42). **Table 2.2** shows that we have significant differences by level of education, with those with the lowest levels of education indicating least levels of importance to parents. This indicates there may be some correlation between how well students do, and how much support for education is expressed by parents. The exception is Aboriginal

Table 2.2: Importance to Parents of Graduating from High School.

	Non-Aboriginal		Aboriginal	
	Female	Male	Female	Male
Below High School Completion	3.67	3.64	3.52	3.72
High School Graduation	3.9	3.90	3.93	3.76
At Least Some Post-Secondary	3.93	3.91	3.98	3.68

Note: 1=not important at all; 4=very important

Table 2.3: Importance to Parents of Education Beyond High School.

	Non-Aboriginal		Aboriginal	
	Female	Male	Female	Male
Below High School Completion	3.3	3.15	2.96	3.04
High School Graduation	3.45	3.33	3.21	3.00
At Least Some Post-Secondary	3.74	3.7	3.53	3.43

Note: 1=not important at all; 4=very important

males with some post-secondary education who report lower parental interest; this may be due to small number effects. We see small differences by gender with females who go on to further education expressing stronger parental support for education. Aboriginal students appear to have lower levels of parental support generally but, overall, they follow the same pattern as the general population.

Table 2.3 reports significant differences by level of parental attitude to increasing one's education, with those with the lowest levels of education indicating lowest levels of parental interest in higher education. In contrast to the attitude of parents to completing high school, we see a substantial increase in positive reinforcement as one moves up the educational continuum. While patterns of increasing interest are similar, Aboriginal youth generally report lower levels of importance than non-Aboriginal students within each level of education. We also note a gender effect. Males tend to report lower levels of importance than females within each level of education (except those who did not finish high school).

Students' Attitudes Toward Schooling

The two indicators included in the YITS regarding students' attitudes toward schooling were: "School was often a waste of time" and "During my last year in high school, junior high, or elementary school, I thought that many of the things we were learning in class were useless." The response to the first of these questions appears in **Table 2.4**, the second in **Table 2.5**.

Table 2.4 suggests that those with higher levels of education are less likely to agree that school was waste of time, although the variability is not large and the results are mixed. We see a gender effect where males are generally more likely

Table 2.4: School was Often a Waste of Time.

	Non-Aboriginal		Aboriginal	
	Female	Male	Female	Male
Below High School Completion	2.06	2.23	2.14	2.12
High School Graduation	1.90	2.04	1.92	2.02
At Least Some Post-Secondary	1.85	1.98	1.87	1.96

Note: 1=strongly disagree; 4=strongly agree

Table 2.5: Thought Many Things Learned in Class were Useless.

	Non-Aboriginal		Aboriginal	
	Female	Male	Female	Male
Below High School Completion	2.45	2.56	2.55	2.55
High School Graduation	2.37	2.46	2.59	2.28
At Least Some Post-Secondary	2.33	2.36	2.41	2.5

Note: 1=strongly disagree; 4=strongly agree

to agree with these statements than females, whatever level of education. Interestingly, we do not see major differences by Aboriginal/non-Aboriginal status.

Table 2.5 indicates that, generally, more students believe that "things learned in class were useless" than "school was often a waste of time." Those with higher levels of education are generally less likely to agree that things learned were useless but again, results are inconsistent and the variability is not large. Finally, males are more likely to agree than females and Aboriginal youth are more likely to agree than non-Aboriginal youth that many things learned in class were of little value. One exception is Aboriginal women who graduated high school. This latter trend may be explained by some of the employment problems encountered when a woman trying to enter the labour force has only a high school diploma.

Students' Social Experiences

Students' social experiences refer to how the respondents perceived their treatment while in school. The two indicators here employed were: "I was treated with as much respect as other students in my class" and "People at school were interested in what I had to say." The responses to question one are reported in **Table 2.6** and the second question in **Table 2.7** (page 44).

Table 2.6 indicates that students with more education were more likely to believe they were treated with the same level of respect as others. That is, as youth continued in school, they perceived less disrespect. There are, however, several anomalies in the table. Aboriginal youth with some post-secondary education were less likely to agree than non-Aboriginals with some post-secondary education, particularly males. Aboriginals with some post-secondary education had profiles similar to both Aboriginal and non-Aboriginal high-school graduates.

Table 2.6: Treated with as Much Respect as Others in my Class.

	Non-Aboriginal		Aboriginal	
	Female	Male	Female	Male
Below High School Completion	2.93	2.93	2.80	2.85
High School Graduation	3.03	3.06	2.94	3.07
At Least Some Post-Secondary	3.25	3.2	3	2.83

Note: 1=strongly disagree; 4=strongly agree

Table 2.7: People at School Were Interested in What I Had to Say.

	Non-Aboriginal		Aboriginal	
	Female	Male	Female	Male
Below High School Completion	2.9	2.90	2.84	2.74
High School Graduation	2.93	2.94	2.98	2.97
At Least Some Post-Secondary	3.07	3.00	2.3	3

Note: 1=strongly disagree; 4=strongly agree

Table 2.7 indicates that those with higher levels of education tended to believe that others were interested in what they had to say despite gender and Aboriginal/non-Aboriginal status. The major exception is Aboriginal females in post-secondary who were among the least likely to believe that others were interested in what they had to say. We do know that many female Aboriginal students tend to leave post-secondary and return later. This migration in and out of formal schooling may be linked to these feelings of not being appreciated. There also may be pressures to build familial relations, care for family, or even start families themselves. These external issues may affect perceptions of people at school.

Conclusions

The roles of students' families' values toward education, and students' levels of connectedness or engagement with schools may be contributing factors to the likelihood of school completion and continuance. The findings from this study suggest that patterns of school completion differ for Aboriginal and non-Aboriginal students. Larger proportions of Aboriginal students drop out of school and smaller proportions continue to the next higher level of education. Employment patterns also differ. In particular, Aboriginal students who drop out of school often have higher relative levels of employment than their non-Aboriginal counterparts. This difference is greater at the lower levels of school attainment. Unfortunately, the relatively small numbers in the sample restrict our ability to conduct a detailed analysis by gender.

The YITS survey provides some further insights into the conundrum of school completion and school-to-workforce transitions among Aboriginal youth. Again, the small sample size and the relative heterogeneity of those self-identifying as Aboriginal limits our depth of analysis. Ideally, future research in this area would see both an increased sample size among the urban aboriginal population and the inclusion of on-reserve youth.

Appendix

Treated with same resepect as others

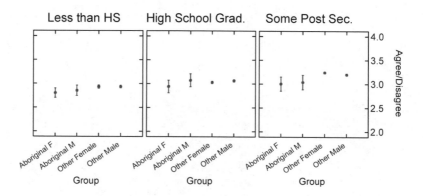

Others interested in what I had to say

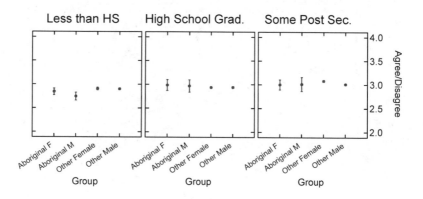

I had friends to talk about personal things

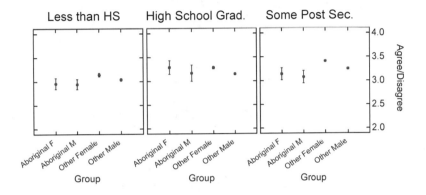

Liked to participate in school activities

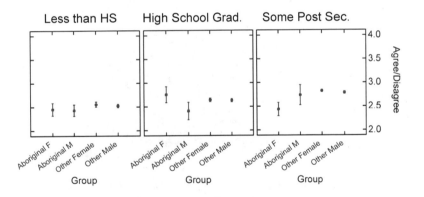

Parents value high school graduation

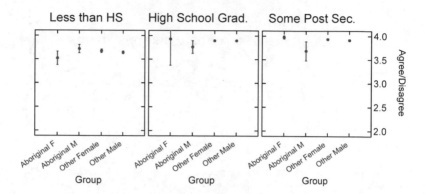

Parents value post secondary schooling

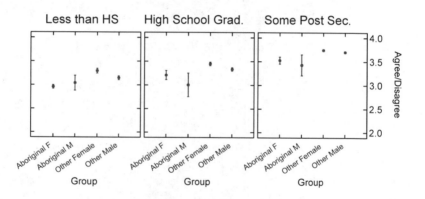

School was often waste of time

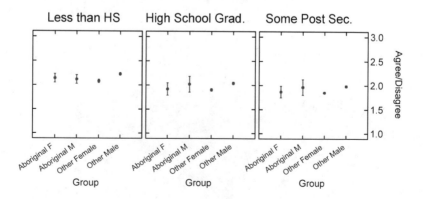

Figure 2.1

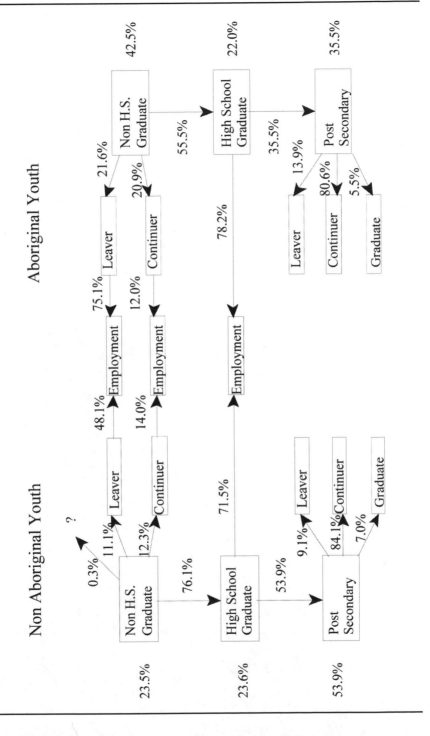

Endnotes

1 Unfortunately, temporal comparisons within this period are complex. Bill C-31 allowed for the reinstatement of "status" to many individuals, particularly women. At the same time, as Guimond (2003) clearly documents, there has been substantial "ethnic drift" which has resulted in many individuals redefining themselves as "Aboriginal" within the census. Higher levels of educational attainment by those reinstated under Bill C-31 and changes in personal definition could account for at least some of the apparent gains in educational attainment within the Aboriginal population.

2 There is a steadily growing body of literature on the experience of Aboriginal youth within the school system (Barman, Hebert and McCaskill, 1986; Battiste and Barman, 1995; Graham, 1997; Binda and Calliou, 2001). Most of this literature, however, is based on individual narrative and qualitative research. It indicates that there are some cultural structural barriers for Aboriginal students, including lack of traditional language availability and culturally inappropriate teaching methods. More empirical studies have mixed results. In the US, Ward (1998) tests and finds some support for the hypothesis put forward by Ledlow (1992) that Indians living in traditional communities confront a persistence in traditional culture and native language that impede their development and educational attainment (see also Shields 1995, 1996, and 1997 and Deyle 1992). Other research indicates otherwise. James et al. (1995) argue that the use of traditional language and traditional affiliation has a positive affect or at least has no negative affect (i.e., does not predict an increase in failure).

3 Collection for Cycle 2 took place from mid-February to mid-June, 2002. Unfortunately, the results from that survey are not currently available for analysis through the RDC.

4 Unlike many of the General Social Surveys, there is no public access to the files through Statistics Canada's Data Liberation Initiative. We produced a proposal to access the YITS Cycle One (18–20 year olds) through the Research Data Centre (RDC) at the University of Western Ontario. We had originally been led to believe that the second cycle of the YITS (20–22 year olds) would be available through the RDC program. In the end this was not the case. We therefore applied for access to Cycle One (18–20 year olds). This was based on two inter-related factors:

1) Cycle One allows us to assess the school graduation, school leaving (graduation or dropout) as well as early transition to the first job. This allows the greatest interface with the non-Aboriginal populations, a large proportion of which have left high school by the age of 20 years.

2) Cycle Two (20–22 year olds) was going to take considerable time to be made available according to those in charge of the RDC process. We still have no access to this data. The proposal for access to the YITS goes through a process similar to a grant application to the SSHRC. The Statistics Canada personnel responsible for the access to data review the proposal for scholarly significance and ethical issues. They also solicit academic reviews of the proposal to ensure it has merit intellectually and will contribute to general knowledge. They are very restrictive about allowing any exploratory investigations. Our proposal for access was accepted after it was clear to them we had a scholarly interest in looking at the Aboriginal data and we had an informed interest in comparing the patterns to other populations.

References

Armstrong, R., J. Kennedy and P.R. Oberle (1990). *University Education and Economic Well Being: Indian Achievement and Prospects*. Ottawa: Indian and Northern Affairs Canada, Quantitative Analyses and Socio-Demographic Research, Finance and Professional Services.

Auditor General of Canada (2000). 2000 Report of the Auditor General of Canada. Ottawa: Government of Canada.

Barman, J. Y. Hebert, and D. McCaskill (1986). *Indian Education in Canada, Volume 1*. Vancouver: UBC Press.

Battiste, M. and J. Barman (1995). *First Nations' Education in Canada: The Circle Unfolds*. Vancouver: UBC Press.

Beavon, D. & M. Cooke (2003). "An Application of the United Nations Development Index to Registered Indians in Canada." In White et al. *Aboriginal Conditions: The Research Foundations of Public Policy*. Vancouver: UBC Press.

Binda, K.P. and S. Calliou (2001). *Aboriginal Education in Canada: A Study in Decolonialization*. Mississauga, Ont.: Canadian Educators' Press.

British Columbia Ministry of Education, Aboriginal Education Branch (2000a). *How are we doing: An overview of Aboriginal educational results 2000–2001*. <**www.bced.gov.bc.ca./abed/results**>

British Columbia Ministry of Education, Aboriginal Education Branch (2000b). *Aboriginal Education Improvement Agreements*. <**www.bced.gov.bc.ca/abed/performance.htm**>

Canada, Secretary of State (1991). *Canada's Off-reserve Aboriginal Population: A Statistical Overview*. Ottawa: Social Trends Analysis Directorate, Department of the Secretary of State.

Deyle, D. (1992). "Constructing Failure and Maintaining Cultural Identity: Navajo and Ute School Leavers." *Journal of American Indian Education* 31, No. 2. pp. 24–27.

Graham, E. (1997). *The Mush Hole: Life at Two Indian Residential Schools*. Waterloo, Ont.: Heffle Publications.

Guimond, E. (2003) "Changing Ethnicity: The Concept of Ethnic Drifters." In White, J.P., P.S. Maxim & D. Beavon (2003) *Aboriginal Conditions: The Research Foundations of Public Policy*. Vancouver: UBC Press.

Hull, J. (2000) Aboriginal Post-Secondary Education and Labour Market Outcomes, Canada, 1996. Ottawa: Indian and Northern Affairs Canada.

Hull, J. (2005) Post-Secondary Education and Labour Market Outcomes, Canada, 2001. Ottawa: Indian and Northern Affairs Canada.

James, K. E. Chavez, F. Beauvais, R. Edwards, and G. Oetting (1995). "School Achievement and Drop-out Among Anglo and Indian Females and Males: A Comparative Examination." *American Indian Culture and Research Journal* Vol.28, pp. 24–30.

Jankowski, W. & B. Moazzami. (1995). "Returns of Education Among Northwestern Ontario's Native People." *Canadian Journal of Native Studies* Vol.15, No.1, pp.104–111.

King, C. (1993). "The State of Aboriginal Education in Southern Canada." RCAP, Public Policy and Aboriginal Peoples 1965–1992.

Kirkness, V. & S. Selkirk Bowman (1992). *First Nations and Schools: Triumphs and Struggles*. Toronto: Canadian Education Association.

Ledlow, S. (1992). "Is Cultural Diversity An Adequate Explanation for Dropping Out?" *Journal of American Indian Education* Vol.31, No.3, pp. 21–36.

MacKay, R. and L. Myles (1989). Native Student Dropouts from Ontario Schools. Toronto: Ontario Ministry of Education.

MacPherson, J. C. (1991). Report on Tradition and Education Towards a Vision of our Future. Ottawa: Department of Indian Affairs and Northern Development.

Maxim, P., J.White & D. Beavon. (2003). "Dispersion and Polarization of Income among Aboriginal and non-Aboriginal Canadians." In White et al. *Aboriginal Conditions: The Research Foundations of Public Policy*. Vancouver: UBC Press.

McDonald, R.J. (1991). "Canada's Off Reserve Aboriginal Population." *Canadian Social Trends* (Winter), pp. 2–7.

Norris, M.J., M. Cooke and S. Clatworthy (2003). "Aboriginal Mobility and Migration Patterns and the Policy Implications." In White, J.P., P.S. Maxim & D. Beavon, *Aboriginal Conditions: The Research Foundations of Public Policy*. Vancouver: UBC Press.

Reyhner, J. (2001). "Family, Community, and School Impacts on American Indian and Alaska Native Students' Success. 32nd Annual National Indian Education Association Annual Convention. **<jan.ucc. nau.edu/jar/AIE/Family.html>**

Reyhner, J. (1991). Plans for Dropout Prevention and Special School Support Services for American Indian and Alaska Native Students. Washington, DC: US Department of Education. ERIC Document Reproduction Service No. ED 343 732.

Shields, C.M. (1997). "Learning About Assessment From Native American Schools: Advocacy and Empowerment." *Theory into Practice* 36, Spring, pp. 102–109.

Shields, C.M. (1996). "Creating a Learning Community in a Multicultural Settings: Issues of Leadership." *The Journal of School Leadership* Vol.6, No. 1, pp. 47–74.

Shields, C.M. (1995). "Context, Culture, and Change: Considerations for Pedagogical Change in a Native American Community." *Planning and Changing* Vol. 26. No. ½, pp. 2–24.

Siggner, A. (1986). "The Socio-demographic Characteristics of Registered Indians." *Canadian Social Trends* (Winter), pp. 2–9.

Statistics Canada (2003). *User Guide. Youth in Transition Survey (YITS) 18–20 Year-old Cohort, Cycle 1*, Ottawa.

Spence, N., Jerry White, and Paul Maxim (2006). *Modelling Educational Success of First Nations Students in Canada: Community Level Perspectives*. Working Paper, First Nations Cohesion Project, University of Western Ontario.

Tait, H. (1999). "Educational Achievement of Young Aboriginal Adults." *Canadian Social Trends* Vol.52, (Spring) pp. 6–10.

Urion, C. (1993). "First Nations Schooling in Canada: A Review of Changing Issues." In *Contemporary Educational Issues 2d ed.*, edited by L. L. Stewin and Stewart J.H. McCann. Toronto: Copp Clark Pitman Ltd.

Ward, C. (1995). "American Indian High School Completion in Rural Southeastern Montana." *Rural Sociology* Vol.. 60, No.3, pp. 416–434.

Ward, C. (1998). "Community Resources and School Performance: the Northern Cheyenne Case". *Sociological Inquiry* Vol.68, No.1, (February), pp. 83–113.

White, J. And P. Maxim (2005). *Preparation of a First Nations' "Youth in Transition Survey"*. Unpublished Paper, submitted to SRAD, Indian Affairs and Northern Development.

White, J.P., P.S. Maxim & D. Beavon (2003) *Aboriginal Conditions: The Research Foundations of Public Policy*. Vancouver: UBC Press.

White, J.P. & P. Maxim. (2002a). "Aboriginal Women and the Economy." *Aboriginal Policy Research Conference*, Ottawa, Nov.26–28, 2002.

White, J. & P. Maxim (2002b) "Correlates of Educational Attainment in First Nations Communities." *Aboriginal Policy Research Conference*, Ottawa , Nov.26–28, 2002.

White, J.P.,P. Maxim and S. Gyimah (2003). "Labour Force Activity of Women in Canada: A Comparative Analysis of Aboriginal and Non Aboriginal Women." *Canadian Review of Sociology and Anthropology* Vol.40, No.4, pp. 395–415.

Wilkinson, R. G. (1997). "Comment: Income, Inequality and Social Cohesion." *American Journal of Public Health, 87*, pp. 1504–1506.

3

Culture-sensitive Mathematics: The Walpole Island Experience

Anthony N. Ezeife

Introduction

Low enrolment in, and phobia toward mathematics, science, and related disciplines have been familiar issues in the academic world for a fairly long time (Ezeife 2004). The research literature is suffused with reports and findings indicating the sad state of affairs in the math/science field. For example, going a little further back to the eighties, the National Research Council, in its 1989 report, stated: "Mathematics is the worst curricular villain in driving students to failure in school. When math acts as a filter, it not only filters students out of careers, but frequently out of school itself" (7). In the same decade, Matthews' (1989, 5) report highlighted the disturbing enrolment and performance situation in science and math in American schools where there had been a dramatic "64% decline in the number of undergraduates entering science teaching ... [and] 30% of science teachers are unqualified to teach the subject."

The unflattering picture that depicted the state of math and science education in the eighties has persisted through the nineties up to the present time (Davison 1992; Backhouse, Haggarty, Pirie & Stratton 1992; Ma 2001; Ezeife 1999, 2003, & 2004; Matang 2001a, 2001b; Mel 2001). The low enrolment and poor performance in math and science that affect schools in several parts of the world assume alarming proportions in ethnic minority and aboriginal cultural populations. MacIvor (1995) has drawn attention to the low enrolment, substandard achievement, and high dropout rates in science, math, and the technological fields of Canadian Aboriginal students. Berkowitz (2001, 17) painted the picture of Aboriginal mathematics and science enrolment in Canadian tertiary education, thusly:

> According to Indian and Northern Affairs Canada, less than 3.2 percent of the 27,000 First Nations students going to university or college full-time on federal funding last year were enrolled in programs leading to careers in science (including agriculture and biological science, engineering and applied science, mathematics and physical sciences, and health professions).

Another researcher (Binda 2001), while studying the situation in schools under local control and jurisdiction (Canadian First Nations schools), observed that performance in mathematics and science is still far below expectation. The researcher noted that schools under provincial management recorded a mean score of 55.6% in mathematics in 1997, the mean score of Aboriginal schools was a meagre 19.6%. In 1998, the situation became even worse as the mean score of provincial schools rose to 61.2%, while the score of First Nations schools dropped to 14.4%. Similarly, O'Reilly-Scanlon, Crowe, and Winnie (2004) have pointed out that the educational attainment levels of Aboriginal students are lower than those of their colleagues from non-Indigenous populations.

The current low enrolment, substandard achievement, and general poor attitude toward school learning of Aboriginal students, especially in the realm of math and science, is a surprising development considering the historical fact that Aboriginal people of old were keen students of nature, astronomy, science, and math. Several authors (Cajete 1994; Hatfield, Edwards, Bitter, & Morrow 2004; Smith 1994) have cited the wealth of experience and accomplishment of various Indigenous populations worldwide. For instance, Smith (1994) narrated the case of the Skidi Pawnee—an Aboriginal group—who in ancient times were not just enthusiastic astronomers but were actually so accomplished that they went as far as identifying and describing the planet Venus. Also, by correctly tracking the movements of the stars and planets, the same group "conceptualized the summer solstice" [and] "... in this way they could predict reoccurring solar phenomena" (Smith 1994, 46).

Why the Decline and Alienation?

So, if their progenitors were pace setters in the fields of math and science, why is it that current Aboriginal students shy away from these areas of study. And why do the few who enrol in math and science perform poorly in examinations? Many researchers have addressed this question, attempting to advance reasons from various perspectives to explain the situation. For example, Sloat and Willms (2000) point to the initial disadvantages that accompany many young Aboriginal learners to school—the lack of appropriate home support and relevant resources, especially scientific and technological toys and learning equipment like computers. Doige (2003) draws attention to the fact that "Aboriginal students are still marginalized in the public school and university systems, through Westernized curricula and pedagogy, even though Aboriginal educators have been overtly calling for a holistic education for their children" (Doige 2003, 145).

In the specific discipline of mathematics/science, several researchers (Cajete 1994; Ezeife 2003; Jegede & Aikenhead 1999: MacIvor 1995; Mel 2001) have all opined that the problem of low Aboriginal enrolment and poor performance arises due to the lack of relevance of mathematics and science taught in school to the Aboriginal learner's everyday life and culture. Drawing the same point, Smith (1994) noted that the mathematics and science taught in Canadian schools are bereft of Aboriginal cultural and environmental content. Thus, Aboriginal students fail to see the relevance of these fields of study to their culture, aspirations, or ways of life, and so they avoid them. In addition, they do not see how they would apply the mathematics and science they study in school to their environment or immediate community, or what benefits would accrue to them if they were to excel in these subjects, so the natural question that runs through their minds is: Why bother?

A Personal Experience

My personal experience as an Indigenous student studying science in high school several years ago in a tropical country exemplifies the frustration non-Western and minority learners face when they are taught science without reference to their culture, tradition, and environment. In my grade 10 physics class, we were learning about the concept of pressure, and its relation to force and area. The teacher used a textbook, obviously written for students in a temperate climate, to teach this topic, and drew his examples and illustrations from this text. I still remember that most of these examples did not make sense to me because they sounded like fairy tales, were foreign, distant, and hence irrelevant to us in the cultural, environmental, and climatic context in which we were learning. One example, in particular, is worth mentioning here. This example used the mechanism of ice skating to illustrate the inverse relationship between pressure and area. Using diagrams from the Western-oriented textbook, the teacher laboured to explain to us how the ice skater exerted a large force (his/her weight) on the skates which have narrow contact edges with the ice (hence, a small surface area), and how this gave rise to a large pressure, which in turn melted the ice, thus enabling the skater to glide smoothly on the ice surface. Once the skater passed a particular area on the ice, the teacher explained, the ice surface was relieved of the pressure, and due to the principle of "regelation" (refreezing), the ice quickly refroze.

Technically, the illustration was apt, but in the situation in which it was used, it was both geographically inappropriate, and culturally meaningless. All the students in my grade 10 physics class were born, and had lived all their life in a tropical, Sub-Saharan African country, where our school was located. None of us had ever seen snow, ice, skating rinks, ice-skaters, or skates. Skating, as a sport, was unknown in our culture, tradition, and environment. And yet we were being taught pressure, force, and area with illustrations and examples meant for students in a Western, temperate country and climate where skating was commonplace and popular. Having undergone that firsthand experience years ago, I can now see exactly what Aboriginal students face in a typical math and science classroom, where they are taught with curriculum materials and resources completely bereft of their culture and environmental content. It took me several years (it was actually when I moved to the Western world for graduate studies), to fully understand the link between pressure, force, and area on the one hand, and ice-skater, his or her weight, and the blades of the skates, on the other. For, it was only in a temperate climate when I saw a skating rink, snow, etc. that the illustrations in my grade 10 physics textbook, which my former teacher laboured in vain to explain so many years ago, made sense to me. However, my grade 10 classmates were prevented from developing an appreciation of physics, given how it was taught. We may have been persuaded to like it, if we had been taught with a culture-sensitive curriculum. This holds true for today's Aboriginal, and other Indigenous learners of science and math.

The Walpole Island Schema-based Math Project

So, what can be done to change the status quo, attract more Aboriginal students to the study of mathematics, and hopefully improve their performance in the subject? Many Aboriginal scholars and Indigenous leaders have emphasized the need to reorient mathematics and science education in Aboriginal schools toward the development of culture-sensitive curricular materials and teaching strategies deemed appropriate for aboriginal students. In Canada for instance, the Assembly of Manitoba Chiefs (1999) suggested incorporating into the curriculum cultural practices, traditional values, ideas, phenomena, and beliefs that would relate the schools to the communities in which they exist and function. Supporting the call for a culture-sensitive curriculum, Kanu's (2002) study identified the Canadian Aboriginal student as a multi-dimensional learner whose competence peaks when instructional material is presented through stories, activities, and traditional practices drawn from the student's culture and schema. In other words, it is implied that Aboriginal students would learn better when a culture-sensitive curriculum is used in teaching them. Calls for an integrative Aboriginal curriculum are prevalent in the research literature (Cajete 1994; Jegede & Aikenhead 1999; Mel 2001, Smith & Ezeife 2000). However, there have not been sustained efforts, especially in the field of mathematics education, to address these calls. Ezeife's (2002) work with Aboriginal pre-service teachers reported the overwhelming interest generated by the culture-based curriculum unit utilized in the project. That study suggested a follow-up work that could integrate culture-sensitive materials into an existing mathematics curriculum, and try out the integrated curriculum in an Aboriginal classroom to determine the efficacy of such integration. This, in brief, is the thrust of the Walpole Island Schema-based Mathematics Project. The study focuses on the development of appropriate culture-sensitive curriculum materials, and their implementation in an Aboriginal setting. The specific objectives of the study are:

1. To compile a list of phenomena, materials, activities, and traditional practices from the culture and immediate environment of a target Aboriginal community (Walpole Island First Nation) that can be used for the teaching and learning of math in the Primary/Junior years (Elementary Grades).

2. To develop model math teaching units that can be incorporated into specific strands of the existing Ontario Grades 1–8 math curriculum, thereby producing an "integrated" curriculum.

3. To set up an experiment pitching the integrated (innovative) curriculum against the existing (regular) one in an Aboriginal school, with a view to determining what impact (if any) this approach would have on math teaching/learning in Aboriginal settings.

Methodology

Phase 1: Compilation of Phenomena, Materials, Activities, Traditional Practices, Folklore, etc.

During this phase of the study, selected elders and educators in the Walpole Island community were interviewed and asked about traditional practices in their culture and environment that have relevance to math. The interview was prompted by the fact that elders in Indigenous communities are known to possess valuable traditional knowledge defined by Bedeau (2006) as "the condition of knowing something with familiarity gained through association and experience" (26). Sites of mathematical interest on the Island were visited and photographed during this phase of the study. Additionally, archives and holdings of the Walpole Island Heritage Centre (Nin Da Waab Jig), a research centre that was set up in 1973, (Jacobs 1992) were thoroughly examined to glean data about past traditional practices in the First Nations community that have relevance to mathematics teaching and learning.

Process of Interview: Most of the interviewees were members of the Walpole Island "Language Advisory Group"—a group of community elders and educators with a high stake in the preservation and transmission of their culture, heritage, and traditional knowledge. Others were distinguished academics on the island, including the then Chief of the community, and the Director of the Heritage Research Centre (Nin Da Waab Jig), which focuses on the preservation of Anishnaabe culture, knowledge, and traditions. All the interviewees willingly and enthusiastically participated in the study.

Interview Format: The interviews were structured in a non-restrictive, open-ended format with leading questions designed to guide the interviewees, and draw them to talk about and comment on certain broad math concepts and topics that relate to Aboriginal (Anishnaabe) counting, record keeping, housing and space allocation, building plans, dimensions of farmlands, hunting and fishing, games, recreational and outdoor activities, and so on. So far, a total of eleven people have been interviewed. The audiotaped interviews were transcribed, and the transcripts given back to those interviewed to read, confirm, or modify as they saw fit, thereby confirming the accuracy of the transcriptions.

Enthusiasm: Some of the interviewees added new material when the transcribed interviews were given back to them. This revealed that they were not only enthusiastic about the project, but were also eager to record and transmit their culture and traditional math knowledge, and most important, see this rich knowledge reflected in the curriculum used to teach math to their children in school. Thus, they expressed immense interest in the study, and volunteered to help in whatever way may be needed to ensure the project is successful.

Table 3.1: Sample Categorizations of Analysed Interviews into Math Strands, Teaching Topics, and Concepts.

Relevant Math Content Gleaned from Interview	Corresponding Math Strand	Applicable Math Topic/Concept
Farmers picking strawberries with large bowls	Measurement	Capacity and volume: Different amounts in different shapes and sizes, for examples, the volumes/capacities of household utensils, cans, cups, cottles, and other everyday containers.
Use of willow to make a "dream catcher" frame	Geometry and spatial sense	Construction; angles involved in the frame; types and measures of angles.
Beadwork, and beads worn by the Anishnaabe	Patterning and algebra	Patterns (in the beadwork, colours and ordering of beads).
Making moccasins— "sometimes requires measuring the feet of someone standing on the hide"	Measurement	Units and standards of units, conversion between different systems of units—The SI system, fps, etc.
"Many," according to the Anishnaabe language "means a whole bunch of something." For example, "in case of berries, it could be a pail full of berries."	Number sense and numeration	Counting, basic units of counting, different base systems.
Flowers in the environment: "Sometimes, we picked flowers and counted the petals."	Number sense and numeration; patterning and algebra	Numeric skills, naturalistic intelligence (Gardner's Multiple Intelligences); patterns in the arrangement of the petals.
Hunting: "The rounded tipped arrows are used for hunting smaller game, while the sharpened tips are used for hunting larger game."	Geometry and spatial sense	Angles, shapes, and velocity of motion. (link the "V" or tip of the arrowhead, which leaves a wake that follows the rest of the arrow to flight of birds in "V" formation—the other birds follow the lead "squad" with less effort).
Housing: "The shape of the lodges is usually circular." "The construction of the lodges is symbolic. At the centre of the lodge is a hold for the fire, and at the top of the roof is a circle for smoke exit. The doorways of the lodges agree with the four directions—East, West, North, and South."	Geometry and spatial sense	Coordinate Geometry: Directions and locations in space. The four cardinal points and the formation of the four quadrants.

Table 3.1: Sample Categorizations of Analysed Interviews into Math Strands, Teaching Topics, and Concepts. (continued)

Relevant math content gleaned from interview	Corresponding math Strand	Applicable math topic/ concept
Fishing: The technique the Anishnaabe use is to make "marsh grass in a circular formation. A hole inside the formation is lined with tunnels; often six or more tunnels are linked to the hole."	Data management and probability	Probability: Its example and application in an everyday life situation. The Anishnaabe technique involves running the fish through several tunnels until they are captured in one. This strategy adopts, and exemplifies the principle of probability.
Burial Traditions: "Burying of a loved one is usually on the 5th day, the body is positioned to the East which symbolizes a new beginning—where the sun rises."	Number sense and numeration	The decimal system of counting contrasted with the base 5 system; the concept and use of "place holder" in counting; cycles and rotations; directions—sunrise and sunset.
Games: "Gaming was a traditional activity, almost like present-day casinos. There were shell games, slide-of-hand [sic] tricks, the moccasin game, etc. In the moccasin game, the target is for each player to correctly guess in which pouch a specially marked marble was hidden."	Data management and probability	Principle of Probability: Games of chance, raffles, lotteries—odds of winning.

Interview analysis: This was a delicate task—to decipher the math content and concepts from the open-ended, free-flowing interviews, and categorize the content and concepts into one or more of the five strands of the Ontario Mathematics Curriculum, Grades 1–8, namely, Number Sense and Numeration, Patterning and Algebra, Geometry and Spatial Sense, Data Management and Probability, and Measurement. The analysis was first undertaken by the Aboriginal graduate students in the research team who were assigned to glean and itemize the math content and concepts into relevant strands, and make a case why they thought each content/concept should belong to the specific strand or strands into which it was put. The final and confirmatory phase of the analysis was done by the researcher who went carefully through the submissions of the graduate research assistants, and made modifications as deemed necessary. Some sample categorizations resulting from the interview analysis are shown in **Table 3.1**.

Figure 3.1–i, ii, iii: Venn Diagram (i), Symbolic Representation (ii), & Composition Chart (iii)

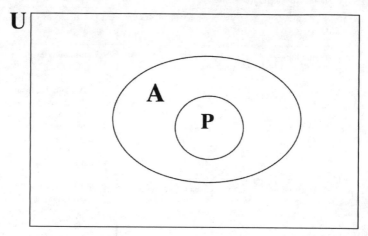

Figure 3.1 i

$$P \subset A \text{ SINCE } P \subseteq A, \text{ AND } P \neq A$$

$$\text{THUS, } \exists\, D = \{x \mid x \in A, \text{ and } x \notin P\}$$

Figure 3.1 ii

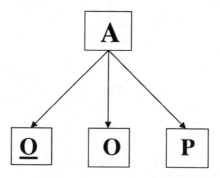

Figure 3.1 iii

U is the universal set (which, in this case, stands for all Canadian Aboriginal people); A (Anishnaabe) is a set in the universal set; and P (Pottawatomie) is a set within the set A.

Phase 2: Integration of Compiled Materials into Existing Curriculum

The integration of cultural and traditional materials into units of the existing Ontario Mathematics curriculum has been done, and actual classroom implementation has started in grades 5 and 6 in the community school on Walpole Island. The implementation will be done in short, interrelated, three-week teaching blocks, taking into cognisance the need to avoid undue, prolonged disruption of the regular school curriculum and class schedules. The unit on Number Sense and Numeration with emphasis on Set Theory has been completed, and the Geometry and Spatial Sense started early in the spring of 2006. Part of the Geometry unit was done in a traditional log house in the island which was made available by a community elder. In teaching the unit on Set Theory, students' prior knowledge and environment, including local examples and illustrations, were used in definitions, and the development and application of math concepts and principles. For instance, for the lesson on **Subsets, Proper Subsets,** and **Complements of a Set,** the typical textbook explanation of these concepts was avoided, and instead local examples and ideas were used. The textbook explanation (Long & DeTemple 2000), which often confuses students, runs like this:

> If two sets A and B have precisely the same elements then they are equal and we write $A = B$. If $A \subseteq B$ but $A \neq B$, we say that A is a proper subset of B and write $A \subset B$. If $A \subset B$, there must be some element of B which is not also an element of A; that is, there is some x for which $x \in B$ and $x \notin A$ (84).

Even for the mathematics student who knows the meanings of the symbols used above and understands that $A \subseteq B$ means "The set A is a subset of the set B", it is usually not easy to fully understand, remember, and apply the concepts as explained in textbooks. Bearing this in mind, I decided to use the Anishnaabe students' prior knowledge and environment in presenting the concepts. The Anishnaabe are an Aboriginal group among Canadian First Nations (Indigenous peoples of Canada). The component groups that make up the Anishnaabe are the Ojibwa ($\underline{O}$), the Odawa (**O**), and the Pottawatomie (**P**), thus forming the "Three Fires Confederacy" of the Anishnaabe group. This is represented in the composition chart, **Figure. 3.1 (iii)**, where:

$$A = \text{Anishnaabe}$$
$$\underline{O} = \text{Ojibwa}$$
$$O = \text{Odawa,}$$
$$P = \text{Pottawatomie.}$$

Thus, in the Venn diagram (pictorial representation of sets) shown in **Figure. 3.1 (i)**, U is the universal set (which, in this case, stands for all Canadian Aboriginal people); A (Anishnaabe) is a set in the universal set; and P (Pottawatomie) is a set within the set A.

Table 3.2: Pre-test Mean Scores of Subjects in Instructional Groups (N = 28)

Groups	Number of Subjects	Curriculum Type	Mean Score
A	14	Regular curriculum	33.85
B	14	Integrated curriculum	35.85
Total	28		34.85

Table 3.3: ANOVA Summary for Pre-test Scores –
F is not significant at 0.05 l.o.s. (Critical value = 4.23)

Source of Variation	Sum of Squares	df	Mean Square	F
Between Groups	28.00	1	28.000	0.284
Within Groups	2,559.429	26	98.440	
Total	2,587.429	27		

Table 3.4: Post-test Mean Scores of Subjects in Instructional Groups (N = 28)

Groups	Number of Subjects	Curriculum Type	Mean Score
A	14	Regular Curriculum	23.85
B	14	Integrated Curriculum	26.42
Total	28		25.14

So, it follows that P is a proper subset of A, since P is not equal to A. Simply, this means that every Pottawatomie is an Anishnaabe, but not every Anishnaabe is a Pottawatomie (recall that there are also the Ojibwa, and Odawa groups).

As expected, the students caught on very quickly to the approach used here in introducing and explaining the concept, because it refers directly to what they are already familiar with as Aboriginal people. Even the mathematical representation of the concepts (as shown in **Figure.3.1 (ii)** – page 60), gave them no problems at all, as they easily moved from the verbal explanation to the symbolic representation of the concept. Subsequently, the same diagram and ideas were used to teach *complement of a set*, and to show the distinction, in a strict sense, between the terms *subset* and *proper subset*. For the major project, a total of five teaching blocks corresponding to the five Ontario math curriculum strands will be used for classroom implementation, which will be done by the same certified teacher, thereby controlling for teacher variability and instructional style.

State of Study and Interim Results

Since the classroom implementation of the integrated curriculum materials for the major project is still ongoing, this paper will only highlight the results of the pilot study that preceded the major project, as reported in Ezeife (2004). As is being done in the ongoing major project, during the pilot study a convenience sample of 28 research subjects was composed from two existing grade 5 classes, and the sample was then divided into two groups, with 14 students in each group. Each of the two groups was then randomly assigned a treatment (curriculum type regular, or integrated curriculum), with the students in the regular curriculum constituting the Control Group (Group A), while their integrated curriculum counterparts formed the Experimental Group (Group B). Subsequently, the two groups were given the same pre-test, and then exposed to treatment as follows: The students in Group A were taught with the existing grade 5 Ontario math curriculum, while those in Group B were taught with the integrated curriculum, which contained culture-prone materials, examples, and illustrations taken from the Walpole Island environment and incorporated into the grade 5 math curriculum. Each of the groups was taught for four weeks by the same instructor. After instruction, each group was given the same post-test. The results of the pilot study are summarized in **Tables 3.2–3.5**.

Summary and Discussion of Results of Pilot Study

Table 3.2 shows that the mean pre-test score of Group A (Control Group) was 33.85, while Group B (Experimental Group) recorded a mean of 35.85 on the same pre-test. An analysis of variance (as summarized in **Table 3.3**) showed that there was no statistically significant difference between these mean scores. The implication of this finding was that there was no significant difference between the mean pre-test score of Group A (Control Group) and that of the Group B (Experimental Group). Thus, on average, the two groups were of the same standard in terms of their "Entry Behaviour," that is, at the time they started the study. No group was at an initial advantageous position over the other because of its mathematics attainment or preparedness. Hence, it was concluded from this finding that the groups were equivalent at the beginning of the study.

From the results in **Table 3.4**, it is seen that the mean post-test score of the Control Group (Group A), taught using the regular/existing curriculum, was 23.85, compared with a mean score of 26.42 for the Experimental Group (Group B), which was taught with the integrated/innovative curriculum. Thus, there was a marginal difference between the means of the two groups in favour of the Experimental Group. One of the null hypotheses to be tested in the ongoing major project would be to see if there would be a significant difference in the achievements of the two groups after sustained teaching that would cover all the strands in the Ontario Grades 1–8 math curriculum. The results of the pilot study, though based on just one out of the five course units that would be used for the major project, are encouraging in that they reveal the fact that the Experimental Group performed better, even if marginally, than the Control Group. The descriptive measures shown in **Table 3.5** (page 64) give more insight into the performance of the two groups. Thus, whereas the standard deviation of the Control Group was 13.4, that of the Experimental Group was 8.6, indicating that the post-test scores of participants in the Experimental Group were closer together than those of the Control Group.

Table 3.5: Descriptive Measures for Post-test Scores by Group (N = 28)

Scores	Group	Measures		Statistic	Std. Error
Post-test Scores	Group A	Mean		23.8571	3.5855
		95% Conf. Int. for Mean	Lower B	16.1112	
			Upper B	31.6031	
		5% Trimmed Mean		23.6190	
		Median		24.0000	
		Variance		179.978	
		Std. Dev		13.4156	
		Minimum		4.00	
		Maximum		48.00	
		Range		44.00	
		Interquartile Range		20.50	
		Skewness		0.290	0.597
		Kurtosis		- 0.704	1.154
Post-test Scores	Group B	Mean		26.4286	2.2984
		95% Conf. Int. for Mean	Lower B	21.4632	
			Upper B	31.3939	
		5% Trimmed Mean		26.1429	
		Median		28.0000	
		Variance		73.956	
		Std. Dev		8.5998	
		Minimum		14.00	
		Maximum		44.00	
		Range		30.00	
		Interquartile Range		16.00	
		Skewness		0.188	0.597
		Kurtosis		-0.148	1.154

This suggests that on the whole, the scores of participants in the Experimental Group—those taught using the integrated/innovative culture-sensitive curriculum—were closer to the mean score of the group, while the scores of participants in the Control Group (taught with the existing/regular curriculum) were more scattered and farther from the group mean. The implication of this is that the Experimental Group showed more consistency and uniformity in the mastery of course content as opposed to the Control Group which displayed heterogeneity, with several cases of high and low scores associated with the group. A comparison of the values of the ranges (30.0 for the Experimental Group, and 44.0 for the Control Group), and interquartile ranges (16.0 for the Experimental, and 20.5 for the Control) further confirms that the post-test scores of participants in the

Experimental Group are closer together than the scores of their counterparts in the Control Group. This implies that on the whole, the integrated/innovative curriculum produced a more homogeneous group, in terms of mathematic achievement, than the regular/existing curriculum. Also, comparing the median scores of the two groups, it was seen that the median of the Experimental Group was 28.0 which was higher that the median of 24.0 for the Control Group. This further points to the situation at the centres of the sets of scores for the two groups—the middle-of-the-pack student in the Experimental Group performed relatively better than a similarly positioned student in the Control Group.

Conclusion

This paper has drawn attention to the low representation, and relatively poor performance of students from Indigenous cultural backgrounds in math and science courses. In the specific example of Canada, Aboriginal students shy away from these courses, and a high percentage of the few brave ones who enrol often drop out, not just from math and science, but eventually out of school itself. The dropout rate has assumed alarming proportions as can be inferred from the statistics cited by Katz and McCluskey (2003, 117), thus:

> In one Manitoba school in 1996, although about 10% of the 700 students were Aboriginal, less than 4% finished grade 12. Of the 23 Native youth who had entered that system in kindergarten, only 1 completed high school. In the same year in another district, only 1 of 25 students who had transferred from northern reserves graduated.

Several researchers have adduced reasons to explain the high dropout rates and poor performance in school of Aboriginal students (Kanu 2002; Simard 1994; Stairs 1995). These studies suggest that the students drop out of school, or perform poorly in some subjects because of their estrangement from the school system, and alienation from subjects such as mathematics, which is completely bereft of their schema, cultural and environmental content, and real-life experiences. It seems to me that many of the Aboriginal students display their frustration with the school system and some school subjects like mathematics and science by purposely engaging in "self-handicapping" tendencies. Dorman and Ferguson (2004) gave some examples of self-handicapping strategies which include "putting off study until the last moment, and deliberately not trying in school" (70). It is my contention that most Aboriginal students are dissatisfied with mathematics, science, and probably many other subjects they are taught in school—they do not see any relevance between these school subjects and their daily lives and aspirations, and so they do not try hard enough, hence they perform poorly, and eventually drop out. A good way to address this problem is to adopt culture-sensitive and holistic curricula in teaching these students—an approach that was initiated in the pilot study of the Walpole Island schema-based math project, and an effort the ongoing major project is continuing with. My decision to involve community members in the project is informed by Gaskell's (2003) well-reasoned stance, articulated as follows: "Broad elements of the community must be engaged in dialogue concerning what knowledge about the natural world is important to whom, and for what purposes" (235). The enthusiastic participation of elders, educators, and other community members of Walpole Island in my project, lends credence to this stance. It is my view that a lot of knowledge, including ethnomathematical knowledge (D'Ambrosio 1985; Shirley 1995), is hidden in most indigenous cultures around the globe. There is urgent need to tap, document, and utilize this abundant knowledge before their possessors, usually community elders, pass away, carrying with them what would, otherwise, have been extremely beneficial to the schools, generations of Indigenous learners of math and science, and indeed, the whole of humankind. My study—the schema-based math project—is engaged in the recovery, tapping, and utilization of the ethnomathematical knowledge of the Anishnaabe people of Walpole Island First Nation.

Acknowledgements

This study is being carried out with a grant from the Social Sciences and Humanities Research Council of Canada (SSHRC)—Aboriginal. The contribution (in kind) of the Aboriginal Education Centre (Turtle Island) of the University of Windsor, is also hereby acknowledged.

References

Assembly of Manitoba Chiefs (1999). *Manitoba First Nations Schools Needs Assessment Report.* Winnipeg: Author.

Backhouse, J., Haggarty, L., Pirie, S., and Stratton, J. (1992). *Improving the Learning of Mathematics.* Portsmouth, NH: Heinemann Educational Books, Inc.

Bedeau, K. (2006). Perceptions of Environmental Pollution Amongst Aboriginal Peoples on the Aamjiwnaang First Nation Reserve. An unpublished MA thesis, Department of Sociology, University of Windsor.

Berkowitz, P. (2001). "Western Science Meets Mi'kmaq Knowledge." *University Affairs,* 42(10), 16–20.

Binda, K. (2001). "Aboriginal Education in Comparative and Global Perspectives: What has Research and Practice Done for Aboriginal Education in Canada?" *Canadian and International Education,* 30(1), 1–16.

Cajete, G.A (1994). *Look to the Mountain: An Ecology of Indigenous Education.* Skyland, N.C.: Kivaki Press.

D'Ambrosio, U. (1985). Ethnomathematics and its Place in the History and Pedagogy of Mathematics. [Online]. Available: <**www.enc.org/topics/equity/articles**>

Davison, D.M. (1992). "Mathematics." In J. Reyhner (Ed.), *Teaching American Indian Students,* 241–250. Norman: University of Oklahoma Press.

Doige, L.A. (2003). "A Missing Link: Between Traditional Aboriginal Education and the Western System of Education." *Canadian Journal of Native Education,* 27(2), 144–160.

Dorman, J.P. & Ferguson, J.M. (2004). "Associations Between Students' Perceptions of Mathematics Classroom Environment and Self-handicapping in Australian and Canadian High Schools." *McGill Journal of Education,* 39(1), 69–86.

Ezeife, A.N. (1999). "Using the Schema Theory in Science Teaching: The Challenge Before the Aboriginal Science Teacher." *WESTCAST conference proceedings,* 43–56. Brandon: Faculty of Education, Brandon University, Manitoba.

Ezeife, A.N. (2000). Middle Years Mathematics Methods course notes. Brandon University Northern Teacher Education Program (BUNTEP), Faculty of Education, Brandon University, Brandon, Manitoba.

Ezeife, A.N. (2002). "Mathematics and Culture Nexus: The Interactions of Culture and Mathematics in an Aboriginal Classroom." *International Education Journal,* 3(3), 176–187.

Ezeife, A.N. (2003). "Using the Environment in Mathematics and Science Teaching: An African and Aboriginal Perspective." *International Review of Education,* 49(3), 319–342.

Ezeife, A.N. (2004). "The Impact of a Culture-sensitive Curriculum on the Teaching and Learning of Mathematics in an Aboriginal Classroom." *Paper presented at the 12th World Congress of Comparative Education Societies (WCCES),* Havana, Cuba, Oct. 25–29.

Gaskell, J. (2003). "Engaging Science Education Within Diverse Cultures." *Curriculum Inquiry,* 23 (3), 235–249.

Hatfield, M.M., Edwards, N.T., Bitter, G.C, & Morrow, J. (2004). *Mathematics Methods for Elementary and Middle School Teachers.* New York: John Wiley & Sons Inc.

Jacobs, D.M. (1992). "Sustaining the Circle of Life." *Proceedings of the Thirteenth North American Prairie Conference,* 1–5. Windsor, Ontario, Canada.

Jegede, O.J. & Aikenhead, G. (1999). "Transcending Cultural Borders: Implications for Science Teaching." *Journal for Science and Technology Education,* 17, 45–66.

Kanu, Y. (2002). "In Their Own Voices: First Nations Students Identify Some Cultural Mediators of Their Learning in Formal School System." *The Alberta Journal of Educational Research,* XLVIII (2), 98–121.

Katz, H. & McCluskey, K. (2003). "Seeking Strength-based Approaches in Aboriginal Education: The 'Three Stars and a Wish' project." *McGill Journal of Education,* 38(1), 116–134.

Long, C.T. & DeTemple, D.W. (2000). *Mathematical Reasoning for Elementary Teachers*. Reading, MA: Addison-Wesley.

Ma, X. (2001). "Stability of Socio-economic Gaps in Mathematics and Science Achievement among Canadian Schools." *Canadian Journal of Education*, 26 (1), 97–118.

MacIvor, M. (1995). "Redefining Science Education for Aboriginal Students." In M. Battiste and J. Barman (Eds.), *First Nations Education in Canada: The Circle Unfolds*, 73–98. Vancouver: UBC Press.

Matang, R.A. (2001a). *An Information Brochure on Glen Lean Ethnomathematics Centre*. Papua New Guinea: University of Goroka.

Matang, R.A. (2001b, July). "The Role of Ethnomathematics in Mathematics Education: Implications for Mathematics Curriculum in Papua New Guinea." *Paper presented at the 11ᵗʰ World Congress of Comparative Education Societies (WCCES)*, Korea National University of Education, Chungbuk, South Korea.

Matthews, M.R. (1989). "A Role for History and Philosophy in Science Teaching." *Interchange*, 2(2), 3–15.

Mel, M. (2001, July). "Teacher as Caregiver: The Introduction of Values Education Through Indigenous Education in Teacher Education at the University of Goroka." *Paper presented at the 11ᵗʰ World Congress of Comparative Education Societies*, Korea National University of Education, Chungbuk, South Korea.

National Research Council (1989). *Everybody Counts: A Report to the Nation on the Future of Mathematics Education*. Washington, D.C.: National Academy Press.

O'Reilly-Scanlon, K., Crowe, C., & Weenie, A. (2004). "Pathways to Understanding: "Wahkohtowin" as a Research Methodology." *McGill Journal of Education*, 39(1), 29–44.

Shirley, L. (1995). "Using Ethnomathematics to Find Multicultural Mathematics Connections." In P.A. House and A.F. Coxford (Eds*.*), *Connecting Mathematics Across the Curriculum*, 34–43. Reston, Virginia: The National Council of Teachers of Mathematics, Inc.

Simard, L. (1994). "Curriculum Adaptation: Just Do It." In K.P. Binda (Ed.), *Critical issues in First Nations Education*, 78–86. Brandon: BUNTEP, Faculty of Education, Brandon University, Brandon, Manitoba.

Sloat, E. & Willms, J. (2000). "The International Adult Literacy Survey: Implications for Canadian Social Policy." *Canadian Journal of Education*, 25(3), 218–233.

Smith, M.R. & Ezeife, A.N. (2000, May). "Using the Environment in Science Teaching: A Cross-cultural Perspective." *Paper presented at the Canadian Society for the Study of Education (CSSE) Conference*, University of Alberta, Edmonton.

Smith, M.R. (1994). "Scientific Knowledge and Cultural Knowledge in the Classroom." In K.P. Binda (Ed.), *Critical Issues in First Nations Education*, 38–54. Brandon: BUNTEP, Faculty of Education, Brandon University, Brandon, Manitoba.

Stairs, A. (1995). "Learning Processes and Teaching Roles in Native Education: Cultural Base and Cultural Brokerage." In M. Battiste and J. Barman (Eds*.*), *First Nations Education in Canada: The Circle Unfolds*, 139–153. Vancouver: UBC Press.

The Ontario Curriculum, Grades 1–8: Mathematics (2005). Toronto: Ministry of Education and Training.

4

A New Approach to Understanding Aboriginal Educational Outcomes: The Role of Social Capital[1]

Jerry White, Nicholas Spence, and Paul Maxim

Introduction

In recent years, social capital has received much attention, and been the subject of great debate in the social sciences and policy arenas. Whether social capital has the capacity and utility to produce meaningful change, in achieving the goals of society, is one focus of that debate.

This paper examines the impacts of social capital on Aboriginal educational attainment in Canada, Australia, and New Zealand. The focus for Canada is First Nations and in other countries it is a similar population. Our aim is to explore how social capital theory has been applied to Aboriginal contexts in each country, and we seek to determine if social capital plays or can play any role in improving educational attainment for Aboriginal populations. Does social capital figure in the formation of programs and policies? Should it be a consideration? What are the specific contexts in which social capital can have an effect on educational attainment? We approached these questions by creating as extensive an inventory of policies and programs as possible for each of the countries. Also, we supplemented our inventory with email, phone, and face-to-face interviews with experts, such as Robert Putnam in the US, David Robinson in New Zealand, Canadian Aboriginal students, and government policy officers in all three countries. We thank everyone who took time to work with us.

We developed a synthesis looking for patterns and distilling the role of social capital. Our research looked at conscious applications of the concept, but also where we could discern its implicit part in educational attainment. In writing our results we chose programs and policies that illustrated our synthesis.

Why Aboriginal Education?

The focus on educational attainment and human capital development is strategic. Much research has illustrated the gap in the standard of living between the greater Canadian society and Aboriginal people, and the foundations for understanding these outcomes (White, Maxim, and Beavon 2004). Recurring themes are the lagging levels of educational attainment, and the consequent poor labour market outcomes among Aboriginals compared to the non-Aboriginal Canadian population. The 2001 Census data demonstrates these gaps clearly. Among the population 15 years of age and over, 48% of Aboriginals have less than a high school graduation certificate compared to 30.8% of the non-Aboriginal population. The percentage of Aboriginals with high school and some post-secondary education is 22.4% compared to 25% for the non-Aboriginal population. For trades or college, 23.7% of Aboriginals possess this credential compared to 25.9% of the non-Aboriginal population. At the high level of attainment—university—only 4.4% of Aboriginals have achieved this credential compared to 15.7% of the non-Aboriginal population (Statistics Canada 2003). The picture is not, however, totally bleak. For example, Indian and Northern Affairs Canada (2004) data shows there have been some improvements in educational attainment over time, but the gaps are still important.

Our paper is anchored by the desire to develop more insight into the solutions to these problems using the social-capital lens. The trends we have documented are not exclusive to Aboriginal Canadians. Indeed, Aboriginal populations across all three countries have less attainment than the general population, and this issue has not gone unnoticed by their governments. Although our preoccupation with this issue originates within the Canadian context, a logical step is to compare the work done in other countries and develop a general framework of social capital as it relates to Aboriginal educational outcomes. This is what we have done.

Defining Social Capital

Conceptually and theoretically, social capital has various faces and dispositions. Recently, there has been a move to arrive at a single conceptualization and definition of social capital—these efforts have met with much resistance. We do not resolve this issue but match our working understanding with the definition set out by some members of the government, including the Policy Research Initiative. We leave the theoretical debates regarding the "correct" definition of social capital for another forum.

We adopt a structural approach to the concept, which emphasizes social networks as the focal point of investigation. Social capital is defined as the networks of social relations within the milieu, characterized by specific norms and attitudes that serve the purpose of *potentially* enabling individuals' or groups' access to a pool of resources and supports. Social capital is conceptualized in three different forms: bonding social capital (intragroup relations), bridging social capital (horizontal intergroup relations), and linking social capital (vertical intergroup relations in a society stratified by class, status, and power relations) (Woolcock 2001).

Outline

In the introduction we have dealt briefly with the focus of the study, our approach to data, and the definition of core concepts. Part I presents our model for understanding how social capital operates in the Aboriginal context we studied. The four dimensions of social capital we identify were derived inductively from the study of policy, practice, and outcomes in our target countries. We integrate a small number of examples into this section to make the model grounded and easier to understand. In Part II we explore some examples of policies and programs that illustrate our synthesis. Finally, we return to the four dimensions, integrate our examples into the model, and draw some further lessons for policy making.

Part I—The Four-Element Model

We can draw the following general conclusions from our study of social capital and Aboriginal educational outcomes: first, social capital is not an extremely powerful explanator. It functions as an independent variable that explains some variance in population and individual outcomes. However, understanding what seems to impact on the effectiveness of social capital provides interesting insights into its potential strengths and weaknesses.

We found that there are four elements that interact to influence the policy-program effects of social capital. They are:

1. Levels of Social Capital

Social capital seems to have more influence at set threshold points. For example, in the case of Port Harrison in Canada, the movement of the community to a new location led to the destruction of social capital as it broke generational ties. Parents and elders used to teach the young how to hunt and build ice houses. The relocation to a place where there were no hunting possibilities led to a breakup of the traditional system where young people traveled with the elder skilled hunters, learning many skills, such as language, traditions, etc., during the hunting season. Prior to the move, this community had high levels of educational attainment because in the off-season the community studied at the school. After the relocation this community spiraled downward as evidenced by many social indicators: suicide increased; school non-attendance became endemic; fertility rates declined; and rates of illness rose (White and Maxim 2003). Thus, the state had destroyed, perhaps inadvertently, the social capital of the community.

As social capital approaches zero, there seems to be a relatively great effect on population outcomes. In communities that are decimated of social capital networks, educational attainment is very low. The rebuilding of social capital in these communities can have a positive effect; however, given the threshold effect, as we build social capital to even moderate levels, the effect may be negligible, or, depending on the existence of the following three other elements, we may see declines in positive outcomes as social capital grows very strong.

2. Norm Effects

Increasing levels of social capital are not necessarily related to increasing educational attainment. This can be understood by examining what we call norm effects.

Simply put, where parents and family have low educational attainment and high levels of bonding social capital, the child's educational attainment is likely to be low. This is why we see a high correlation between mothers' and children's educational attainment (White and Maxim 2002). The post-secondary students we interviewed for this study all came from communities where their family-clan networks had relatively high educational attainment. Ward's (1992) work examining the Cheyenne found that the level of educational attainment in the clan group is critical to the educational success of the children. In another US examination of policy, Ward (1998, 102) notes that the more successful community Busby and its tribal school utilize the highest educational achievers where "adults with education are the role models and sources of support for students." This is a case where the norms available for the child are critical, and substituting higher norm adults for the bonded network of the family has positive effects.

Where we have low educational norms embedded in a child's family, it is counter productive to build bonding social capital. The higher the bonding social capital, the more the low norms are reinforced, and the lower the educational attainment is likely to be. In Part II we have several indications of this process. In Queensland, Australia, they had truancy problems and developed a program whereby buses went to the homes of every Aboriginal student to get them in the morning. They discovered that the parents who had little schooling would not wake the children to get on the bus—they preferred to have them sleep.

3. Cultural Openness Contexts (Building Relationships Based on Cultural Context)

Where bonding social capital networks are integrated into wider society (either bridged or linked), there is greater potential for increasing educational attainment. Even remote communities can experience more improvement if culturally open. Open cultures can exist in a few ways. For example, where language use includes dominant languages, people engage in the wider economy, and traditions are not exclusionary. Openness is a relative concept; hence, if that which is "outside" can be made more like the target group's culture it simulates a more open situation, and allows bridging and linking. Highly closed dominant cultures and marginalized or non-integrated ethnic groups can have high levels of social capital and very low educational attainment. Integrated and open cultural contexts that have much lower social capital will have more potential for educational attainment.

This phenomenon can be understood in different ways. For example, if we look at the more successful endeavors in our target countries, we can understand the process as one where the dominant cultural group gathers a clear appreciation of the Aboriginal culture. This appreciation is translated into behaviours that are consistent with the norms within the Aboriginal culture, which facilitates the development of relations and allows linking and bridging to take place. We find this process most clearly manifested in New Zealand. Williams and Robinson (2002) have sought to identify Indigenous applications of social capital.

Interestingly, they argued that "the nature of social capital in New Zealand can only be understood by taking into account elements of social capital important to the Maori," which led to their development of a Maori concept of social capital (ibid, 12). Robinson and Williams (2001) argued that there were nine key factors or emphases in a Maori concept of social capital. Our review of their work indicates that the key differences involve the role of primary network. For example, in their estimation social capital is not produced outside of family. The extended family in Maori thinking is the community. Imposition of networks outside the family or community are deemed to be less functional. Robinson and Williams (2001, 55–60) outline their theory:

> A Maori concept of social capital emphasises the following elements: Extended family relationships are the basis for all other relationships. The whanau [family] is the nucleus of all things. Maori community values and norms come from traditional values that are rooted in the whanau ... It is essential to have knowledge of, and to know one's place in ... the hierarchy of whanau, hapu and iwi[2] ... Relationships in Maori society develop around informal association rather than formal organisations ... The connectedness that is derived from this association ... The holistic, integrating nature of relationships and networks are of primary importance, while their use or functional activity is secondary ... Family, tribal and community networks may take priority over functional contracts with specified agencies such as health, education or welfare ...

> Membership in customary Maori associations is based on an exchange of obligations and acceptance by the group. Conditions for joining are verbal, implicit and obligation-driven—rather than rule-driven, specified and written down ... The concept ... includes obligations based on a common ancestry and the cultural dimension that obliges one to act in certain ways that give rise to the development of social capital. Key concepts of Maori society that relate to social capital include hapai (the requirement to apply the concept of uplifting/enhancement) and tautoko (providing support within the community).

So New Zealand views of social capital imply that relationships must be built through informal associations as opposed to formal institutionalized structures, and the informal relations that lead to the connectedness and networks that are created have specific functions and expectations at the family kin group (whanau), sub tribe (hapu), and tribal (iwi) level. According to Williams and Robinson (2002) these relationships take precedence over formalized contractual relations in things such as education. The traditional culture has two social capital related processes that New Zealand policy can utilize: hapai (bridge or connect) and tautoko (support or commitment) which we will see in the form of drawing the family into pre-school.

From a practical point of view, the problem is how to utilize the strong bonding capital networks within the community at the family and clan level to enhance population outcomes. The simple approach to this would have included bridging and linking them to wider social capital networks. Robinson (2004) notes that success depends on two factors: creating or drawing on a collective historical memory of relations held by the iwi (tribe) with another community that facilitates the bridging process (i.e., the memory and history of relations with the central government in this case); and the perception of, or lack of, shared understandings. These are assessed and developed through interaction. Interaction takes place in traditional forums such as the hui—a ceremonial gathering that allows people to get to know each other in a recognizable context. It seems from our assessment that this recognition can, therefore, manufacture a collective knowledge/memory of shared understandings which permits linkages.

New Zealand has developed a Maori concept of social capital where it is only produced in the extended family (whanau), and cannot be created for the Maori from the outside through linking or bridging networks. Thus, programs that involve the imposition of networks outside the family or community are deemed to lack functionality. Success rests on bridging networks based on relationships that must be built through engagement in informal associations at the whanau (family), hapu (clan), or iwi (tribe) level. Informal associations that work can eventually be translated to more formal institutionalized structures.

The Maori have specific practices where whanau, hapu, and iwi levels develop understandings of each other. These specialized meeting and exchange structures, such as the hui, are used to create higher level linkages and bridges between social capital networks. You will see, in the program and policy examples below, how this has been utilized.

So in New Zealand, we found that government policy and program development was preceded by an understanding of Maori culture. The implementation of the programs to help with educational attainment issues could only be done by creating the conditions for bridging and linking, which meant opening the cultural context by adopting the Maori ways.

There are many examples around the world where Aboriginal cultures have changed and become more open. Exogamy creates more openness for example. In Australia and Canada, the residential schools were an attempt to force assimilation. We can see that these attempts to create linkages are very destructive.

4. Community Capacity

Strong bonding social capital networks, with high attainment members, that are bridged to school networks and linked to resources seem to have a positive effect on the transitions to high school and post-secondary institutions, graduate rates, and overall educational success. The context within which social capital works seems much more important than the "strength" or "level" of the bonded network. Networks cannot hold all the resources necessary to ensure educational attainment. They must operate in capital-rich environments; that is, they require other forms of capital in order to have a positive influence on educational attainment. This is why we observe that communities with low economic development (high unemployment) have low educational attainment. Those willing or able to integrate with wider capital formations (e.g., physical capital), or who have the capacity to develop such capital based on their infrastructures tend to have high educational attainment.

Our investigation of Australia demonstrated this dimension very clearly. Stone, Gray, and Hughes (2003) argue that using social capital generated by low-capacity communities can reinforce low capacity. They are looking at this in the context of job searching, but it has implications for education. Interventions to network low-achievement parents with the schools may encourage a reproduction of the lower achievement according to the Australian approach.

Hunter (2000) notes that unemployment of adults is a key problem in creating and sustaining poor educational results for children. Community capacity is once again seen as playing a fundamental role in educational processes. Hunter's study of social capital concludes that reinforcing social capital in a community with low employment levels reinforces lower norms of achievement, and leads to children uninterested in educational attainment.

A study by the Centre for Aboriginal Economic Policy Research (Hunter 2000), however, does call for Australia to vet all policies (as per Putnam's call) to determine the effects on social capital, and how to ensure that policies increase the involvement and connection of Aboriginal society with wider Australian society. This "connectiveness" may actually increase integration and mitigate the effects of high levels of bonding capital, which works with low education norms to reinforce separateness. There has been considerable research on Portes's four negative attributes of social capital and their application to the Australian Aboriginal context. Hunter (2004) notes that the "exclusion of outsiders" prevents access to services, especially in the area of education; "excessive claims on group members" plays out as "demand sharing" that may undermine educational involvement by youth; "restrictions on group members' freedom" can undermine autonomy where norms dictate non-involvement; and "downward leveling of norms" creates a non-achievement context as we noted in the previous studies.

The Australians are developing a theoretical model that differs from the one used in New Zealand and advocates the need to intervene to build community capacity, including at the level of network construction. They have also placed cultural specificity at the core of approaching the issue of social capital and educational attainment, but it appears somewhat differently (more interventionist) in practice as we will see in the policies we review in Part II.

Conceptual Modelling of the Four Elements

If we examine some combinations of cases, the interrelationships and impacts of the four dimensions may become clearer:

> *Scenario 1*: Aboriginal children with moderate to high social capital, where educational attainment norms in their networks are moderate to high, who live in communities with cultural openness and low unemployment levels, will have high educational attainment.

> *Scenario 2*: Aboriginal students who have high levels of social capital with low educational attainment norms in their network and low economic

development, will have low educational attainment. This scenario is often compounded by being resilient to outside network bridging and linking—a result of being culturally closed.

Scenario 3: Aboriginal children with zero or extremely low social capital will have no educational attainment norms to draw upon and will have low educational attainment. In this case alone, building social capital is a key prerequisite to increasing educational attainment.

Part II—Selected Policy and Program Examples in New Zealand, Australia, and Canada

Part II explores some of the policies and programs aimed at confronting problems of educational attainment among Aboriginals in New Zealand, Australia, and Canada. This is not designed to be an exhaustive review of the activities in each region; instead, it examines some key illustrations of the four dimension model we presented earlier.

New Zealand

New Zealand has targeted educational attainment for the Maori as the key to reversing the negative population indicators all too common among Indigenous populations worldwide. The New Zealand Ministry report small yet positive improvements based on two identified factors that have made the biggest difference in engaging students and raising their achievement: the quality of teaching and the relationship between whanau/home and school (New Zealand Ministry of Education 2003). We will concentrate on the second issue, the relationship between family and school, because this is clearly connected to the use of social capital to increase educational outcomes, and provides the clearest indication of opening relationships based on cultural context.

Since 1988 the New Zealand Government has moved to "hand over responsibility for governing educational institutions to the local community and make communities accountable ... reforms have encouraged more innovative ways for communities and education institutions to work together" (Ministry of Maori Development 1997,10). The evaluation of the reforms overall, cited that the successful initiatives occurred when there was a developed community-school co-operation, and when the community families proposed, developed, or participated in and supported the programs (ibid.).

One of the first policies developed and translated into programs was the stepwise creation of pathways for parents to be involved in supporting their children's learning. The Parent Support and Development Program (PSDP), Study Support Centres (SSC), and Parents as Mentors (PAM) initiatives were set up as partnerships between schools, whanau (family), and communities. If social capital is created in the kin group (whanau), and social capital in the form of networks of support are key to improving school achievement, then building network connections between schools and whanau would be the way to proceed. This is exactly what they have done. The building block of their improvement program is increasing Maori involvement, but that cannot be done top down but only bottom up (recall our discussion in Part I).

The Parents as First Teachers (PFT) program is one of the most illustrative. It focused on providing support and guidance to parents with children zero to three years of age. Maori children tend to come less prepared for elementary school, which leads to performance and discipline issues. This led to a widespread discussion between those running the program and the whanau and communities about establishing and running preschools in those communities to increase the preparedness of the children. From our modeling perspective we have to ask: "How did the Ministry get the whanau to be involved?" The Ministry set up stalls at community events, attended *hui* (special meetings with dialogue), etc., and the Ministry networks became "known" to the Maori. Recall that relationships in Maori society develop around informal association rather than formal organizations, and so family, tribal, and community networks may take priority over functional contracts with specified agencies. Thus, building the personal informal links was a precursor to more formalized relations. After being known to Maori families, the New Zealand Ministry explained the benefits of preschool, and helped parents set up their own early childhood programs, or helped children enroll in the founding ones. In 2003, 3,000 Maori families were involved in the PFT program (Farquhar 2003; New Zealand Ministry of Education 2003).

The case of New Zealand illustrates the need to build culturally sensitive pathways that open the bonding social capital networks up to linking and bridging resource-rich networks. Also demonstrated is the role of norms and the relative unimportance of levels of social capital in the basic bonding networks.

Australia

In this section we want to highlight what is distinctive in the Australian approach and point out how their understanding contributes to our model. While the Australians have launched a myriad of programs to improve teacher cultural understanding, train new teachers, develop preschools, and integrate parents, they see building community capacity as integral to making education relevant to Indigenous peoples. Thus, jobs and access to markets are the foundation of success. They also see that the skills of the labor force have to increase in order to take advantage of any development. There is little evidence that the Australians are looking at any particular strategies that involve utilizing or developing social capital in this process. Some exceptions are, however, notable. The Gumala Mirnuwarni (Coming Together to Learn) Program, West Australia, was established in 1997. The House of Representatives Standing Committee (2004,189) reports that the impetus for this program was the community's desire to see their children more actively participate in school: "It has involved collaboration and partnership between children, parents, schools, State and Commonwealth education authorities, three resource partners and a philanthropic organization, in a program designed to improve educational outcomes for local Indigenous students." A representative of Rio Tinto outlined one element of the project, it is a personal commitment contract that reads: " 'I, the child, agree to go along to school and I, the family member, agree to support my child going to school. ... ' If the child does not participate in school, then they are not welcome at the after-school program ... that has been set up for them. So there is an expectation that their participation in school will lead to enhanced benefits"[3] (House of Representatives Standing Committee 2004, 189).

The Gumala Mirnuwarni has been successful because of the attempts to link family networks, students, and school networks together utilizing reciprocity mechanisms. The Government noted that they recognize the success of the project, and have proceeded to use it as a foundation for other initiatives. They have developed the notion of compacts around the country in which diverse stakeholders forge beneficial working relations, for example, families with schools and industry (House of Representatives Standing Committee 2004). This has the effect of increasing the apparent benefits of school. The use of networks in the community is less developed and less widespread than in New Zealand; however, an analysis of policy development does show the employment of networks. The Australians are cautious on social capital issues.

The Australian experience indicates the relationships between the goals of being educated and the motivation to be involved in the process of being educated. Where there is development in the community (higher capacity) there is a tangible reward or return for the work of going to school. Where there are no opportunities for work or societal involvement, the rewards are unclear and involvement in the educational process diminishes.

Canada

The last set of examples we will cover are from Canada. This section is broken into two parts as we want to look at examples from National program and policy, delivered under the auspices of Indian and Northern Affairs Canada (INAC), and some provincial examples.[4]

National Policies in Canada

INAC operates two major sets of programs. First, The Elementary/Secondary Education National Program aims to "provide eligible students living on reserve with elementary and secondary education comparable to that required in provincial schools ... where the reserve is located" (INAC 2003a, 3). Funding is transferred to a variety of deliverers that can include the Bands (communities) themselves, the provincial school boards if they are delivering the services, or federal schools maintained by the government. INAC outlines the expenditures acceptable for funding. Second, the Post-Secondary Education Program's objective is to "improve the employability of First Nations people and Inuit by providing eligible students ... access to education and skill development opportunities at the post-secondary level" (INAC 2003b, 3). Moreover, this program aims to increase participation in post-secondary studies, post-secondary graduation rates, and employment rates (ibid).

Canada launched a review in 2002 to identify and address the factors of a quality First Nations education (INAC 2002). Several initiatives have been started in the past few years, but more time will have to elapse before we can evaluate these initiatives. However, we can see that many of these initiatives parallel those that have been successful in other countries.

Provincial Initiatives

There are many policies and programs across the country affecting Aboriginal people that are aimed at enhancing their educational and labour market outcomes. We look at only a few illustrative examples in British Columbia, where the work that has been done is quite extensive.

The Best Practices Project by the First Nation Schools Association and First Nations Education Steering Committee of British Columbia (1997) is a very successful initiative. For example, the First Nations Role Model Program in School District 52 (Prince Rupert) involves the use of very successful First Nations role models in the classroom. The goal is to promote awareness of First Nations cultures and issues for all students and teachers, while promoting self-esteem and pride in cultural heritage. There is a benefit to the school and students as the mentor links the students to the resources of the outside world, and they substitute for the low educational norm context of the parental networks. Not only can the mentor's resources be potentially drawn upon, but they establish a relationship that is grounded in a culturally familiar context. The provision of a higher norm model substitutes for lower attainment levels in the child's bonding capital group (family) while fostering openness. The key is not building bonding social capital, which can reinforce low attainment (scenario 2).

The Summer Science and Technology Camps Initiative, funded by INAC and coordinated by the First Nations Education Steering Committee, targets First Nations youth to engage them in science and technology issues, and expose them to the numerous education and career opportunities available. The program includes local elders and other community members through the process of having First Nations communities and organizations develop the initiatives in accordance with their local priorities. Through partnerships with institutions outside of the community, such as BC Hydro, BC Gas, Ministries of Fisheries and Forestry, Science World BC, and the University of British Columbia, the reason for education becomes clear. In a way, this initiative connects the students directly to the job market, and makes education seem to have a purpose. In that respect, it plays the role that higher levels of community capacity and development would play. This is an illustration of what the Australians are arguing, concerning the need for resource-rich environments for social capital to operate. As well, links are forged between the communities (children) and resource-rich institutions. The immediate effects are increased interest in science subjects, and the long-term establishment of relations between the community and the labor force.

Policy and Program Implications

As we developed Parts I and II above we drew some tentative linkages between the policy and program initiatives, and the four elements that we feel interact to enhance success generally and optimize social capital based initiatives particularly. We can draw some more general conclusions in this section, and push a little deeper into how we can approach the critical issue of Aboriginal educational attainment. Policy and program success seems highly sensitive to context.

In New Zealand where the Maori are a large proportion of the population, we find well-developed programs to build educational attainment levels. They are also based most closely on a homegrown, culturally specific notion of social capital. As we noted, New Zealand has determined that social capital is only created in the communities at the family level. Given that the families and sub-clans all have high-bonding social capital levels, and that the higher tribal organizations are built on this social capital base, any bridging or linking that is going to take place must be rooted in the core family networks. They have a restricted yet functional view of using social capital, where the high levels of bonding social capital must be shaped and utilized in the wider institutions to promote the norms of external networks. We saw for example that the programs began at the preschool with the families running the preschool, which changed attitudes towards schooling. Parents (the whanau) became involved in preparing children for school, which was often done in the school setting, by passing school skills onto them. It is through this process that the school system becomes a part of the family. The school networks, including teachers, principals, etc., became "known" and began to "share a history" with the Maori while developing "knowledge of the customs and norms." This process allowed the whanau to be bridged and linked to the educational institutions, which precipitated the flow of the bridged and linked resources. The policy aimed at creating a context of cultural openness in this case.

Openness can be created in two ways. First, one can transform aspects of the cultural norms of the target populations, although this is the most difficult and runs the risk of being seen as assimilationist. A second approach is to make sure the program is delivered in a way that is not challenging to the Aboriginal culture, using the ways of the people to the greatest possible degree. This has the effect of making the institution, such as a school, more like the people and less "outside." A closed cultural context is one that has two approaches that are culturally distant. Narrowing the gap through the introduction of Aboriginal language, community elder participation, and using the forums that are acceptable (e.g., the hui in New Zealand) helps create a more open context.

Specific policies and programs across our three countries all reinforce the importance of this condition being fulfilled. Many have aspects of their programs tailored, albeit often unconsciously, to reinforce openness. This process is clearly seen in initiatives such as "Teaching the Teachers" which teaches Aboriginal culture as well as programs that integrate community cultural leaders and make use of family and Elders.

The Australians have a greater focus on economic development as a necessary condition for improving educational attainment. They are generally more skeptical of the concept noting that the high levels of bonding social capital combined with poor norms around schooling reinforce non-attainment. Australia seeks a more step-wise process to improving educational attainment where the key is community development and improved community capacity. Having access to jobs enables citizens to understand the utility of education. Also, this strategy retains those with human capital in communities, which in turn provides better norm models. Recall, Queensland had a problem with school attendance and developed a program to have buses drive to each student's house every morning to take them to school. The result was poor because the parents would not wake the kids if they were sleeping. Attendance, leading to graduation, leading to jobs was the needed understanding. The successful programs have developed partnerships with the business community, creating job opportunities. These partnerships around the country link industry and community interests, giving meaning to educational attainment. They created the integration of the family bonding capital networks with the resources that made education more important. In these cases it was the building of community capacity that was key, and the other elements, while important, needed to be less prominent. Building social capital at the community level (bonding) was of little importance, and may have been detrimental in the absence of economic development given the low educational norms.

Using our framework, and incorporating the Australian experience, we might argue, given our examination of initiatives, that in the unsuccessful programs, the parents were not easily involved because they had little understanding of the importance of schooling, given their low educational attainment. Given the low community capacity in terms of economic development, the purpose for supporting the schools and promoting higher educational attainment for the children was unclear to both the community and the students. The more successful programs were, indeed, linked to job paths.

In Canada, at the federal level, some of the recent initiatives that have been started in the past few years parallel initiatives that have been successful in other countries. These initiatives have not had sufficient time to develop and evaluate at this stage. The provinces have developed programs that address specific local needs. The provincial programs that are most successful target the specific problem associated with our model. For example, in the Science and Technology Camps, the inclusion of local elders and other community members as teachers led to the First Nations communities and organizations developing the initiatives in accordance with their cultures; consequently, family networks were bolstered by having adult participants that came back and encouraged support for education. In the case of the First Nations Role Model Program, the mentors substituted for the low educational norm context of the parental networks. Other initiatives examined but not reported showed similar patterns.

In conclusion, we would argue that understanding social capital is important in promoting educational attainment. However, it has a moderate influence, and rarely acts alone. It influences outcomes for Aboriginal educational attainment in conjunction with other resources (human and economic/physical capital). It is contingent on the context and this can be assessed by using the four elements we have discussed throughout our paper. We have argued the following:

1. It is key to identify the specific context and interrelation of the four identified elements, and address programming toward the specificity of the situation. Just building social capital would rarely be the most effective strategy. Where communities, families, and clans face grave social problems and have low bonding social capital, then it is appropriate to build that resource. It could, however, under certain conditions, be the wrong strategy.

2. Where there are very low educational norms in the child's networks, reinforcing social capital in those networks is the wrong approach. It will reinforce low norms and non-attainment strategies. Substituting higher norm roles is one strategy for overcoming this problem; however, that involves bridging and linking to the child and their networks, which depends on the appropriateness of strategies and the degree of openness of communities to outsiders.

3. The ability to engage children depends on how open their communities are. Schools, ministries of education, federal departments, and teachers will have to depend on the target groups having accepted or incorporated aspects of the dominant culture and goals in order to connect with their programs and resources; or the dominant culture and its institutions can adopt, and adapt to, the Aboriginal minority culture, and create an openness context to connect in that manner. Such adaptation must be context specific. However, even where connections can take place, there is no guarantee of any "buy-in" to goals of educational attainment.

4. Enthusiasm for education is linked to seeing a purpose for the effort. This point is key particularly where past experience has been negative for the parents. For example, residential schooling in Canada and Australia created a legacy of mistrust and anger among Aboriginal peoples. The key to providing purpose is related to the development of community or related capacity.

Future Research

The development of a better understanding of the interrelationship between the four identified elements is the next step. This should involve two separate processes. First, the development of methods to measure the different elements will allow us to produce useful diagnostic tools. The second process is to develop a simple planning tool that gives its user a way to draw conclusions about the relative problems across the four dimensions: levels of social capital, norms effects, cultural openness, and community capacity. The planning tool could be a crude guide to assess existing programs, diagnose problems, and design improvements.

Endnotes

1   This is a revised version of a paper originally published in the Policy Research Initiative's *Social Capital Thematic Studies Book* in 2005.

2   Whanau is family, hapu is sub clan, and iwi is tribe.

3   "The programs involved Education Enrichment Centres where students can study after school, with supervision and support. Homework and individual tutoring was undertaken. The centres were set up with educational resources including computers with internet access ... Students were assigned a school-based mentor ... who also worked on well-being. Extracurricular activities could be arranged to develop confidence and abilities including ... visits to industry ... and cultural awareness camps ..."(Western Australia Department of Education n.d.)

4   In Canada education falls under provincial jurisdiction in the Constitution. However, note that INAC funds basic elementary and secondary education for the 120,000 students who live on-reserve (INAC 2004). The federal government also provides funding that supports roughly 26,000 First Nation and Inuit students in post-secondary education each year. About 4,000 of these students graduate annually (ibid).

References

Farquhar, Sarah Eve (2003). *Parents as First Teachers: A Study of the New Zealand PAFT Program.* Wellington, New Zealand: Early Childhood Development.

First Nations Schools Association and First Nations Education Steering Committee (1997). *First Nations Education: Best Practices Project Volume 1.* Vancouver, British Columbia: First Nations Schools Association and First Nations Education Steering Committee.

House of Representatives Standing Committee on Aboriginal and Torres Strait Islander Affairs (2004). *Many Ways Forward: Report of the Inquiry Into Capacity Building and Service Delivery in Indigenous Communities.* Canberra, Australia: The Parliament of the Commonwealth of Australia.

Hunter, Boyd H (2000). "Social Exclusion, Social Capital, and Indigenous Australians: Measuring the Social Costs of Unemployment." Technical Report Discussion Paper No.204, Centre for Aboriginal Economic Policy Research, Australia National University.

Hunter, Boyd H (2004). "Taming the Social Capital Hydra? Indigenous Poverty, Social Capital Theory and Measurement." Retrieved October 2, 2004 <**www.anu.edu.au/caepr/Publications/topical/ Hunter_social%20capital.pdf**>.

Indian and Northern Affairs Canada (2002). *Our Children–Keepers of the Sacred Knowledge: Final report of the Minister's National Working Group on Education.* Ottawa, Canada: Government of Canada.

Indian and Northern Affairs Canada (2003a). *Appendix A: Elementary and Secondary Education– National Program Guidelines.* Ottawa, Canada: Government of Canada.

Indian and Northern Affairs Canada (2003b). *Appendix B: Post Secondary Education–National Program Guidelines.* Ottawa, Canada: Government of Canada.

Indian and Northern Affairs Canada (2004). Personal Communication. November 11.

Ministry of Maori Development (1997). *Making Education Work for Maori: Talking Points for Parents and Whanau.* Wellington, New Zealand: Government of New Zealand.

New Zealand Ministry Of Education (2003). *Nga Haeata Maturauranga: Annual Report on Maori Education.* Wellington, New Zealand: Government of New Zealand.

Robinson, David and Tu Williams (2001). "Social Capital and Voluntary Activity: Giving and Sharing in Maori/Non Maori Society." *Social Policy Journal of New Zealand* 17:51–71.

Robinson, David (2004). "Forming Norms and Implementing Sanctions–Deliberation and Sustained Dialogue in a Social Capital Framework." Notes prepared for panel presentation at ISTR Conference, Toronto, July 11–14, 2004.

Statistics Canada (2003). "Selected Educational Characteristics, Aboriginal Identity, Age Groups, Sex, and Area of Residence for Population 15 Years and Over, 2001 Census – 20% Sample Data." Ottawa: Statistics Canada. Catalogue #: 97F0011XCB01042.

Stone, Wendy, Matthew Gray, and Jody Hughes (2003). *Social Capital at Work: How Family, Friends and Civic Ties Relate to Labour Market Outcomes.* Research Paper 31, Australian Institute of Family Studies, Melbourne.

Ward, Carol (1992). "Social and Cultural Influences on the Schooling of Northern Cheyenne Youth." PhD dissertation, University of Chicago.

Ward, Carol (1998). "Community Resources and School Performance: The Northern Cheyenne Case." *Sociological Inquiry* 68(1):83–113.

Western Australia Department of Education. *GUMALA MIRNUWARNI–*"Coming Together to Learn." Retrieved September 20, 2004 <**www.dest.gov.au/archive/iae/analysis/learning/1/gumala.htm**>.

White, Jerry and Paul Maxim (2002). "Correlates of Educational Attainment in First Nations Communities." *Aboriginal Policy Research Conference*, Ottawa, Nov. 26–28, 2002.

White, Jerry and Paul Maxim (2003). "Social Capital, Social Cohesion, and Population Outcomes in Canada's First Nations Communities." Pp. 7–34 in *Aboriginal Conditions: Research as a Foundation for Public Policy*, eds. White, Jerry, Paul Maxim, and Dan Beavon. Vancouver: UBC Press.

White, Jerry, Paul Maxim, and Dan Beavon (editors) (2004). *Aboriginal Policy Research: Setting the Agenda for Change. Volumes I & II.* Toronto, ON: Thompson Educational Publishing.

Williams, Tu and David Robinson (2002). "Social Capital Based Partnerships, A Maori Perspective – A Comparative Approach." in *Building Social Capital,* edited by David Robinson. Victoria, New Zealand: Institute of Policy Studies Victoria University.

Woolcock, Michael (2001). "The Place of Social Capital in Understanding Social and Economic Outcomes." Pp. 65–88 in *The Contribution of Human and Social Capital to Sustained Economic Growth and Well-Being.* HRDC and OECD.

5

Aboriginal Occupational Gap: Causes and Consequences

Costa Kapsalis

Introduction

While significant improvements in the labour market outcomes of Aboriginal people have been achieved over the last decade, they remain among the most marginalized and vulnerable groups in Canada. Previous studies have shown that, in general, "Aboriginal people have a lower labour force participation rate, a higher rate of unemployment, less representation in higher paying occupations, and not surprisingly, lower average wage rates than other workers" (DeSilva 1999). Low education has been identified as the key factor in explaining the relatively weak performance of Aboriginal Canadians in the labour market (Comfort, et al. 2005). Consequently, skills development has been identified as "the most fruitful approach to raising the standard of living of Aboriginal Canadians" (DeSilva 1999).

This study attempts to determine to what extent the weaker labour market performance of Aboriginal Canadians is due to the type of occupations they have, and why their occupations differ from the rest of Canadians. In particular, the study poses the following questions:

1. What kind of jobs do Aboriginal workers have, compared to those of non-Aboriginal workers?

2. What is the impact of occupational differences on wage differences between the two groups of workers?

3. What are the main factors behind their occupational and wage differences?

Methodology

The analysis is based mainly on special tabulations from the 2001 Census. The Census 2001 Public Use Mircrodata Files (PUMF) was used primarily for initial explorations. The sample selected for our analysis was restricted as follows:

1. Age 18–64 in 2000, excluding full-time students; and

2. Had only paid work in 2000, and worked full-time (i.e. 30 or more hours weekly) for at least 26 weeks during the year.

Figure 5.1: Definition of NOC Skill Levels

High-skill occupations	Skill level 0	**Managerial occupations:** No education requirements or skill levels assigned, although they are often treated as high-skill occupations.
	Skill level A	**Professional occupations:** Usually require university education.
	Skill level B	**Skilled admin, technical, paraprofessional:** Usually require college education or apprenticeship training.
Low-skill occupations	Skill level C	**Clerical, health support, intermediate sales, machine operators:** Usually require secondary school and/or occupational specific training.
	Skill level D	**Elemental sale, trades helpers, labourers:** Usually require on-the-job training only

Figure 5.2: Distribution of Workers by Occupational Skill Level and Aboriginal Identity, 2000

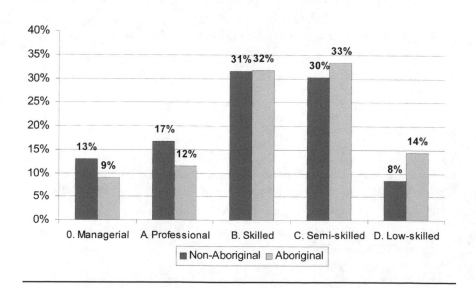

The reason for the sample restrictions was to focus the analysis on those with a significant amount of work during the year.[1] The restriction to those with paid work only was imposed because self-employment income presents more measurement challenges (such as the presence of negative earnings). However, sensitivity analysis shows that a broader or narrower sample selection leads to similar results.

The occupational classification is based on the National Occupational Classification (NOC).[2] For some parts of the analysis, we used all 520 NOC categories. However, most of the time we used the five skill levels identified by NOC (**Figure 5.1**); and 19 clusters of major NOC groups. Following convention, we define high-skill occupations as managerial occupations (level 0), professional occupations (level A), and skilled occupations (level B). We define low-skill occupations as semi-skilled (level C) and low-skilled (level D). The term skill gap refers to the difference between the percentage of Aboriginal and non-Aboriginal workers with high-skill occupations—managerial, professional (level A) and skilled (level B) occupations. The industry classification is based on the North American Industry Classification System (NAICS). We distinguished occupations into two broad groups: public and private sector. The public sector is broadly defined as public administration, education, health, and social assistance while, the private sector is everything else.

Occupational Gap

Aboriginal Versus Non-Aboriginal

First, we compare the distribution of Aboriginal and non-Aboriginal workers by type of occupation. The main focus is on differences in the percentage of the two groups with high-skill jobs (referred to here as skill gap). Aboriginal individuals are less likely to have a significant amount of work than non-Aboriginal individuals. On average, the employment rate (full-time/26+ weeks) of Aboriginal individuals is about three-quarters that of non-Aboriginal individuals (43% vs. 56%). The difference is smaller in the case of Métis (50% vs. 56% non-Aboriginal). One possible reason is that Métis are more likely than other Aboriginal individuals to live in large urban areas.

Aboriginal workers are less likely than non-Aboriginal workers to have a high-skill occupation (**Figure 5.2**). In particular:

1. Aboriginal workers are under-represented in managerial occupations and professional occupations (which usually require university education) (20% vs. 30%);

2. They are roughly equally represented in skilled jobs (which usually require college education) and semi-skilled occupations (32% vs. 31%); and

3. They are over-represented in semi-skilled and low-skilled occupations (47% vs. 38%).

Aboriginal workers are most under-represented in high-skill jobs in the private sector, including:

1. Private sector managerial positions
2. Professional occupations in business and finance, engineering and computers, and medicine
3. Skilled technicians and technologists in engineering, computers and health

They are overrepresented in the following occupations:

1. Public sector managers
2. Skilled workers in government and the cultural industry (e.g., paralegal, library technicians, etc.)
3. Semi-skilled workers in trades and low-skill workers in sales and labour

Aboriginal Identity

The percentage of workers with high-skill occupations is similar across all Aboriginal identities **(Figure 5.3)**. However, if it were not for public sector occupations, the Aboriginal skill gap would be larger. Over-representation of Aboriginal workers in the public sector high-skill occupations reduces the overall skill gap of Aboriginal workers. This is particularly true of the Inuit, half of whom are working in the public sector.

Gender

The skill rate among Aboriginal men is 51%, and 52% among Aboriginal women. This means that there is no male–female skill gap among Aboriginal workers. By contrast, the male–female skill gap among non-Aboriginal workers is 6 percentage points (64% male vs. 58% female). However, were it not for public sector employment, there would be a skill gap between Aboriginal men and Aboriginal women (37% vs. 20%). Women are over-represented in the public sector relative to men. The difference is particularly pronounced in the case of Aboriginal workers.

Wage Gap—Aboriginal Versus Non-Aboriginal

Next, we compare the average weekly wage rates of Aboriginal and non-Aboriginal workers. The reader should be reminded that our sample includes only full-time paid workers. Wage gap refers to the percentage wage difference between Aboriginal and non-Aboriginal workers.

Aboriginal workers earn 23% less on average than non-Aboriginal workers. Within each broad occupation group, Aboriginal workers earn less than non-Aboriginal workers. Moreover, the higher the skill level, the larger the wage gap **(Figure 5.4)**. A more detailed comparison of average wages within each of the

Figure 5.3: Percentage of Workers with Private and Public Sector High-skill Occupations by Aboriginal Idenity, 2000

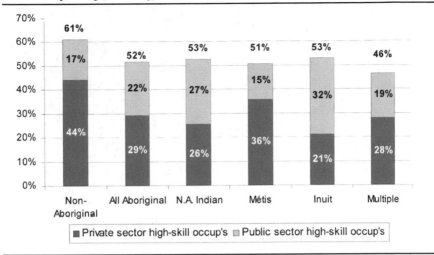

Figure 5.4: Average Weekly Wages by Skill Level and Aboriginal Identity, 2000

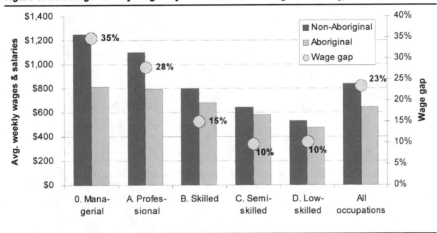

520 NOC codes shows that in 96% of the cases, Aboriginal workers earned less on average in their occupational category than non-Aboriginal workers.

We reweighted Aboriginal workers across all 520 NOCs (shift-share analysis) so that their occupational distribution would be the same as that of non-Aboriginal workers. Because there is an Aboriginal/non-Aboriginal wage gap within virtually all occupational categories, even when Aboriginal workers were redistributed among the 520 NOC's occupations, the wage gap was still 17%. The result was that only about one-third of the wage gap disappeared. A possible explanation of this finding is that wage differences hide further occupational differences within the 520 codes.

Figure 5.5: Average Weekly Wages by Aboriginal Identity, 2000

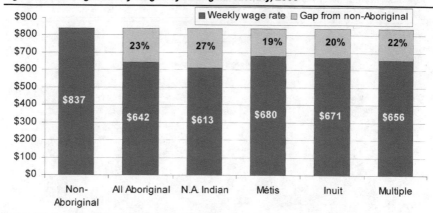

Figure 5.6: Distribution by Level of Education and Aboriginal Identity, 2000

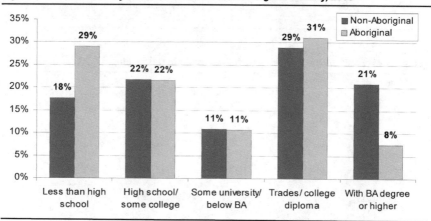

Figure 5.7: Percentage with Post-secondary Degree/Diploma by Aboriginal Identity, 2000

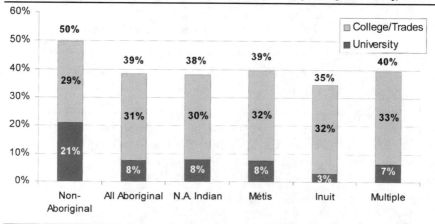

Aboriginal Identity

There are also small variations in the wage gap according to Aboriginal identity. The wage gap is largest in the case of North American Indians (27%) and smallest in the case of Métis (19%) **(Figure 5.5)**.

Gender

Aboriginal women earn less per week than non-Aboriginal women ($549 vs. $677). Similarly, non-Aboriginal men earn more than Aboriginal men ($957 vs. $719). Although Aboriginal women earn less than Aboriginal men, their wage gap compared to non-Aboriginal women is smaller (19%) than the corresponding gap among men (25%). A possible explanation is that in both groups more female workers are clustered near minimum and entrance level wages. As a result, their wage distribution tends to be "flatter," which leads to a smaller gap between both Aboriginal men and women, and non-Aboriginal men and women.

Worker Characteristics

Next, we explore the main differences in characteristics between Aboriginal and non-Aboriginal workers. We focus primarily on education, place of residence, and sector of work in order to examine the impact of these differences on the occupational and wage gap between Aboriginal and non-Aboriginal workers.

Education

The percentage of Aboriginal workers with a high school or college education is similar to that of non-Aboriginal workers. However, Aboriginal workers are less likely to have a university degree than non-Aboriginal works (8% vs. 21% respectively) and more likely to have less than high school education (29% vs. 18%) **(Figure 5.6)**. Also, Aboriginal workers with a post-secondary diploma or degree tend to be somewhat under-represented in the highest paying fields of study, such as business and financial management, engineering, mathematics, and the applied, computer and physical sciences. As a result, differences in the level of education between Aboriginal and non-Aboriginal workers understate the full extent of differences in educational qualifications between the two groups.

Among Aboriginal identity groups, Inuit have the lowest rate of university degrees (3%) compared to the average Aboriginal rate (8%) and non-Aboriginal rate of (21%) **(Figure 5.7)**. One possible factor that accounts for the low incidence of university degrees among the Inuit may be that most live in Nunavut, which is far from universities. Past research has shown that distance from post-secondary institutions is a significant barrier to higher education.

In general, women are more likely than men to have a university degree, particularly among Aboriginal workers. Aboriginal women are twice as likely to have a university degree than Aboriginal men (10% vs. 5%). The higher education level of Aboriginal women relative to that of Aboriginal men is a likely reason why there is no skill gap between the two of them and why the wage gap is not as large as between male and female non-Aboriginal workers.

Place of Residence

Half of all Aboriginal workers live in rural and small urban areas (under 10,000 population), compared to one-quarter of non-Aboriginal workers (**Figure 5.8**). Among Inuit workers, 98% live in rural communities. This difference works to the disadvantage of Aboriginal workers. The reason is that although the incidence of high-skill jobs is similar by size of area, wages are about 12% lower in smaller areas.

Sector of Work

About 35% of Aboriginal workers work in what can be broadly defined as the public sector (i.e., public administration, education, health, or social services) compared to 23% of non-Aboriginals (**Figure 5.9**). The percentage working in the public sector is particularly high among the Inuit (51%). The public sector has a higher incidence of high-skill jobs. This helps raise the occupational skill rate among Aboriginal workers and reduce their skill gap from non-Aboriginal workers.

Explaining the Occupational and Wage Gap

In this section, we examine the factors behind the occupational and wage gap between Aboriginal and non-Aboriginal workers. We will show that educational differences explain most of the occupational differences between Aboriginal and non-Aboriginal workers. However, we will also show that educational differences leave a big part of the wage gap unexplained.

Figure 5.10 (page 96) shows that within each level of education, Aboriginal and non-Aboriginal workers have a roughly equal chance of being in a high-skill occupation. The implication is that, if Aboriginal workers had the same level of education as non-Aboriginal workers, the percentage with high-skill jobs would be the same as that for non-Aboriginal workers.

Given the above results, it is not surprising that shift-share analysis shows that if there were no educational differences between Aboriginal and non-Aboriginal workers, the occupational mix of the two groups would have been more equalized (**Figure 5.11** – page 97). For example, the percentage of Aboriginal workers with managerial occupations would have been 11% rather than 9% (still somewhat lower than the non-Aboriginal rate of 13%). In the case of professional jobs, the percentage of Aboriginal workers would have actually surpassed that of non-Aboriginal workers.

Figure 5.8: Distribution of Aboriginal and Non-Aboriginal Workers by Size of Area, 2000

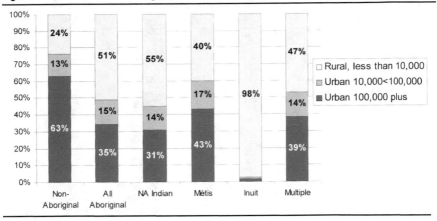

Figure 5.9: Distribution of Aboriginal and Non-Aboriginal Workers by Sector, 2000

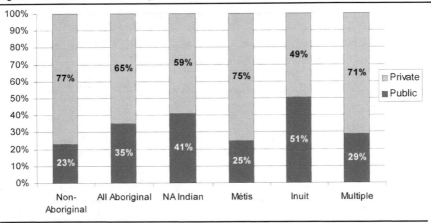

Using logit regression, we probed further the two top types of high-skill occupations: managerial and professional (which usually require a university degree). As we discussed earlier, Aboriginal workers are under-represented in these two groups of occupations (20% vs. 30%). The regression results show that educational differences fully explain why Aboriginal workers have a lower incidence of occupations (**Table 5.1** – page 96). However, although closing the educational gap between Aboriginal and non-Aboriginal workers would have eliminated their skill-gap, a significant portion of the wage gap would have still persisted. Ordinary Least Squares (OLS) regression analysis attributed 36% of the wage gap to educational differences. The younger age of Aboriginal workers explained another 8% of the wage gap, while 3% was attributed to the fact that Aboriginal workers tend to live in smaller areas (**Table 5.2** – page 97). About half of the wage gap is due to factors not taken into account in our analysis, such as quality of education, discrimination, and social factors. The persistence of a wage gap, even after the effect of apparent education differences is removed requires further investigation.

Figure 5.10: Incidence of High-skill Occupations by Level of Education and Aboriginal Identity, 2000

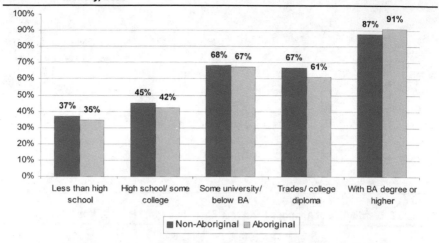

■ Non-Aboriginal ▨ Aboriginal

Table 5.1: Logit Regression Analysis of Determinants of Incidence of Managerial/Professional Occupations Among Aboriginal Workers, 2000

Independent variables	b-coeffic.	Stand.error	t-statistic	Odds ratio
Constant	-3.050	0.190	-16.086	0.047
Education				
- Less than high school (reference catego|	na	na	na	na
- High school/some college: <13 yrs	0.258	0.236	1.094	1.295
- High school/some college: 13+ yrs	0.926	0.214	4.337	2.526
- Some university/below BA: <16 yrs	1.548	0.209	7.409	4.704
- Some university/below BA: 16+ yrs	2.393	0.278	8.597	10.942
- Trades/college diploma: <14 yrs	0.058	0.194	0.297	1.059
- Trades/college diploma: 14+ yrs	1.601	0.182	8.785	4.960
- With BA degree or higher: <19 yrs	3.917	0.284	13.802	50.229
- With BA degree or higher: 19+ yrs	4.183	0.391	10.711	65.546
Area				
- 100K plus	-0.429	0.132	-3.249	0.651
- 15K to less than 100K	-0.563	0.186	-3.021	0.570
- Less than 15K (reference category)	na	na	na	na
Sector				
- Private (reference category)	na	na	na	na
- Public	0.814	0.124	6.593	2.258
Gender				
- Male	-0.038	0.119	-0.321	0.963
- Female (reference category)	na	na	na	na
Age				
- Under 35 (reference category)	na	na	na	na
- 35-49	0.640	0.128	4.998	1.896
- 50+	0.948	0.177	5.364	2.580
Nagelkerke R Square:	35%	Unweighted count:		2,920
- Non-Aboriginal: Actual incidence				30%
- Aboriginal: Actual incidence..				19%
- Aboriginal: Hypothetical incidence if education the same...........................				32%

Figure 5.11: Occupational Profile Before/After Removing Educational Differences Between Aboriginal and Non-Aboriginal Workers, 2000

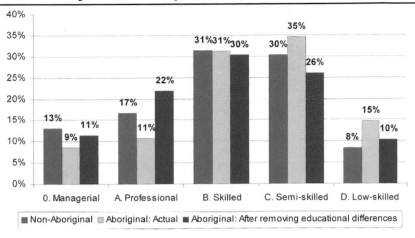

Non-Aboriginal ▢ Aboriginal: Actual ■ Aboriginal: After removing educational differences

Table 5.2: OLS Reggression Analysis of Determinants of Weekly Wages among Aboriginal Workers, 2000

Independent variables	b-coeffic.	Stand.error	t-statistic
Constant	306.989	9.329	32.909
Education			
- Less than high school (reference categor	na	na	na
- High school/some college: <13 yrs	60.972	11.781	5.175
- High school/some college: 13+ yrs	68.956	11.088	6.219
- Some university/below BA: <16 yrs	146.742	13.561	10.821
- Some university/below BA: 16+ yrs	216.006	20.632	10.469
- Trades/college diploma: <14 yrs	106.166	9.571	11.093
- Trades/college diploma: 14+ yrs	180.576	10.521	17.164
- With BA degree or higher: <19 yrs	411.570	16.669	24.691
- With BA degree or higher: 19+ yrs	460.067	23.116	19.902
Area			
- 100K plus	23.900	7.373	3.241
- 15K to less than 100K	43.950	9.871	4.452
- Less than 15K (reference category)	na	na	na
Sector			
- Private (reference category)	na	na	na
- Public	-13.742	7.712	-1.782
Gender			
- Male	208.403	6.836	30.488
- Female (reference category)	na	na	na
Age			
- Under 35 (reference category)	na	na	na
- 35-49	162.542	7.033	23.113
- 50+	188.849	10.138	18.629
Adjusted R-squared	50% Count		2,613

Conclusions

There are significant occupational differences between Aboriginal and non-Aboriginal workers. Aboriginal workers are under-represented in managerial and professional occupations, which usually require a university degree. The under-representation is mostly concentrated in the private sector.

Educational differences explain most of the occupational differences between Aboriginal and non-Aboriginal workers. This means that closing the education gap between the two groups would eliminate most of the occupational differences. However, almost two-thirds of the wage gap between the two would still persist. Nevertheless, education remains the most promising policy lever. Two priorities are apparent:

1. Promote culturally sensitive programs that combine work and learning to reduce the Aboriginal high school drop-out rate, which will in turn increase the potential pool of post-secondary students; and

2. Offer more innovative ways of making university more accessible and enticing to Aboriginal youth (e.g. distance education).

Endnotes

1 A similar definition of significant work was used recently in a study of the working poor by Fleury and Fortin (2004).

2 For more details on the National Occupational Classification system please visit the HRSDC website at <**www23.hrdc-drhc.gc.ca/2001/e/groups/index.shtml**>.

References

Comfort, Derrick, Michael DeJong and John Kozij (2005): *A Portrait of the Labour Market Outcomes of Aboriginal Canadians*. Human Resources and Skills Development Canada, Aboriginal Affairs Directorate Research Note.

DeSilva, Arnold (1999). "Wage Discrimination Against Natives." *Canadian Public Policy*, vol. XXV, no. 1.

Fleury, Dominique and Myriam Fortin (2004): "Canada's Working Poor." *Horizons*, PRI, December, vol. 7, no. 2.

Hull, Jeremy (2005). *Post-Secondary Education and Labour Market Outcomes Canada, 2001*. Indian and Northern Affairs Canada.

Mendelson, Michael (2004). *Aboriginal People in Canada's Labour Market: Work and Unemployment, Today and Tomorrow*. Caledon Institute of Social Policy.

Mendelson, Michael (2005). *Aboriginal Peoples and Post-Secondary Education in Canada*. Indian and Northern Affairs Canada.

Part Two:
Dimensions of Socio-economic Well-being

6

Responding to Climate Change in Nunavut: Policy Recommendations

James Ford and Johanna Wandel

Introduction

Climate change is considered to be a significant challenge for Inuit (Duerden 2004; ACIA 2005; Ford et al. 2006a). Communities, governments, and regional and national Inuit organizations have expressed their concern over the risks posed by climate change, and the urgency of taking action to address the problem (NTI 2001; GN 2003; Shirley 2005; Watt-Cloutier et al. 2005). Existing policy responses to climate change have largely focused on reducing greenhouse gas emissions, also referred to as climate change mitigation. Even under the most aggressive emission control measures, however, current greenhouse gas emissions commit the earth to continued climate change (Hansen et al. 2002; Wigley 2005). The likelihood of adverse impacts has created a growing urgency for measures to reduce or moderate the expected negative effects of climate change (known as adaptation). To identify adaptation needs and facilitate adaptation policy, we need to know the nature of community vulnerability, in terms of who and what are vulnerable to what stresses, in what way, why, and what capacity exists to cope with change (Burton et al. 2002; IISD 2003; Ford & Smit 2004; Schroter et al. 2005).

This paper outlines potential policy responses to reduce the vulnerability of Inuit communities to climate change, focusing on hunting livelihoods, which form the basis of Inuit living and culture. The paper begins by reviewing policy approaches to climate change at international, federal, and territorial levels, arguing for the development of adaptation policy. Drawing upon specific work conducted in partnership with the communities of Arctic Bay and Igloolik, Nunavut, and general research from Nunavut, we identify key drivers of climate change vulnerability. The paper concludes by identifying entry points for policy aimed at increasing adaptive capacity and/or reducing exposure to climate change.

Climate Change Policy

The United Nations Framework Convention on Climate Change (UNFCCC) and national governments have focused on two broad policy areas to address climate change: mitigation and adaptation (Ford & Smit 2004). Mitigation relates to efforts to reduce or stabilize greenhouse gas emissions to abate, moderate, or alleviate changes in the climate. Adaptation refers to consciously planned adjustments in a system to reduce, moderate, or take advantage of the expected negative impacts of climate change (IPCC 2001). Academic and political attention has largely focused on mitigation as a response to climate change, evident in the UNFCCC and Kyoto Protocol (Burton et al. 2002; Huq & Reid 2004; Burton & Lim 2005). Adaptation is also recognized in the UNFCCC as a component of climate change policy, the importance of which is increasingly being recognized (EC 2002; Huq et al. 2003; Smith et al. 2003; C-CIARN 2004; Ford et al. 2006; Fussel & Klein 2006). In Canada, the federal government has supported research activities on adaptation, including the creation of the Canadian Climate Impacts and Adaptation Research Network (C-CIARN). The Government of Nunavut has also indicated its intention to promote adaptation to climate change with the release of the Nunavut Climate Change Strategy, in which the development and promotion of adaptation are key goals (GN 2003).

The increasing importance of adaptation relates, in part, to the recognition that even under the most aggressive emission control measures, current greenhouse gas emissions commit the earth to continued climate change (Hansen et al. 2002). Furthermore, it is also recognized that climate change is already occurring in some regions where populations are vulnerable (Huq et al. 2003; ACIA 2005). This is particularly relevant in the Arctic, where evidence already points to the impact of climate change on local weather patterns and livelihoods (Ford 2005; Ford et al. 2006a, b). Regional organizations, governments, and communities in the Arctic have stressed the necessity and importance of developing adaptive options that address current and future climate-related vulnerabilities (Cohen 1997; DSD 2003; GN 2003; ICARP 2005; NTI 2005; Shirley 2005; Streicker 2005).

Adaptation Policy

Adaptation research has traditionally focused on identifying potential measures for adapting to climate change (O'Brien et al. 2004). Burton et al. (2002) term this "first generation" adaptation research, and it has formed the basis of several studies including the US Country Studies Program and UNEP Country Studies (Burton & Lim 2005). Identified adaptation options are predominantly technological and engineering based, including the construction of sea defences to provide protection from rising sea levels and development of irrigation schemes in areas predicted to experience increased drought occurrence (Smith & Lenhart 1996; O'Brien 2000; Stuczyinski et al. 2000). The focus of these studies is largely biophysical, using scenarios of climate change to model biophysical system responses, with corresponding adaptation options designed to reduce exposure to climate change impacts. In the Arctic too, adaptation research has focused on specifying technical adjustments required to reduce exposure to climate change (Maxwell 1997; Johnson et al. 2003; Instanes 2005).

Experience, however, indicates that policy targeting climate change alone may be neither optimal nor successfully incorporated into the decision-making process (O'Brien, 2000; Newton 2001; Dowlatabadi 2002; Handmer 2003; Huq et al. 2003; Smit & Pilifosova 2003; Niang-Diop & Bosch 2005). Climate change is one stress among many; social, cultural, and economic stresses are often considered more important to decision makers and communities. Policy aimed specifically at addressing climate change is further limited by its focus on future conditions—such approaches do not necessarily address immediate and pressing needs. In Nunavut, for example, policy priorities established by communities relate to other problems, including suicide prevention, cultural preservation, education and training, and employment creation (RT & Associates 2002; NEDS 2003; Boyle & Dowlatabadi 2005; Ford 2005; Shirley 2005).

Within the climate change adaptation field, there is growing consensus that enhancing adaptive capacity is as central to adaptation as the identification of particular adaptation measures specific to climate change (Smit & Pilifosova 2001, 2003; O'Brien et al. 2004; Burton & Lim 2005). Enhanced adaptive capacity can be achieved by addressing non-climatic determinants of vulnerability and integrating them into ongoing decision-making and policy processes, thereby serving immediate needs, providing immediate benefits, and reducing vulnerability to current climatic conditions (Agrawala 2004; Huq & Reid 2004). Enhancing capacity to deal with present conditions strengthens community resilience to longer-term climate change (IISD 2003; O'Brien et al. 2004; Pielke & Sarewitz 2005; Thomas & Twyman 2005). Known as "mainstreaming," this approach to climate change adaptation policy is increasingly well recognized and utilized in planning (Pouliotte 2005).

A Conceptual Approach for Adaptation Research

The identification and characterization of vulnerability in communities is crucial for identifying adaptation needs, opportunities, and constraints to adaptation, and for informing the development of policies that reduce risks associated with climate change (Burton et al. 2002; Ford & Smit 2004; Burton & Lim 2005; Schroter et al. 2005). Vulnerability refers to the susceptibility to harm in a system in response to a stimulus or stimuli (Smit & Pilifosova 2003). It is widely accepted that vulnerability is conditioned by the nature of biophysical conditions and the human system (Turner et al. 2003; Duerden 2004; Ford & Smit 2004; O'Brien et al. 2004; Robards & Alessa 2004). Ford et al. (2006a, b) conceptualize vulnerability as a function of exposure and adaptive capacity. Here, exposure reflects the susceptibility of people and communities to hazardous conditions, and adaptive capacity reflects a community's potential or ability to address, plan for, or adapt to exposure-sensitivity. In a similar manner, Turner et al. (2003), O'Brien et al. (2004), and ACIA (2005) frame vulnerability in terms of exposure, sensitivity, and resilience or capacity to adapt. Common to these approaches, vulnerability at a local level is viewed as being affected by social, economic, cultural, political and biophysical conditions and processes operating at multiple scales over time and space. Adaptation policy must take into account cross-scale linkages which will influence success of policy and determine policy entry points.

Vulnerability analysis starts by examining past and present experience and response to climate variability, change, and extremes in order to characterize current levels of vulnerability. This addresses important concerns for adaptation policy, including:

1. Identification of those conditions that represent risks to community members;

2. Characterization of how communities manage and experience climatic risks;

3. Identification of those processes and conditions that influence exposure to climatic hazards and determine the efficacy, availability, and success of past and present adaptations;

4. Identification of opportunities and constraints to adapting to climate change; and

5. Identification of points of entry for adaptation policy.

Analysis of current vulnerability provides an empirical foundation for developing adaptation policy, identifying opportunities to reduce vulnerability by increasing adaptive capacity and/or reducing exposure-sensitivity. Future vulnerability is assessed by analyzing how climate change will alter the nature of the climate-related risks, and whether the communities' coping strategies will have the capacity to deal with these risks. This is used to set the context for adaptation policy and help assess policy options.

Nunavut

The Canadian territory of Nunavut, which became an official and independent territory in 1999, covers 1,994,000 square kilometres of Arctic Canada carved out of the Northwest Territories by the Nunavut Land claims Agreement. This agreement provided the territory's Inuit population—who make up 85% of Nunavut's population of 26,000—with control of more than 350,000 square kilometres of land, and set up a territorial government with wide ranging powers. Nunavut's 26 communities range in size from Bathurst Inlet (population 25) to the capital, Iqaluit (population 6,500). The economy is based on the harvesting of renewable resources, estimated to be worth at least $40–$60 million annually, which provides many families with an affordable and important source of food (Furgal et al. 2002; NEO 2002; Duhaime et al. 2004). Harvesting is supplemented by mineral exploration, extraction activities, tourism, sales of Inuit art, and government employment.

Communities in Nunavut have experienced rapid social, cultural, economic, and political changes over the last 50 years (see Wenzel 1991; Damas 2002), including the development of a wage-based economy alongside the informal harvesting economy, integration of and dependence on external markets, sedentarization of previously semi-nomadic hunting groups, imposition of southern education and cultural values, and changes to the technology used in hunting. Climate change is superimposed upon, and exacerbated by, these social changes (Krupnik & Jolly 2002; DSD 2003; ACIA 2005; Nickels et al. 2005; Ford et al. 2006a, b). Continued climatic change will contribute to background variability and community hazard, and can be expected to increasingly test the adaptive capacity of Inuit livelihoods in Nunavut (ACIA 2005).

Vulnerability to Climate Change in Nunavut

Current State of Vulnerability Research in Nunavut

Vulnerability assessments have only been conducted in a limited number of communities in Nunavut, especially assessments of the harvesting sector (Shirley 2005). There is need for more community case studies to identify how local geography, community history, and social, political, economic, and biophysical conditions shape vulnerability. However, completed climate change vulnerability analyses by Ford (2006 a, b) and Ford et al. (2006 a, b), in partnership with the communities of Igloolik and Arctic Bay, Nunavut, identify key trends and drivers of vulnerability. Emerging research indicates these key trends are comparable in small Inuit communities across the Canadian Arctic (Berkes & Jolly 2002; Gagnon 2005; Laidler 2005; Nickels et al. 2005; Pearce 2005a, 2005b). In absence of more detailed case studies, and in light of ongoing and predicted rapid climate change, these trends can identify key themes for targeted adaptation policy.

Key Vulnerability Trends

High Level of Adaptive Capacity

Analysis of past and present response to, and experience of, climate variability, change, and extremes indicates significant adaptability among Inuit in Nunavut (Ford et al. 2006 a, b). **Table 6.1** (page 116) shows how Nunavut communities are currently responding to climate change; responses are largely behavioural, and include risk minimization, risk avoidance, and the sharing of risk. The ability of Inuit in Nunavut to cope or deal with changing exposure is indicative of their adaptive capacity. This capacity is facilitated by traditional Inuit knowledge, strong social networks, flexibility in seasonal hunting cycles, and economic and institutional support.

From knowledge passed down through the generations—and from personal experience—hunters have knowledge of the dangers of hunting, how to evaluate risks, what preparations to make before hunting, and what to do in emergency situations. As a repository of accumulated experience and knowledge of changing conditions and successful adaptations, this knowledge is drawn upon to minimize the risks of hunting and maximize the opportunities. It is a highly experiential form of knowledge, continually updated and revised in light of observations, trial and error experience, and incorporation of non-traditional knowledge alongside the traditional (Stevenson 1997; Berkes 1999; Ford et al. 2006). For example, increasing unpredictability of biophysical conditions, documented by community members in recent years, is now part of the collective social memory that frames individual practice and decision making (Ford et al. 2006). This ability to learn and combine new experiences with traditional knowledge confers significant adaptability.

In Igloolik and Arctic Bay, Nunavut, Ford et al. (2006 a, b) demonstrated the importance of social networks in facilitating adaptive capacity to environmental stress. These networks included a high level of interdependence within the extended family unit, and a strong sense of collective community responsibility and mutual aid. Sharing remains an affirmation of Inuit identity, and the responsibility is taken seriously. These networks facilitate the sharing of food, equipment, and knowledge, and ensure rapid response to crisis. The sharing of food in the extended family unit, for instance, underpins the food security of those who do not have the time, money, or knowledge to hunt in light of community documented climate change. The importance of social networks in community life and in dealing with stress has been demonstrated across Nunavut (Wenzel 1991, 1995; Oakes & Riewe 1997; Damas 2002; DSD 2002; NEO 2002).

Inuit hunting is opportunistic, a necessity given the inherent variability of Arctic environments. While there are preferred seasons and locations to hunt, hunters will harvest what is available, whenever and wherever it is available. In Arctic Bay, for instance, if the caribou hunt in August and September fails, other species, such as seal, will be harvested (Ford et al. 2006a). Substitution allows people to cope with variations in animal numbers, and also enables them to manage changes in the accessibility of hunting locations. Similar flexibility has been documented by Wenzel (1995) in Clyde River, Nunavut, and Nickels et al. (2005) throughout Nunavut.

Monetary transfers from the federal government, and emerging institutional support from the Nunavut government and Inuit institutions, play an important role in providing financing to cover the purchase of equipment to cope with the changing climatic conditions. This is particularly important in an Arctic context, where high levels of unemployment, and limited opportunities to earn money limit the extent to which hunters can purchase safety equipment.

Emerging Vulnerabilities.

Strategies by which Inuit deal with climate variability, change, and extremes are not without their costs, and the ability to respond is unequal (**Table 6.1** – page 116). Technological adaptations, for instance, are available only to those who can afford them, and there is evidence that technological developments may increase inequalities within communities (DSD 2002; Ford et al. 2006). Quota systems on certain animal species restrict the flexibility with which hunters can respond to changing accessibility of hunting areas and abundance of animals. The effectiveness of adaptation also varies. Some adaptation technologies can increase exposure to climatic hazards by encouraging risk taking behaviour (Aporta & Higgs 2005; Ford et al. 2006 a, b).

In other areas, characteristics of Inuit society that traditionally facilitated adaptability have been altered as a result of changing livelihoods during the last half of the twentieth century. Over time, this has resulted in the emergence of vulnerable groups, specifically younger generation Inuit and those without access to economic resources. An erosion of traditional Inuit knowledge and land-based skills—through which hunting risks are managed—has been documented among younger generation Inuit in Nunavut (Rasing 1999; Aporta 2004; Takano 2004; Ford et al. 2006 a, b), and throughout the Canadian Arctic (Condon et al. 1995; Newton 1995; Collings et al. 1998). While subsistence activities remain important to younger generation Inuit, fewer are displaying the same degree of commitment or interest in harvesting. This has been attributed to: southern educational requirements that result in decreased time to participate in hunting, increased dependence on waged employment, a general shift in social norms, and intergenerational segregation between young and older generations (Condon et al. 1995; Kral 2003; Takano 2004; Ford et al. 2006). Consequently, certain skills necessary for safe and successful harvesting have been lost, including traditional forms of navigation and the ability to make snow shelters. Other skills have been inadequately developed, including how to dress appropriately, what equipment to take along on trips, and the ability to identify precursors to hazardous conditions. This has increased the vulnerability of young hunters when they travel and hunt without experienced hunters (Ford et al. 2006).

The functioning of social networks has been affected by a decrease in the importance of the extended family, the emergence of intergenerational segregation, decline in practice of traditional cultural values, concentration of resources in fewer hands, and the emergence of social tension (Oakes & Riewe 1997; Wenzel 1995; Kral. 2003; Kishigami 2004). The increasing importance of money has created division and social tension, and has entered into previously non-monetary sharing practices. The sharing of equipment, in particular, is practised less today, although traditional foods are still widely shared (Wenzel 1995; Ford et al. 2006). The increasing importance of money has also resulted in economic dependence on the volatility of external markets and government support. The recent closure of the Nanisivik mine near Arctic Bay, for example, forced many former employees to sell their hunting equipment, which they can no longer afford (DSD 2002). For young Inuit, in particular, the lack of monetary resources limits their opportunities to take part in harvesting activities, further reinforcing the decline in participation in and erosion of traditional skills (Collings et al. 1998; NEO 2002). Weakened social networks compromise the capacity of individuals to cope with changing climatic conditions.

Institutional support and new technology have, to an extent, emerged to compensate for the weakening of social networks and erosion of traditional knowledge. GPS for instance, means that knowledge of traditional navigational skills is no longer required for safe travel. Snowmobiles permit hunters to travel long distances quickly, without the knowledge required to operate a dog team. New technology, however, has increased risk-taking behaviour and dependency on monetary resources (Aporta & Higgs 2005). Institutional support is also important: people no longer starve in years when there are no animals, as happened occasionally in the past. In addition, there is also evidence that such support has heightened some inequalities in the community, further reinforcing a weakening of social networks (Ford et al. 2006a, b).

Specific Adaptation Policy Options

Climate change vulnerability assessments were conducted by Ford (2006 a, b) and Ford et al. (2006 a, b) in partnership with the communities of Arctic Bay and Igloolik, Nunavut, using data gathered from 112 interviews in 2004/05. Specific measures to address current vulnerabilities were identified by community members during this research. These included: subsidies to cover the purchase of extra supplies and safety equipment necessary in light of more hazardous conditions; affordable insurance to cover equipment lost or damaged in climate-related hunting accidents; increased search-and-rescue capability in light of more dangerous hunting conditions; resources to help hunters learn how to properly use new hunting technology; the development of inter-community trade to help those with country food shortages; enhanced awareness and understanding of climate change so that people know how it might affect them; and construction of a bridge from Igloolik Island to the mainland to allow access to hunting areas on the mainland in light of changes in the sea ice.

> "[We need] more coast guard ships close by to the community so they can rescue stranded hunters."—Atagutak Ipeeleee, Arctic Bay

> "We need bigger boats in order to cope with [the stronger] winds [in the summer]."—Anonymous, Arctic Bay

> "We have to get insurance to help those people who [lose] equipment ... because of [unusual] ice conditions or if they are stranded on the floe edge [due to unpredictable weather]."—Koonoo Muckpaloo, Arctic Bay

> "The Nunavut Government should supply [safety] equipment to the hunters [because it is now more dangerous to hunt]."—Elizabeth Awa, Igloolik

> "[With the ice freezing up later] it would be a lot easier if they put a bridge over [to] the mainland."—Elizabeth Awa, Igloolik

These measures are largely technological/financial, are specific to climate change, and address current climatic risks, the responsibility for which lie with the territorial government and Inuit organizations. While they are specific to Arctic Bay and Igloolik, research indicates similar recommendations elsewhere in Nunavut (DSD 2003; Nickels et al. 2005).

Mainstreaming Adaptation

Given the importance of competing priorities for the Government of Nunavut, policy targeting climate change alone may not be successfully incorporated into the decision-making process. This section identifies potential for adaptation "mainstreaming" in Nunavut, where policy addresses non-climatic determinants of climate change vulnerability, which can be included in the routine development of policy. Policy entry points include existing programs relating to cultural preservation, wildlife management, community well-being, education, and community economic development. While all these entry points are addressed, the discussion largely focuses on the preservation and promotion of cultural values.

Preservation and Promotion of Traditional Knowledge, Culture, and Values

Opportunities exist for actions to address social issues, which will also increase the adaptive capacity and reduce exposure of communities to cope with future climate change. Policies are needed to promote and preserve traditional Inuit knowledge, culture, and values, and increase safe hunting practices, especially among youth; many hunting accidents today are associated with a lack of land-based skills and knowledge of the environment.

> "It is more dangerous [for the younger generation] because they don't know the conditions, what to avoid."—Kautaq Joseph, Arctic Bay

> "I think we have lost the skills so much, I mean what would have not been dangerous for a man 50 years ago is now dangerous ... because we have lost so many skills."—James Ungallak, Igloolik

> "If you don't know the traditional knowledge you won't last very long, you will freeze to death if you don't know how to survive."—David Kalluk, Arctic Bay

Reducing exposure and increasing adaptive capacity of youth today will reduce vulnerability to future climate change.

Traditional Inuit knowledge also forms the basis of Inuit cultural identity, spirituality, and values, the preservation and promotion of which can reinforce other factors relevant to climate change. Kral's (2003) work in Nunavut, for instance, indicated strong links between the promotion of traditional knowledge and cultural values, and suicide prevention. Similarly, Kirmayer et al (1998, 2000) in their work among small Inuit communities in Nunavik, northern Quebec, demonstrate that greater engagement with a community and family network reduces suicide risks among youth aged 15–25. The work of Condon et al. (1995) and Collings et al. (1998) in the Inuit community of Holman, shows a strong relationship between subsistence activities and mental health and self-esteem.

"My main concern is passing on traditional knowledge in terms of the weather, hunting, and so on, the social knowledge, the Inuit traditional knowledge."—Koonark Enoogoo, Arctic Bay

"It is a real concern [to people in the community] that these general skills and ability to read the weather are not being passed on to the young as they should be."—John MacDonald, Igloolik

"I wish that we could start teaching the traditional way of the Inuit ... I would prefer that we used Inuit traditional knowledge to be utilized in the wellness teaching."—Anonymous, unspecified Nunavut community (from Kral 2003).

Efforts to promote traditional Inuit knowledge and values are ongoing in Nunavut. In Igloolik, the Inullariiat Society, a not-for-profit entity formed in 1993, promotes Inuit culture and heritage within the community. "Land Camps" whereby elders and experienced hunters take young Inuit on the land for weeks at a time are offered throughout the year by the Society. Teaching replicates the way in which knowledge and values were traditionally passed down: participants learn by doing, watching, and being on the land. This program has not only helped participants to develop essential survival and safety skills, but has also allowed young people to strengthen their relationships with each other, elders, and their cultural heritage (Wachowich 2001; Takano 2004). Other programs offered in Igloolik include classes that demonstrate preparation of animal skins, how to make traditional clothing, and how to build igloos. Kral (2003) identifies these activities as essential to community well-being, serving to strengthen community social networks and increase individual self-esteem. Lack of funding however, remains an issue constraining the development of such initiatives elsewhere in Nunavut, and has limited the programmes in Igloolik (Takano 2004). Residents in Arctic Bay, for instance, expressed the need for such a program in their community:

"If they set up a camp here for young people, that could be used to revive the traditional skills"—Leah Kalluk, Arctic Bay

"I think [they] should have more kids going out with older people. They should have more of those kinds of activities in the community." —Martha Attitaq, Arctic Bay

Strengthening of financial support from the Government of Nunavut and Inuit organizations is required to meet these needs. This falls within their mandate; maintaining and promoting Inuit knowledge and culture:

- Is established in the Nunavut Political Accord, the Nunavut Land Claims Agreement, and the Bathurst Mandate;
- Has been identified as a policy priority by communities throughout Nunavut and one that must be taken into account in community economic development;

- Forms a central objective of regional and national Inuit organizations (NEO 2002; NEDS 2003; Nickels et al. 2005; GN 2004; ITK 2006); and
- Is central to the current mandate of the Government of Nunavut.

Wildlife Management

Opportunities exist to address climate change vulnerability in policy development and programming in wildlife management. Quota systems, which limit the number of animals that can be caught (narwhal, polar bear) and, in some instances, the timing at which they can be caught (polar bear), have the potential to reduce the flexibility with which hunters can respond to climate change. Quota systems have also been linked to conflicts between community members with conflicting goals, with consequences for the strength of social networks.

> "[The quota] angers a lot people ... old and young. They fight amongst each other, they divide families, because [of] disagreement how they should distribute the quotas "— James Ungallak, Igloolik

Emerging co-management agreements over the allocation of harvesting quotas, however, have significantly increased the flexibility of quota systems, creating an enabling framework where conflicts can be resolved. For example, since 1999, narwhal quotas have been determined in a co-management body composed of the local Hunters and Trappers Organization, the Nunavut Wildlife Management Board, Nunavut Tunngavik Incorporated, and the Federal Department of Fisheries and Oceans (DFO). Although the fixed level of the quota is set by the DFO, there is flexibility: the community has the opportunity to carry over the total allowable harvest from the previous year or borrow for the next years limit (Armitage 2005). Flexible, multi-level governance is important in facilitating the ability of management systems to deal with change, promoting the sharing of information between decision makers at different scales, linking scientific and traditional management systems, permitting greater opportunity to address conflicts over competing vision or goals, and providing an arena to solve conflict (Berkes et al. 2003; Armitage 2005; Diduck et al. 2005), which is important in light of predictions of changing migration and accessibility of narwhals. Similar co-management arrangements exist for polar bears (Diduck et al. 2005).

While existing experience of wildlife co-management in Nunavut is encouraging, technical, methodological and political differences between actors remain. Relationships between actors, for example, remain hierarchical with conflicts over the use of scientific and traditional knowledge. In 2000, in the community of Qikiqtarjuaq, Nunavut, the DFO decided to close the narwhal hunt on the basis of scientific stock assessments, creating significant conflict among partners in the co-management arrangement who were not consulted. If current co-management systems are to adapt to change, better coordination and communication across levels will be required (Armitage 2005; Diduck et al. 2005).

Economic Development

Sustainable economic development in the north includes community participation, equitable distribution of economic benefits within communities, and allocation of increased importance to land based economies in development decisions. Past experience with economic development in Arctic Canada, particularly resource development, has been mixed (Myers and Forest 1997; DSD 2002). For example, the operation of, and subsequent closure of, the Nanisivik mine near Arctic Bay. The mine acted as an important source of income during its operation, but created wage dependency in the community, contributed to social problems including drug and alcohol abuse, created inequities in income distribution, and contributed to the emergence of conflict in the community (DSD 2002; Ford et al. 2006). If future development increased disparities, this could increase vulnerability to climate change. Since the opening of the Nanisivik mine in the 1970s, however, significant advances have been made. Inuit in Nunavut now have a central role in setting economic priorities, power has been devolved to allow Inuit to have greater control over how development proceeds, and ensuring that benefits are spread equally is a major goal in development planning—these are enshrined in the Nunavut Economic Development Strategy, Nunavut Land Claims Agreement, and the mandate of the current Government of Nunavut. If economic development occurs within this context, then adaptive capacity can be strengthened. It is important therefore that these priorities are maintained in light of significant development pressure from mining and oil, and gas companies.

Conclusion

In light of competing policy priorities, if climate change adaptation policy is to be successful, it needs to serve immediate needs, bring immediate benefits, and enhance the ability to cope with current climatic conditions. Drawing upon the author's own work, and that of others' in Nunavut, this paper has demonstrated that adaptation policy can be informed and guided by the assessment of non-climatic determinants of vulnerability. These include an erosion of traditional Inuit knowledge, weakening of social networks, and reduced harvesting flexibility, which have increased exposure to climatic hazards and reduced adaptive capacity over time. Such measures will strengthen livelihoods and the ability to respond to current stressors, and increase capacity to adapt to climate change. These issues are key community concerns for which the Government of Nunavut has a mandate to address. Potential policy directions to reduce vulnerability to climate change include: expansion of cultural preservation programs, strengthening of wildlife co-management arrangements, and community-based economic development.

Acknowledgements

The insights and generous hospitality provided by residents of Arctic Bay and Igloolik are gratefully acknowledged, particularly the contributions of Mishak Allurut, Harry Ittusujurat, John MacDonald, Kevin Qrunnut, Leah Otak, and Kik Shappa. Thanks to Lea Berrang Ford and Barry Smit for academic input. The research was supported by ArcticNet, a Seed Grant from the Integrated Management Node of the Ocean Management Research Network, and the Social Sciences and Humanities Research Council of Canada. The research was undertaken as part of the Global Environmental Change Research Group at the University of Guelph, and was conducted under Nunavut Research Institute License #0203204N-M.

Table 6.1: Adaptive Strategies Employed by Inuit in Nunavut to Deal with Climate Change and Associated Cost

Climate Change Related Risks	Adaptive Strategies	Adaptation Costs
Unpredictability of the weather, wind, ice	• Hunters are taking extra food, gas, and supplies in anticipation of potential dangers • Hunters are making sure that they travel with others when possible • Some hunters are being risk averse, avoiding travelling on the land or water if they have reason to believe the weather is going to be bad • Use of weather forecast on the TV and radio to complement traditional forecasts • New equipment taken along e.g. personal location beacons, immersion suits, satellite phones	• Costs of purchasing extra supplies prohibitive for many who have limited income • Avoiding travelling at certain times results in shortages of some traditional foods and need to purchase more store food • New equipment is often expensive
Waves/stormy weather for summer boating	• Identification of safe areas prior to travel where shelter can be found • Waiting in the community for adequate conditions	• Waiting results in reduced harvests and need to purchase more store food • Avoiding certain areas can result in higher gas costs and add more time onto hunting trips (a problem for those with full-time jobs)
Snow covered thin ice	• Avoidance of snow covered areas • Extra care while travelling	• Avoiding certain areas can result in higher gas costs and add more time onto hunting trips (a problem for those with full-time jobs)
Reduced accessibility to hunting areas	• Waiting in the community until hunting areas are accessible • Switch species and location • Sharing of country food • Development of new access routes – e.g. overland travel instead of ice travel	• Waiting results in reduced harvests and need to purchase more store food • Not all have the hunting skills to switch species • New routes can be more time consuming, have higher fuel costs, and be more damaging on equipment

Source: Adapted from Fox 2002; Thorpe et al. 2002; Nickels et al. 2002, 2005; DSD 2003; Ford 2005, 2006; Ford et al. 2006 a, b; Laidler 2005

References

ACIA (2005). *Arctic Climate Impacts Assessment.* Cambridge University Press, Cambridge, UK.

Agrawala, S. (2004). "Adaptation, Development Assistance and Planning: Challenges and Opportunities." *IDS Bulletin 35*, 50–54.

Aporta, C. (2004). "Routes, Trails and Tracks: Trail Breaking among the Inuit of Igloolik." *Inuit Studies 28*, 9–38.

Aporta, C. & Higgs, E. (2005). "Satellite Culture: Global Positioning Systems, Inuit Wayfinding, and the Need for a New Account of Technology." *Current Anthropology*, 46, 729-753.

Armitage, D. R. (2005). "Community-based Narwhal Management in Nunavut, Canada: Change, Uncertainty, and Adaptation." *Society and Natural Resources, 18*, 715–731.

Berkes, F. (1999). *Sacred Ecology: Traditional Ecological Knowledge and Resource Management,* Taylor and Francis, London.

Berkes, F. & Jolly, D. (2002). "Adapting to Climate Change: Social-ecological Resilience in a Canadian Western Arctic Community." *Conservation Ecology 5*, [online] <**www.consecol.org/vol5/iss2/art18/**>

Berkes, F., J. Colding, & C. Folke. (2003). *Navigating Social-ecological Systems: Building Resilience for Complexity and Change.* Cambridge University Press, Cambridge, UK.

Boyle, M., Dowlatabadi, H., Rowley, S. & Kandlikar, M. (2004). "Learning from History: Lessons for Cumulative Effects Assessment and Planning." *Meridian Fall/Winter*, 6–12.

Burton, I., Huq, S., Lim, B., Pilifosova, O. & Schipper, E. L. (2002). "From Impacts Assessment to Adaptation Priorities: The Shaping of Adaptation Policy." *Climate Policy 2*, 145–159.

Burton, I. & Lim, B. (2005). *Adaptation Policy Framework for Climate Change,* Cambridge University Press, Cambridge, UK.

C-CIARN. 2004. *Climate Change Impacts and Adaptation.* Climate Change Impacts and Adaptation Research Network, Ottawa.

Chandler, M. J., & Lalonde, C. (1998). Cultural Continuity as a Hedge against Suicide in Canada's First Nations." *Transcultural Psychiatry, 35,* 191–219.

Cohen, S. (1997). *Mackenzie Basin Impact Study.* Atmospheric Environment Services, Environment Canada, Downsview, Ontario.

Collings, P., Wenzel, G. & Condon, R. (1998). "Modern Food Sharing Networks and Community Integration in the Central Canadian Arctic." *Arctic 51*, 301–326.

Condon, R., Collings, P. & Wenzel, G. (1995). "The Best Part of Life: Subsistence Hunting, Ethnicity, and Economic Development among Young Adult Inuit Males." *Arctic 48*, 31–46.

Damas, D. (2002). *Arctic Migrants/Arctic Villagers.* McGill-Queen's University Press.

Derocher, A., Lunn, N. J. & Stirling, I. (2004). "Polar Bears in a Warming Climate." *Integrative Comparative Biology 44*, 163–176.

Diduck, A., Bankes, N., Clark, D. & Armitage, D. R. (2005). "Unpacking Social Learning in Social-ecological Systems." In Berkes, F., Diduck, A., Fast, H., Huebert, R. & Manseau, M., *Breaking Ice: Integrated Ocean Management in the Canadian North.* University of Calgary Press, Calgary, 269–290.

Dowlatabadi, H. (2002). "Global Change: Much More than a Matter of Degrees." *Meridian Spring/Summer*, 8–12.

Downing, T. & Patwardhan, A. (2005). "Assessing Vulnerability for Climate Adaptation." In: Huq, S. and Lim, B. *Adaptation Policy Framework for Climate Change.* Cambridge University Press, Cambridge, UK.

DSD. (2002). *The Nanisivik legacy in Arctic Bay: A Socio-economic Impact Study.* Prepared for Department of Sustainable Development Government of Nunavut by Brubacher Associates, Ottawa.

DSD. (2003). *Inuit Qaujimajatuqangit of Climate Change in Nunavut: Summary Report of Activities January 2001 to March 2003.* Department of Sustainable Development, Government of Nunavut, Iqaluit, Nunavut.

Duerden, F. (2004). "Translating Climate Change Impacts at the Community Level." *Arctic 57*, 204–212.

Duhaime, G., Serles, E., Usher, P.J. & Frachette, P. (2004). "Social Cohesion and Living Conditions in the Canadian Arctic: From Theory to Measurement." *Social Indicators Research 66*, 295–317.

EC. (1998). "Climate Change Impacts on Permafrost Engineering Design." In: Environment Canada, *Environmental Adaptation Research Group*, Downsview, Ontario.

EC. (2002). *Climate Change Plan for Canada.* Environment Canada, Ottawa.

Ford, J. (2005). "Living with Change in the Arctic." *World Watch, September/October,* 18–21.

Ford, J. (2006a). "Sensitivity of Hunting to Hazards Associated with Climate Change: Iglulingmiut Perspectives." In *People and Environmental Change in the Hudson's Bay Region: Beginning the Next Step*, Aboriginal Issues Press, In Press.

Ford, J. (2006b). "Hunting on Thin Iice: Changing Risks Associated with the Arctic Bay Narwhal Hunt." In *People and Environmental Change in the Hudson's Bay Region: Beginning the Next Step, Aboriginal Issues Press*, In Press.

Ford, J. & Smit, B. (2004). "A Framework for Assessing the Vulnerability of Communities in the Canadian Arctic to Risks Associated with Climate Change." *Arctic 57*, 389–400.

Ford, J., Smit, B., & Wandel, J. (2006a). "Vulnerability to Climate Change in the Arctic: A Case Study from Arctic Bay, Nunavut." *Global Environmental Change*, In Press.

Ford, J., MacDonald, J., Smit, B., & Wandel, J. (2006b). "Vulnerability to Climate Change in Igloolik, Nunavut: What We Can Learn from the Past and Present." *Polar Record*, 42(2), 1–12.

Furgal, C., Innes, S. & Kovacs, K. M. (2002). "Inuit Spring Hunting Techniques and Local Knowledge of the Ringed Seal in Arctic Bay (Ikpiarjuk), Nunavut." *Polar Research 21*, 1–16.

Fussel, H. M. & Klein, R. T. J. (2006). "Climate Change Vulnerability Assessments: An Evolution of Conceptual Thinking." *Global Environmental Change*, In Press.

Gagnon, C. A. (2005). "Collecting Inuit Local Ecological Knowledge in the Context of Ecological Research and Ecosystem Management: The Case of Sirmilik Canada National Park." Poster presentation at the ArcticNet Annual General Meeting, Banff 2005.

GC. (2005). *Moving Forward on Climate Change: A Plan for Honouring our Kyoto Commitment.* Government of Canada, Ottawa.

GN. (2004). *Pinasuaqtavut 2004–2009*. Government of Nunavut, Iqaluit.

Handmer, J. (2003). "Adaptive Capacity: What Does it Mean in the Context of Natural Hazards." In Smith, J., Klein, R. T. J. and Huq, S., Climate Change, *Adaptive Capacity, and Development.* Imperial College Press, London.

Hansen, J., Sato, M., Nazarenko, L., Ruedy, R., et al. (2002). "Climate Forcings in GISS SI2000 Simulations." *Journal of Geophysical Research – Atmospheres 107*, 4347–4384.

Houghton, J. T., Ding, Y., Griggs, D. J., Noguer, M., van der Linden, P. J., Dai, X., Maskell, K. & Johnson, C. A. (2001). *Climate Change 2001: The Scientific Basis. Contribution of Working Group I to the Third Assessment Report of the Intergovernmental Panel on Climate Change,* Cambridge University Press, Cambridge, United Kingdom.

Huq, S. & Burton, I. (2003). *Funding Adaptation to Climate Change: What, Who and How to fund?* International Institute for Environment and Development, London.

Huq, S., Rahman, A., Konate, M., Sokona, Y. & Reid, H. (2003). "Mainstreaming Adaptation to Climate Change in Least Developed Countries." International Institute for Environment and Development Climate Change Program. London, 38.

Huq, S. & Reid, H. (2004). "Mainstreaming Adaptation in Development." *IDS Bulletin: Climate Change and Development 35*, 15–21.

ICARP. (2005). ICARP II: *Working Group 10 - A Research Plan for the Study of Rapid Change, Resilience and Vulnerability in Social-ecological Systems of the Arctic.* Report from working group 10 of International Conference on Arctic Research Planning, <**www.icarp.dk/WCreports/WC10report. PDF**>, accessed 20 January 2006

IISD. (2003). *Livelihoods and Climate Change: Combining Disaster Risk Reduction, Natural Resource Management and Climate Change Adaptation in a New Approach to the Reduction of Vulnerability and Poverty.* International Institute for Sustainable Development, Winnipeg.

Instanes, A. (2005). "Infrastructure: Buildings, Support Systems, and Industrial Facilities." In: *Arctic Climate Impact Assessment Scientific Report*. Cambridge University Press, Cambridge, UK.

IPCC (2001). *Climate Change 2001: Impacts, Adaptation and Vulnerability*. A report of Working Group II of the Intergovernmental Panel on Climate Change.

ITK. (2006). *Aims and Objectives*. Inuit Tapiriit Kanatami, Ottawa.

Johannessen, O. M., Bengtsson, L., Miles, M. W., Kuzmina, S. I., Semenov, V. A., Alekseev, G. V., Nagurnyi, A. P., Zakharov, V. F., Bobylev, L. P., Pettersson, L. H., Hasselmann, K. & Cattle, H. P. (2004). "Arctic Climate Change: Observed and Modelled Temperature and Sea Ice Variability." *Tellus 56A*, 328–341.

Johnson, K., Solomon, S., Berry, D. & Gramah, P. (2003). "Erosion Progression and Adaptation Strategy in a Northern Coastal Community." 8th International Conference on Permafrost, Zurich.

Kattsov, V. M. & Kallen, E. (2005). "Future Climate Change: Modeling and Scenarios for the Arctic." In: *Arctic Climate Impact Assessment Scientific Report*. Pre-release version of chapters, **www.acia.uaf.edu/pages/scientific.html**, accessed 25 May 2005, pp. 99–150.

Kirmayer, L., Boothroyd, L., & Hodgins, M.D. (1998). "Attempted Suicide among Inuit Youth: Psychosocial Correlates and Implications for Prevention." *Canadian Journal of Psychiatry*, 43, 816–822

Kirmayer, L., Brass, G.M., & Tait, C.L. (2000). "The Mental Health of Aboriginal Peoples: Transformations of Identity and Community." *Canadian Journal of Psychiatry, 45(7)*, 607–616

Kishigami, N. (2004). "A New Typology of Food Sharing Practices among Hunter Gatherers, with a Special Focus on Inuit Examples." *Journal of Anthropological Research 60*, 341–358.

Kral, M. (2003). *Unikkaartuit: Meanings of Well-being, Sadness, Suicide, and Change in Two Inuit Communities*. Final Report to the National Health Research and Development Programs, Health Canada.

Krupnik, I. & Jolly, D. (2002). *The Earth is Faster Now: Indigenous Observations of Climate Change*. Arctic Research Consortium of the United States, Fairbanks, Alaska.

Laidler, G. (2005). "Sea Ice Variability and Change: Exposure and Risk in Three Nunavut Communities." Poster presentation at the ArcticNet Annual General Meeting, Banff 2005.

Maxwell, B. (1997). *Responding to Global Climate Change in Canada's Arctic*. Volume II of the Canada country study: Climate Impacts and Adaptation. Environment Canada, Downsview, Ontario.

McBean, G., Alekseev, G. V., Chen, D., Forland, E., Fyfe, J., Groisman, P. Y., King, R., Melling, H., Vose, R. and Whitfield, P. H. (2005). "Arctic Climate—Past and Present." In: *Arctic Climate Impact Assessment Scientific Report*. Pre Release Version of Chapters, **www.acia.uaf.edu/pages/scientific.html**, accessed 25th May 2005, pp. 22–60.

Myers, H. & Forrest, S. (1997). "Making Change: Economic Development in Pond Inlet, 1987 to 1997. *Artic 53*, 134–148.

NEDS. (2003). *Nunavut Economic Development Strategy*. Government of Nunavut, Iqaluit.

NEO. (2002). *Nunavut Economic Outlook. Economic Services*. The Conference Board of Canada, Ottawa.

Newton, J. (1995). "An Assessment of Coping with Environmental Hazards in Northern Aboriginal Communities." *The Canadian Geographer 39*, 112–120.

Newton, J. & Burton, I. (2001). *An Exploration of Potential Directions for Climate Change Policy in Northern Canada*. Climate Change Impacts in Northern Canada: Assessing Our Current Knowledge. Whitehorse, Yukon.

Niang-Diop, I. & Bosch, H. (2005). "Formulating an Adaptation Strategy." In Huq, S., and Lim, B. *Adaptation Framework for Climate Change*. Cambridge University Press, Cambridge, UK.

Nickels, S., Furgal, C., Buell, M. & Moquin, H. (2005). *Unikkaaqatigiit—Putting the Human Face on Climate Change: Perspectives from Inuit in Canada*. Joint publication of Inuit Tapiriit Kanatami, Nasivvik Centre for Inuit Health and Changing Environments at Université Laval and the Ajunnginiq Centre at the National Aboriginal Health Organization, Ottawa.

NTI. (2005). *What if the Winter Doesn't Come?: Inuit Perspectives on Climate Change Adaptation Challenges in Nunavut*. Nunavut Tunngavik Incorporated, Iqaluit, Nunavut. 9.

GN. (2003). *Nunavut Climate Change Strategy*. Government of Nunavut, Iqaluit.

Nuttall, M. (2005). "Hunting, Herding, Fishing and Gathering: Indigenous Peoples and Renewable Resource Use in the Arctic." In *Arctic Climate Impact Assessment Scientific Report. Pre-release version of chapters*, <**www.acia.uaf.edu/pages/scientific.html**>, accessed 25 May 2005.

Oakes, J. & Riewe, R. (1997). *Culture, Economy, and Ecology.* The Cider Press, Millbrook, Ontario.

O'Brien, K., Sygna, L. & Haugen, J. E. (2004). "Resilient or Vulnerable? A Multi-scale Assessment of Climate Impacts and Vulnerability in Norway." *Climate Change, 64,* 193–225.

O'Brien, K. (2000). *Developing Strategies for Climate Change: The UNEP Country Studies on Climate Change Impacts and Assessment.* Report 2000-02. CICERO, Oslo, Norway.

Overland, J., Spillane, M. C. & Soreide, N. (2004). "Integrated Analysis of Physical and Biological Pan-Arctic Change." *Climatic Change 63,* 291–322.

Pearce, T. (2005a). "Living with Climate Change in Ulukhaktok." Poster presentation at the ArcticNet Annual General Meeting, Banff 2005.

Pearce, T. (2005b). "Living with Climate Change in Ulukhaktok (Holma, NT)." *Weathering Change Spring 2005,* 6.

Pielke, R. A. (2005). "Misdefining Climate Change: Consequences for Science and Action." *Environmental Science and Policy 8,* 548–561.

Pouliotte, J. (2005). *Environmental Change and Dynamic Vulnerability in Subarnabad Village, Bangladesh.* MSc Thesis, University of Guelph.

RT & Associates (2002). *Igloolik Community Economic Development Plan.*

Rasing, W. (1999). Hunting for Identity. Thoughts on the Practice of Hunting and its Significance for Iglulingmiut Identity." In: Oosten, J. and Remie, C., *Arctic Identities: Continuity and Change in Inuit and Saami Societies.* University of Leiden, Leiden, Netherlands, 79–108.

Robards, M. & Alessa, L. (2004). "Timescape of Community Resilience and Vulnerability in the Circumpolar North." *Arctic 57,* 415–427.

Schroeter, D., Polsky, C. & Patt, A. G. (2005). "Assessing Vulnerabilities to the Effects of Global Change: An Eight Step Approach. *Mitigation and Adaptation Strategies for Global Change 10,* 573–595.

Shirley, J. (2005). C-CIARN North—Nunavut Community Research Needs Survey. North-Nunavut, C.-C.

Smit, B. & Pilifosova, O. (2001). "Adaptation to Climate Change in the Context of Sustainable Development and Equity." In: McCarthy, J., Canziani, O. F., Leary, N. A., Dokken, D. J. & White, K. S., *Climate Change 2001: Impacts, Adaptation, Vulnerability. Contribution of working group II to the third assessment report of the Intergovernmental Panel on Climate Change.* Cambridge University Press, 876–912.

Smit, B. & Pilifosova, O. (2003). "From Adaptation to Adaptive Capacity and Vulnerability Reduction." In: Smith, J., Klein, R. T. J. and Huq, S., *Climate Change, Adaptive Capacity, and Development.* Imperial College Press: London, 9–28.

Smith, J. B., Klein, R. T. J. & Huq, S. (2003). *Climate Change, Adaptive Capacity, and Development.* Imperial College Press, London.

Smith, J. B. & Lenhart, S. S. (1996). "Climate Change Adaptation Policy Options." *Climate Policy 62,* 193–201.

Stevenson, M. G. (1997). "Indigenous Knowledge in Environmental Assessment." *Arctic 49,* 278–291.

Streicker, J. (2005). "Adaptation on the Horizon." *Weathering Change, 3(5),* 1–2.

Stuczyinski, T., G. , Demidowicz, T., Deputat, T., Górski, S., Krazowicz & Kus, J. (2000). "Adaptation Scenarios of Agriculture in Poland to Future Climate Changes." *Environmental Monitoring and Assessment 61,* 133–144.

Takano, T. (2004). *Bonding with the Land: Outdoor Environmental Education Programmes and their Cultural Contexts.* PhD. University of Edinburgh, Edinburgh.

Thomas, D. S. G. & Twyman, C. (2005). "Equity and Justice in Climate Change Adaptation amongst Natural-Resource-Dependent Societies." *Global Environmental Change 15,* 115–124.

Turner, B., Kasperson, R. E., Matson, P. A., McCarthy, J., Corell, R., Christensen, L., Eckley, N., Kasperson, J. X., Luers, A., Martello, M. L., Polsky, C., Pulsipher, A. & Schiller, A. (2003). "A

Framework for Vulnerability Analysis in Sustainability Science." *Proceedings of the National Academy of Sciences 100*, 8074–8079.

Wachowich, N. (2001). *Making a Living, Making a Life: Subsistence and the Re-enactment of Iglulingmiut Cultural Practices.* PhD Thesis. Department of Sociology and Anthropology, University of British Columbia, Vancouver.

Watt-Cloutier, S., Fenge, T. and Crowley, P. (2005). *Responding to Global Climate Change: The Perspective of the Inuit Circumpolar Conference on the Arctic Climate Impact Assessment.* Inuit Circumpolar Conference, Ottawa. **<www.inuitcircumpolar.com/index.php?ID=267&Lang=En>**

Wenzel, G. (1991). *Animal Rights, Human Rights,* University of Toronto Press, Toronto.

Wenzel, G. (1995). "Ningiqtuq: Resource Sharing and Generalized Reciprocity in Clyde River, Nunavut." *Arctic Anthropology 32*, 43–60.

Wigley, T.M.L. (2005). "The Climate Change Committment." *Science 307*, 1766–1769.

7

Policies and Practices Affecting Aboriginal Fathers' Involvement with their Children

Jessica Ball and Ron George[1]

Introduction

This paper offers Aboriginal fathers' perspectives on how policies and practices of federal and provincial agencies and in-community programs affect their involvement with their children. Canadian history has included a series of legislative acts that have ingrained racism and contributed to the social exclusion of many Aboriginal individuals and groups. Systemic racism occurs when institutions such as government agencies and organizations responsible for developing and maintaining public policy, health care, education and social services function in ways that limit rights or opportunities on the basis of ethnic identity (Moffatt & Cook 2005). Provisions in the *Indian Act* effectively work to diminish the population eligible for federal entitlements as Status Indians. Jurisdictional ambiguity for First Nations peoples' health and social services has reduced the transparency and accessibility of services. Domination of social services by non-Aboriginal agencies and personnel has limited the cultural acceptability of services to Aboriginal children and families. In addition to being harmed by racist legislation, insufficient funding and lack of appropriately trained personnel has meant that even when promising policies are in place, service systems frequently fail to deliver assistance to families in timely and needed ways.

Within this difficult context, Aboriginal fathers have been especially excluded, both as a stakeholder group and as a resource for their children. Recently, steps have been taken to improve developmental conditions for Aboriginal children, for example, through targeted infant development programs, innovative Maternal and Child Health programs, and Aboriginal Head Start. Yet, the contributions that Aboriginal fathers can make to their children's health and development have yet to be recognized. The Grand Chief of the First Nations Summit in British Columbia, Ed John, asserted in a recent forum:

> Fathers may very well be the greatest untapped resources in the lives of Aboriginal children. If we could support them to get involved and stay connected with their children, that would be a big protective factor for these youngsters as they grow up. (Aboriginal Early Childhood Development Leaders Forum, Vancouver, April 27, 2004, quoted with permission).

Research involving non-Aboriginal fathers shows clear correlations between fathers' involvement and developmental outcomes for children, mothers, fathers, families, and communities (Lamb 2004; Marsiglio, Day, & Lamb 2000; Flouri & Buchanan 2004), as well as improvements in fathers' mental health (Milkie, Bianchi, Mattingly, & Robinson 2002) and fathers' social well-being (Pleck & Masciadrelli 2004). Steps need to be taken to reduce systemic barriers and create supportive environments for Aboriginal fathers to initiate and sustain positive relationships with their children.

An opportunity to conduct the first research study of First Nations and Métis fathers in Canada came through a networked study of seven populations of fathers, including Aboriginal fathers, initiated by the Father Involvement Research Alliance of Canada. The study explored fathers' involvement with their children, and their views about needed reforms to legislation, public policies, community resources, and supports (Daly & Ball 2005).

Method

Research ethics: Conceived as part of a larger agenda of reparative social justice (Ball 2005a), the study was guided by principles and protocols suggested by Indigenous scholars for research involving Indigenous peoples (Castellano 2004; Interagency Advisory Panel 2003; Piquemal 2000; Ten Fingers 2005; University of Victoria Indigenous Governance Program 2003). Community relevance, respectful partnerships, and research capacity building were seen as ethical prerequisites for participating in the national fatherhood study. An urgent need to understand and support Aboriginal fathers had already been expressed by the national office of Aboriginal Head Start, and by agencies in British Columbia serving Aboriginal children and families. Low participation of First Nations and Métis fathers in children's programs was found in previous research (Ball 2005b), and unsuccessful efforts to involve Aboriginal fathers are a frequently reported concern among health-care and child-care practitioners. Thus, Aboriginal practitioners in several community-based agencies readily engaged as community partners in the research.

Due to time and budget constraints, the study was conducted only in B.C. Community-university partnership agreements were negotiated with one First Nation reserve, and two community-based agencies serving First Nations and Métis children in Prince George. After news of the study spread, the research team received an outpouring of requests from First Nations and Métis fathers, communities, and agencies to participate. Hence, the study expanded to include two more First Nations and two urban-Aboriginal program partners, as well as 18 fathers without partner affiliations who asked to contribute their stories.

Research plan: Two First Nations fathers and one woman of Aboriginal descent worked on the study team with the co-authors, contributing variously to the design, collection, transcription, and interpretation of data, and to sessions with community partners to confirm understandings and plan strategies for mobilizing knowledge gained from the research. Information gathering had three components: (1) a demographic profile of Aboriginal fathers in Canada using census data; (2) a questionnaire asking each father about their involvements with their children, their roles in relation to their children's other relatives, and their use of community programs; and (3) a 60-minute conversational interview with each father that was audiotaped and transcribed (Ball 2006).

Participant recruitment: The study recruited 80 self-identified First Nations and Métis fathers, including biological fathers, regardless of their degree of involvement with their children, and men engaged in fathering roles with children of current or former partners. Because community partners wanted to know about Aboriginal fathers with young children, the study recruited fathers with at least one child less than seven years of age.

Data analysis: Analysis of the interview transcripts used a grounded theory approach demonstrated in family interaction research by one of the authors (Ball, Cowan, & Cowan 1995).

Results

Participants

Among the 80 fathers who volunteered for the study, 72 were First Nations (90%), seven were Métis (9%), and one was a non-Aboriginal father of First Nations children. The sample was fairly representative of Aboriginal men in Canada with reference to characteristics of men self-reporting Aboriginal ethnic origins in the 2001 census (Statistics Canada 2001). These characteristics are summarized in **Table 7.1** (page 126).

Long and Winding Roads to Becoming Fathers

Nearly all of the fathers described a gradual process of identifying with fatherhood and learning to be positively involved with their children. Nearly half of the fathers had little or no contact with their first-born child, or with children from an earlier partnership until these children were adolescent or older. In contrast, studies of European-heritage fathers indicate that the birth of their first child has an immediate, momentous impact on them (e.g., Palkovitz, Copes, & Woolfolk 2001).

Many study participants described needing time to *"get up the courage to reach out to my kids"* and *"to try to get to know them, and let them get to know me."* Some also explained that in order to sustain contact with their children, they needed time to learn to manage relationships with their children's mothers, extended families, foster parents, and family service workers. Although most fathers in the study were actively involved with children who had come later, usually through a

Table 7.1: Self-Reported Demographic Characteristics of Participants

Characteristics	%	Frequency	M	SD
Identity as First Nations	90.0	72		
Identity as Métis	8.75	7		
Living On-Reserve	43.8	35		
Living Off-Reserve	52.5	42		
Age			38.00 11.89	
Number of children identified as theirs			3.29	2.13
Number of children in home			2.08	1.49
Number of adults in home			2.11	0.90
Living with a spouse or partner	55.0	44		
Highest level of education				
Some high school	36.4	29		
High school diploma	21.3	17		
Trade/college certificate or diploma	2.5	18		
Some university	11.3	9		
Bachelor's degree or higher	5.1	4		
Other	3.8	3		
Total household income				
Under $10,000	15.0	12		
$10 – 19,000	12.5	10		
$20 – 39,000	20.0	16		
$40 – 59,000	13.8	11		
$60 – 79,000	10.0	8		
$80 – 99,000	2.5	2		
Over $100,000	2.5	2		
Refused	23.8	19		
Receiving institutional financial assistance	32.5	26		
Partner receiving institutional financial assistance	8.8	7		
Currently employed or self-employed with an income	61.3	49		
Partner currently employed outside the home	37.5	30		
Physical or mental disabilities or special needs	27.5	22		

subsequent partnership, nearly half of the fathers said they wished for more involvement with their children. What are some of the barriers that make the transition to fatherhood and the goal of sustaining desired levels of involvement with their children so challenging for Aboriginal fathers?

Disrupted Intergenerational Transmission of Fathering

Aboriginal fathers' accounts of historical trauma and ongoing racist legislation and polices pointed to a monolithic set of causal factors shaping their experiences of being fathered, and of becoming fathers.

> One thing I notice is a lot of non-Aboriginal fathers going out with their kids, doing stuff with their kids and it is something I don't really see Native guys doing. [Why do you think that is?]
>
> I think it has a lot to do with how they were raised and how they grew up in their own family. I was never taught those things. I never did those things with my family. It is kind of hard.

Most fathers referred to various government policies that have disrupted teaching and learning about positive fathering from one generation to another.

> I didn't have the affection of a loving father-child relationship, like kissing your younger children. So back when my child was born, I had no communication skills. I only learned years later what it takes to love a child. Over the years, I have learned to love myself. Then I'll be able to learn to love my child. There was nothing like that when I was growing up in a residential school. Because I was in residential school until I was eighteen years old, so I really didn't learn anything. No love and no hugs from the priests or the nuns. I just came out cold.

Government policies have resulted in the dispersion of children and extended family groupings through residential schooling, foster care, adoption, forced relocations of villages, and incentives for assimilation and urbanization. For example, one father described visits he has now with a daughter he had with a non-Aboriginal mother whose family members had arranged to have his daughter adopted.

> It makes me feel so happy to be called 'Dad.' With my older children, I did not have a chance to be part of their lives. My oldest daughter lives with her grandparents in [another province] and I haven't seen her since she was a newborn.

Many of the fathers were displaced geographically from their communities of origin, and expressed regret about not being able to share their cultural and linguistic heritage with their children.

> Knowing about your culture has a huge impact on your parenting because if you have no knowledge of where you come from or your roots, it leaves a gap in your child's upbringing, their identity, self-esteem, and self-worth.

Aboriginal scholars have chronicled the devastating effects of colonial government policies that were aimed, first, at segregating Native peoples from colonial society through a reservation system, and subsequently, at forcing Aboriginal peoples either to assimilate into colonial society or subsist on its margins (Fournier & Crey 1997; Grant 1996; Ing 2000; Lawrence 2004; Miller 1996; York 1990). Over the course of seven generations, systems of tribal community governance and extended family life were broken down, and the transmission of cultural knowledge and skills for living on the land was disrupted (Chrisjohn & Young 1997; Smolewski & Wesley-Esquimaux 2003). Urbanization has disconnected Aboriginal people from their heritage language, culture, and clans (Brown, Higgitt, Wingert, Miller, & Morrissette 2005; Jantzen 2004; Lawrence 2004; Newhouse & Peters 2003). As a result of colonial efforts to sever ties between Aboriginal children and parents, most Aboriginal adults today have not enjoyed the kinds of experiential learning, affection, and play that are considered foundations for eventual parenting (Cassidy & Shaver 1999; Lamb 2004).

> My father was not involved in my life. He was abusive. I was only a year old when he left, and so I don't know if I ever saw it or experienced it [being fathered]. He left … I can remember seeing him and wishing he were more involved. After he died, I had dreams of him and he didn't recognize me. There was a lot of stuff that I had to deal with as I grew up. But, I knew that was not what I wanted for my children. I wanted my children to have a father and to understand the joys and rewards of having both parents in their lives.

Institutional Barriers

Aboriginal fathers also perceived several institutional barriers to sustained and satisfying involvement with their children, including: legislation and practices affecting establishment of paternity; mother-centred programs of support for parenting, child care, education, and health; legal and community-level custody and guardianship decisions favouring care by mothers or mothers' extended family members; lack of Aboriginal child welfare agencies, and disruptions in family care caused by non-Aboriginal welfare agencies.

Establishing Paternity

Paternity designation has implications for determination of Aboriginal identity and, in the case of First Nations people, registration under the 1985 *Indian Act*. Research with non-Aboriginal fathers has shown that fathers who voluntarily establish their paternity on their child's birth record are more likely to provide financial support and to be involved with their child (Argys & Peters 2001; Bergman & Hobson 2002), even after parents separate (Mincy, Garfinkel, & Nepomnyaschy 2005). One study in the US shows that among 217,798 infants, those without a father's name on their birth certificate (17.9 %) were 2.3 times more likely to die in the first year of life compared to those with paternity designation on their birth certificate (Gaudino, Jenkins, & Rochat 1999). According to Clatworthy (2004), nearly one in five children born to Registered Indian women between 1985 and 1999 did not have a father of record on official documents.

Various people may play a role in this omission, including fathers themselves, mothers, community health care and hospital staff, provincial birth registrars, First Nations regional administrators, and federal regional managers of Indian registration involved in the birth registration process. Clatworthy found higher rates of unstated paternity in communities that do not have community-based maternity facilities, and where maternity facilities are far from communities and fathers may not be present to sign birth documentation. In Clatworthy's study, First Nations registration officers attributed lack of paternity designation to a number of factors, including: fathers' denial of paternity to avoid responsibility for the mother or the child; fathers' lack of understanding about the registration process and the importance of paternal designation for establishing a child's entitlement to registration under the *Indian Act*; mothers' wishes, based on concerns about safety for themselves or the child, or their desire to hide the child's paternity from family and community; and financial costs to amending birth registration that may prohibit delayed paternity designation.

Paternity designation may also be influenced by the ways in which fatherhood is constructed and held in the community. For example, in some First Nations communities that are traditionally matrilineal, mothers and their families may view children as belonging most importantly to the mother and her family, and may regard paternity designation as less important. Prevalent social stereotypes of First Nations fathers as deadbeat dads may encourage mothers to avoid registration of paternity. Some fathers in the current study explained that they had not claimed paternity on birth records for one or more of their children because they felt undeserving: in their own evaluation, they had nothing to offer their child, or wanted to hide their ethnic or personal identity in an effort to save their child from stigma. Some First Nations women who commented on the study findings noted that, in addition to birth registry, legal marriage is an institution that was introduced by Europeans. Traditionally, among Aboriginals neither marriages nor births were matters of legal, written record.

One tool that has been used to erode traditional roles for fathers within First Nations family systems and communities is legislation in the *Indian Act* that has caused people to have their Indian Status denied or revoked if they do not live on-reserve in their communities of origin. Without status, many are forbidden to live on-reserve with their cultural and linguistic community. This process consists of a kind of legislated forceful relocation, similar in effect to the better known forced relocations of the communities of Davis Inlet and Cheslatta. Partly as a result of enfranchisement[2] and forced relocation, a majority of Aboriginal people live off-reserve, and are not entitled to the unique benefits and supports that the federal government is obligated to provide to Status Indians living on-reserve, including funding for programs specifically designed to support Aboriginal families, including fathers.

Hastening the decline of First Nations family and community unity and support has been legislation in the *Indian Act* that causes women who marry non-Aboriginal men to have their status revoked, precluding entitlements for children whose fathers were not registered as status Indians. Common sections of the *Indian Act* pre-dating 1985 were Sections 12(1)b, which caused loss of status to women marrying non-Indians, or Métis, and non-status Indians, and Section 12(1) a: 4, or the double mother clause, which caused children to lose status at the age of 21 years if their mother and their father's mother were non-Indian.[3] The *Indian Act* continues to differentiate between Status, Non-Status, and off-reserve Indians. In so doing, the Act can be viewed as violating the United Nations Covenant of Civil and Political Rights (1976), that guarantees all citizens the rights to community, culture, and language.

The effects of these colonial policies are felt by mothers and fathers, as well as by their children. Numerous position papers have advised changes to the *Indian Act* that would result, in principle, in greater equity and government accountability to Aboriginal peoples (e.g., Quebec Native Women's Association 2000). However, even when needed policy reforms have been achieved, for example, in the case of Bill C-31, whereby certain Aboriginal people living off-reserve acquired status, resources have often not been committed to make these changes meaningful in the lived experiences of Aboriginal families. Meanwhile, the system invites manipulations in order to reduce the derogatory and debilitating effects of the *Indian Act*. For example, there are anecdotal reports of paternity being designated as a Status Indian man who is not actually a child's father but who is able to secure a child's entitlement to registration as a Status Indian under provisions of the *Indian Act*. As one father noted:

> The *Indian Act* is a breeding formula, with recipes for what needs to show up on birth records in order to produce a Status Indian child who may be able to pass on their status to their own offspring, depending on the status of the person they have the child with. That's why we're called alphabet Indians. Some Indians have learned their alphabet and use paternity designation to spell entitlements for their children.

Poverty

Among broad determinants of Aboriginal fathers' involvement with their children, one of the most significant is poverty. In the current study, although 61% of the fathers had at least some part-time work, 37.5% were living far below the poverty line, based on their family size, size of community of residence, and household income. This is consistent with 2001 census data (Statistics Canada 2001), which show that although 68% of Aboriginal men are employed part time, only 29% have full-time employment. Census data also show a higher prevalence of inadequate housing and food among Aboriginal families living both on- and off-reserve, compared to non-Aboriginal families. Fathers in the study who identified poverty as a barrier to fathering and family well-being attributed this to various government policies and intervention.

We don't have much. We are losing our rights. Whether it be hunting or fishing, we lose everything. And our people seem to be getting poorer and poorer. There is no end in sight. Soon as you get a little bit ahead, the government puts up a policy. A never ending battle with colonialism.

Poverty marginalizes fathers' involvement through both direct and indirect effects. For fathers living apart from their children, poverty often means that they are unable to relocate to live near their children, unable to cover transportation costs to visit their children regularly or at all, and unable or less inclined to access programs that may be available for fathers or families.

The poverty and the cultural aspect make it a little harder to access services. Aboriginal young families, in general, in my own experiences I have found that they are a little more transient, moving from town to town or house to house. They are not as fixed, regardless of how many kids they have. And the poverty issue makes for the same hardships as for non-Aboriginal families who are poor, but culturally Aboriginal families are less apt to go for services that are not specifically for Aboriginals.

Some of the fathers in the study described feeling inadequate, or ashamed of not being able to provide a suitable living space, food, clothing, recreation or entertainment for their children. Over one-quarter of the fathers in the study did not have a phone, many did not have driver's licenses, and few owned their own vehicle. Several had changed addresses within six months after their interview. Four had no home at all and were "couch surfing," living in temporary shelters, or on the streets. One was living in a halfway house. All of these manifestations of poverty contribute to the challenges that many Aboriginal fathers encounter in trying to maintain contact with their children, and engage comfortably and in suitable settings with them.

Poverty also reduces the prospects of fathers or mothers being able to retrieve a child who has been placed in the care of the government. When a child is removed, parents receiving income assistance are cut back to the level for accommodating a single person, making it difficult to provide a suitable home for the return of the child. When parents are separated, mothers who retain custody of children and who are poor may be highly transient, making it difficult for a father to find his children in order to sustain his relationship with them.

Dislocations from the World of Work

Jobs that traditionally enabled Aboriginal men to be family breadwinners, and provided a context for fathers to teach skills and transmit stories to their children, have diminished as access to land, and jobs in industries depending on natural resources have diminished. Few Aboriginal fathers have the means to take their children out on trap lines, fishing boats, or hunting grounds, or to teach them their ancestral language. At the same time, 51% of First Nations men in Canada have not completed high school (Statistics Canada 2001) and may be out of step with their children's achievements or goals in formal schooling.

The Aboriginal male, their job title used to be hunting and gathering. They used to have to hunt and if you weren't hunting or fishing you were preparing to go hunting, fishing, gathering food, making shelters and doing all those things. So, that whole thing with the Europeans coming in and wiping it all out … First it was the residential school and they took away the language, or tried to take the language away. They took the entire role of the male in the Aboriginal community away so that left a big empty gap for males. They didn't know what to do, where to go, what to say, when to say it, or anything. They had to be fit in and women had to play another role in telling the male what to do, but the women kept their jobs. The women looked after the kids; they did all the food preparations and things like that. That stayed. The women fit in a lot easier than the men I think. It wasn't easy for women, but they had certain jobs that they were able to do. Whereas the men, they had to go off, they had to go and learn how to build certain kind of houses and they had to relearn how to live in society, how to get a wife and what to do as a husband, as a father and as a member of a community.

Mother-centric Outreach and Services

Some fathers in the current study perceived that there are currently more opportunities for women to enter the work force in office jobs, especially in urban centres, and to receive funding and support for vocational training and education.

I'll go out and try looking for a job and they tell me I don't have the right education … they give me the run around. All the education programs are geared towards single mothers and they tell me that they can't help me.

While a large proportion of Aboriginal men have been dislocated from the world of work, it appears that more fathers have become very involved in domestic life, including a few who are primary or lone caregivers.

Now, we have moved to such a society that women are more in the limelight of career opportunities. That's a great thing. Now there's a shift going on, where there has to be a balance where both parents have equal involvement in their kids' lives. I think it's the economy that dictates how it's being done … There's a lot more fathers staying home now, instead of going to work. I'm a stay-at-home dad and my brother just became a stay-at-home dad.

Yet, most fathers in the study expressed their acute sense of social exclusion in what seems to them to be a mother's world of prenatal care and education, child care, parent education, health services, home-school liaison, social services, and other forms of support for parenting.

There needs to be provided more male-based information, programs and workshops for men. I went there [to a parent support program] and there were all mothers. When I go to things like that, I just do not feel comfortable. I was going to go to the "Nobody's Perfect" program, but it is nothing but females in there! I would like to go in there and just start advocating for the fathers. I want to go in there and say, 'This is a good program, but you have to expand it to include the father's point of view, give them a voice.' And when I try to speak up about it, people just brush it off. They say they have 'enough work to do' and 'we only have a certain amount of time to talk about these issues and maybe we'll just talk about it next time.' Nothing happens.

Indeed, community-based program managers who were interviewed in another study (Ball 2005b) commented that, until now, Aboriginal fathers have not been seen as a source of support for infants, children and mothers. One parent support worker admitted: "It's not so much that we have failed to reach Aboriginal dads. It's more that we have never tried."

Virtually all fathers in the study identified a need for more support to learn to be a father. Mothers have overwhelmingly been beneficiaries of parenting outreach, support, and education programs.

> It should be equal rights for the male and the female ... She (my child's mother) had so much support from the Ministry and through the parenting programs; she had it all set up for her. But then, when we split up, all that left with her.

Fathers most frequently identified a need for information packets and DVD programs explaining child health, safety, dental care, teaching techniques for preschoolers, and ways for fathers to handle new situations with their children, especially with daughters (e.g., bathing, toileting, leisure time interests, and puberty).

> I think that father's support is big and being able to see how other fathers handle different situations. Because honestly, there are a lot of fathers out there who weren't raised by a father, or were raised by an abusive father, and don't know how to be a father. Like me—my father was not around, so you have to learn right from the beginning, when you have a baby sitting right there in front of you and you have to be a dad.

Fathers wanted these resources to be specifically tailored for Aboriginal fathers.

> I know that John Howard has that but it is not specifically for Aboriginal fathers. I think that there is a high degree of cultural shame amongst Aboriginal people and I think that if they [Aboriginal fathers] could identify with other Aboriginal fathers, share their experiences, share their strengths, then maybe they could step out of that and teach their children how to be proud of who they are.

Fathers variously asserted that they were not "irrelevant" or "indifferent," as schools, health centres, and courts often seem to view them, and they suggested that institutions have policies that require practitioners to keep a record about how to reach a child's father, and to contact fathers, as well as mothers, about significant events (e.g., accident reports, achievements), appointments (e.g., parent-teacher meetings, diagnostic assessment reports, immunization visits), and achievement (e.g., report cards).

> For years it has been the single mother. So the people that are trained to deal with parenting and children are so focused on the woman. If there is policy for mothers, there needs to be policy for fathers. You know—family support workers, education, daycare workers and people like that need to be trained to deal with fathers. They need to know that there are fathers out there that are trying and they should be pushing for that.

In addition to exclusionary practices in institutions, fathers described settings and events where they experienced socially hostile or dismissive attitudes, as if they were intruders in their child's life. For example, one father described how he feels like he is being looked at with suspicion when he walks down the city street with his four year old daughter: "as if I might be abducting her." Another father reported that he had been pointedly asked at the community swimming pool where his daughter's mother was. Most fathers described situations where they had felt uncomfortable or unwelcome because the program was expecting mothers rather than fathers (e.g., Mother-Tot program, Mothers' Morning Out, Mother Goose, Maternal and Child Health Programs).

Four fathers in the study were raising their children as lone parents, and were particularly vocal in expressing the sense of being left without help to figure out how to raise their child: "Nobody has even tried to talk to us; they haven't made an effort."

Separated and Divorced Aboriginal Fathers

Fair, equitable access to children by Aboriginal fathers after separation or divorce is an area where policy reforms are needed, and commitments of funding are required to implement provisions that may already be articulated. The appearance of bias in favour of awarding custody to mothers is pervasive in Canada. For Aboriginal fathers of children whose mother is non-Aboriginal, historically mothers are given custody. Several fathers who had lost custody of one or more children expressed their view that: "*When you go to court, it doesn't matter what the situation is, the courts are always in favour of the women.*"

Two of the lone fathers in the study were raising their young daughters after their child's mother had gone missing. Both were isolated on small rural reserves, and reported that they had received little or no support from health, education, or social services. Another lone father described a lack of acknowledgement for his role as primary caregiver with only occasional appearances by the child's mother.

> I had already had our daughter for nearly two years before this court case happened ... Her mother had only been around for three days, but the social workers assumed that she was the one that was bringing her up. I know that there are a lot of single mothers out there, but for my case, they sort of just left me high and dry. There was no support for me. I just want them to understand what I have to do to bring this child up.

First Nations child and family service agency staff who were consulted for this study noted several ways that Aboriginal fathers are currently under-represented in custody decision making, and where there are gaps in services. For example, Shelly Johnson, Executive Director of Victoria's Surrounded by Cedar Child and Family Services Agency, identified a litany of barriers to sustained father-child relationships in situations involving child welfare interventions: long wait lists for separation and divorce mediation; lack of Aboriginal court workers; reluctance of mediators to take cases involving alcohol or other substance abuse; minimal legal representation; lack of appropriate education to inform fathers about their rights to legal aid; lack of staff to supervise father–child visits; lack of suitable, accessible places for supervised visits; lack of training for staff to supervise visits; and lack of clarity and follow-up when a non-Aboriginal mother refuses an Aboriginal father access to children (S. Johnson, personal communication 2006). In a survey done by the Victoria Urban Aboriginal Steering Committee Society, separation and divorce mediation counselling was identified by First Nations people living on- and off-reserve as one of their program priorities (Johnson 2001).

Jurisdictional Ambiguities in Access to Support Services

For Aboriginal fathers, access to resources, programs and services is more complicated than for non-Aboriginal fathers. There are several levels of government involved in providing funding, services, and other resources for Aboriginal peoples, including federal, provincial, and First Nations self-government, and First Nations or Inuit specific legislation. There are different policy frameworks in each provincial and territorial government for the administration of government services to Aboriginal peoples, and different fiduciary responsibilities with respect to different populations of Aboriginal people. For example, the federal government provides a wide range of services to First Nations on reserves and to Inuit, primarily through Indian and Northern Affairs Canada, and Health Canada. Apart from this unique relationship, provincial governments have jurisdiction over health services, housing, education, and child and family services for Aboriginal peoples living off-reserve. Thus, the specific designation of the father's Aboriginal identity, as well as the geographic location(s) in which a father and his child reside, influence what kinds of services are available as well as how to access them. The situation is doubly complex when a child has a different identity with regard to Aboriginality or status, and/or lives in a different geographic location under a different jurisdiction.

Jurisdictional confusions, overlaps, and gaps reflecting the multiple levels of government involvement in financing and delivering programs and services cause fragmentation, redundancies, inconsistencies, instability, and lack of transparency of services for Aboriginal fathers and their families. "Client-centred" or "customer-service" orientations are not characteristic of most child and family service agencies. In particular, social assistance and child protection services tend to be more professional-oriented, and designed to meet the needs of the government system and its preoccupation with standards and liability, rather than the family system, with its preoccupation to survive and provide some quality of life for family members. Navigating and negotiating needed resources and services requires far more tenacity, ingenuity, time, and resources than most men or women have at their disposal. In addition to the labyrinthine nature of services for Aboriginal peoples, many First Nations and Métis people find the system especially intimidating because of the history of oppressive relations between government and Aboriginal peoples, and the lack of culturally competent staff or a cultural frame around services.

Child Welfare: Least Disruptive Interventions

Removal of children from their homes and communities is a common cause of disrupted father-child relationships. Several fathers in the study described this as the primary reason for lack of contact with one or more of their children. Aboriginal children are demographically over-represented in the child welfare system. The national First Nations Child and Family Caring Society estimates that 30–40% of children in the care of child welfare agencies across Canada are Aboriginal. According to this Society, Aboriginal children are most often identified as needing care as a result of neglect (almost twice the rate of non-Aboriginal children removed for reasons of neglect) as opposed to abuse or other concerns. Neglect is often a result of poverty, lack of education, poor parenting skills, and/or father's or mother's stress or illness.

Within the context of Canadian legislation recognizing certain special rights and legal status of Aboriginal people, government child welfare policies have gradually provided for Aboriginal people to assume authority over child welfare services for Aboriginal children. The extent and type of services offered by Aboriginal child and family welfare agencies depends upon the identity of the child, where he or she lives, and the type of agreement in place in that particular jurisdiction.

In general, a "kith and kin" approach is consistent with Aboriginal perspectives on caring for children within extended family networks, and with the child welfare principle of using "least disruptive interventions." In a kith and kin approach, children considered to be in need of an increased level of resourced care or protection are kept in their own homes, with extra supports, or in the homes of relatives or friends close to home. This approach increases opportunities for continuous relationships between children and their parents. However, there is inadequate funding to implement least disruptive service policies. According to a study by the First Nations Child and Family Caring Society and the Department of Indian and Northern Affairs federal child welfare agencies, children and families on reserves receive 22% less funding than their provincial counterparts (Blackstock, Clarke, Cullen, D'Hondt & Formsma 2004; FNCFCS 2005). In B.C., guardians of children living in the home of a relative for purposes of child protection receive a lower rate of pay and receive no support services compared to if the child is placed in a foster home with a non-relative. This policy means that children who are retained closer to home and family are more likely to live in poverty without needed supports. Thus, there is a financial disincentive for relatives to keep children within their family network.

First Nations control over welfare services to children and families living off-reserve is disputed in many parts of Canada (Gough, Blackstock, & Bala 2005).

Again, jurisdictional ambiguities have resulted in limited or restricted access to services that fathers need in order to maintain contact with their children either when their relationships with the child's mother is ruptured, or the child is deemed in need of protective custody. Fathers in the study who had lost custody of their children as a result of divorce, foster care, or adoption, described feeling caught in an uninterpretable web with no legal representation or program support. They pointed to unanswered questions such as: What exactly constitutes adequate care and protection? What constitutes a suitable home in which to place a child for alternative care? What do fathers need to do to be eligible for supervised access to their children? Apprehension about dealing with government authorities, low levels of literacy, lack of transportation, language barriers, and personal difficulties interfering with effective participation in the deliberations with professionals are just some of the barriers that fathers described as factors compounding the challenge of navigating the complexities of child welfare services.

Recommendations

Implement Recommendations in the Royal Commission on Aboriginal Peoples.

The Royal Commission on Aboriginal Peoples (RCAP 1996) is a public policy landmark that can serve as a primary reference point for deliberating steps towards policy reform and provision of needed resources and services to promote social justice for Aboriginal peoples in general, and for Aboriginal fathers specifically. This five-volume, 4,000-page report has 440 recommendations. Volume 2 builds on the historical review provided in Volume 1 by making the case for Aboriginal self-government within the Canadian context as the primary means for Aboriginal people to gain control over their affairs, including matters of child care, protection, and family well-being. Implementation of the recommendations in this report, deliberated over six years of consultations, would significantly improve conditions for Aboriginal children and families. While nation-to-nation negotiations are the preferred approach to renewing relationships between Aboriginal Peoples and provincial, federal, and territorial governments in Canada, many recommendations in this document could be implemented while this larger agenda unfolds.

Reduce Systemic Barriers to Social Inclusion.

Progress needs to be made to reduce systemic barriers to Aboriginal fathers' social inclusion. Poverty, racism, negative social expectations, and policies that prevent Aboriginal fathers from establishing paternity and sustaining connections with children as family circumstances change combine to perpetuate Aboriginal fathers' social exclusion and a vacuum of support. The multigenerational perspective that Aboriginal fathers in the study brought to their understandings of fathering casts the need for policy reforms and systemic program solutions within a post-colonial social justice agenda that requires a long-term commitment.

Facilitate Paternity Designation.

There are legal rights and responsibilities, as well as familial, social, emotional, and cultural implications, that flow from the designation of paternity on a birth certificate—perhaps no more so than for Aboriginal peoples, given the distinctions among Aboriginal peoples constructed by the *Indian Act*. Steps are needed to ensure that both fathers and mothers are aware of the process of registration and the implications of unstated paternity. Opportunities for paternity registration need to be made readily accessible and free of charge to fathers at the time of a child's birth as well as for an extended period subsequent to the birth. Special efforts need to be made to reach out to fathers in rural and remote areas where maternity facilities are far from home, fathers may be working far from home, and there may be limited ability for fathers to travel to be present at their child's birth.

Support Cultural Continuity.

Disrupted father-child relationships exacerbate the challenges for both Aboriginal children and their fathers to elaborate cohesive and positive Aboriginal identities, especially for those living off-reserve, away from their cultural and language community. Continuity of father–child relationships means that children are continuously given opportunities to learn and consolidate Aboriginal cultural knowledge and identity. Following the diminution of intergenerational cultural learning as a result of residential schooling, foster care and adoption, resources are needed to enable Aboriginal fathers to restore their cultural roots and re-constitute culturally meaningful roles for fathers, and to involve their children in learning their culture, for example, through Native Friendship Centres and other Aboriginal community programs. The Canadian Constitution affirms children's right of cultural continuity, stating that: "First Nations children have a right to learn, maintain, and preserve their language(s) and cultures." The United Nations Convention on the Rights of the Child also recognizes that "traditional cultural values are highlighted as essential for the protection and harmonious development of children."

Commit Resources for Outreach and Support Programs for Aboriginal Fathers.

Many practitioners recognize the deficiencies of the motherhood-first paradigm and the need for its transformation (Rohner & Veneziano 2001). Policy and program development to enhance Aboriginal fathers' involvement needs to occur at the level of communities or community agencies representing the particular needs, goals, and circumstances of particular Aboriginal groups. Fathers in this study articulated a mandate for community-based agencies, as well as political bodies, to get involved in supporting healing programs, reducing negative stereotypes of Aboriginal fathers and families, and actively reaching out to support fathers in their fatherhood journeys. These initiatives are best directed by Aboriginal people themselves.

Increase Transparency and Aboriginal Control of Child Welfare Services.

There is an immediate need to fund and support the development and operation of Aboriginal-controlled child and family service agencies. Policy reforms in some provinces are responding to calls by Aboriginal leaders to embrace a 'least disruptive interventions' approach, including kinship care, whereby children requiring protective guardianship are placed in the homes of relatives (Gleeson 1996). Policy reform is needed to provide for equivalent levels of funding and access to support services (e.g., counselling, respite, transportation) as are available when children are placed in the care of non-relatives. The kinship care approach needs to be given time to mature, and evaluated with a view to improvements in implementation.

While Aboriginal-controlled child welfare agencies are evolving, existing service agencies can be improved by increasing the cultural competence of staff, providing culturally appropriate supports and interventions around services, and providing language interpreter services and outreach. Existing systems of services for Aboriginal children and families can be made more transparent, accessible, and father-friendly through appropriate print materials and Aboriginal staff who can serve as guides to help fathers navigate the child welfare system. Funding to deliver training in communities and Indigenous post-secondary institutions can strengthen the Aboriginal work force available to assume positions of child welfare agencies. Parent support programs, legal consultations, mediation, and family intervention services need to be offered in settings that are accessible and sensitive to the legacy of residential schools and other government interventions.

Fund Research Focused on Aboriginal Fathers

Aboriginal fathers' voices have rarely been heard in community programs or research. Practitioners have called for more knowledge about Aboriginal fathers' intentions in regards to parenting, their living circumstances, needs, and goals in order to inform community outreach efforts. Community response to this exploratory study and insights gleaned from fathers' stories suggest that research about Aboriginal fathering can fill a distinct gap in knowledge about fathering, which primarily represents men of western-European heritage. One father reflected the importance of listening to fathers:

> I think it's really important that Aboriginal people are heard in this survey and I'm honoured to be asked to take part in this. The more that we do this, the more that we work on hearing the voices of Aboriginal males and other males in Canada then the government will get a better understanding of what it is they're dealing with … instead of telling us what we need to be doing, asking us what we, you know asking for input from us and getting out of what I'm saying and all the other men that your going to talk to or listen to or read about, put it all together and you're going to get some answers, and programs and services are going to be put together in a way that's going to come from down in the ground here.

There are over 600 culturally distinct First Nations in Canada, and many sources of variation among Aboriginal peoples living in urban centers across the country. There are significant differences in polices affecting different Aboriginal populations and significant variations in policies across provinces and territories. In particular, access to resources varies greatly between the largely urban, off-reserve population and the more rural on-reserve population of First Nations men. To avoid an overgeneralized, 'pan-Aboriginal' interpretation of Aboriginal fathers' experiences and changes needed to policy and practice, future research should explore the constitution of fathering and patterns of fathers' involvement across specific cultural groups and settings with varied historical and current circumstances.

Conclusions

Aboriginal fathers in Canada remain very much on the margins of mainstream society with no focused social advocacy or previous research. There are monumental challenges facing Aboriginal fathers and families. However, several fathers who took part in the current study referred to themselves as "success stories," and were proud of the quality of relationships with their children that they had achieved with little help from community programs, child welfare services, or society as a whole. Their stories suggest the potential for a new generation of positively involved Aboriginal fathers that urgently needs to be recognized and supported through policy reforms and resources to put policies into practice.

Acknowledgments

Research for this paper was supported by funding from the Social Sciences and Humanities Research Council of Canada, Community-University Research Alliances program (File No. 833-2003-1002) and by the British Columbia Ministry of Children and Family Development through the Human Early Learning Partnership. The views presented here are those of the authors and do not represent provincial or federal funding agencies or Aboriginal organizations.

The authors thank the First Nations fathers who participated in the research; the B.C. community partners in the research: Lil'wat Nation, Little Hands of Friendship and Power of Friendship Aboriginal Head Start Programs in Prince George, the Terrace Child Development Centre Dad's Group, and Esketemc Aboriginal Head Start; contributions by team members Candice Manahan and Leroy Joe; and the Fathers Involvement Research Alliance of Canada, CURA project, directed by Kerry Daly.

Endnotes

1 We welcome comments and requests for more information about the study discussed in this paper. Address correspondence to: Jessica Ball or Ron George, Early Childhood Development Intercultural Partnerships, University of Victoria, School of Child and Youth Care, Box 1700 STN CSC, Victoria, B.C., Canada V8W 2Y2. Tel: 250-472-4128 Fax: (250) 721-7218. Email: jball@uvic.ca; tsaskiy@uvic.ca Web site: **www.ecdip.org**.

2 Enfranchisement refers to losing the status of being "Indian," under the law. When one was enfranchised, it meant they gained the franchise to vote in Federal elections. Up until 1960 it was not possible for status Indians to vote unless they revoked, lost, or were taken off the Indian status list of the *Indian Act*. There were both voluntary or involunatary provisions under which this could happen; however, in 1984, a presentation read into the standing committee hearings, (The United Native Nations Presentation to the Parliamentary Standing Committee on Indian Affairs Respecting Bill C-31) proved that all provisions were involuntary, and that they were all coercive and enticing. Thus all those who once had status and lost it or were entitled, were eligible for reinstatement under Bill C-3, the act amending the *Indian Act*.

3 This term originally meant no Indian blood, but it turned out that if the mother were Indian with no status, it applied as well. So the term used in this sense, is the legal term Indian, one registered under the Indian Act. The term Indian is not synonymous with having Indian blood, only that they are registered as Indian. A non-Indian woman (no Indian blood) gained status upon marriage to a status Indian man prior to April 17, 1985. The real reason for enfranchisement was to diminish Canada's legal and fiscal responsibility to Section 91(24) of the BNA Act obligations to "Indians and lands reserved for Indians."

References

Argys, L.M., & Peters, H.E. (2001). "Interactions between Unmarried Fathers and their Children: The Role of Paternity Establishment and Child-support Policies." *The American Economic Review*, 91 (2), 125–129.

Ball, J. (2006). Indigenous Fathers Involvement project description. Retrieved February 15, 2006 from **<www.ecdip.org/fathers/index.htm>**

Ball, J. (2005a). "'Nothing about us without us': Restorative Research Partnerships involving Aboriginal Children and Communities in Canada." In A. Farrell (Ed.) *Exploring Ethical Research with Children*. (pp. 81–96) Berkshire, UK: Open University Press/McGraw-Hill Education.

Ball, J. (2005b). "Early Childhood Care and Development Programs as Hook and Hub for Inter-sectoral Service Delivery in Aboriginal Communities." *Journal of Aboriginal Health, 1*, March, 36–49.

Ball, J., Cowan, P., & Cowan, C. (1995). "Who's got the power: Gender Differences in Experiences of Marital Problem Solving." *Family Process, 34(3)*, 303–322.

Bergman, H., & Hobson, B. (2002). "The Coding of Fatherhood in the Swedish Welfare State." In B. Hobson (Ed.). *Making Men into Fathers*. (pp. 92–124) Cambridge, UK: Cambridge University Press.

Blackstock, C., Clarke, S., Cullen, J., D'Hondt, J., & Formsma, J. (2004). *Keeping the Promise: the Convention of the Rights of the Child and the Lived Experience of First Nations Children and Youth*. First Nations Child and Family Caring Society of Canada. Retrieved February 1, 2006 from **<www.fncfcs.com/docs/KepingThePromise.pdf>**

Brown, J., Higgitt, N., Wingert, S., Miller, C., & Morrissette, L. (2005). "Challenges Faced by Aboriginal Youth in the Inner City." *Canadian Journal of Urban Research, 14* (1), 81–106.

Cassidy, J. & Shaver, P. (Eds.). (1999). *Handbook of Attachment Theory and Research*. New York: Guilford.

Castellano, M. B. (2004). "Ethics of Aboriginal research." *Journal of Aboriginal Health, 1*(1), 98–114.

Chrisjohn, R., & Young, S., with Maraun, M. (1997). *The Circle Game: Shadows and Substance in the Indian Residential School Experience in Canada*. Penticton, BC: Theytus Books.

Clatworthy, S. (2004). "Unstated Paternity: Estimates and Contributing Factors." In J.P. White, P. Maxim, & D. Beavon (Eds.), *Aboriginal Policy Research: Setting the Agenda for Change, Vol. II*. (pp. 225–244). Toronto: Thompson Educational Publishing.

Daly, K. J. & Ball, J. (2005). *Fathers' Involvement with their Children: Presentation on the First Canadian National Study of Fatherhood*. Paper presented at the Seminar Series on Research on Early Education and Child Health, University of Victoria, Canada, April 14. Retrieved October 1, 2005 from **<www.ecdip.org/fathers/index/htm>**

First Nations Child and Family Caring Society of Canada (2005). *"A Chance to Make a Difference for this Generation of First Nations Children and Young People: The UNCRC and the Lived Experience of First Nations Children in the Child Welfare System of Canada."* A submission to the Standing Senate Committee on Human Rights, February 7, 2005. Retrieved February 2, 2006 at **<www.fncfcs.com/docs/CommitteeOnHumanRightsFeb2005.pdf>**

Flouri, E., & Buchanan, A. (2004). "Early Father's and Mother's Involvement and Child's Later Educational Outcomes." *British Journal of Educational Psychology, 74*, 141–153.

Fournier, S. & Crey, E. (1997). *Stolen from our Embrace: The Abduction of Aboriginal Children and the Restoration of Aboriginal Communities*. Vancouver, BC: Douglas & McIntyre.

Gaudino, J.A., Jenkins, B., & Rochat, F.W. (1999). "No Father's Names: A Risk Factor for Infant Mortality in the State of Georgia, USA." *Social Science and Medicine, 48*, 253–265.

Gleeson, J. P. (1996). "Kinship Care as a Child Welfare Service: The Policy Debate in an Era of Welfare Reform." *Child Welfare, 75*(5), 419–449.

Gough, P., Blackstock, C., & Bala, N. (2005). *"Jurisdiction and Funding Models for Aboriginal Child and Family Service Agencies."* Centre of Excellence for Child Welfare, Information Sheet #30E. Toronto, ON, Canada: University of Toronto. Retrieved February 10, 2006 from **<www.cecw-cepb.ca/DocsEng/JurisdictionandFunding30E.pdf>**

Grant, A. (1996). *No End of Grief: Indian Residential Schools in Canada.* Winnipeg: Pemmican Publications.

Ing, N. R. (2000). *Dealing with Shame and Unresolved Trauma: Residential School and its Impact on the Second and Third Generation Adults.* Unpublished doctoral dissertation, Department of Educational Studies, University of British Columbia.

Interagency Advisory Panel on Research Ethics (2003). "Section 6: Research Involving Aboriginal Peoples." In *Tri-Council Policy Statements: Ethical Conduct for Research Involving Humans.* Ottawa, ON. Retrieved October 1, 2005 from <**www.pre.ethics.gc.ca/english/policystatement/section6. cfm**>

Jantzen, L. (2004). "Top Seven Aboriginal Census Metropolitan Areas: Similar Issues and Different Circumstances." *Our Diverse Cities, 1,* 76–85.

Johnson, S. (2001). *Victoria Urban Aboriginal Steering Committee Society Pre-Planning Report.* Unpublished report. Surrounded by Cedar Child and Family Services Agency. Victoria, B.C.

Lamb, M. E. (Ed.). (2004). *The Role of the Father in Child Development* (4th ed.). Hoboken, NJ: John Wiley & Sons.

Lawrence, B. (2004). *"Real" Indians and Others: Mixed-blood Urban Native Peoples and Aboriginal Nationhood.* Vancouver: UBC Press.

Marsiglio, W., Day, R. D., & Lamb, M. E. (2000). "Exploring Fatherhood Diversity: Implications for Conceptualizing Father Involvement." *Marriage & Family Review. Special Issue: Fatherhood: Research, Interventions, and Policies, 29,* 269–293.

Milkie, M.A., Bianchi, S.M., Mattingly, M. J., & Robinson, J. P. (2002). "Gendered Division of Childrearing: Ideals, Realities, and the Relationship to Parental Well-being." *Sex Roles, 47,* 21–38.

Miller, J.R. (1996). *Shingwauk's vision: A History of Native Residential Schools.* Toronto: University of Toronto Press.

Mincy, R., Garfinkel, I., & Nepomnyaschy, L. (2005). "In-hospital Paternity Establishment and Father Involvement in Fragile Families." *Journal of Marriage and Family, 67,* 611–626.

Moffatt, M.E.K., & Cook, C. (2005). "How Can the Health Community Foster and Promote the Health of Aboriginal Children and Youth?" *Paediatric Child Health, 10* (9), 549–552.

Morrissette, P.J. (1994). "The Holocaust of First Nations People: Residual Effects on Parenting and Treatment Implications." *Contemporary Family Therapy, 16,* 381–392.

Newhouse, D. & Peters, E. (Eds.). (2003). *Not Strangers in these Parts: Urban Aboriginal Peoples.* Ottawa, ON: Policy Research Initiative, Indian and Northern Affairs Canada.

Palkovitz, R., Copes, M.A., & Woolfolk, T.N. (2001). "It's like ... you discover a new sense of being": Involved fathering as an evoker of adult development. *Men and Masculinities, 4,* 49–69.

Piquemal, N. (2000). "Four Principles to Guide Research with Aboriginals." *Policy Options, 21*(10), 49–51.

Pleck, J. H. & Masciadrelli, B. P. (2004). "Paternal Involvement: Levels, Sources, and Consequences." In M.E. Lamb (Ed.), *The Role of the Father in Child Development* (4th ed., pp. 222–271). Hoboken, NJ: John Wiley & Sons.

Quebec Native Women's Association (2000). "Brief: Changes Proposed to the *Indian Act* and the Administration of the *Indian Act*." Retrieved January 19, 2006 from <**www.faq-qnw.org/ Indian%20Act/Brief_indian_act_2000.pdf**>

Rohner, R. P., & Veneziano, R. A. (Eds.). (2001). "The Importance of Father Love: History and Contemporary Evidence." *Review of General Psychology, 5,* 382–405.

Royal Commission on Aboriginal Peoples (1996). *Report of the Royal Commission on Aboriginal Peoples.* Ottawa, ON: Canada Communication Group. Retrieved February 13, 2006 from <**www.ainc-inac.gc.ca/ch/rcap/sg/sgmm_e.html**>

Siggner, A.J. (2003). "Urban Aboriginal Populations: An Update Using the 2001 Census Results." In D. Newhouse & E. Peters (Eds.) *Not Strangers in These Parts: Urban Aboriginal Peoples* (pp. 15–19). Ottawa, ON: Policy Research Initiative, Indian and Northern Affairs Canada.

Smolewski, M., & Wesley-Esquimaux, C. C. (2003). *Historic Trauma and Aboriginal Healing.* Ottawa, ON: Aboriginal Healing Foundation Research Series.

Statistics Canada (2001). *Census of the Population 2001.* Ottawa, ON: Statistics Canada.

Ten Fingers, K. (2005). "Rejecting, Revitalizing, and Reclaiming: First Nations Work to Set the Direction of Research and Policy Development." *Canadian Journal of Public Health, 96* (Jan/Feb supplement), S60–S63.

University of Victoria Indigenous Governance Program (2003). Protocols and Principles for Research In An Indigenous Context. Victoria, B.C.: Author. Retrieved November 13, 2006 <**web.uvic.ca/igov/ programs/masters/igov_598/protocol.pdf**>

United Nations International Covenant of Civil and Political Rights (1976) Retrieved January 15, 2006 from <**www.ohchr.org/english/law/pdf/ccpr.pdf**>

York, G. (1990). *The Dispossessed: Life and Death in Native Canada*. Toronto: Little, Brown and Company.

8

Building Governance Capacity: The Case of Potable Water in First Nations Communities

John Graham and Evlyn Fortier

Introduction

There is a near consensus among development experts, both in this country and abroad, that governance is a critical component in improving individual and community well-being.[1] Not surprisingly, a growing number of organizations in Canada focus on building governance capacity of Aboriginal communities as a critical element of their mandate. Some of these organizations are run by Aboriginal people. One of the newest is the recently constituted National Centre for First Nation Governance, which has a broad mission for stimulating improvements in Aboriginal governance. And there are many others—from training organizations to educational institutions to special purpose bodies like the National Aboriginal Health Organization.

Furthermore, many federal and provincial government departments would claim to be in the capacity-development business, with Indian and Northern Affairs Canada as one of the most important players. Its capacity mandate is wide and includes implementing claims and self-government agreements; assisting First Nations in administering certain sections of the *Indian Act*; improving financial management; and assisting communities and governments in the northern territories.

But despite the importance of governance and the prevalence of governance capacity building, there appears to be much confusion about what the term capacity building encompasses; what approaches are effective and in what circumstances; what are important preconditions for success; and what constraints exist for organizations funding capacity building approaches.

The purpose of this paper is to help fill this knowledge gap. In the following, we present a model for capacity development that outlines the various approaches, goals, and considerations for strategies to develop capacity. We examine the advantages and disadvantages for each of the possible approaches. To illustrate this model, we apply it to a case study—potable water in First Nations communities. Finally, we conclude with "lessons learned" from the application of this model to the case study.

What Is Capacity Building?

Among the acknowledged leaders in the field of capacity development and building governance capacity is the United Nations Development Program (UNDP). Most recently, the UNDP has implemented a program called Capacity 2015 to build capacity at the local level through partnerships. The object of this program is to realize the Millenium Development Goals. The various initiatives of Capacity 2015 are designed to support processes leading to increased incomes, and link local communities to the global economy.

The UNDP uses this definition for capacity development:

> Capacity is the ability of individuals, organizations and societies to perform functions, solve problems, and set and achieve goals. Capacity Development (CD) entails the sustainable creation, utilization and retention of that capacity, in order to reduce poverty, enhance self-reliance, and improve people's lives.[2]

This definition has considerable merit. It puts the emphasis on ultimate objectives—improving well-being—and contains the notion of sustainability as critical to capacity building. Nonetheless, the very breadth of the definition is challenging in that it could encompass anything from training a single individual to a massive project, such as introducing the rule of law into China, an exercise that one commentator has called "one of the largest social infrastructure projects in the history of mankind."[3]

International Experience

The next question to consider is what has been the experience internationally in building governance capacity. This has been an important priority of many international development agencies, including the World Bank. Every year the World Bank publishes a document called "Governance Matters." In May 2005, their document "Governance Matters IV" looked at governance indicators in 209 countries.[4] The salient conclusions of this paper include the following:

- Wealth is not a precondition of good governance.
- The most important causal relationship is good governance leading to good outcomes.
- Corruption is of critical importance to society's investment climate.
- Relatively rapid improvement in governance is rare but possible.
- The worldwide average of a host of good governance indicators has not improved over the past eight years, despite significant investments from aid agencies.
- "The importance of political commitment from the top has been underplayed …"

These conclusions contain much that is encouraging, but also much that is worrisome. The fact that wealth is not a precondition for good governance is good news, given the need for good governance in countries with poor economic conditions. The causal relationship is actually the other way—that is, good governance leads to improved outcomes in the form of economic and social well-being.

However, the fact that rapid improvement is rare but possible sounds a cautionary note. Furthermore, the fact that the worldwide average of good governance indicators has not improved over the past eight years, despite substantial investments, is discouraging to say the least. And the last bullet points to one reason for the lack of progress—that is, the need for political commitment from the top as a necessary precondition for realizing progress in improving governance.

The conclusions of this World Bank report are significant for the case study that follows.

Developing a Capacity Building Plan

The following model is adapted from a similar analytical tool developed by the UNDP:

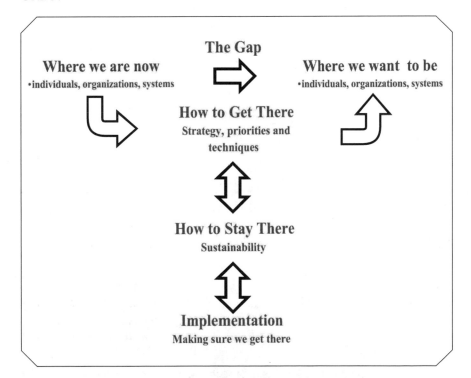

Several aspects of this model deserve further elaboration. One of its critical elements is the gap analysis between "where we are now" and "where we want to be." This paper will not address various approaches for undertaking this gap analysis. Suffice it to say that this is a complex undertaking meriting a paper in its own right. That said, the Institute has developed several tools for effecting such an analysis and these tools are built on good governance principles.[5]

The sustainability part of the model is also very important. Sustainability will figure prominently in the case study featured in the latter part of this paper.

Finally, the gap analysis situates the issue as a matter involving individuals, organizations, or systems. This tripartite view of building capacity allows analysis of the three approaches, the strategies and techniques for each, and their advantages and disadvantages. And it is to this that we now turn.

Individuals

A common approach to capacity building focuses on individuals. That is, the critical issue from this perspective is developing the skills, knowledge, and values of individual people, and giving them the tools to do their jobs. Indeed, for many, capacity development boils down simply to training.

Even from within the confines of individual approaches to capacity building there is a richer array of approaches than just training. For example, establishing a professional association is a common strategy among a wide range of public service disciplines. For First Nations, there are more and more professional associations being set up, such as associations of financial officers, economic development officers, and water operators. Other strategies include establishing certification requirements, changing incentives such as pay and recognition, and providing better tools such as computers.

Using the approach of focusing on individuals is popular with funders. There are advantages such as low cost, quick and measurable results, low political risk, and well-defined roles for funders. However, the disadvantages are also compelling. Governance capacity issues are seldom confined to individuals, and sustainability is an issue when using these strategies. In short, despite the fact that this approach involves low risk, it also involves low reward.

Organizational

A second approach to capacity building concentrates on the organization. According to the rationale for this approach, improvement in the organization is required because it lacks a clear mission, has poor morale, lacks policies, has poorly defined roles and so on. In the case used as an example below, the organization could be the First Nations public works function, including the Chief and Council, and staff.

Strategies and techniques for this approach are well known. One strategy uses an "outsider" to conduct a policy or program review or study. Another involves leadership change. Certification for the organization is a third technique, which is relevant for First Nations issues. For example, the Membertou First Nation has an ISO certification and the Institute on Governance has advocated such a system for improving financial management.[6] Furthermore, the *First Nations Fiscal and Statistical Management Act* sets up a First Nations-run certification scheme for First Nations interested in property tax and borrowing, using the income stream from property taxes as collateral. Other strategies for the organizational approach involve organizational development workshops, and twinning with an outside organization.

There are a number of advantages to focusing on the organization. Building capacity at the organizational level is more likely to address underlying governance issues. There are potentially high payoffs to such an approach. Finally, if the organization is improved, this can provide incentives for individual skill building. For example, an ISO certification will require using certified individuals for certain functions in order to maintain certification. This provides an ongoing incentive for individual capacity building.

However, the disadvantages need to be considered. Focusing on the organization can involve higher costs and longer timetables. There is uncertainty about how long these exercises will take, and their status when they end. Furthermore, an organizational approach is riskier in that it might imply change to the existing power structures. And sustainability is an issue. Leadership change, for example, can set the organization backward dramatically.

Finally, the funders' role becomes more problematic because projects focusing on the organization start to change power relationships and this presents problems for public servants or NGO officials wary of getting involved in community or organizational politics.

System-wide

The last category involves a system-wide approach. In this case, the focus is on relationships among organizations in a system. So, for example, in a First Nations context, we would examine the set of relationships the First Nation would have with other governments—federal, provincial, municipal—and with other organizations such as Tribal Councils, service organizations, etc.

The issues prompting a system-wide approach could include poor legal or regulatory systems, inadequate system resources, poor relationships among players, and so on. To tackle these issues, capacity-building strategies might implement new or enhanced regulatory systems, new coordinating machinery and agreements, or dispute resolution systems. The Social Union Framework Agreement (SUFA)[7] is an example of new coordinating machinery and agreements struck between the federal and provincial/territorial governments. Another strategy might employ adding more resources to the system, and there have been many examples of this technique. A final technique uses system-wide review and advocacy. A Royal Commission, such as the Romanow Commission, is an example of such an approach.

There are potential benefits, but also potential costs, to a focus on a governance system. One advantage is that this is the only sustainable strategy, assuming a gap analysis identifying system-wide problems is correct. There are also high potential payoffs in the long term. Furthermore, a system-wide approach can provide incentives for organizational and individual approaches. For example, the Navajo in the United States, with a population of 140,000 on a reservation the size of West Virginia, embarked on an eight-year plan to build their own Environmental Protection Agency (EPA) with the help of the US Environmental Protection Agency. This plan involves a system-wide focus that stimulates incentives for tribal organizations to conform to environmental regulations and individuals to become properly qualified to perform certain functions.

However, there is an important precondition in that a system-wide approach requires a high degree of political commitment from all of the critical players involved. The disadvantages include high cost, and the fact that a system-wide approach is time consuming and high risk. Money alone may not solve the problems, and there is an increasingly uncertain role for funders.

In sum, system-wide approaches involve potentially substantive changes in power relationships and long-term commitments with uncertain outcomes. For these reasons, they tend not to be favoured by funders.

Considerations—A Look Back at the World Bank Findings

The above analysis of the three approaches to capacity building helps illuminate the World Bank's gloomy findings. One of these was that rapid change is rare, and we can see why. System-wide changes—those with the biggest impact and potentially the most sustainable results—are premised on political commitment and moreover take considerable time. Furthermore, the long time frames and uncertain results present significant problems for funding agencies. Demonstrating results, especially in the short term, is not likely possible.

An example of a system-wide approach illustrates the dilemmas involved. Hernando de Soto, the Peruvian economist, notes that developing countries are much richer than we give them credit for, but they suffer from what he calls "dead capital" because of the lack of a land registry system. Thus, in these developing countries, financial institutions have no way of taking property as collateral to finance small business loans, because of the lack of a registry. But small business loans are the most important source of capital for small businesses. Thus putting in place a land registry system in a country like Egypt can be crucial for economic development by leveraging the country's considerable housing capital. Nonetheless it's an undertaking that can take decades. Just imagine the number of land disputes involving such matters as ownership and land boundaries in a city as complicated as Cairo!

This and other examples of system-wide changes are important reminders that too often, citizens of first world countries take complex governance systems for granted. These systems function below the radar screen unless something drastic goes wrong, as in the case of Walkerton, Ontario. However, when they are not in place, a country or society faces formidable challenges to build them.

The following case study will explore this theme in more depth.

Case Study—Safe Water in First Nation Communities

The model developed in the previous section can be applied to a pressing problem—safe drinking water on First Nations reserves. A large number of First Nations reserves have poor quality drinking water, a fact that is now well understood. In March 2006, over 10% of First Nations communities (79 of the 755 community water systems identified by the Department of Indian and Northern Affairs on reserves across Canada) faced boil water advisories. Furthermore, 193 water systems were identified as high risk, 312 as medium risk and 250 as low risk.[8]

The gap analysis for this situation reveals problems at all three levels.

- **Individual**: many water operators on reserves are uncertified; some leaders lack knowledge and commitment
- **Organizational**: some water plants on reserves are not well maintained; water systems suffer from early rust-out; community budgeting issues sometimes restrict the ability to address problems
- **System-wide**: there are unclear standards for water quality on reserves; inspections are insufficient; enforcement of standards is limited; resources are insufficient; there are few communities with user fees despite the requirement for such in agreements with INAC. Such fees might help curb consumption and provide a source of additional funding for maintenance; and roles of the key players are poorly defined.

The story of water problems at the Kashechewan reserve brought the issue of unsafe water in First Nations communities to national prominence late in 2005, but the issue has had a long history. Following the outbreaks of water-borne illnesses at Walkerton in 2000 and North Battleford in 2001, the federal government announced a seven-point strategy with elements aimed at individuals (primarily training and certification of operators); organizations (more funds and other approaches to encourage better maintenance); and some system-wide deficiencies (e.g., attempts to introduce standards and enforcement measures).

In March of 2006, the new Conservative government announced a five-point plan to tackle water issues on reserves, a plan that in many ways repackaged the former government's seven-point strategy but with one significant difference: it made a commitment for a legislated regulatory system.

It is worth examining the elements of the seven-point strategy ("Strategy 7") and five-point plan ("Plan 5") in more detail.

Individual Approaches

One important part of both Strategy 7 and Plan 5 is aimed at water operators. That is, they both include a program to train and certify operators. The program has provided circuit rider training in all areas of Canada, training that originated in Ontario with the Ontario First Nations Technical Services Corporation. Efforts have also been directed at educational materials for the Chiefs, Councils, and members. Public education efforts have also begun in certain regions.

The most significant issue for this approach involves problems around certification. The original objective was to have 100% of operators certified by 2006. This objective has been restated by the current government.

However, the 100% certification target is unattainable, assuming that the approach is to recruit and train members of First Nation communities. Why is this so? The answer relates to the stringent education and experience requirements, along with certification exams. Take Ontario as an example. Like most jurisdictions in North America, Ontario follows the ABC standard of water-operator certification, which involves four levels or classes: water treatment plants, water distribution, waste water treatment and waste water distribution. In Ontario there were 134 First Nations operated plants in 2004—71 were Class I, 54 were Class II, and 7 were Class III. Certification requirements for these three classes of plants are as follows:

- Class I: Grade 12; 1 year experience; 70% on exam

- Class II: Grade 12; 3 years experience; 70% on exam; must have Class I licence

- Class III: Grade 12 plus 2 years of additional education; 4 years experience (at least 2 years as operator in charge); must have a Class II licence

For many communities the educational requirements represent a major hurdle. Furthermore, the time necessary to become certified, especially for the Class II and III plants, is so long that replacing a certified operator who retires or leaves with another community member who is certified to the appropriate level is not practical. Therefore, the whole notion of having trained First Nations operators, employed by their communities, is very much in question. Kashechewan provides definite proof of the weakness of this strategy.

Fortunately, the new Conservative government's five-point plan recognizes the problem, and proposes another approach based on the use of outside suppliers with certified operators to oversee First Nations plants in situations where the First Nation cannot provide its own certified operators.

In conclusion, the approach to training and certifying operators, in each community, manifests many of the advantages and disadvantages predicted by the UNDP-based capacity building model. This approach has proven popular with both funding agencies and with First Nations and their organizations (tribal councils and technical organizations). Few would argue against more training and better qualified operators.

Nonetheless the disadvantages of pursuing this route outside the ambit of more systemic changes—such as the introduction of a regulatory system that would make the certification of operators legally mandatory—are equally glaring. Thus it has taken over three years to realize that relying on First Nation members to be trained and certified will not meet the goal of having certified operators in every community in a sustainable manner. Furthermore, even with certified operators in place, other critical elements are required to match the situation off-reserve: dedicated budgets and sufficient funding for operations and maintenance; political leaders aware of and committed to their responsibilities; legally enforceable standards; sufficient information available to the public to track performance; and inspections with appropriate penalties.

It is to some of these elements that we now turn.

Organizational

Both Strategy 7 and Plan 5 have also focused on a number of organizational approaches. For example Strategy 7 included more funding for maintenance and, in some regions, stringent audit requirements. It also included better commissioning of plants and increased testing and inspection. Plants must undergo evaluations by third parties every three years, and funding for plants not meeting standards is a number one priority. In addition to these measures the new government's Plan 5 calls for specific remedial plans for First Nations communities with serious water issues.

Once again, the predictions of the UNDP-based model appear to be borne out. Without more systemic reforms, the appropriate incentives are not in place to realize significant, sustainable change. For example, those First Nations which do the worst job of running their plants become the highest priority recipients for new funding. Furthermore, the more heavy-handed federal officials become in insisting that new funding for water-related initiatives be spent effectively by First Nations—through increased audits and inspections, for example—the more strained the relationship becomes between the partners in this joint endeavour to ensure safe water for First Nation communities.

So organizational capacity building efforts, even when combined with activities aimed at key individuals like water operators, are not sufficient to deal with the safe water problems on-reserve. More systemic approaches—approaches that alter the incentives for both First Nations and their federal counterparts—are required.

System-wide

In relation to system changes, Strategy 7 did mention the introduction of standards, but stated this in very tepid terms. For example, it talked about developing a stronger, transparent inspection, reporting and compliance regime, and establishing national standards and protocols. But until the Kashechewan crisis, the federal government had demonstrated little appetite for a legislative approach for a variety of reasons—not the least of which, no doubt, is the political challenge of introducing legislative change affecting all First Nations across Canada. When the Kashechewan situation became well known, the Martin government announced their intentions to introduce legislated federal standards. And the new government, as noted above, has continued this commitment.

But the World Bank experience, buttressed by other attempts at large-scale systemic change, suggests that any attempt to introduce such a regulatory system will be a long, arduous process. In the remainder of this section we canvass the reasons why this will indeed be the case.

What's Involved in the Regulation of Water?

To begin, the principle elements of a regulatory system for water quality would include the following:

- Legislative base
- Standards—source protection; water quality; system type; plant commissioning and certification; operators; maintenance; lab certification; testing; public disclosure; inspections; general standard of care
- Arms-length regulatory bodies (likely two—one for public health, a second with an environmental focus), inspection powers, enforcement options, and penalties
- Emergency procedures
- Public education

Several points require elaboration. First, regulation of water is a complicated business, highly scientific in nature, and one where there are multiple standards. Furthermore, water acts and their accompanying regulations are hundreds of pages in length, and call for some judgment in even identifying what standards exist.

But regulation is also very much an art form. The issue comes down to managing risk and allocating scarce resources to keep the risk of something going wrong at acceptable levels. This requires considerable experience and years of practice. And it necessitates identifying and working with allies.

Finally, regulation can become politically charged. No one likes being regulated, especially if the reporting burden is high, and the possibility of fines, or even jail terms is real.

Why Legislation?

Legislation is the preferred base for such a system for a variety of reasons:

- Legislation forces needed clarity and transparency into the murkiness of unclear roles and accountabilities that characterize the current situation.

- Legislation is more likely to encourage sustainability. Courts do not look kindly on governments which establish regulatory regimes and then do not manage or resource them adequately.

- Legislation provides an easy out for politicians to deal with the politics of regulatory regimes. Faced with pressures to "let up," politicians have a ready response: "I have no choice but to enforce the law."

- Inspection and enforcement powers can be draconian, and regulators need the certainty and force of legislation to do their jobs properly. For example, a provincial officer in Ontario has the authority to conduct an inspection without a warrant, or enter without a warrant any place that he or she reasonably believes contains part of a drinking water system. Along with broad powers of entry, they also have the power to take and remove documents, make inquiries, make excavations, and require tests to be performed. A provincial officer can also issue a compliance order requiring a person to repair, maintain, or operate a drinking-water system, water testing equipment or a laboratory in such a manner and with such equipment as may be specified in the order, among other things.

- Penalties are also significant. Again, using Ontario as an example, enforcement of water quality can lead to convictions involving five years in prison and $6 million in fines. These penalties must have a legislative base.

- A well-designed regulatory regime, as opposed to the contractual approach that has been utilized, would have a much wider variety of responses to water problems, responses varying from traditional enforcement techniques to negotiation, education and other voluntary approaches.

What Should Be the Scope of the Legislation?

Should the government establish a combined regulatory system for water and waste water? The Sustainable Development Commissioner recommended a regulatory system for water only,[9] but the experiences of North Battleford and Kashechewan suggest that any initiative should encompass waste water as well. Furthermore, there are practical reasons for a combined system because the same inspectors are involved. That said, federal and provincial/territorial leaders have already embarked on a Canada–wide exercise to harmonize waste water treatment standards. Thus, coordination is required between this exercise and any attempt to develop a safe water regime for First Nations.

Which Standards Should Be Adopted—Federal or Provincial?

Another issue involves using provincial versus federal standards. There are strong reasons to use provincial standards. The provinces already have education and certification systems based on provincial standards for operator training and certification. Furthermore, the construction industry will be familiar with these provincial standards. However, some provinces and territories do not yet have regulatory systems for water—for example, New Brunswick, Newfoundland and Labrador, and the Yukon. So federal standards or other provincial standards will be necessary for these jurisdictions.

What Should Be the Role of the Federal Partners—INAC, Health Canada and Environment Canada?

The role of federal departments in regulation of water is an issue. Federal departments, such as INAC, Health Canada and Environment Canada, should not be regulators. In some instances, they may actually be the regulatees. Do federal departments provide enough funds? Are they doing a good job when they approve plant designs, and so on? Regulators should pose these and other questions to the federal departments.

The issue of adequate funding for First Nations will be a major obstacle to overcome. It will not be tenable for First Nations leaders to assume the same liabilities as their non-Aboriginal counterparts in local governments across Canada, and yet not have some reasonable guarantee of adequate funding. This will be, indeed, a tough nut to crack.

Who Should Be the Regulatory Authority?

There are three options: a new federal authority, existing provincial authorities or some newly established First Nations authority. The obvious answer is to build on the provincial experience and have provincial authorities acting as agents of the federal government. Furthermore, within each provincial regulatory authority, there could be units specifically established for First Nations. All of this would take considerable negotiation, involving First Nations and the other two levels of government in each province and territory. And the issues will not be easy, funding being a key obstacle to overcome. Also, there is still the question of what to do in provinces without existing regulatory regimes.

How to Bridge this New Regime to Self-government?

Implementing regulatory systems for potable water involve questions about the roles of the different levels of government, but for First Nations, the issue is also about building an important bridge to self-government. An ideal situation, as noted above, would involve a negotiated agreement with each province to establish a special inspection and enforcement unit to be staffed primarily by personnel recruited from First Nations. This would be more acceptable to First Nations communities in administering what is essentially a provincial regime. Also, at some point in the future, the First Nation unit could become part of some First Nation government and would bring with it the experience, skills and contacts that would otherwise take years to build.

What about Existing Self-government Agreements?

Unfortunately, existing self-government agreements, such as those involving Yukon, Cree-Naskapi and Nisga'a First Nations and the *First Nations Lands Management Act*, have not addressed the issue of potable water well.[10] Often, these agreements provide First Nations with the jurisdiction to deal with potable water but do not ensure that they have a fully functioning regulatory regime. Furthermore, the large majority of agreements do not provide an appropriate governmental structure for an effective regulatory system for potable water. In essence the self-governing entities would both operate water systems and regulate themselves. These agreements need to be reviewed, and future agreements should be developed with greater attention to the regulatory function.

What about Powers and Penalties?

Inspection powers and penalties comprise yet another area of potential concern. Post Walkerton, provincial penalties have stiffened considerably, and some adjustments may be necessary in the First Nations context. Furthermore, there may ways to develop sanctions more in keeping with First Nations culture than simply reverting to fines and jail terms.

What Should Happen to Existing Plants that Don't Meet Standards?

Another issue involves the relationship of regulation to plant conditions and operators. Many plants are not up to standard at present, and will require significant investments to upgrade them. These plants might require a transition stage.

Looking toward the future, there is an additional dilemma facing federal funders, assuming the federal legislation adopts provincial standards, and it is this: the regulation of water is a dynamic area of public policy with ever-evolving regulatory standards. To meet new standards will likely cost money. And yet, both federal and First Nations governments would not be in control of the development or adoption of these standards. This is not a position in which governments like to find themselves.

What about Other Regulatory Voids Affecting First Nations Communities?

Any solution for setting up a regulatory system for clean potable water on reserves could provide some routes to deal with other environmental and health-related voids.[11] These are considerable:

- Environmental protection relating to water and land (solid waste recycling, contaminated sites, hazardous waste, nutrients, pesticides)

- Resource management (land use, water use, forestry, fish, wildlife, agriculture, minerals, aggregates)
- Environmental assessment
- Health, safety, and transportation (hazardous substances, fire safety, spill responses, dangerous goods)

To avoid dealing with these voids implies health and environmental conditions on reserves well below those found in other Canadian communities. Furthermore, the road to self-government will be a long, rocky one. It is asking a lot for new self-governing entities to address the enormity of the challenges these voids present.

Conclusions

In this paper, we have examined a model that outlines three possible strategies for building governance capacity: individual, organizational and system-wide. We have argued that there is a program bias among funders of capacity building activities towards individual strategies. Organizational and system-wide strategies tend to be costly, risky, longer-term, and dependent on political commitments. Also, the roles of funding agencies are more uncertain in these latter approaches.

It is clear from the potable water case study we presented that a reliance on individual or even organizational strategies will not suffice to deal adequately with the problems facing First Nations in providing this basic necessity to their citizens. Furthermore, communities in the greatest need of reform for their water systems are often the least likely to be equipped to lead such reforms.

So putting in place a regulatory system akin to that found in non-Aboriginal communities across Canada is clearly the way to proceed. But having said this, the difficulties of addressing the array of issues in implementing such a systemic change should not be underestimated. Indeed, this may well be a five-to-ten-year exercise, involving significant changes to existing incentives. Readers may recall television clips of the Chief of the Kashechewan First Nation returning to a hero's welcome to his community after negotiating a deal with Ottawa for significant housing and other upgrades to his community. Had the Chief been a mayor of an adjacent non-Aboriginal community, rather than being seen as a hero, he and his fellow councillors would have been subject to significant fines and even jail terms for allowing E.coli into their community's drinking water.

With so much at stake, and with the wide range of difficult issues to address, the question becomes whether there will be significant political will on the part of all parties—First Nation, federal, and provincial/territorial—to stay the course. For the sake of some of Canada's poorest communities and most vulnerable citizens, let's hope the answer is yes.

Endnotes

1 For a review of some of the evidence for this statement, see John Graham, Bruce Amos and Tim Plumptre. "Governance Principles for Protected Areas in the 21st Century." June 2003. <**www.iog.ca/publications/PA_governance.pdf**>

2 <**www.capacity.undp.org**>

3 Dr. Zhenim Wang. "Developing the Rule of Law in China." *Harvard Asia Quarterly*. Autumn 2000. p. 7.

4 <**www.worldbank.org/wbi/governance/pubs/govmatters4.html**>

5 See, for example, John Graham and Jake Wilson. "Towards Sound Government-to-Government Relationships with First Nations." Policy Brief No. 21, October 2004. <**www.iog.ca/publications/fn_govtogov_rel.pdf**> and John Graham. "Managing the Relationship of First Nation Political Leaders and Their Staff." March 30, 2006. 40–42. <**www.iog.ca/publications/2006_ fnleader_staff_rel.pdf**>

6 See John Graham. "Getting the Incentives Right: Improving Financial Management of Canada's First Nations." Policy Brief No. 8, May 2000. <**www.iog.ca/publications/policybrief8.pdf**>

7 <**www.unionsociale.ca/news/020499_e.html**>

8 <**www.ainc-inac.gc.ca/nr/prs/j-a2006/2-02757_e.html**>

9 Report of the Commissioner of the Environment and Sustainable Development, 2005 Report. "Drinking Water in First Nation Communities." <**www.oag-bvg.gc.ca/domino/reports.nsf/ html/c20050905ce.html**>

10 See John Graham. "Rethinking Self-Government Agreements: The Case of Potable Water." Policy Brief No. 12, November 2001. <**www.iog.ca/publication/policybrief12.pdf**>

11 The reason for such voids results from section 91.24 of the Constitution Act 1867 where the federal government has exclusive legislative authority for "Indians and lands reserved for Indians." Section 88 of the *Indian Act* only provides for provincial laws of general application to apply to "Indians" but not "lands reserved for Indians."

9

A Glass Half Empty: Drinking Water in First Nations Communities

Sarah N. Morales[1]

Introduction

Water is an essential part of life, especially for First Nations citizens as it contributes not only to their physical survival but their cultural survival as well. Virtually all rights of Aboriginal peoples depend on a viable and sufficient quantity and quality of water. For example, water is essential to the Aboriginal rights to fish, hunt, and trap. Water is also essential as a means of transportation for many Aboriginal people. In fact, the absolute necessity of water to the lives of Aboriginal people has made it a significant part of their spiritual and cultural existence as well. It is for these main reasons that many Aboriginal leaders advocate the recognition of an Aboriginal right to govern this resource within their traditional territories.

All communities rely on sources of potable water for drinking and household use. Native communities that manage their own water systems may face specific problems, as alternative sources of potable water may not be available. The production and delivery of potable water is often taken for granted until problems occur, sometimes with tragic consequences. After incidents in Walkerton, Ontario, in 2000, North Battleford, Saskatchewan, in 2001, and more recently in the First Nations community of Kashechewan, Ontario, in 2005, improving the safety of drinking water has become a priority in Canada, especially in First Nation communities.[2] Providing safe drinking water involves complex technical, human, financial, and regulatory factors. In First Nations communities, the relationship between the federal government and First Nations, and the unique situation of each First Nation add to this complexity.

Federal programs and funding related to drinking water on reserves are based on government policy adopted in the 1960s and 1970s, and parliamentary appropriations. The objective of the government policy is to ensure that people living on-reserve attain a comparable level of health and have access to water facilities comparable to those of other Canadians living in communities of similar size and location. However, these very government policies often prevent this objective from being attained. This is mainly due to the fact that these policies lack input from Aboriginal communities and fail to take into consideration the unique circumstances and issues that these communities face. Until a regulatory regime which takes Aboriginal concerns and values into consideration is in place, INAC and Health Canada cannot ensure that First Nations people living on-reserve have access to safe drinking water.

This paper first explores the current federal policy adopted by government to deal with the issue of safe drinking water in First Nations communities, and the insufficiencies of this policy. Secondly, it suggests two working approaches to water quality in these communities. The first is the creation of a co-management regime between the federal government and First Nations governments. The second is a recognition of an Aboriginal right to govern the water resources within their traditional territory.[3]

Unique Susceptibility of First Nations Communities and Their Members to Pollutants

The economic condition and health status of Aboriginal peoples are among the lowest of any ethnic or minority group in Canada. Poverty, poor health, and more limited access to health care all make Aboriginal Canadians more susceptible to adverse impacts from pollution.[4] Although fiduciary duties, treaties, and the *Indian Act* obligate the federal government to provide health-related services to First Nations, shamefully, government departments responsible for these services have a history of being grossly under-funded and under-staffed.

Traditional, cultural, and subsistence uses of, and strong dependencies on, natural resources such as water make First Nations especially susceptible to adverse health affects from pollution. In many cases, First Nations "have greater exposure risks than the general population as a result of their dietary practices and unique cultures that embrace the environment."[5] Hunting, gathering, and fishing are necessary not only for survival, but also for maintaining the cultural, social, spiritual, and economic aspects of Aboriginal communities. Frequently, the right to engage in gathering, hunting, and fishing is legally protected by treaty. First Nations and their members also use water, plants, and animals in religious, traditional, and cultural ceremonies and practices. When pollutants contaminate the air, water, soil, plants, and animals, these pollutants will likely accumulate in the people through consumption, ingestion, contact and inhalation.[6]

A recent example of the tragedy that can occur when pollutants go unchecked occured in the Aboriginal community of Kashechewan. Kashechewan's water treatment plant, funded in 1995 by Indian and Northern Affairs Canada (INAC), was designed by out-of-town consultants. It was placed downstream from an existing sewage lagoon. This essentially means that contaminants flow past the intake pipe that feeds raw water into the complex system to be treated for drinking. In 2004, Indian Affairs spent $500,000 for upgrades, but did not move the intake pipe.[7] Furthermore, Band leaders say that they never received proper training, or enough funding to run the plant, which requires 24-hour maintenance.[8] In late October 2005, the evacuation of more than 1,000 community members began as the situation descended into crisis when federal officials warned of high *E. coli* levels in tap water. Almost all of these residents were evacuated due to scabies, impetigo and other health-related problems from *E. coli*-laced water.

Unfortunately, the threat of such contamination is not only limited to the health of Aboriginal communities, but extends also to the health and well-being of future generations. Several studies have shown that children are particularly susceptible to the effects of pollution. For example, industry has devastated the traditional lifestyle of the Mohawk community on the Akwesasne reservation. Core samples of the St. Lawrence River bottom have found over 6,000 ppm of polychlorinated biphenyls ("PCBs").[9] However, while the PCB concentrations in the breast milk of Mohawk women decreased over time, their infants' urine PCB levels were ten times higher than that of their mothers.[10]

Situations such as these indicate that oftentimes it is the people who are most at risk who should be entitled to determine the relevant environmental standards that will govern their resources. However, as the next section will demonstrate, Aboriginal peoples have little decision-making authority under the current federal policy governing drinking water quality on reserve lands.

Current Jurisdictional Responsibilities and Policy Over Water Quality

It is current government policy that the management of potable drinking water and waste water on First Nation reserves, from source to tap, is a shared responsibility between First Nations and the federal government. First Nations Band councils, INAC (advised by Environment Canada), and Health Canada provide programs and services that are meant to ensure safe, clean, and secure water on reserves.

Indian and Northern Affairs Canada (INAC) has the primary authority for fulfilling the federal government's constitutional, treaty, political, and legal responsibilities for First Nations. Since the early 1960s, the department has provided support to assist individuals living on-reserve in accessing basic infrastructure services, i.e. water, waste water treatment, roads, bridges, schools etc.[11] In addition, the department is authorized to provide funding assistance to operate and maintain these assets. INAC's primary role today is satisfied through the provision of funding and advisory activities.[12]

INAC funding for infrastructure services is provided through a variety of funding arrangements. These funding arrangements include terms and conditions, and reporting requirements that INAC uses to ensure that First Nations meet program requirements. For example, subject to approval, based in part upon a review of the First Nation's financial management track record, and the availability of funds, finances are provided to reserve communities for capital construction and upgrading, operation and maintenance, and water and waste water plants through INAC's Capital Facilities and Maintenance Program. However, INAC's funding to subsidize the operation and maintenance of water treatment and distribution systems is in accordance with an established formula. The remaining funding is to be provided locally from user fees or other revenue sources.[13] INAC also provides funding to First Nations to share services, such as water, with neighboring municipalities through municipal-type agreements when this is a cost-effective and practical solution.

Health Canada's general mandate regarding the protection of public health is found in the *Department of Health Act*,[14] 1996. This legislation delineates the health matters in which the Minister may act, while respecting provincial jurisdiction. These matters include, but are not limited to, investigations and research into public health, monitoring of diseases, providing public-health information, establishing safety standards for consumer products, and co-operating with provincial authorities to coordinate efforts to preserve and improve public health.[15]

Health Canada, in collaboration with INAC, is responsible for ensuring safe drinking water in First Nation communities south of 60°. As part of the Environmental Health Program, and through the Drinking Water Safety Program, Health Canada is responsible for working with First Nations to monitor drinking water quality in distribution systems with five or more connections and cisterns in First Nation communities. Water quality sampling, testing, and interpretations are to be done according to the *Guidelines for Canadian Drinking Water Quality*, Sixth Edition, Health Canada.

Environment Canada's main responsibility in regards to safe drinking water in First Nations communities is with respect to waste water management. Environment Canada provides advice and technical expertise to INAC on assessments under the *Canadian Environmental Assessment Act*, and on requirements related to the *Canadian Environmental Protection Act, 1999*, and the *Fisheries Act*. Environment Canada develops standards, guidelines and/or protocols for waste water systems on federal and Aboriginal lands, including effluent limits.

INAC policy states that on-reserve waste water treatment systems are to be designed and operated in such a way that effluent quality meets the requirements of the latest edition of the *Guidelines for Effluent Quality and Waste water Treatment at Federal Establishments*, established by Environment Canada, and other applicable provincial/territorial requirements, if these are stricter.[16] It is important to note that First Nations values and ideas are not taken into consideration under this current government policy.

Under current government policy, First Nations are responsible for ensuring that water and waste water systems are planned, designed, constructed, and maintained and operated according to funding agreement conditions.[17] First Nations are legally required to comply with all program and financial terms and conditions in their funding agreements. However, there is very little room for First Nations to vary the structure of these agreements to meet local needs and concerns.

All proposed capital projects for water and waste water systems, funded by INAC, must comply with the terms and conditions of the funding agreement under the Capital Facilities and Maintenance Program. For all INAC-funded capital projects, First Nations are responsible for:

- Project identification;
- Feasibility (engineering) studies;
- Environmental assessments;
- Project design;
- Project construction;
- Plant classification; and
- Commissioning.[18]

First Nations are required to:

- Follow INAC's tendering policy;
- Conduct regular site inspections;
- Provide construction and financial progress reports;
- Submit a project completion report;
- Secure "as build" drawings for future reference; and
- Develop site-specific maintenance management plans.[19]

First Nations require INAC approvals for all capital project components from the feasibility stage to the commissioning stage as per INAC policy.

Under current government policy, First Nations must follow INACs and Health Canada's monitoring and inspection regimes. All sampling and testing procedures performed during monitoring activities must be carried out as defined in the monitoring and inspection regime, including the use of accredited laboratories. If a First Nation does not follow this regime, and depending on the level of risk to health, gradual compliance assurance will be started by INAC.[20] This will include things such as written warnings; holdbacks from "non-essential" funding; and ultimately, third-party management.

INAC provides a funding subsidy to First Nations for the operations and maintenance (O&M) of water and waste water facilities on reserves. First Nations Chief and Council are responsible for assuming partial financial responsibility for the remaining funding through user fees and/or other revenue sources. However, funding for O&M must be used for the purposes described in the funding agreements, and First Nations are responsible for demonstrating that these funds were spent on INAC's intended purposes, regardless of what the First Nation views to be an intended purpose.

As demonstrated by this policy model, currently First Nations have very little flexibility in creating standards or regulations to ensure high water quality in their communities. Under section 81(1) of the *Indian Act*,[21] a Band council is given the power to make by-laws for a number of different purposes. The provision of section 81(1) which could give a Band council jurisdiction over water quality management is section 81(1)(l)—the construction and regulation of the use of public wells, cisterns, reservoirs, and other water supplies.

However, bylaws can be disallowed by the Minister of Indian Affairs and Northern Development. Once passed, a bylaw must be forwarded to the Minister, and it automatically comes into force after forty days unless it is disallowed [s. 82(2)]. A further problem, discussed below, is that the by laws are limited in their geographic scope. In other words, by laws only apply on the reserve. Even if a water body or fishery is near the reserve and affects a Band's on-reserve water quality, the bylaw-making power is strictly confined to the physical boundaries of the reserve. Another limitation is that Band Councils do not have the power to make bylaws in relation to "navigable" rivers, even if a river is physically on the reserve.

Another limitation is that the bylaw-making power of Band councils is largely restricted to regulatory and administrative matters. This restriction may prevent the adoption of a proper water management scheme on reserve lands. For example, it is doubtful whether a Band bylaw which attempted to say that all waters are in the control of a Band would be valid. This would be seen as an illegal expropriation.

As a result, drinking water quality on reserves is governed by current federal policy. However, currently there is no regulatory regime in place to deal with this resource. Therefore, funding arrangements seem to play a large role in dictating water quality standards and requirements. As the next section will demonstrate, this policy model creates significant issues in the provision of safe drinking water on reserves.

Issues with the Current Policy Model

Regulatory Gap for Drinking Water on Reserves

In its recent report, the Commissioner of the Environment and Sustainable Development found that INAC, Health Canada, and First Nations do not operate under a regulatory regime as most provinces do. There is no effective legislative base for regulating potable water on reserves. The operative federal standards, set out in the Guidelines for Canadian Drinking Water Quality, are just that—guidelines with no legislative teeth. Instead, INAC and Health Canada use funding arrangements with First Nations, and administrative documents as the means to set and enforce requirements for water quality and safety.

INAC attempts to fill this "regulatory gap" by referring to provincial legislation and regulation in its policies and administrative guidelines, and in funding arrangements with First Nations. However, the Report of the Commissioner of the Environment and Sustainable Development ("the Report") found that important elements covered in most provincial regulatory regimes are missing from the guidelines and funding arrangements.[22] These include the approval and licensing of water treatment plants, ongoing monitoring, public reporting requirements, and compliance and enforcements mechanisms. In practice, this means, for example, that where a province requires water treatment plants to be licensed or certified, the plants located in First Nations communities face no such regulation from the provinces.

The Report also found that INAC administrative guidelines are not consistently implemented.[23] These guidelines require, among other things, that new water systems meet provincial regulations, except where they are less stringent than those of the federal government. Department officials informed the Commissioner of the Environment and Sustainable Development that they do not feel obliged to comply fully with or enforce provincial regulations.[24] They also stated that they do not have the human resources and capacity that the provinces have to support and enforce them.[25]

INAC is drafting new administrative guidelines for drinking water systems in First Nations communities as a component of the First Nations Water Management Strategy. However, the Commissioner of the Environment and Sustainable Development reviewed the document, and found that it falls short of providing an effective regulatory regime because the guidelines apply only to INAC officials.[26] Furthermore, the Report found that it will not be enforceable through legislation or regulations, and how it will apply to First Nations remains unclear.[27]

Most frequently, INAC relies on funding arrangements with First Nations to define drinking water requirements on reserve lands. However, the language in the arrangements is general and does not specifically refer to water systems.[28] In 2001, in a submission to the Walkerton Inquiry, the Chiefs of Ontario stated: "First Nations, their consultants, and federal officials are left to discern the applicable standards from vague and conflicting language in funding conditions, guidelines and manuals."[29] Unfortunately, even with the First Nations Water Management Strategy, this situation has not changed significantly.

Funding arrangements between INAC and First Nations require First Nations to adhere to all applicable codes and standards, and preserve health and safety. However, it is not clear whether and how the First Nations are to incorporate all the elements found in provincial legislation and regulations in the management of their drinking water. The Chiefs of Ontario also commented, in a submission to the Walkerton Inquiry, that "The question of 'which law applies' is inherently uncertain for most activities that take place on reserves because of the judicially undefined scope of Aboriginal rights and the vague and subjective tests which govern the division of powers impacting on 'Indianness.'"[30]

Currently, there is no legislation requiring that drinking water quality and safety in First Nations communities be monitored. More importantly, there is no First Nations–specific legislation on water quality of environmental standards in Canada. It is Health Canada's policy that it has no statutory- or regulatory-based enforcement or inspection powers for water quality on reserves.[31] Therefore, departmental staff members are not legally empowered to ensure that all required tests are carried out. In addition, First Nations are not legally empowered to test their drinking water. Consequently, residents in First Nation communities do not benefit from testing practices comparable to those in non-reserve communities.

Under the Drinking Water Safety Program, Health Canada enters into funding arrangements with most First Nations, or contracts with individuals, to test drinking water as recommended under the *Guidelines for Canadian Drinking Water Quality*. However, under these arrangements, the only consequence for failing to carry out tests is that funds are withheld.[32]

Water Systems Do Not Meet All Applicable Codes and Standards

The Report of the Commissioner of the Environment and Sustainable Development found that INAC has no comprehensive list of codes and standards applicable to the design and construction of water systems.[33] Codes and standards are set out in various documents, funding arrangements, administrative documents, and project briefs. In these documents, the definitions of codes and standards range from the requirement to meet "all applicable codes and standards" to references to either a general or specific list of codes and standards.[34] It is unclear which definitions are applicable and will be applied to a given project.

This issue can have consequences for the quality or safety of drinking water. INAC's 2001 assessment of water systems found many design or construction faults. In fact, these faults explain a portion of the 75% of water systems that were classified as risky.[35] As history has demonstrated, these deficiencies can result in risks to operator safety, failure to achieve the treatment performance, or inability to produce the expected water quantity.

Under the First Nations Water Management Strategy, INAC has committed to ensuring that all water systems on reserves are built to standards. It has developed draft administrative guidelines to define it own requirements. In their current form, these guidelines clarify some requirements, but it is not clear how First Nations will implement them.[36]

Water Testing is Inconsistent

It is well known that drinking water needs to be tested regularly as a final check on the safety of the supply chain for drinking water, and to protect public health. However, regular tests of drinking water are not carried out in most First Nation reserve communities.[37]

Although Health Canada's overall target is to reach the testing frequency recommended in the *Guidelines for Canadian Drinking Water Quality* by 2008, as late as November 2005, the department had yet to develop a comprehensive plan, with specific target dates, to meet this overall target.[38] In addition, it does not ensure that First Nations test their drinking water as required in the funding arrangements, contracts and Health Canada procedure manual.[39] Although Health Canada does not provide funds when tests are not carried out, the absence of tests hampers Health Canada's and First Nations' ability to detect potential water quality problems and make timely and informed decisions to deal with these issues.

As previously stated, Health Canada's policy is that it has only an advisory role to First Nations when tests show that the drinking water is not safe to drink. At its discretion, the Department may recommend that a First Nation issue a boil-water advisory to users. According to Health Canada, First Nations have the authority to put in place and lift advisories, and they have the responsibility, with assistance from INAC, Health Canada, tribal councils, and other support organizations, to correct the underlying causes. However, some advisories have been in place for many years.[40]

Support and Capacity Development is Inadequate

The Report of the Commissioner of the Environment and Sustainable Development found that INAC's programs are limited in scope, and that the technical help available to First Nations to support and develop their capacity to provide safe drinking water is fragmented.[41] The report identified weaknesses in three main areas: operators, funding, and information and monitoring.

Operators

Most water treatment plant operators in First Nations communities do not posses the knowledge and skills required to operate their plant safely. The 2001 assessment found that approximately 10% of the operators on reserves met the certification requirements of their respective province.[42] Under the First Nations Water Management Strategy, INAC introduced a requirement that all on-reserve operators be certified to the level of complexity of their water treatment plant, in accordance with the rules applicable in their province. The target is to certify all operators or ensure that uncertified operators are directly supervised by a certified operator by 2006.

INAC's statistics indicate that at the end of March 2005, about 40% of the operators were certified.[43] However, for one region included in these statistics, the Commissioner of the Environment and Sustainable Development found that although many of the operators were trained and had passed exams, they were not certified.[44] In addition, the statistics do not indicate if the operators are certified to the level of complexity of their plants. Furthermore, as provincial certification and training requirements are becoming more stringent, many First Nations operators have difficulty meeting educational and experience requirements. Also, for more complex water treatment plants, a minimum number of years of experience operating such a facility under appropriate supervision is required before certification.

As previously stated, the main support available to operators comes from the Circuit Rider Training Program funded by INAC in all regions. However, this type of support and training is not mandatory or accessible to all First Nations.[45] In addition, INAC does not require a training plan to be in place.[46] Also, a lot of the trainer's time is spent resolving immediate technical problems rather than providing training.[47] In summary, the Report indicates that there is a high probability that the certification target will not be met.[48]

Funding

INAC does not use a consistent method to fund First Nations for the operation and maintenance (O&M) of their water systems. Its policy is to allocate O&M funds on the basis of a formula. The amount allocated to each First Nation should cover 80% of the estimated O&M costs of drinking water systems. However, the formula has not been updated for many years. In some regions, the Department does not use the formula, and provides some First Nations with 80% of their actual O&M costs if they can provide sufficient evidence of paying these costs.[49]

Under the First Nations Water Management Strategy, INAC is implementing a new method to estimate O&M costs and allocate funds. This method takes into account the characteristics of each water system, and as a result, many First Nations are eligible for additional funding. However, it is not clear whether this method will apply to all First Nations, or if actual costs will continue to be paid in some cases.[50]

INAC does not know whether all funds for operation and maintenance are used for this purpose. Under the applicable funding conditions, First Nations have the flexibility to use O&M funds for other purposes, and INAC has limited assurance that they are used for the intended purpose. At this time, it is not clear whether INAC will make funding conditions uniform under the First Nations Water Management Strategy, and how it will obtain assurances that the funds are being used as intended.

Another issue related to operation and maintenance funding of water systems is based on the fact that under INAC's O&M guidelines, First Nations are expected to cover 20% of the O&M costs of water systems through user fees or other sources. In practice, few First Nations collect user fees.[51] Moreover, INAC does not take into consideration whether First Nations have other resources to meet this requirement, and has no means to enforce it.[52]

Information and Monitoring

INAC has limited information on whether First Nations meet the conditions of their funding arrangements, and whether its programs and funding result in safe drinking water. To monitor the state of water systems, INAC requires First Nations to provide information annually on their O&M plans and activities, and the results of an inspection of the condition of their water systems every three to five years.

However, in many cases, INAC does not know whether regular maintenance identified by First Nations was completed, or whether urgent maintenance or repair projects are needed.[53] Some reports requested by INAC are not provided by all First Nations, even though they would be useful to both INAC and the First

Nations. For example, First Nations are supposed to have maintenance management plans in place for their water systems. However, INAC does not require evidence that these plans are in place and used.[54] In addition, regions are supposed to ensure that annual maintenance inspections are completed. These are not being done systematically.[55] Moreover, periodic inspections are not always carried out when due, and some inspection reports provided by First Nations contain poor-quality information.[56] As a result, the information system in place to record the results of water system inspections is not reliable.

As a result of their funding arrangements, when deficiencies in a water system are noted in a report to INAC, First Nations are responsible for correcting them. However, there is no effective means to inform INAC that the deficiencies are corrected, and the Department has limited means to ensure that a First Nation has addressed the deficiencies. Furthermore, INAC cannot threaten to withdraw O&M funding to facilitate a correction because drinking water is an essential service.[57] Under the First Nations Water Management Strategy, INAC has undertaken a review of its information needs and data collection processes for drinking water, but it is yet to be seen whether this review will be successful and what actions will result from it.

Co-management as a Solution

As the previous section has demonstrated, significant regulatory changes need to be made in order to ensure that Aboriginal communities are receiving good quality water. However, if these changes are to be effective, they must be created and implemented with the participation and support of the Aboriginal communities which they affect. In recent decades, there has been considerable attention paid to co-management as an important mechanism for the effective management of natural resources. The term "co-management" refers to a wide range of organizational arrangements, functions, and levels of power-sharing. It encompasses everything from relatively simple arrangements with government managers sharing power with users over limited resources and geographic areas, to legislated arrangements evolving from Aboriginal self-government negotiations.[58] As a result, this paper adopts Notzke's general definition: "'Co-management' broadly refers to the sharing of power and responsibility between government and local resource users. This is achieved by various levels of integration of local and state level management systems."[59]

Aboriginal support for a co-management role over water and other natural resources is aimed at the recognition and integration of Aboriginal concerns, Aboriginal rights, and Aboriginal expertise into the management and policy arenas concerning water resources. Aboriginal governments argue that the era of paternalistic, unilateral decision-making by the federal government is over, super-ceded by the more forward-looking policy of encouraging the exercise of Aboriginal rights and Aboriginal self-determination. Co-management is one approach that fits within this era of recognition and reconciliation of Aboriginal rights with the rights of the Canadian population at large.

Integration of First Nations as co-managers provides an effective means of addressing some of the complex issues discussed above concerning the provision of safe drinking water to Aboriginal communities in Canada. Integration of tribes as co-managers moves the major parties closer to developing more effective measures to deal with the difficult scientific and policy issues involved with water quality. Co-management provides a unique opportunity for the application of Aboriginal traditional ecological knowledge to increasingly complex problems that require a broader and deeper understanding of the phenomena at issue.[60] As previously stated, often times it is the community most affected by an issue which is in the best position to come up with the most effective and appropriate means to deal with the problem.

The 1987 amendments to the United States' *Clean Water Act*[61] demonstrate an example of one of the highest forms of co-management—one that has been enshrined in federal legislation. The 1987 amendments to the *Clean Water Act* provide the Environmental Protection Agency (EPA) with the authority to approve a tribe for treatment as a state for certain purposes enumerated in the act.[62] One of the enumerated sections for which tribes may seek approval is Section 303, the water quality standard provision of the act. Section 303 permits a state, or a tribe treated as a state, to establish water quality standards for the water resources within the state's or the tribe's governmental jurisdiction. However, a tribe must first demonstrate four categories of authority and capability in order to be treated as a state by the EPA. First, the tribe must be one that is recognized by the Department of the Interior.[63] Second, the tribe must have a governing body carrying out substantial governmental duties and powers.[64] Third, the functions to be exercised must concern the management and protection of the water resources which are held by an Indian tribe, held in trust by the United States for Indians, held by a member of an Indian tribe subject to a restriction, or otherwise within the borders of an Indian reservation.[65] Finally, the tribe must show that it is reasonably expected to be capable, in the Administrator's judgment, of carrying out the functions to be exercised.[66]

Water quality standards establish the desired ambient nature of a water body.[67] Under this co-management system, the appropriate state or tribal authority establishes designated beneficial uses for the water resources under its jurisdiction, then develops narrative and numerical criteria to protect the designated uses.[68] Each set of standards must contain an anti-degradation clause, intended to prohibit further polluting of the water.[69]

Once established and approved, these water quality standards apply to lakes, rivers and streams, or portions thereof. If there is a discharge into a segment of the water body, the required permit issued to the discharger must nominally meet any applicable water quality standards.[70] A permit cannot be issued if the discharge would violate these standards.[71] When drafting a permit, the EPA seeks certification from the state or from a tribe that the limitations in the proposed permit will not violate existing water quality standards.[72] Moreover, a discharge permit must be conditioned so as not to violate downstream stands.[73]

These aspects of tribal power under the *Clean Water Act* have been upheld by United States courts. For instance, in New Mexico, the Isleta Pueblo, an Indian tribe downstream from the City of Albuquerque on the Rio Grande, was granted *Clean Water Act* tribes-as-states status, and adopted water quality standards more stringent than those of the state of New Mexico.[74] Albuquerque challenged the EPA's approval and subsequent enforcement of those standards—which included requiring changes to Albuquerque's National Pollution Discharge Elimination System (NPDES) permit for an upstream waste water treatment facility—on a variety of grounds, including challenging the authority of EPA to implement more stringent tribal standards against non-Indian entities off-reservation.[75] The court upheld the EPA's application of the tribe's standards, expressly holding that the Isleta Pueblo's right to adopt water quality standards more stringent than those of an upstream state was rooted not just in the *Clean Water Act*, but also in the tribe's "inherent sovereignty."[76]

There is no one-size-fits-all approach to co-management. Each First Nation, as a unique, self-determining community, has developed its own institutions, resources, and procedures. Each First Nation's rights are based on legal documents, i.e. treaties, and histories specific to that community. Furthermore, the local situation within which each First Nation is embedded is unique, with particularized landscapes, resource issues, and user groups. Therefore, the means by which a particular First Nation can be integrated into a decision-making process for water and waterways needs to be developed on a First Nation–specific basis.

Nonetheless, there are some fundamental, overarching principles that can govern each co-management agreement regarding water quality. First, the role that First Nation governments play in a co-management regime must be developed within a framework that recognizes that they are in fact governments, accountable for the health and welfare of their membership. Such recognition can serve to ensure the protection of the Aboriginal interest in resources critical to the long-term economic security, political integrity, and health and well-being of their communities.

Second, First Nations should be made an integral part of the decision-making process. The very term co-management means that First Nations participate in the decision-making process. First Nations should be sitting at the table from the earliest stages of policy formulation, problem identification, and development of solutions to water quality. In order to effectively deal with the water quality issues within Aboriginal communities, their leaders or representatives need to be included at the very beginning of the decision-making process. Such front loading of First Nation participation not only reduces the potential for long-term, disruptive conflict over policies and proposed solution, but it also facilitates the incorporation of critical information and technical expertise possessed by the Aboriginal communities.

Third, the input provided by tribes should be considered expert information, and given a certain degree of deference. Traditional Aboriginal knowledge of ecological systems, developed from generations of interaction with the environment, influences tribal beliefs regarding resource use and management.[77] Aboriginal environmental knowledge is integrated with tribal religious beliefs and world view in many different ways.[78] While current economic, social, and political factors affect Aboriginal world views,[79] there is a certain consistency of traditional environmental knowledge influencing First Nation environmental decision-making.[80] A water resource co-management approach is an important tool because it offers First Nations the opportunity to integrate traditional Aboriginal values and knowledge with contemporary resource management policies.

Fourth, a co-management system should incorporate mechanisms for resolving disputes, and differences in opinion and approach among the co-managing parties. As diverse stakeholders with interests and perspectives that might be at odds, the parties to a co-management regime must develop methods and mechanisms to deal with disputes. Unilateral decision-making by one party upsets the power balance between the co-managing powers. One useful model for integrated decision-making and dispute resolution is the Columbia River Fisheries Management Plan (CRFMP), a complex arrangement for the management of Indian and non-Indian fisheries on the Columbia River that involves four Indian tribes, three states and two federal agencies. The CRFMP contains detailed provisions for dispute resolution among the parties, recognizing the likelihood of disagreement on technical and policy matters.[81] The CRFMP provides for an internal dispute resolution mechanism through which policy or technical disputes are brought before the Policy Committee, a body comprised of representatives appointed by each party, and charged with the task of "facilitating cooperative action by the Parties."[82] Moreover, the CRFMP remains under the continuing jurisdiction of the federal district court for Oregon, and a special magistrate is available to hear and resolve disputes between the parties that cannot be resolved through the internal dispute resolution process.[83]

Though a co-management regime is not without its faults, a co-management regime for water resources offers several advantages to First Nations, including the opportunity to participate in and influence the development of water quality policies that affect them. Once First Nation governments gain "a seat at the table," they have the opportunity to integrate Aboriginal beliefs and management practices with mainstream policies on water quality. At the same time, co-management approaches also help water quality policymakers learn about the values, culture and way of life of Aboriginal people. This is important because it helps government policymakers understand traditional Aboriginal views, and avoid potential disputes and tragedies, such as the recent incident at Kashechewan.

Self-governance as a Solution

Though co-management is a desirable objective for First Nation governments, arguably many leaders are advocating for a system of self-governance to rectify issues in their communities, such as water quality. A definition of Aboriginal "self-government" is difficult to formulate, as the term has been used to describe many different types of political systems. Essentially, self-government arrangements grant Aboriginal people some degree of decision-making power in specified areas. In *Delgamuukw v. The Queen*[84] the Gitskan and Wet'suwet'en people claimed ownership and jurisdiction, including self-government, over a territory in central British Columbia. In dissent, British Columbia Court of Appeal Justice Lambert articulated the plaintiffs' claim for self-government as a claim for a "right of self-regulation of themselves and their institutions."[85]

Self-government is critical to Aboriginal culture. The plaintiffs in *Delgamuukw* argued that self-government is necessary "in order to determine their development and safeguard their integrity as Aboriginal peoples" and "to preserve and enhance their social, political, cultural, linguistic, and spiritual identity."[86] Since contact, Aboriginal communities have done everything humanly possible to maintain the integrity and vitality of their own traditions, languages, ceremonies, and other authoritative internal arrangements, and to continue fulfilling their ancestral obligations to one another and the rest of creation,[87] despite immense changes to their physical and economic circumstances, and pressures from non-Aboriginal institutions.[88] Arguably, ensuring high water quality is necessary to preserve Aboriginal traditions and customs, as well as to preserve the health and well-being of the communities themselves. This, combined with the fact that the current federal policy on drinking water quality on reserves lacks a sufficient regulatory regime, makes it clear why First Nation governments would find a right to govern water quality preferable.

If First Nations were able to prove an Aboriginal right to self-governance, then this right would receive protection through s. 35(1) of the Constitution Act, 1982. This section reads:

35. (1) The existing Aboriginal and treaty rights of Aboriginal peoples of Canada are hereby recognized and affirmed.

However, as case law has demonstrated, proving an Aboriginal right to self-governance is not an easy right to prove. Courts have yet to articulate a clear statement on the legal status of the right to self-government, let alone on the scope of the right and its relationship to federal and provincial laws.[89]

R. v. Van der Peet[90] sets out the test for determining the practices, customs, and traditions which fall within s. 35(1) and, as such, provide the legal standard against which a claim to regulate water quality as a part of self-government must be measured. In *Van der Peet*, the test for identifying Aboriginal rights was said to be as follows: "... in order to be an Aboriginal right an activity must be an element of a practice, custom, or tradition integral to the distinctive culture of the Aboriginal group claiming the right."[91] In applying this test, the court must first identify the exact nature of the activity claimed to be a right, and must then go on to determine whether, on the evidence presented to the trial judge, and on the facts as found by the trial judge, that the activity could be said to be "a defining feature of the culture in question" prior to contact with Europeans.[92]

In turning to the first part of *Van der Peet*, the court held that:

> To characterize an applicant's claim correctly, a court should consider such factors as the nature of the action which the applicant is claiming was done pursuant to an Aboriginal right, the nature of the governmental regulation, statute or action being impugned, and the practice, custom or tradition being relied upon to establish the right.[93]

In *R. v. Pamajewon*[94] the court considered whether the right to self-government falls within the scope of the Aboriginal rights recognized and affirmed by s. 35(1) of the Constitution Act, 1982. In making its decision, the court assumed, without deciding, that s. 35(1) encompasses claims to Aboriginal self-government; however, the applicable legal standard is that laid out in *Van der Peet*. Speaking for the court, Lamer, C.J. stated:

> Assuming s. 35(1) encompasses claims to Aboriginal self-government, such claims must be considered in light of the purposes underlying that provision and must, therefore, be considered against the test derived from consideration of those purposes. This is the test laid out in *Van der Peet*. In so far as they can be made under s. 35(1), claims to self-government are no difference from other claims to the enjoyment of Aboriginal rights and must, as such, be measured against the same standard.[95]

The court found that to recognize "a broad right to manage the use of their reserve lands" would be to cast the court's inquiry at a level of excessive generality.[96] Therefore, the right to self-government must be looked at in light of the specific history and culture of the Aboriginal group claiming the right.[97] The right to self-government, according to the test laid out in *Van der Peet*, must be considered at the appropriate level of specificity.[98]

According to these tests, the correct characterization of the right put forward is that of a right to regulate water quality as part of self-government. Therefore, individuals and First Nations' government advocating for recognition of this right must first prove that the practice of managing water quality was exercised prior to the contact. Though little physical evidence is likely to exist to demonstrate this fact, oral histories and the "common law" practices of these groups could be used to demonstrate that this right existed, and that it was exercised prior to European contact. However, under the tests enunciated in these cases, First Nations must also prove that regulating water quality was integral to their distinctive cultures. As previously stated, water is the lifeblood for many of these communities. It is used to not only meet physical needs, but cultural and sacred needs as well. Many

Aboriginal villages were traditionally located on waterways, and this resource was depended upon for food, household needs, travel, and ceremonial practices. Arguably, ensuring water quality was "integral to the distinctive culture(s)" of these Aboriginal groups and should be found "worthy" to merit the constitutional protection of s. 35(1).

Even if courts were to recognize an Aboriginal right to regulate water quality, this will not necessarily solve all the issues outlined in the first part of this paper. As this paper has demonstrated, one of the major issues affecting water quality on First Nation reserves is capacity building. Even if First Nations were to gain ownership and control of this resource, this in itself, would not be enough to solve this problem. In fact, some may even argue that this change in ownership and jurisdiction would do more to reduce capacity building than develop it. Some critics of Aboriginal self-governance argue that Aboriginal communities have too few members with sufficient leadership skills, technical expertise, or practical experience to meet the collective's needs in these highly complex and difficult circumstances.[99]

However, aggregation could be used by First Nations to help improve and build capacity within their communities. The Royal Commission on Aboriginal Peoples (RCAP) commented extensively on this issue and argued that individual Aboriginal communities are too small to develop the necessary capacity to govern the many jurisdictions often contemplated by the negotiating parties.[100] RCAP recommended that these governance functions be carried out by Nations, rather than individual Aboriginal communities. However, RCAP's Nation-based solution would represent a radical departure for a great majority of Aboriginal groups across the country. Thus, while sympathetic to the commission's premise that the community may not represent the ideal governing building block for all jurisdictions, many involved in self-government negotiations are discussing other aggregation options.

One type of aggregation that could be used to more effectively govern water in Aboriginal communities is a two-tier level of aggregation. Two-tier aggregation involves a number of governments coming together and forming a second level, "regional" government to deal with those issues that are beyond the capacity of any of them to handle individually.[101] In doing so, the participating governments aggregate a number of their governance structures, processes, and functions upwards to the newly formed body.[102] The strength of the two-tier government lies in the framework it provides for: a) local Aboriginal communities to work together to deliver services; b) the formalization of the political relationships amongst local Aboriginal communities; and c) the establishment of a mechanism for joint decision-making.[103] In looking at well-established, non-Aboriginal two-tier aggregation models, it has been observed that, "the inherently flexible, non-interventionist approach and the gradual expansion of activities in response to local decisions have resulted in a system that is accepted, practical, and functional."[104]

One must also consider the benefit of a two-tier system, in that it could be structured to permit the assignment of operating responsibilities to one tier and regulatory responsibility to the other. Brian Crowley, president of the Atlantic Institute for Market Studies, a Halifax-based think tank, stated:

> When the government is a supplier of a service, such as water, it tends to be a poor regulator of quality. Regulator and supplier often work in the same department, may belong to the same union, and are both responsible to the same elected officials—who want to avoid unpleasantness and conflict. Problems are bushed up or ignored with a wink and a nod. Governments can be far more rigorous regulators when they are at arm's length from the supplier.[105]

However, whether such delegation will be used with potable water, whether it would be sustainable given that delegated responsibilities can be withdrawn and whether a large Aboriginal body, such as a tribal council, is of sufficient size and independence to exercise regulatory responsibilities is still unknown.[106]

Other potential weaknesses of this type of aggregation include that they are not easy to understand and therefore reduce accountability to citizens or membership.[107] This could pose an even greater disadvantage in Aboriginal communities where citizens, on average, have lower education levels, and where accountability of government institutions is very important. Secondly, two-tier aggregation requires a lot of effort to ensure that there is good coordination among the various levels.[108] As was previously mentioned, Aboriginal communities are already struggling with capacity and resource issues. Finally, these types of systems are costly to run[109] and First Nation governments are often working from very limited funding arrangements.

Instead of a tiered governance structure, aggregation can take many other forms. A less "ambitious" form of aggregation, some may argue, is through special purpose bodies that have the following characteristics:

- They usually focus on one area of public concern, such as education, policing and water etc.;
- Unlike governments, they do not have the power to legislate;
- Any powers they do have are established in legislation of some level of government; and
- The leadership of the body is not necessarily elected by citizens at large.[110]

These special purpose bodies could have legislated powers, or they could not. Those without any real powers tend to be advisory or advocacy in nature, and in many instances they provide services to governments.

It has been stated that "in the everyday world of Canadian municipal government, especially in the rural areas of the smaller provinces, inter-municipal problems are not solved by establishing new tiers of government or by drastically altering municipal boundaries."[111] In fact, local governments have found many advantages to using special purpose bodies to carry out their governance functions. For example, local governments can remain distinct and responsible for the things that they do best on their own. At the same time, they can join with other local governments to undertake the delivery of services that are better or more efficiently done in concert. Protection service, such as fire and ambulance, sewage and waste disposal, and planning services are examples of services most commonly delivered by joint agreements. However, this does not mean that potable water could not fit within this realm as well. This service is greatly related to sewage and waste disposal. In many instances these agreements can provide an expanded level and variety of services to rural residents.[112] Other reasons local governments find this aggregation attractive are that they can save on costs by either sharing expensive services, or by obtaining volume discounts.[113] Furthermore, "joint hiring practices allow small local governments to recruit and share professional and technical staff."[114]

These advantages do not mean that this type of governance structure is not without its disadvantages. However, it has been stated that these types of agreements are most effective in the provision of regional services in either of two situations: 1) they are effective in predominately rural areas where services are limited, and there is economic and demographic stability; or 2) they are effective where a second tier of government takes responsibility for them.[115] Therefore, this might suggest that if Aboriginal governments were to gain jurisdiction and control over water, a combination of a two-tier government system and a special purpose body might be the most effective way to manage and regulate the resource.

Though recognizing a right to regulate water quality provides one potential solution for drinking water quality on reserves, it is not without its own set of potential obstacles and concerns. Currently, many Aboriginal communities do not have the capacity or financial resources to effectively manage this resource. However, there are steps these communities could take to increase their capacity and resources to a higher level. One potential solution is aggregation. However, because benefits tend to be over-estimated and costs tend to be under-estimated,[116] this solution would have to be carefully studied before Aboriginal communities committed to it.

Conclusion

Currently, Indian and Northern Affairs Canada, Health Canada, and First Nations do not operate under a regulatory regime for drinking water as most provinces do. As this paper has demonstrated, there are also many weaknesses in program management in federal departments. As a result, when it comes to the safety of drinking water, residents of First Nations communities do not benefit from a level of protection comparable with that of Canadians living off-reserve. This is not acceptable. Aboriginal Canadians, including Indigenous people living on "land reserved for Indians," are residents of the country, and should be entitled to safe drinking water on the same terms as those prevailing in other similarly placed communities.

Water and water quality has always played an integral role in the lives of Canada's Aboriginal peoples. For many First Nations, water is a sacred element in their existence, and forms an important part of their understanding of who they are as a people. Based on these traditions, it is not inconceivable to consider that Aboriginal peoples in Canada could have a right to manage this resource, or at the very least a right to co-manage this resource. Though it would be naïve to believe that all the issues surrounding water quality in First Nation communities will simply disappear through a transfer or sharing of jurisdiction, it is not inconceivable to think that because of their vested and personal interest in this resource, First Nation communities would be more willing to create regulatory structures to govern this vital resource. If such a transfer were to occur, arguably aggregation could prove to be a useful tool for these communities.

Not all First Nations communities may wish to have jurisdiction over this resource, and, in reality, many may not be in a position to take over responsibility for safe drinking water in their communities. Co-management then offers a unique solution in which Aboriginal communities work together with government players to help ensure the provision of quality water in these communities. One thing is clear, however, if First Nation communities are to have quality drinking water—comparable to other mainstream Canadian communities—changes have to be made to the current government policy on safe drinking water. The creation of legislation and an adequate regulatory body must be a priority for all parties responsible for this resource. To deal with such a complex set of issues all major players and their political representatives will need to be involved. Only then can a policy be created which recognizes and addresses all the concerns of the parties involved—one that will ensure the provision of safe drinking water equally to all Canadians.

Endnotes

1 LL.M. candidate, University of Arizona.

2 In 2000, the deaths of seven people from *E.coli* contamination in Walkerton's drinking water, and illnesses in that community and others affecting approximately 2300 others put the spotlight on Canada's capacity to provide its citizens with safe drinking water. See Ontario, Ministry of the Attorney General, *Part Two: Report of the Walkerton* Inquiry, Chapter 15 (Ottawa: Queen's Printer for Ontario, 2002) (Commissioner: Dennis R. O'Connor). The Battleford area of Saskatchewan experienced an outbreak of gastroenteritis between late March and early May 2001. An estimated 5,800 to 7,100 people from the Battleford area were affected along with hundreds of visitors from other parts of Saskatchewan, Alberta, Manitoba, and British Columbia. By May 2001, *C. parvum* infection was confirmed in 275 people. See Public Health Agency of Canada, *Canada Communicable Disease Report*, Volume 27–22, available at **http://www. phac-aspc.gc.ca/publicat/ccdr-rmtc/01vol27/dr2722.html** (last accessed February 11, 2006). In 2005, approximately 1000 members of the Kashechewan First Nation were evacuated due to high *E. coli* levels in tap water. See note 6.

3 Although the author recognizes that the issue of water quality encompasses many aspects of First Nations lives, this paper will focus mainly on drinking water as a case study of this issue.

4 J. Walker, J. Bradley & T. Humphrey, Sr., "Environmental Justice: A Closer Look at Environmental Injustice in Indian Country" (2002) 1 *Seattle J. Soc. Just.* 379 at 386.

5 National Environmental Justice Advisory Council, *Integration of Environmental Justice in Federal Agency Programs* 46 (May 2002), available at **http://www.epa.gov/compliance/ resources/publications/ej/**.

6 *Supra* note 4 at 386.

7 S. Bailey, "Indian Affairs Minister Visits Remote Reserve Battling Waterborne Hazards" *Maclean's* (October 19, 2005), available at: **www.macleans.ca**.

8 *Ibid.*

9 Laduke, W. (1999). *All Our Relations: Native Struggles for Land and Life*. Cambridge: South End Press. 18 (the Mohawk PCB standard was 0.1 parts per million).

10 *Ibid.* 11–23.

11 Canada. (2001). *Safe Drinking Water on First Nation Reserves: Roles and Responsibilities*. Ottawa: Indian and Northern Affairs Canada. 2.

12 *Ibid.*

13 *Ibid.* 3.

14 *Department of Health Act*, R.S.C. 1996, c. 8.

15 *Ibid.* s. 4.

16 *Supra* note 11 p. 14.

17 *Ibid.*

18 *Ibid.* 9.

19 *Ibid.*

20 *Ibid.* 11.

21 *Indian Act*, R.S.C. 1985, c. I–5.

22 Canada, Office of the Auditor General of Canada. (2005). *Report of the Commissioner of the Environment and Sustainable Development—2005*, "Chapter Five—Drinking Water in First Nations Communities" Ottawa: Minister of Public Works and Government Services Canada. 10.

23 *Ibid.* 11.

24 *Ibid.*

25 *Ibid.*

26 *Ibid.*

27 *Ibid.*

28 *Ibid.*

29 *Ibid.*

30 Ontario, Ministry of the Attorney General. (2002). *Part Two: Report of the Walkerton Inquiry,* Chapter 15 Ottawa: Queen's Printer for Ontario. (Commissioner: Dennis R. O'Connor). 492.

31 *Supra* note 22 p. 11.

32 *Ibid.* 12.

33 *Ibid.* 15.

34 *Ibid.*

35 *Ibid.*

36 *Ibid.* 16.

37 *Ibid.*

38 *Ibid.*

39 *Ibid.*

40 *Ibid.* In one First Nation community, a section of the community had been under a boil-water advisory for over three years before the corrective actions were taken and the advisory lifted.

41 *Ibid.* 17.

42 *Ibid.*

43 *Ibid.* 18.

44 *Ibid.*

45 *Ibid.*

46 *Ibid.*

47 *Ibid.*

48 *Ibid.*

49 *Ibid.* 19.

50 *Ibid.*

51 *Ibid.*

52 *Ibid.*

53 *Ibid.* 20.

54 *Ibid.*

55 *Ibid.*

56 *Ibid.*

57 *Ibid.*

58 E. Peters, "Organisational Design for Co-Management: Comparing Four Committees in Nunavik" 44 C. de D. 667 at 669.

59 C. Notzke. (1995). "A New Perspective in Aboriginal Natural Resources Management: Co-management." 26 (2) *Geoforum* 187.

60 See generally Rebecca L. Tsosie. (1996). "Tribal Environmental Policy in an Era of Self-Determination: The Role of Ethics, Economics, and Traditional Ecological Knowledge." 21 Vt. L. Rev. 225 (describing function and value of tribal traditional ecological knowledge in dealing with contemporary environmental problems).

61 *Clean Water Act* 33 U.S.C. (1988).

62 33 U.S.C. 1377(a) (1988).

63 33 U.S.C. 1377(h)(2) (1988).

64 33 U.S.C. 1377(e)(1) (1988).

65 33 U.S.C. 1377(e)(2) (1988).

66 33 U.S.C. 1377(e)(3) (1988).

67 33 U.S.C. 1313 (1988) The rules and regulations for establishing, submitting, and approving standards are in 40 C.F.R. 131 (1993).

68 33 U.S.C. 1313(c)(2)(A) (1988).

69 *Ibid*. Anti-degradation measures provide that existing uses may not be lowered, very high quality waters must be maintained and protected, and high quality waters in state and national outstanding resource areas must be maintained and protected.

70 33 U.S.C. 1341(a) (1988).

71 33 U.S.C. 1341(a)(2) (1988).

72 *Ibid*. The certifying authority is the governmental entity with legal jurisdiction over the water body where the discharge originates, and which has water quality standards. A permit cannot be issued if the certifying authority determines that the discharge will violate the standards.

73 40 C.F.R. 131.10(b) (1993).

74 See *City of Albuquerque v. Browner*, 97 F.3d 415, 419 (10th Cir. 1996).

75 *Ibid*.

76 *Ibid*. 423. However, the court noted that the tribe was not regulating the City of Albuquerque, but rather that EPA was "exercising its own authority in issuing NPDES permits in compliance with downstream state and tribal water quality standards." *Ibid*. 424.

77 *Supra* note 60 at 272–76.

78 *Ibid*. 274.

79 D. Martinez, "American Indian Cultural Models for Sustaining Biodiversity," available at **www.fs.fed.us/pnw/pubs/gtr63/gtrwo63g.pdf** (last visited January 31, 2006) at 115–16.

80 *Ibid*. at 110, 115.

81 Columbia River Fish Management Plan (Oct. 7, 1988) at 54–56.

82 *Ibid*.

83 *Ibid*. 7 & 56.

84 *Delgamuukw v. The Queen*, [1993] 5 W.W.R. 97 (British Columbia Court of Appeal).

85 *Ibid*. 348.

86 *Ibid*. 149.

87 See generally J.J. Borrows. (1992). "A Genealogy of Law: Inherent Sovereignty and First Nations Self-Government" 30 *Osgoode Hall L.J.* 291 (Anishnabek).

88 J.R. Miller. "The Historical Context of the Drive for Self-Government." in R. Gosse, J. Youngblood Henderson & R. Carter, eds. (1999). *Continuing Poundmaker and Riel's Quest.* Saskatoon: Purich Publishing. 41 at 42.

89 B. Morse. (1997). "Permafrost Rights: Aboriginal Self-Government and the Supreme Court in R. v. Pamajewon." 42 *McGill L.J.* 1011 at 1016.

90 [1996] 2 S.C.R. 507 [hereafter *Van der Peet*].

91 *Ibid* at para. 46.

92 *Ibid* at para. 59.

93 *Ibid* at para. 53.

94 [1996] 2 S.C.R. 821 [hereafter *Pamajewon*].

95 *Ibid* at para. 24.

96 *Ibid* at para. 27.

97 *Ibid*.

98 *Ibid*.

99 K. Wilkins. (2000). "Take Your Time and Do It Right: Delgamuukw, Self-Government Rights and The Pragmatics Of Advocacy." 27 *Man. L. J.* 241 at 253.

100 Institute on Governance. (1998). *Self-Government Agreements and the Pubic Works Function.* Ottawa: The Institute on Governance. 3.

101 Institute on Governance. (2000). *Governance Models to Achieve Higher Levels of Aggregation: Literature Review.* Ottawa: The Institute on Governance. 14.

102 *Ibid.*

103 *Ibid.* 18.

104 *Ibid.*

105 Institute on Governance. (2001). *Re-thinking Self-Government Agreements: The Case of Potable Water.* Ottawa: The Institute on Governance. 3.

106 *Ibid.*

107 *Supra* note 101 at p. 18.

108 *Ibid.*

109 *Ibid.*

110 *Ibid.* 30.

111 *Ibid.* 36.

112 *Ibid.*

113 *Ibid.*

114 *Ibid.*

115 *Ibid.* 37.

116 *Supra* note 101 at 48.

References

Bailey, S. (2005). "Indian Affairs Minister Visits Remote Reserve Battling Waterborne Hazards." *Maclean's* (October 19), online: <**www.macleans.ca**>.

Borrows, J. (1992). "A Genealogy of Law: Inherent Sovereignty and First Nations Self-Government." 30 *Osgoode Hall L.J.* 291.

Canada, Office of the Auditor General of Canada. (2005). *Report of the Commissioner of the Environment and Sustainable Development—2005.* "Chapter Five—Drinking Water in First Nations Communities." Ottawa: Minister of Public Works and Government Services Canada.

Canada. (2001). *Safe Drinking Water on First Nation Reserves: Roles and Responsibilities.* Ottawa: Indian and Northern Affairs Canada.

City of Albuquerque v. Browner, 97 F.3d 415, 419 (10th Cir. 1996).

Columbia River Fish Management Plan (Oct. 7, 1988).

Delgamuukw v. The Queen, [1993] 5 W.W.R. 97 (BCCA).

Government of Canada. (1985). *Indian Act*, R.S.C., c. I–5.

Government of Canada. (1988). *Clean Water Act* 33 U.S.C.

Government of Canada. (1996). *Department of Health Act*, R.S.C., c. 8.

Institute on Governance. (2000). *Governance Models to Achieve Higher Levels of Aggregation: Literature Review.* Ottawa: The Institute on Governance.

Institute on Governance. (2001). *Re-thinking Self-Government Agreements: The Case of Potable Water.* Ottawa: The Institute on Governance.

Institute on Governance. (1998). *Self-Government Agreements and the Pubic Works Function.* Ottawa: The Institute on Governance.

Laduke, W. (1999). *All Our Relations: Native Struggles for Land and Life.* Cambridge: South End Press.

Martinez, D. "American Indian Cultural Models for Sustaining Biodiversity," available at <**www.fs.fed.us/pnw/pubs/gtr63/gtrwo63g.pdf**> (last visited January 31, 2006).

Miller, J.R., "The Historical Context of the Drive for Self-Government" in R. Gosse, J. Youngblood Henderson & R. Carter, eds. (1994). *Continuing Poundmaker and Riel's Quest.* Saskatoon: Purich Publishing.

Morse, B. (1997). "Permafrost Rights: Aboriginal Self-Government and the Supreme Court in R. v. Pamajewon." 42 *McGill L.J.* 1011.

National Environmental Justice Advisory Council, *Integration of Environmental Justice in Federal Agency Programs* 46 (May 2002), available at <**www.epa.gov/compliance/resources/publications/ej/nejac/cover-contents-fed-integration-030102.pdf**>

Notzke, C. (1995). "A New Perspective in Aboriginal Natural Resources Management: Co-management." 26 2 *Geoforum.*

Ontario, Ministry of the Attorney General. (2002). *Part Two: Report of the Walkerton Inquiry, Chapter 15.* Ottawa: Queen's Printer for Ontario (Commissioner: Dennis R. O'Connor).

Peters E., "Organisational Design for Co-Management: Comparing Four Committees in Nunavik" 44 *C. de D.* 667.

Public Health Agency of Canada. *Canada Communicable Disease Report*, Volume 27-22, available at <**www.phac-aspc.gc.ca/publicat/ccdr-rmtc/01vol27/dr2722ea.html**> (last accessed February 11, 2006).

R. v. Pamajewon, [1996] 2 S.C.R. 821.

R. v. Van der Peet, [1996] 2 S.C.R. 507.

Tsosie, R. (1996). "Tribal Environmental Policy in an Era of Self-Determination: The Role of Ethics, Economics, and Traditional Ecological Knowledge." 21 *Vt. L. Rev.* 225.

Walker, J., Bradley J. & T. Humphrey, Sr. (2002). "Environmental Justice: A Closer Look at Environmental Injustice in Indian Country." 1 *Seattle J. Soc. Just.* 379.

Wilkins, K. (2000). "Take Your Time and Do It Right: Delgamuukw, Self-Government Rights and The Pragmatics of Advocacy." 27 *Man. L.J.* 241.

10

Inuit Research Comes to the Fore

Robert M. Bone

Introduction

In the post-Inuit-land-claim world, four political regions emerged. These are Nunavik (1975), the Inuvialuit Settlement Area (1984), Nunavut (1999), and Nunatsiavut (2005). In April 2005, the federal government formed the Inuit Relations Secretariat (IRS) to provide Inuit organizations with a "window" into Indian and Northern Affairs Canada (INAC). In turn, IRS, as a unit with Indian and Northern Affairs Canada, was responsible for providing information on the Inuit population to senior officials in INAC. Such information was normally organized by the four land claim regions because each region had its own particular circumstances. For example, IRS prepared its education, health, and housing decks for the First Ministers Meeting in Kelowna (November 2005) by the four land claim regions. While utilizing a wide range of information, IRS relied heavily on the 2001 census. Unfortunately, the geographic organization of the 2001 census does not match the boundaries of three of the four land claim regions. Nunavut, being a territory, forms one of the Census regions, but, even in this case, Statistics Canada does not present the data by Inuit identity population. Instead, the census data by subject matter, such as education or housing, is organized by total population, and by Aboriginal identity population.

Purpose of this Paper

IRS recognized that the misalignment of the 2001 census for three of the four land claim regions needed to be correct in order for IRS to provide more precise and geographically correct census data in its briefing reports for INAC policy-makers. Custom tabulations from Statistics Canada were designed to provide census data by (1) Inuit Identity Population, (2) Canada and the four land claim regions, and (3) those residing outside of the four land claim regions. These three elements comprise the core of the Inuit Database which is being created from these custom tabulations of the 2001 Census. Census subject matter for the Inuit Database was selected on the basis of the mandate of IRS. Subject matter includes population counts, age and sex, language, education, income, labour force, occupation, industry, housing and dwelling conditions by total population, Aboriginal population, Inuit population by ancestry, and Inuit population by identity.

In this paper, the power of the Inuit Database is demonstrated by 12 tables. Ten tables present Inuit Identity population by population size, age, and sex for

Table 10.1: Inuit Identity Population by Regions

Region	Population	Percent
Nunatsiavut	2,345	5.2
Inuvialuit Settlement Area	2,975	6.6
Nunavik	8,705	19.3
Nunavut	22,560	50.1
Total in land claim regions	36,585	81.2
Total outside of land claim regions	8,485	18.8
Canada	45,070	100.0

Source: Statistics Canada. 2001 Census. Custom Table Prepared for INAC. Requested by IRS.

Table 10.2: Inuit Identity Population Outside of Land Claim Regions

Urban Population	Population	Percent
Census Metropolitan Areas	3,300	38.9
Other urban centres	5,185	61.1
Total outside of land claim regions	8,485	100.0

Source: Statistics Canada. 2001 Census. Custom Table Prepared for INAC. Requested by IRS.

the five Inuit regions, while two tables focus on urban Inuit population. A 1996 custom tabulation permits a comparison between selected urban centres from 1996 to 2001.

Initial Results by Inuit Identity Population

1. Population Size

Population counts by Inuit identity were completed by November 2005. **Table 10.1** represents a basic summary of population by regions. The total number of Inuit recorded in the 2001 Census was 45,070. Regional variations existed with Nunatsiavut having the smallest number of Inuit at 2,345 (5.2%) and Nunavut having the largest number at 22,560 (50.1%). The total number of Inuit residing within the four land claim regions was 36,585 or 81.2%. The Inuit population residing outside of the four land claim regions totaled 8,485 or 18.8%. In examining those living outside of the land claim regions, just over 60% (5,185) resided in smaller urban centres such as Happy Valley-Goose Bay and Yellowknife while the remaining 39% (3,300) lived in large cities known as Census Metropolitan Areas (**Table 10.2**).

2. Age and Sex: Basic Comments

Age and sex are the most basic characteristics of a population. Every population has a different age and sex composition—the number or proportion of males and females in each age group. The age/sex structure of a population has implications for its economy and society. Such implications are revealed by examining three

Table 10.3: Inuit Identity Population by Age and Sex

Age Cohorts	Population	Percent	Male %	Female %
0 -14	17,460	38.8	51.0	49.0
15-64	26,200	58.1	49.2	50.8
65 & over	1,410	3.1	54.6	45.4
Canada	45,070	100.0	50.1	49.9

Source: Statistics Canada. 2001 Census. Custom Table Prepared for INAC. Requested by IRS

Table 10.4: Comparison of Inuit and Canada's Population by Age

Age Cohorts	Inuit Percent	Canada Percent
0 -14	38.8	19.4
15-64	58.1	68.4
65 & over	3.1	12.2
Canada	100.0	100.0

Source: Statistics Canada. 2001 Census. Custom Table Prepared for INAC. Requested by IRS

classic age groups (cohorts). The three cohorts contain the age groups 0 to 14; 15 to 64; and 65 and over. This traditional arrangement of age cohorts means that those between the ages of 15 and 64 represents the potential labour force, which is sometimes referred to as the productive age group. The other two age cohorts (those under 15 years of age and over 65 years of age) are considered "dependent" or non-productive members of society because they are either in the education system or retired.

The number of males and females is normally balanced. At birth, the ratio of males to females is higher because more males than females are born. After birth, the proportion of males to females varies because of different patterns of mortality (young males tend to die more often than young females, and the life span of females is longer than males) and migration (females tend to move more readily than males).

3. Age and Sex of the Inuit Population

The age and sex composition for the Inuit population in Canada is shown in **Table 10.3**. The first observation is that the percentage of Inuit under the age of 15 is extremely high at 38.8%. For comparison purposes, the total population of Canada illustrates strikingly different percentages (**Table 10.4**). For example, the national population under the age of 15 is 19.1%. On the basis of this information, demographers would classify the Inuit population as "young" and the Canadian population as "old." A young population is associated with a high fertility rate while an old population has a low fertility rate. Demographers would also note that such a large proportion of the population in one sector leaves fewer for the other two age categories. Not surprisingly then, the second observation is that a

Table 10.5: Nunatsiavut: Inuit by Age and Sex

Age Cohorts	Population	Percentage	Male %	Female %
0 -14	800	34.1	48.8	51.2
15-64	1,430	61.0	52.8	47.2
65 & over	115	4.9	56.5	43.5
Nunatsiavut	2,345	100.0	51.4	48.6

Source: Statistics Canada. 2001 Census. Custom Table Prepared for INAC. Requested by IRS

Table 10.6: Inuvialuit Settlement Area: Inuit by Age and Sex

Age Cohorts	Population	Percentage	Male %	Female %
0 -14	1,010	34.0	50.5	49.5
15-64	1,820	61.2	49.7	50.3
65 & over	145	4.8	55.2	44.8
Inuvialuit	2,975	100.0	50.3	49.7

Source: Statistics Canada. 2001 Census. Custom Table Prepared for INAC. Requested by IRS

Table 10.7: Nunavik: Inuit by Age and Sex

Age Cohorts	Population	Percentage	Male %	Female %
0 -14	3,645	41.9	51.3	48.7
15-64	4,790	55.0	50.5	49.5
65 & over	270	3.1	53.7	46.3
Nunavik	8,705	100.0	51.0	49.0

Source: Statistics Canada. 2001 Census. Custom Table Prepared for INAC. Requested by IRS

relatively small proportion of Inuit fall within the so-called productive age group of 15 to 64 years of age. As **Table 10.4** indicates, 58.1% of the Inuit population falls within this category compared to 60% for all Canadians. Similarly, only 3.1% of the Inuit population is in the 65 years of age and older category compared to 12.9% for Canada.

4. Age and Sex by Regions

Overall, the five Inuit regions exhibit youthful populations. Yet there are regional differences. Two Inuit regions, Nunavik and Nunavut, have similar age charac-teristics compared to those for Nunatsiavut, Inuvialuit, and those living outside of the four land claim regions. For example both Nunavik and Nunavut have very high percentages of their population under the age of 15. As shown in **Table 10.5** and **10.6**, these figures are 41.9% and 41.4% respectively. In compari-son, the figures for Nunatsiavut, Inuvialuit, and those living outside of the four land claim regions are much lower at 34.1%, 34%, and 31.5% respectively. Some Inuit residing outside of the four land claim regions are in large cities (Census Metropolitan Areas). These southern urban Inuit have the lowest proportion of their population under 15 years of age at 31.4% (**Table 10.10**).

Table 10.8: Nunavut: Inuit by Age and Sex

Age Cohorts	Population	Percentage	Male %	Female %
0 -14	9,345	41.4	51.3	48.7
15-64	12,595	55.8	49.8	50.2
65 & over	620	2.8	59.5	40.5
Nunavut	22,560	100.0	50.7	49.3

Source: Statistics Canada. 2001 Census. Custom Table Prepared for INAC. Requested by IRS

Table 10.9: Inuit Residing Outside of Land Claim Regions by Age and Sex

Age Cohorts	Population	Percentage	Male %	Female %
0 -14	2,675	31.5	50.2	49.8
15-64	5,560	65.5	45.5	54.5
65 & over	250	3.0	44.0	56.0
Rest of Canada	8,485	100.0	46.9	53.1

Source: Statistics Canada. 2001 Census. Custom Table Prepared for INAC. Requested by IRS

Table 10.10: Inuit Residing in Census Metropolitan Areas by Age and Sex

Age Cohorts	Population	Percentage	Male %	Female %
0 -14	1,035	31.4	53.1	46.9
15-64	2,220	67.3	42.8	57.2
65 & over	45	1.3	55.5	44.5
Census Metropolitan Areas	3,300	100.0	46.2	53.8

Source: Statistics Canada. 2001 Census. Custom Table Prepared for INAC. Requested by IRS

All Inuit regions have much higher proportions of their population in this young age group compared to the national figure of 19.1%.

The four land claim regions all exhibit a higher percentage of males. In striking contrast, the Inuit population residing outside of the land claim region is predominately female (**Table 10.9**). The likely explanation is a larger number of females than males moved from the land claim regions to towns and cities.

5. Urban Inuit Residing Outside of their Land Claim Regions

While census data on urban centres within the four land claim regions is readily available through a number of Statistics Canada products, including their website for Aboriginal Population Profiles, little is known about the size and distribution of Inuit in centres outside of the land claim regions. Yet, in 2001, almost 19% of Inuit (8,485) lived outside of the four land claim regions (**Table 10.11** – page 192). Nearly 40% (3,300) of these Inuit resided in Canada's largest cities, the Census Metropolitan Areas (Statistics Canada 2006). Even so, Dr. Michalowski and her associates (2005:23) reported that between 1996 and 2001, the Inuit migration rate was the lowest of the three Aboriginal peoples.

Table 10.11: Inuit Residing Outside of Land Claim Regions by Selected Urban Centres, 1996 and 2001

Major Inuit Urban Centres (with 100 or more Inuit in 2001)	1996	2001	% Change 1996 to 2001
Happy Valley-Goose Bay (CA)	1,225	1,100	(10.2)
Yellowknife (CA)	545	660	16.8
Edmonton (CMA)	205	465	126.8
Ottawa/Hull (CMA)	220	455	106.8
Montreal (CMA)	340	435	27.9
Toronto (CMA)	175	355	102.9
Vancouver (CMA)	110	260	136.4
St. John's (CMA)	135	210	55.5
North West River (CA)	195	195	0.0
Calgary (CMA)	185	195	5.4
Winnipeg (CMA)	120	185	54.1
Halifax (CMA)	75	165	126.7
Saskatoon (CMA)	85	120	41.2
Whitehorse (CA)	85	125	35.3
Wood Buffalo (CA) (Fort McMurray)	15	115	666.7
Hay River (CA)	65	105	61.5
Total in Major Inuit Centres	3,780	4,820	27.5
Total in Minor Centres*	3,520	3,665	4.1
Total Urban Inuit	7,300	8,485	16.2

*Defined as under 100 Inuit in 2001 Census

Sources: Statistics Canada. 2001 Aboriginal Population Profile. http://www12.statcan.ca/english/Profil01ab/PlaceSearchForm1.cfm; and Statistics Canada. Custom Table Prepared for INAC. Requested by IRS

To address this issue, IRS requested custom tables on Inuit residing in Census Subdivisions (CSDs). From these custom tables, a more detailed breakdown of urban centres with larger Inuit populations (at least 100 Inuit) was produced (**Table 10.12**). In 2001, the largest number of Inuit outside of the four land claim regions lived in Happy Valley-Goose Bay (1,100) and Yellowknife (660) while 14 other urban centres had at least 100 Inuit recorded by Statistics Canada (**Table 10.5**). The 2001 Census also recorded Inuit residing in over 100 urban centres with populations under 100 Inuit. (Statistics Canada 2006). Of this group of urban centres, most had 10 or less Inuit by identity in their populations. Six cities, however, had between 40 and 60 Inuit. They are: Red Deer (60), Kitchener (55), London (55), Victoria (55), Kingston (40), and Kamloops (40) (Statistics Canada 2006).

Why have Inuit located in these centres? Happy Valley-Goose Bay and Northwest River have long attracted Inuit from Nunatsiavut. In fact, the Nunatsiavut government has located some of its offices in these two communities, thus providing employment opportunities. Further south, Edmonton, Ottawa/Hull, and Montreal had the largest number of Inuit (**Table 10.12**). No doubt, the north/south transportation links from these three metropolitan centres to the four land

Table 10.12: Inuit Residing in Selected Census Metropolitan Areas, 1996 and 2001

Selected Census Metropolitan Areas*	1996	2001	% Change 1996 to 2001
Edmonton	205	465	126.8
Ottawa/Hull	220	455	106.8
Montreal	340	435	27.9
Toronto	175	355	102.9
Vancouver	110	260	136.4
St. John's	135	210	55.5
Calgary	185	195	5.4
Winnipeg	120	185	54.1
Halifax	75	165	126.7
Saskatoon	85	120	41.2
Total	1,650	2,845	72.4

*CMAs with Inuit Populations 100 or more in the 2001 Census.

Sources: Statistics Canada. 2001 Aboriginal Population Profile. http://www12.statcan.ca/english/Profil01ab/PlaceSearchForm1.cfm; and Statistics Canada. Custom Table Prepared for INAC. Requested by IRS.

claim regions helps to account for the relatively large number of Inuit. Edmonton provides ready access to the Inuvialuit Settlement Area while Montreal and Ottawa/Hull services Nunavik, Nunavut, and Nunatsiavut.

As **Tables 10.11** and **10.12** indicate, the number of urban Inuit is rapidly growing. From 1996 to 2001, the Inuit identity population in Canada increased from 40,220 to 45,070 or by 12%, while those residing in urban centres outside of the land claim regions grew at the higher rate of 16.2%. The highest rates of increase from 1996 to 2001 took place in Fort McMurray (667%), Vancouver (136%), Edmonton (127%), Halifax (127%), and Ottawa/Hull (107%). Equally remarkable, the Inuit population in the leading ten Census Metropolitan Areas increased by 72.4% (**Table 10.12**). The proportion of urban Inuit to those residing in the four land claim regions is shifting in favour of the urban Inuit. In 1996, 18.1% of the Inuit population resided outside of the four land claim regions. By 2001, this percentage had increased to 18.8%. Again, the growing number of urban Inuit does not mean that the populations within the four land claim regions are diminishing. Quite the contrary—the population of these four regions are increasing, but at a slower rate for the period 1996 to 2001.

Conclusion

In the preparation of documents for senior INAC officials, the 2001 Census remains the key source of data. IRS recognized that the development of an Inuit Database compiled from the 2001 Census was required for IRS to provide more precise census data in its briefing reports. Three key elements comprise the Inuit Database. They are (1) realigning existing 2001 census boundaries to fit the four land claim regions, (2) presenting census data by Inuit identity population, and (3) establishing a fifth Inuit region comprising those Inuit residing outside of the four land claim regions.

In this paper, the 12 tables illustrate the nature of the Inuit Database, and the text provides an elementary analysis. For ten tables, the census data is arranged by the five Inuit regions which reveal strong regional differences. Nunavut has the largest population of the five regions while Nunatsiavut has the smallest. In terms of age structure, close similarities are found between Nunavut and Nunavik, and between the Inuvialuit Settlement Area and Nunatsiavut. The age and gender structure of the Inuit population residing outside of the four land claim regions is different from the four land claim regions in two ways. First, the urban region has a larger percentage of its population in the so-called productive age category. Second, the urban region has a larger percentage of females than males. The last two tables (**Tables 10.11** and **10.12**) describe the number of Inuit residing in urban centres outside of the four land claim regions. These tables provide an insight into the differing rates of urban Inuit population increase from 1996 to 2001.

The 2001 Inuit Database is composed of census data by total population, Aboriginal identity population, and Inuit ancestry population. At this point in time, the subject matter consists of age and sex, language, and Inuit residing in urban centres. Statistics Canada is expected to make the remaining custom tabulations on education, income, labour force, occupation, industry, household, and dwellings available soon. At that time, basic tables on these subject matters will be prepared.

References

Bell, Jim. (2003). "One in 10 Inuit Live in the South, Census Shows." *Nunatsiaq News*. January 24.

Carpenter, Mary. (1993). "Urban Inuit." *Inuktitut*. 76:62–69.

George Jane. (2001). "Ottawa Shelter Opening for Homeless Inuit: Pigiarvik House Will Open Its Doors in June." *Nunatsiaq News*. June 1.

_____. (2004). "Living in Qallunajatut: Real People Populate New Isuma Documentary." *Nunatsiaq News*. October 8.

Inuit Tapiriit Kanatami and the Minister of Indian Affairs and Northern Development. (2005). *Partnership Accord*. Ottawa: Indian and Northern Affairs Canada.

Kishigami, Nobuhiro. (1999). "Why do Inuit Move to Montreal?" *Étude/Inuit/Studies*. 23 (1/2): 221–227.

_____. (1999). "Life and Problems of Urban Inuit in Montreal, Report of 1997." Research, *Journal of Liberal Arts*. No. 68:81–109.

_____. (2002). "Inuit Identities in Montreal, Canada." *Étude/Inuit/Studies*. 26 (1):183–191.

_____. (2002). "Urban Inuit in Canada: A Case from Montreal." *Indigenous Affairs*, 3/4: 55–59.

Indian Register Population by Sex and Residence. (2004). <**www.ainc-inac.gc.ca/pr/sts/rip/rip04_ e.html**>

Inuit Tapiriit Kanatami and Strategic Research and Analysis Directorate of the Department of Indian Affairs and Northern Development. Forthcoming. "Determining the Inuit population: definitional issues and differences. No. 1." Social Trends Profile Series. Ottawa: Indian and Northern Affairs Canada.

_____. Forthcoming. "Inuit in Canada: Regional distribution and demographic changes from 1981 – 2001. No. 2." Social Trends Profile Series. Ottawa: Indian and Northern Affairs Canada.

Mesher, Jr., Victor. (2000). "No Longer Alone: A Haven of Happiness with the Association of Montreal Inuit." *Makivik Magazine*. 54:57–67.

Michalowski, Margaret, Shirley Loh, Ravi Verma, Marie-France Germain, and Claude Grenier. (2005). *Projections of the Aboriginal populations, Canada, provinces and territories: 2001 to 2017*. Statistics Canada. 91-547-SCB.

Norris, M.J., Cooke, M., Beavon, D., Guimond, E., and Clatworthy, S. (2003). "Registered Indian Mobility and Migration in Canada: Patterns and Implications Migration." In *Population Mobility and Indigenous Peoples in Australasia and North America*. Taylor, J. and Bell, eds. New York: Routledge Press.

Ravenstein, E.G. (1876). "The Laws of Migration." *Journal of the Statistical Society*. 48:167–227.

_____. (1876). "The Laws of Migration." *Journal of the Statistical Society*. 52:214–301.

Roy-Sole, Monique and David Trattles. (2005). "Urban Inuit." *Canadian Geographic*. July/August issue: 74–82.

Siggner, Andrew J. and Rosalinda Costa. (2005). "Aboriginal Conditions in Census Metropolitan Areas, 1981–2001." Statistics Canada. 89–613. <**dsp-psd.pwgsc.gc.ca/Collection/Statcan/89-613-MIE/89-613-MIE2005008.pdf**>

_____. (2001). *Aboriginal Population Profile*. <**www12.statcan.ca/english/profil01ab/Place SearchForm1.cfm**>

_____. (2003). "2001 Census: Age and Sex. Topic Based Tabulation 5. Age (122) and Sex (3) for Population, for Canada, Provinces, Territories, Census Metropolitan Areas and Census Agglomerations, 2001 Census - 100% Data." <**www12.statcan.ca/english/census01/products/standard/ themes/RetrieveProductTable.cfm?Temporal=2001&PID=55437&APATH=3&GID**>

_____. (2005). Custom Tables from the 2001 Census prepared for INAC Requested by IRS. Age and Sex, and Language.

_____. (2006). Custom Table from 2001 Census prepared for INAC Requested by IRS. List of CSDs listed and ranked by Inuit population greater than 0, 2001 Census from core table #37.

_____. (2006). Custom Tables from the 2001 Census prepared for INAC Requested by IRS. Education, Income, Labour Force, Occupation, Industry, Households, and Dwellings.

Statistics Canada. (1982). *Indian and Northern Affairs Canada. Living in the South.* 39 pp.

Statistics Canada. (2003). "Aboriginal Mobility and Migration Within Urban Canada: Outcomes, Factors and Implications by Mary Jane Norris, Indian and Northern Affairs Canada, and Stewart Clatworthy." Four Directions Project Consulting.

Statistics Canada. (2006). Indian and Northern Affairs Canada. Federal Interlocutor for Métis and Non-Status Indians. Urban Aboriginal Strategy. <**www.ainc-inac.gc.ca/interloc/uas/cit_e.html**>

11

Aboriginal Languages in Canada: Trends and Perspectives on Maintenance and Revitalization

Mary Jane Norris[1]

Introduction

Across Canada, languages indigenous to this country are many and diverse, with some 50 individual languages belonging to 11 Aboriginal language families or isolates,[2]—10 First Nations, Inuktitut, and Métis.[3] These languages reflect a diversity of distinctive histories, cultures, and identities; linked in many ways to family, community, the land, and traditional knowledge. And, these many languages and their communities also differ widely in their state and conditions, with varying degrees of vitality—some flourishing, others endangered, and some close to extinction.

Unlike most Canadians, Aboriginal people are confronted with the issue that many of their languages are in the process of disappearing and nearing extinction. The implications of language maintenance and revitalization are profound for Aboriginal languages. In June 2005, the Task Force on Aboriginal Languages and Cultures presented its report to the Minister of Canadian Heritage, entitled "Towards a New Beginning: A Foundation Report for a Strategy to Revitalize First Nation, Inuit, and Métis Cultures." This report addresses issues and makes recommendations concerning strategies to preserve, revitalize, and promote Aboriginal languages and cultures.

In its discussions, the Task Force emphasized that a strategy to support First Nation, Inuit, and Métis peoples to revive, maintain, and strengthen their languages must reflect the great variety of language conditions; and that these complexities and variations in language conditions can impact on planning and programs at the local, regional, and national levels. Also, during consultations, the need for a community-driven revitalization strategy was stressed in identifying priorities and developing plans to revitalize their languages, along with the recognition that community needs and plans would differ from community to community, depending on the state of their languages and resources. (Canadian Heritage, 2005, 33, 63).

This paper first discusses the current state of First Nations, Inuit, and Métis languages, together with recent trends, from various perspectives including communities, cities, regions, and the specific languages themselves. Discussion is necessarily focused on community-level indicators in relation to the need for community-driven language planning and strategies—be they associated with preservation, maintenance, or revitalization. The paper then explores long-term trends over the past 20 years, and future prospects in maintenance and revitalization, germane to language planning, programs, and policies that address the challenges of protecting and promoting Aboriginal languages. The research utilizes data on Aboriginal languages from Canada's censuses from 1981 through to 2001.

State of First Nations, Inuit, and Métis Languages, 2001

Of the 976,000 people who identified as Aboriginal in the 2001 Census, just under a quarter (235,000) said that they had knowledge[4] of, or ability to converse in, an Aboriginal language. Some 21% of the Aboriginal population learned an Aboriginal language as their first language or mother tongue,[5] but only 13% reported speaking an Aboriginal language most often in their home. New information from the 2001 census indicates that an additional 5% do use an Aboriginal language regularly, if not mainly, at home.[6] This may be relevant for endangered languages where the languages are used less frequently.

The 2001 census data reflects the outcomes of long-term language erosion. For the first time since 1981, the total population with an Aboriginal mother tongue declined from 208,600 in 1996 to 203,300 in 2001.[7] Prior to 1996, the population speaking an Aboriginal language at home was declining, but the mother tongue population still grew. However, data now show that the number of people with an Aboriginal mother tongue is decreasing instead of growing.

State of Languages: Selected Indicators

Home Language of Today: Mother Tongue of Tomorrow

Although population size is an important consideration in determining the health of a spoken language, if it is not being spoken within the family home it is less likely to be the mother tongue of the next generation. The viability or continuity of a language is dependent on it being used on a daily basis, ideally as the major home language (Report of the Royal Commission on Aboriginal Peoples (RCAP) 1996). The prospects of transmitting a particular language as the mother tongue of the next generation can be assessed on the basis of an indicator, the continuity index. The continuity index of a language measures current home use relative to first-language speakers, based on the ratio of the number of people who speak the language at home for every 100 persons who speak that language as their mother tongue.[8]

Declines in Language Continuity

Trends indicate that many Aboriginal languages—even ones with large mother tongue populations—will be confronted with the challenges of continuity for the next generation. For example, even though Ojibway has a sizable population of first-language speakers, representing the third largest Aboriginal mother tongue in Canada today, trends indicate that the number of Ojibway first-language speakers are aging and declining, and that the use of Ojibway as a major home language is diminishing. For most Aboriginal languages, the transmission of Aboriginal mother tongues (first languages) to younger generations is declining due to their decreasing use as major home languages. Overall, the 1981 to 2001 period saw steady erosion in home language use, with decreased continuity, and increasingly older populations of speakers. For language survival, the impact of the long-term decline in continuity, or transmission to children, is now being felt more profoundly than ever.

Children are the future speakers of Aboriginal languages; their language outcomes are critical to the maintenance and revitalization of their languages. Language outcomes of children today have significant implications for the language status of future generations. According to the United Nations Educational Scientific and Cultural Organization (UNESCO), a language is considered endangered if it is not learned by at least 30% of children in a community. The 2001 census indicated that only 15% of Aboriginal children in Canada under the age of five had learned an Indigenous mother tongue. Children are the major source of growth for the Aboriginal mother tongue population in Canada. The decrease in the numbers of first-language speakers since 1996 attests to the impact of declining continuity. Lowered rates of language transmission to younger generations seem to no longer be offset by still relatively high levels of Aboriginal fertility.

The average age of the population with a given Aboriginal mother tongue is a significant indicator of the health and future prospect of languages because it reveals the extent to which it has been transmitted to younger generations. The higher the average age, the fewer young people have learned or still understand the language and the older the people who still speak it. When these older people die, so may the languages.

For Aboriginal languages overall, the average age of the speakers have been increasing. This trend is due to decreasing shares of children acquiring an Aboriginal mother tongue, and, to some extent, to declining fertility rates, which although still high, eventually translate into relatively fewer children. The twenty year period from 1981–2001 saw an erosion of home language use, and an aging population with Aboriginal mother tongues. Over this period, the index of continuity decreased from about 76 to 61; the average age of the mother tongue population rose by 5.5 years to 33 in 2001 (**Figure 11.1** – page 200).

Also, corresponding to long-term trends of declining continuity and aging first-language speakers, the proportion of children in the population with an Aboriginal

Figure 11.1: Aboriginal Languages: Index of Continuity and Average Age of Mother Tongue Population, Canada, 1981–2001

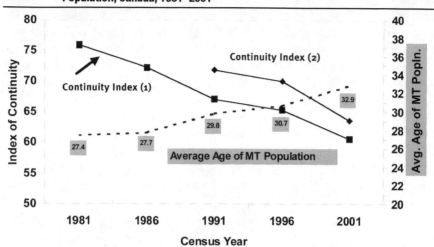

(1) Based on Single responses to language (MT, HL) questions.
(2) Based on Single and Multiple responses.
Source: 1981–2001 Censuses, Norris 2003

mother tongue has been diminishing. Between 1986 and 2001, the percentage of first-language speakers aged 0 to 19 declined from 41 to 32%. In the opposite direction, the percentage of adults aged 55 and over increased from 12 to 17% (**Figure 11.2**).

Shifts from First to Second Language Acquisition

Age and continuity factors do not tell the whole story, however, since second language acquisition is prevalent among younger generations. With the declining use of Aboriginal languages as the major home language, younger generations of speakers are increasingly likely to acquire their Aboriginal language as a second language rather than as a mother tongue. For example, the Kutenai language family has one of the oldest mother tongue populations and lowest continuity indexes but the index of ability or second language acquisition[9] indicates that there are two people (usually younger) who speak the language for every one individual with a mother tongue, suggesting that younger generations are more likely to learn Kutenai as a second language. Second language acquisition patterns are also more highly pronounced off-reserve, especially among youth in urban areas (Norris and Jantzen 2002). It should be noted though, that with respect to second-language acquisition, varying degrees of fluency could be represented among census respondents reporting knowledge of the language—that is, the ability to conduct a conversation in an Aboriginal language—suggesting some caution in considering the implications of second language acquisition for transmission and continuity.

Figure 11.2: Children and Seniors as Percentage of Population With an Aboriginal Mother Tongue, 1986 to 2001

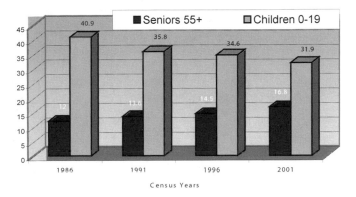

Children's & Seniors' Share of Aboriginal Mother Tongue Population

Source: 1986–2001 Censuses, Norris 2003

Most languages over the 1996 to 2001 period, experienced greater growth in the numbers of speakers overall who could carry on a conversation, regardless of how they learned the language, compared to the growth of their first language only speakers. These trends suggest that some languages are gaining speakers at a faster rate through second-language acquisition than through mother tongue transmission. Learning an Aboriginal language as a second language appeared to be on the rise between 1996 and 2001 for most Aboriginal languages, based on the index of second language acquisition. Some languages saw a growth in their numbers of total speakers, while others experienced declines overall because of shrinking mother tongue populations.

First Nations, Inuit, and Métis Languages: Distinct States

Significant differences in the state of First Nations, Inuit, and Métis languages, in their home communities and in cities, reflect in part the differences among these groups in the degree of their urbanization. Groups that live in remote communities or in settlements with concentrated populations of Aboriginal speakers, such as registered Indians on-reserve or Inuit, generally find it easier to retain their language than other groups like non-status Indians or Métis, who have higher proportions of their population residing in urban areas. Census data illustrate the sharp contrast across Aboriginal groups in the state of their languages. For 2001, the proportions of populations with an Aboriginal mother tongue are highest among Inuit (66%), followed by First Nations (26%), and lowest among Métis (4%). First Nations, Inuit, and Métis also differ in the transmission and acquisition of their languages for the next generation. Inuit languages show the

Figure 11.3: Percentage of Aboriginal Identity Population with an Aboriginal Mother Tongue, Canada, 1996 and 2001

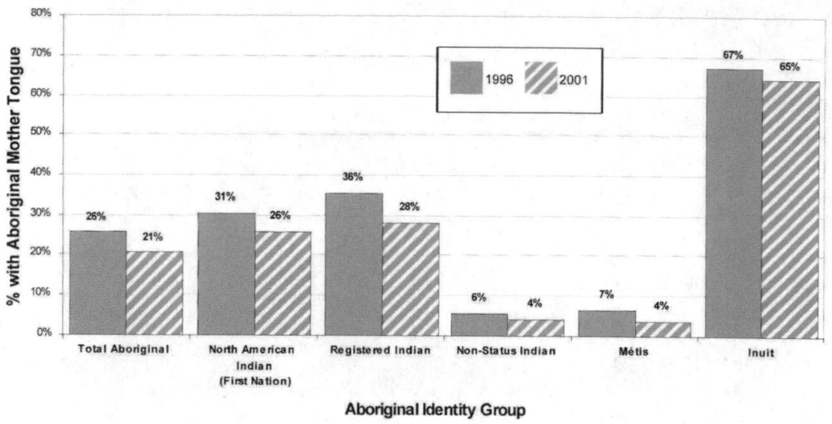

Aboriginal Identity Group

Source: 1996 and 2001 Censuses, Norris 2003

greatest continuity, being most likely to be transmitted as the mother tongue of future generations, followed by First Nations languages. While Inuit speakers are most likely to have learned their languages as their mother tongue, Métis speakers are most likely to learn their languages as second languages. (Norris and Jantzen 2002). Despite their differences, First Nations, Inuit, and Métis languages experienced similar trends between 1996 and 2001, of declining shares of populations with an Aboriginal mother tongue (**Figure 11.3**), decreased continuity, and increased second language acquisition.

The State of Aboriginal Languages Within Communities and Cities

Aboriginal languages appear to fare much better within Aboriginal communities as opposed to outside, especially in larger urban environments. The transmission of Aboriginal languages as a mother tongue from parent to child is clearly jeopardized in an urban environment given the small share of Aboriginal persons speaking an Aboriginal language at home, and findings suggest that urban Aboriginal people continue to be confronted with considerable challenges in maintaining their Aboriginal languages where the dominant languages (English or French) prevail (RCAP 1996; Norris and Jantzen 2002). The 2001 census suggests overall continued patterns of erosion of Aboriginal language use and maintenance within cities.

Aboriginal communities, including First Nations reserves and northern Inuit communities, can serve as enclaves for the maintenance and survival of their languages, especially those with sizable mother tongue populations and high

Figure 11.4: Percentage of Aboriginal Identity Population with Aboriginal Mother Tongue, Home Language or Knowledge by Place of Residence, Canada, 1996

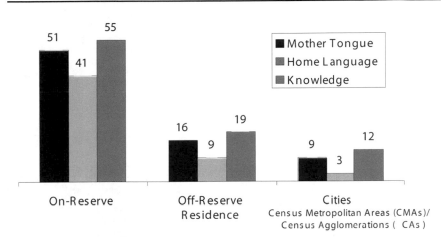

Source: 1996 Census, Norris 2003

continuity. In 1996, half of the Aboriginal population residing in reserve communities had an Aboriginal mother tongue. Some 55% had the ability to speak an Aboriginal language, and nearly 40% spoke their Aboriginal language most often at home. In sharp contrast, much smaller proportions of Aboriginal people residing in cities had an Aboriginal mother tongue (9%), spoke their language as the major home language (3%), or had the ability to converse in their language (12%) (**Figure 11.4**).

Yet, language situations of communities can differ significantly in their outlook depending on their location, degree of remoteness, or urbanization (even among the same language). The more viable languages tend to be spoken in isolated and/or well-organized Aboriginal communities with large numbers of resident speakers. Compared to speakers in Aboriginal communities, those in cities are less likely to use their languages as the major language in the home, and are also more likely to learn their language as a second language.

The next section explores the state and conditions of the many and diverse Aboriginal languages from a number of different perspectives.

Diversity: Perspectives on State, Community, Urbanization, and Regions

Language planning, strategies, programs, and policies associated with the promotion, preservation, maintenance, and revitalization of the many and diverse Aboriginal languages in Canada need to be developed from a variety of perspectives. A range of perspectives and measures are examined in relation to indi-

Figure 11.5: Percentage of Aboriginal Identity Population[10] with Aboriginal Mother Tongue, Home Language or Knowledge by Place of Residence, Canada, 1996

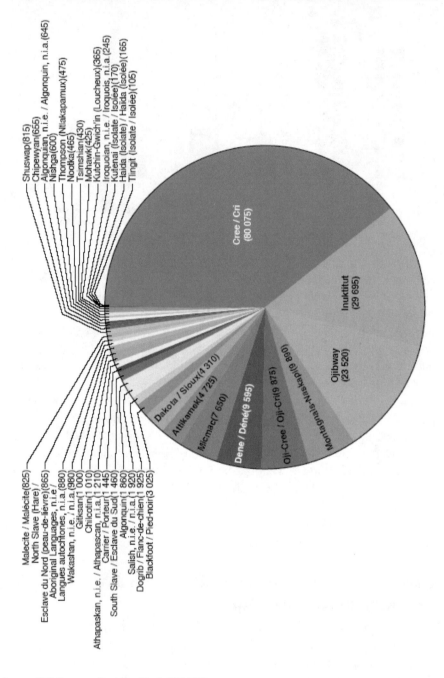

Source: 2001 Census, updated from Norris 1998,2005

vidual languages: the size of speaker populations and state of intergenerational transmission, the numbers of communities, the degree of urbanization, and regional characteristics. From this multi-dimensional approach, a more complete picture is emerging about the range and extent of maintenance and revitalization requirements at the level of specific languages and their communities. Analyses of the size of languages and their shares according to these different perspectives could have significant implications for planning and allocation of resources associated with various language revitalization strategies.

Viable and Endangered Aboriginal languages

Aboriginal languages differ significantly in their state, and in their trends and outlook, and as such they can be classified accordingly. On the basis of a classification by Kinkade (1991), they can be divided into five groupings: already extinct; near extinction; endangered; viable with a small population base; and viable with a large population. Languages classified as near extinction[11] may be beyond the possibility of revival. As only a few elderly people speak these languages, there may only be enough time to record and archive them. Endangered languages are spoken by enough people to make survival a possibility, given sufficient community interest and concerted educational programs. They tend to have small populations, older speakers, and lower rates of language transmission. Many of the smaller languages, often with fewer than 1,000 persons, have very low prospects for ongoing transmission across generations. This is particularly relevant to the situation in British Columbia where many of the languages found there have very low prospects for continuity, and are either endangered (e.g. Nishga, Haida) or near extinction. Viable small languages generally have more than 1,000 speakers, and are spoken in isolated or well-organized communities with strong self-awareness. In these communities, language is considered one of the important marks of identity. A language can be considered viable if its continuity is high and it has relatively young speakers, for example, Attikamek and Dene. Viable large languages have a population base large enough that long-term survival is likely assured. Cree, Inuktitut, and Ojibway are the only viable languages with large population bases. Large or small, viable languages tend to have relatively young speakers, compared to endangered languages. Census data are available for viable and endangered languages, but are not available separately for languages near extinction owing to their small numbers of speakers.

The following provides a summary of the state of these viable and endangered languages along selected dimensions of population size, continuity, number of communities, and urbanization to illustrate how individual languages differ in their situations depending on the perspective considered.

By Mother Tongue Population, 2001 Census

In Canada's 2001 census, 203,300 persons reported an Aboriginal language as their mother tongue. The Algonquin, Inuktitut, and Athapaskan language families

Figure 11.6: Index of Continuity by Aboriginal Languages, Canada, 2001

Index (No. of persons with home language per 100 with mother tongue)

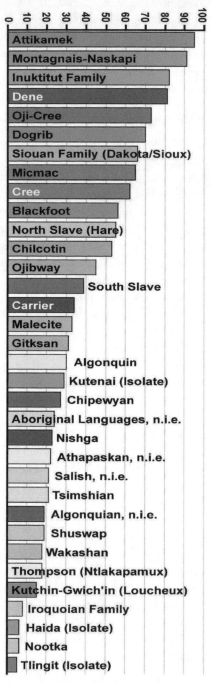

Source: 2001 Census, Updated from Norris 1998, Norris and Jantzen, 2002

have the largest mother tongue populations; together, they represent 94% of the total Aboriginal mother tongue population. In contrast, the eight other language families account for the remaining 6% of the Aboriginal mother tongue population, including many smaller languages in British Columbia. According to the 2001 census, the five largest individual Aboriginal languages, all considered to be viable, are Cree (39%), Inuktitut (15%), Ojibway (12%), Montagnais-Naskapi (5%), and Dene (5%), which, when combined, account for 76% of the total population of Aboriginal mother tongue speakers (**Figure 11.5** – page 204).

By Strength—Continuity of Language, 2001 Census

As noted previously, the state of a language is not just linked to population size; continuity is also an indicator of vitality. From the perspective of intergenerational transmission, a different picture emerges compared to population size alone. Those languages with the greatest prospects for transmission as the first language of the next generation are some of the smaller viable languages: Attikamek, Montagnais-Naskapi, Inuktitut, Dene, and Oji-Cree (**Figure 11.6**). These continuity measures suggest that the two larger languages—Cree and Ojibway—are less likely to be passed on as a mother tongue compared to these smaller viable languages.

By Number of Communities,[12] 2001 Census

From the perspective of the sheer number of communities, clearly a different picture emerges with respect to British Columbia. Although BC languages are characterized by small populations and weak prospects for continuity, they are nevertheless many in number, and associated with a disproportionately large number of communities where the languages, are or have been, spoken. The five languages with the largest number of communities, out of a total of 879 communities in Canada, are Cree (23%), all Salish languages (17%), Ojibway (16%), Inuktitut (6%), and Micmac (4%). These five languages account for 60% of all communities in which an Aboriginal language is spoken or was the original language.

By Urban Areas, 2001 Census

Not all Aboriginal people reside in predominantly Aboriginal communities. Close to 39,000 people, or almost one in five who reported speaking an Aboriginal mother tongue, resided in major cities across Canada. In terms of the urban situation, clearly not all Aboriginal languages are similar in their degree of urbanization. For example, even though Inuktitut comprises the second largest share (15%) of Canada's Aboriginal mother tongue population, only 3% of Inuktitut first language speakers reside in cities. In 2001, the five languages comprising the largest populations and shares of first-language speakers residing in urban areas were: Cree (36%), Ojibway (18%), Micmac (10%), Montagnais-Naskapi (6%), and Salish (4%).

Regional Perspectives: Distribution of First Nations, Inuit, and Métis Languages

Regional perspectives are important because the size, diversity, and state of First Nations, Inuit, and Métis languages differ significantly across provinces and territories. This has implications for understanding differing regional needs in language maintenance and revitalization. The current geographic distribution and size of Aboriginal languages, and a variety of geographical, cultural and historical factors reflect the different situation of First Nations, Inuit, and Métis languages. First Nations languages comprise the vast majority of Aboriginal languages spoken in Canada, with their more populous languages tending to be the most widely dispersed across Canada. Algonquian, the largest language family, extends from the Atlantic region to the Rocky Mountains. Although home to at least half[13] of Canada's Aboriginal languages, British Columbia accounts for just 6% of first language speakers in Canada. Languages spoken by Métis people are mainly concentrated in Manitoba, Saskatchewan, and Alberta, and to some extent in parts of the NWT, British Columbia, Ontario, and Labrador. These include Dene (Athapaskan family), Cree and other Algonquian languages, and Michif, considered the historical and cultural language of the Métis. Manitoba (37,085), Quebec (36,535) and Saskatchewan (33,330) have the largest populations of Aboriginal first language speakers. Combined, they represent just over half (52%) of the 203,000 people in Canada who reported speaking an Aboriginal language as their first language. Smaller populations of first language speakers are found in Alberta (13%) and Ontario (10%). Inuktitut is distributed widely across northern Canada, including northern Northwest Territories, Nunavut, northern Quebec, and Labrador.

Linguistic Diversity in Provinces and Territories: From Few to Many Different Languages

The range in the regional diversity of Aboriginal languages is considerable: from only one or two Aboriginal languages spoken in some provinces/territories to a multitude in British Columbia. In both Nunavut (Inuktitut) and Nova Scotia (Micmac), practically all the first-language speakers speak just one language, making them the two most linguistically homogenous areas in Canada. In most provinces, the three largest Aboriginal languages generally account for at least 80% of the province's total population of first-language speakers. In contrast, in British Columbia where 20 languages make up the total population with an Aboriginal mother tongue, the three largest Aboriginal languages—Salish, Cree, and Carrier—account for only 38% of the province's first-language speakers. The next most diverse area is the Northwest Territories, where 10 different Aboriginal languages account for 67% of that territory's population of first-language speakers.

Provinces and Territories Differ Broadly in the State of their Languages

Various census-based measures and indicators demonstrate the substantial differences that exist across provinces and territories in the state, maintenance, and revitalization of Aboriginal languages. In 2001, about one in five Aboriginal people (21%) in Canada reported an Aboriginal mother tongue. Regionally this share ranged from a low of 7% in British Columbia to a high of 84% in Nunavut. Between these extremes, nearly one in two (46%) Aboriginal people in Quebec reported an Aboriginal mother tongue, followed by about 25–30% of Aboriginal populations in each of the NWT, Saskatchewan, Manitoba, and Nova Scotia.

In some regions where intergenerational transmission remains strong, children are still highly likely to learn an Aboriginal language as their mother tongue, and less so as a second language. Owing to the linguistic vitality of languages like Inuktitut, Attikamek, and Montagnais-Naskapi, practically all the speakers of Aboriginal languages in Quebec, Nunavut, and Labrador have learned their language as a mother tongue. And, it appears that younger generations continue to do so, having some of the youngest first-language speakers in Canada, with ages ranging on average from the mid- to late-twenties. In sharp contrast, some of the oldest populations of first-language speakers are found in British Columbia and Yukon, averaging over 40 years of age. For many of the endangered languages in these areas, the prospects of being transmitted as the mother tongue of the next generation are extremely low, although it appears that young people may be learning some of these languages as their second language.

The next section explores most recent short-term trends over the 1996–2001 period for different Aboriginal languages with respect to their continuity, transmission, and acquisition.

Recent Trends in Selected Viable and Endangered Aboriginal Languages: 1996–2001

Between 1996 and 2001, the average age of mother tongue speakers rose, even in cases where an Aboriginal language is not the only mother tongue of the respondent, but can be a "multiple."[14] As with long-term trends, aging was less pronounced for those languages that had been spoken frequently at home. For example, the average age of first-language speakers increased only slightly, remaining in the early- to mid- twenties, for the Montagnais-Naskapi, Attikamek, and Inuktitut languages, with only slight declines in their high continuity over the 1996–2001 period, (from 94 to 91; 97 to 95; and 86 to 82 respectively). By contrast, those languages that experienced a steady long-term decline in home use and in continuity, exhibited significant aging of their first language speakers. Even larger languages, such as Ojibway, experienced a sharp increase in the average age of first language speakers, from 36 to 40 years between 1996 and 2001.

Figure 11.7: Distribution of Aboriginal Communities* by Continuity Index of Aboriginal Language, Canada, 1996 and 2001

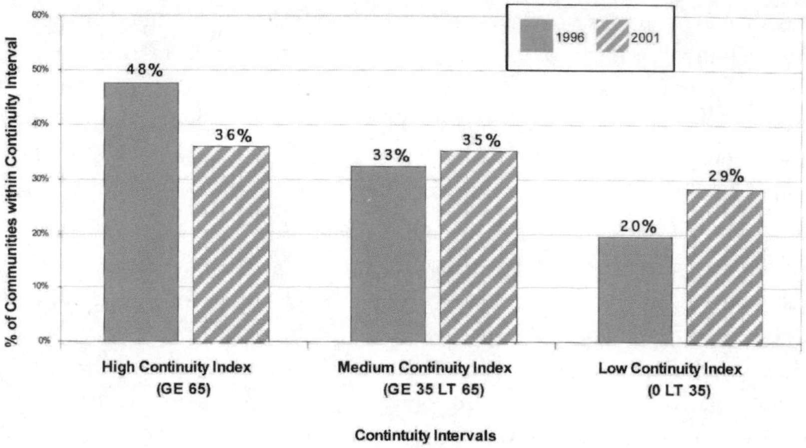

*Number of comparable communities between 1996 and 2001 = 390.

Source: 1996 and 2001 censuses, updated from Norris 2002, 2003

Intergenerational Transmission Contributes to Growth of Mother-tongue Population

While the population with an Aboriginal mother tongue declined overall between 1996 and 2001, some languages experienced growth in the number of speakers, with the strongest growth observed for those with high continuity levels of at least 80. In 2001, a total of 29,700 people reported Inuktitut as their mother tongue, up 7% from 1996. Even stronger growth in mother tongue populations was observed for the smaller high continuity languages such as Attikamek (18%), and Montagnais-Naskapi (9%). Other languages that showed increases in mother tongue included Dene, Micmac, Oji-Cree, and Dakota/Sioux.

While it is not surprising that populations of endangered mother tongues shrunk over the 1996–2001 period, it perhaps seemed more unexpected that some of the larger more viable languages, like Cree and Ojibway, also decreased, by 3% and 10% respectively. This reflects the impact of long-term declines in continuity and in aging first language speakers, and demonstrates that population size is not the only contributing factor to the health and vitality of a language.

Trends: Transition from First-language Transmission to Second Language Acquisition

Between 1996 and 2001, there was greater growth in the number of people who were able to converse in their language, irrespective of whether the language was learned as a first or second language, compared to the growth of first language speakers. These patterns suggest greater growth among those who reported learning an Aboriginal language later in life—that is, as a second language. For

Figure 11.8: Distribution of Aboriginal Communities* by Index of Second Language Acquisition, for Aboriginal Language, Canada, 1996 and 2001

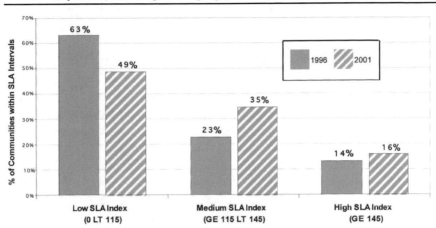

Second Language Acquisition (SLA) Intervals

*Number of comparable communities between 1996 and 2001 = 390

Source: 1996 and 2001 censuses, updated from Norris 2002, 2003

those languages that experienced declines in their mother tongue populations, the extent of the overall decline in speakers tended to be less, being offset by the addition of second-language learners. For Attikamek, between 1996 and 2001, the population with the ability to speak the language increased 21%, compared to 18.5% for its mother tongue population. Similarly for Dene, knowledge of the language increased 10%, while mother tongue speakers increased only 6%. For Blackfoot, while the mother tongue population declined by 27%, the total population of speakers declined to a lesser extent, by 20%, over the same period, with losses offset by the addition of second-language speakers.

Trends in second language learning are increasing, especially among endangered languages, and are most pronounced among youth. For example, among the smaller Salish languages in British Columbia, there are signs that revitalization is occurring among youth. By 2001 the second-language index increased to 156 from 132 in 1996, while the average age of all Salish speakers (including second language learners) is notably younger at 42 years of age, compared to 50 years for the population with a Salish mother tongue.

Community Perspectives on Maintenance and Revitalization

Clearly, the census information demonstrates that Aboriginal communities play a critical role in the maintenance and revitalization of their languages. Yet many communities have stated that their languages are eroding, mirroring the trends of declining continuity and diminishing prospects of intergenerational transmission, and shifts towards second-language learning. As with their languages, this transition is just beginning for some communities, is well underway in others, and completed in some communities, especially for endangered languages that are being learned increasingly as second languages.

Community Shifts 1996–2001: Lowered Continuity, Increased Second-language Acquisition

The prospects for a community's language being transmitted as a mother tongue can be assessed using the continuity index, while the extent to which the community language is being learned as a second language can be assessed using the index of second-language acquisition. Comparisons between 1996 and 2001 for the same set of comparable communities (with a minimum mother tongue population of 30 in 2001 and enumerated in both 1996 and 2001)[15] showed an overall shift to lower continuity; that is, decreased prospects for intergenerational transmission, and over the same period, an overall shift towards second-language acquisition. **(Figures 11.7** and **11.8** – pages 210 and 211).

In 1996, practically half, 49% of communities experienced relatively "high" levels of continuity (indices of greater than or equal to 65); another 29% experienced "medium" continuity (indices between 35 and less than 65); and 22% experienced "low" continuity levels (indices of less than 35). By 2001, the percent of communities in the "high" continuity category fell significantly to just 34%, while in contrast, the "medium" and "low" categories of continuity saw increased shares of 38% and 28% respectively. Corresponding to this overall shift in the distribution, while many communities (59%) remained within the same range of continuity levels over this period, another 30% shifted into ranges of lower continuity, while 11% saw shifts into higher ranges.

Similarly, in 1996, with respect to the index of second-language acquisition, close to two out of three communities (64%) had "low" second-language acquisition indices (less than 115), implying that most community speakers had learned their language as a mother tongue. Another 28% of communities fell into "medium" ranges (greater than or equal to 115 and less than 145), while the remaining 8.5% displayed high indices (greater than 145), suggesting that a significant proportion of their speakers would have acquired their Aboriginal language as a second language. By 2001 these distributions shifted notably, such that now less than half, 45%, of communities had measures of second-language acquisition in the low range; in contrast the percent of communities with second language measures in the "medium" category increased to 38% while the percent with relatively "high" levels of second-language acquisition doubled from 8.5% to 17%. Corresponding to this shift in the overall distribution, second-language indexes remained within the same range for most communities (54%) while 34% of communities saw their indexes shift into higher ranges of second-language acquisition, with the remaining 13% shifting into lower ranges.

Community-driven Revitalization Strategy

In the Task Force report, those consulted about a community-driven revitalization strategy stressed that the community must play a central role in revitalization, and that planning should be community-driven, by the needs and aspirations of each First Nations, Inuit, and Métis community. The involvement and participation of all community members from all age groups are required if a language revitalization plan is to be realistic and achievable.

> It was recognized that plans would vary from community to community, depending on the state of the language and the resources available in each. Some languages may have a large number of speakers and be widely spoken: here efforts would focus on maintaining and expanding the language. In other communities, only a few elderly speakers may be remaining; efforts here would need to concentrate on preserving the language (Canadian Heritage 2005, 63–64).

The Task Force pointed out that few fluent speakers are left in many communities, and that it is not unusual for a language to be spoken in only one or two communities within the territory in which the language had been spoken, especially in British Columbia. Even languages with many speakers encounter difficulties, such as losing the names and uses of local flowers, and forgetting ways of describing kinship relationships (Canadian Heritage 2005, 65).

From a planning and policy perspective, demographic research on the conditions and characteristics of Aboriginal languages at the community level can help inform the development of language strategies, through the use of various measures and indicators relative to the type and extent of language-related activities—be it preservation, revitalization or promotion across First Nations, Inuit, and Métis communities.

Communities in Transition: A Continuum of Transmission, Acquisition, and Decline

From the 2001 census data, 879 communities have been identified as Aboriginal—specifically First Nations, Inuit, and Métis, and by major language, based on criteria first established using 1996 census data (Norris 1998; Norris and Jantzen 2002 a&b). Communities were classified by language states using various indicators of maintenance and revitalization. These indicators included: the community's continuity index cross-classified by its second-language index, by population size of first-language speakers, by ages of all speakers, and by first-language speakers. Apart from population size, the other indicators were restricted to the 445 communities with a minimum mother tongue population of 30 or more first-language speakers. The measures are not reliable for communities with small population sizes. In summary, all 879 communities are classified into nine mutually exclusive and exhaustive categories, which yield a continuum of categories of communities by differing language states. These categories range from "communities with flourishing languages and young first language speakers" (category 1) to "communities with no first-language speakers" (category 8). Category 9 consists of those communities for which census data is unavailable. These categorizations may provide some insight into the type, range and extent of appropriate community-level interventions and activities. The categories and demographic implications are summarized in the following:

1. Communities with Flourishing Languages, Young First-language Speakers (116)

There are 116 communities in this category. The language situation for communities in this category could be considered to be ideal in terms of language maintenance and transmission. Revitalization does not appear to be an issue at this time. About one out of every four communities with a mother tongue population of at least 30 or more speakers fit this category. These 116 communities can generally be characterized as having "high continuity, low second-language acquisition," with large populations of first-language speakers, numbering 500 or more, and mainly very young, with average ages of between 15 and 24 in about half of communities. Children in these communities learn their language almost exclusively as a mother tongue. Communities in this category are First Nations (70%), Inuit (27%), and Métis (3%), with five languages accounting for nearly 90% of the communities: Cree (34%), Inuktitut (27%), Dene (10%), Montagnais–Naskapi (8%), and Ojibway (6%). Ojibway communities are under-represented in this category given their 16% share of communities; while Inuktitut speaking communities are over-represented with a share of 6%. These communities are concentrated in the eastern Arctic, Quebec, and the interior and northern areas of the Prairie provinces. None are found in British Columbia, or in southern Ontario.

2. Communities Beginning Transition: From First- to Second-language Acquisition Among Youth and Young Adults; Middle Aged First-language Speakers (39)

The 39 communities in this category can be characterized as having "high continuity, medium to high second-language acquisition," with medium to large Aboriginal mother tongue populations (between 100 and 500 first language speakers), who are mainly middle aged (between 35 and 54 years of age). The community's language has been learned mainly as a mother tongue, but there are also beginning signs of shifts from first-language transmission to second language acquisition among youth and young adults. Nearly all (97%) of communities in this category are First Nations. Some 85% of these communities are accounted for by three major language groupings: Cree (36%), the Athapaskan family of languages (28%), and Ojibway (28%). The shares of Ojibway and Athapaskan communities in this category are disproportionately high. Most communities tend to be located in the more southerly Prairie province areas and in the Northwest Territories. None are found in British Columbia, and few exist further east than Manitoba.

Owing to their demographics, these communities have a high prospect for revitalization of their language, especially for young adults in their child-bearing years, who, if motivated, are likely to transmit their language to their children, as a first language.

3. Communities Already in Transition: Decline in First Language, but Young Adults Acquiring Second Language; Middle Aged First-language Speakers (116)

The 116 communities in this category are characterized as having medium continuity, and medium to high second-language acquisition, with a medium to large mother tongue population, and predominately middle aged first-language speakers. The community's language had been learned previously as a mother tongue, as evidenced by older first-language speakers, but there are indications that the transition from first to second language acquisition is well underway, and has been occurring for some time among young adults. Communities include First Nations (83%), Métis (12%), and Inuit (5%). While about 64% of communities are Cree (44%) or Ojibway (19%), communities from the Salish language family are also represented. Largely concentrated in the Prairies provinces, these communities are also found in parts of British Columbia, all Territories, Ontario, and Atlantic Canada.

From a demographic perspective, given the long-term decline in mother tongue transmission already evident in older generations, second-language acquisition will become an increasingly important factor in offsetting declines in first language transmission.

4. Communities That Have Completed Transition: Predominately Second-language Acquisition; Middle Aged and Older Speakers (81)

The 81 communities in this category are characterized as having low continuity, and medium to high second-language acquisition, with small (between 30 to 100 persons) Aboriginal mother tongue populations and many middle aged and older speakers. In these communities, children are no longer learning the Aboriginal language as their mother tongue, since many of the older first-language speakers are beyond child-bearing years, and the language is being spoken infrequently in the home. Learning the language as a second language appears to have been occurring for some time, particularly among middle aged adults. Communities include First Nations (82%), Métis (12%), and Inuit (6%), and represent a number of languages, including Cree (28%), Ojibway (19%), Inuktitut (6%), and some endangered languages such as Salish (10%) and Wakashan (7%). These languages tend to be distributed across all the Western provinces, from Manitoba westward, the Northwest and Nunavut Territories, southern Ontario, and Atlantic Canada.

Intergenerational transmission has clearly declined. Given that most of the remaining first-language speakers are older and beyond the parenting years, prospects for transmitting the community language as the mother tongue of the next generation are low. From a demographic perspective, this would suggest that languages in these communities would be increasingly likely to be learned as second languages, especially among younger generations. Also, these communities have older populations of first-language speakers—implying that community elders could be potential sources for language learning.

5. Communities in Decline: Decline in First-language Transmission, No Second-language Acquisition; Middle Aged First-language Speakers (50)

There are 50 communities in this category. They can be generally characterized as having medium continuity and low second-language acquisition, with medium to large Aboriginal mother tongue population, and mostly older middle aged speakers. The language is still learned to some extent as a mother tongue, but relatively little second-language acquisition is occurring, even among younger generations. There are no indications of second-language acquisition among any age group even as mother-tongue transmission declines. Communities comprise First Nations (88%), Métis (8%), and Inuit (4%), and two thirds of the communities are Cree (44%) and Ojibway (22%). They are located mainly in the Prairie provinces and in the interior of British Columbia.

From a demographic perspective, intergenerational transmission is in decline, because the mother tongue populations of these communities are aging. Second-language speakers, even among younger generations, are not making up the number of speakers.

6. Communities Where Languages are Most Endangered and Fading: No First- or Second-language Acquisition; Few and Aging Speakers (43)

There are 43 communities in this category. They can be generally characterized as low continuity, low second-language acquisition. The community's language is not being transmitted as a mother tongue, or as a second language. Aboriginal mother tongue populations tend to be older and small, between 30 and 100 first-language speakers. All speakers, not only first language learners, are relatively old, and it appears that few in these communities are acquiring their language as either a first or second language. The distribution of these communities includes First Nations (86%), Inuit (9%), and Métis (5%). Their linguistic composition is heterogeneous, with representation not only from endangered language communities, but also from communities with languages that otherwise are viable overall such as Inuktitut. Nevertheless these communities are struggling. These communities include: Cree (28%), Ojibway (12%), Salish family (14%), Inuktitut (9%), and Tsimshian (6%). Communities tend to be located mainly in British Columbia, the western Artic, and in southern areas of the Prairie provinces.

From a demographic perspective, these communities face the prospect of ongoing decline in the numbers of speakers. It appears that their languages are not being learned as either first or second languages. The situation is urgent, particularly for those communities with already endangered languages, where the few speakers that are left are probably elderly.

7. Communities with Few First-language Speakers (174)

Among the 619 communities with Aboriginal mother tongue populations, 174, or 28%, have very small populations of less than 30 persons reporting an Aboriginal first language. These communities are liable to be losing most if not all of their first-language speakers over the next few years. Almost all of these communities (95%) are First Nations, and most have endangered languages. These communities are concentrated mainly in British Columbia, and in some of the more urban areas of Saskatchewan and Ontario. About 30% of the communities that have very few first language speakers are Salish, a disproportionately high share considering that 16% of all Aboriginal communities are Salish. Conversely, there are few communities in this category with the more viable languages.

From a demographic perspective, intergenerational transmission is not viable, and the remaining speakers are few in number and probably elderly. Hence, preserving the language would likely be a major consideration.

8. Communities with No First-language Speakers (90)

No Aboriginal mother tongues were reported in 90 of the 709 Aboriginal communities that were enumerated in the 2001 census—in other words, nearly 13% of enumerated communities have no first language speakers. Practically all of these communities (98%) are First Nations and are concentrated in British Columbia. Most of these communities are associated with the Salish family of languages[16]— again emphasizing their high degree of endangerment[17]. This category raises more questions than answers with respect to the types of appropriate interventions. How many of them have recently lost their first language speakers? How many have simply not had any speakers for decades? For example, there are at least 40 communities that did not report any Aboriginal mother tongue population in 2001, but did have first language speakers in 1996. About half of these communities are from the smaller endangered Salish language categories. From a demographic perspective, apart from the obvious loss in speakers, it is difficult to assess the long-term implications for community prospects.

9. Unknown: Communities with No Census Data on State of Their Language (170)

Census language data are not available for about one in five (19%) of the 879 Aboriginal communities. In the 2001 census, 170 communities either did not participate, that is they were incompletely enumerated, or their data were suppressed due to data quality issues. Consequently, there is little if any information from the census about the language situation of these particular communities. These missing communities are largely First Nations (82%) and Métis (18%). There are no Inuit communities in this category—consequently we have an accurate as possible picture from the census for most Inuktitut language communities. Though the affected communities are relatively widespread, not all languages and regions are equally affected. For example, none of the Mohawk- Iroquoian-speaking[18] communities participated in the census, and other missing communities include Ojibway (25%), Salish family (22%), and Cree (12%). Thus, gaps exist in the community picture for some of these languages, and the entire picture is lost in the case of the Mohawk/Iroquoian family. Regions with communities most affected by incomplete enumeration/suppression include Atlantic Canada, Ontario, Saskatchewan, Alberta, and British Columbia.

Clearly these categories of "community language conditions" reveal significant variations by Aboriginal groups, languages and regions. Consequently, language planning and strategies need to take into account these complexities and variations in order to gain insights into effective courses of action across First Nations, Inuit, and Métis communities and languages. Finally, it should be emphasized that the role of this analysis and exercise is strictly informative—not prescriptive—in its approach. The community ultimately identifies the priorities and determines the appropriate course of language strategies. The objective here is to provide a demographic overview of language conditions of languages at the community level, through a variety of indicators that can inform language planning at all levels—community, regional and national.

The next section explores long-term trends in intergenerational transmission, examines factors and processes underlying those trends, especially in relation to family and community, and, based on their implications, considers the outlook for the maintenance and revitalization of Aboriginal languages.

Long-Term Trends 1981–2001 and Outlook

Trends in Continuity and Aging for Viable and Endangered Languages: 1981–2001

Declining Continuity for Most Languages, Especially Endangered

Over the 20-year period from 1981 to 2001, most Aboriginal languages, both viable and endangered, have experienced long-term declines in their continuity.[19] Although most languages experienced steady erosion in linguistic continuity, endangered ones suffered the most. Several of the more viable languages, such as Inuktitut, appear to have retained their linguistic vitality. Even the larger viable languages like Cree and Ojibway posted steady long-term declines in the intergenerational transmission of their mother tongues. Continuity indices for Cree declined from 78 in 1981 to 58 in 2001. The same indices for Ojibway declined even more sharply, from 66 to 39. In contrast, the continuity of Inuktitut appears to be relatively stable, showing only a slight decline to 82 by 2001.

Among endangered languages, the isolates of Haida, Kutenai, and Tlingit have experienced ever-decreasing prospects of transmission to the next generation, declining from already low 1981 levels of continuity of 40, 50, and 30, respectively, to practically nil by 2001. These languages now have fewer than 200 first language speakers. Within the home, only 50 people report Kutenai as their major home language, and virtually no one speaks Haida or Tlingit at home.

By 2001, for every 100 speakers with an Aboriginal mother tongue, viable language groups have an average index of nearly 70, compared with 30 or less among endangered groups.

Aging Mother Tongues: Seniors are the Main First-language Speakers of Endangered Languages

The average age of language speakers and rates of population aging vary significantly due to differences in intergenerational transmission of languages and fertility. For viable languages, the average ages of mother tongue populations tend to fall within the young adult ages, between 25 and 40 years of age. For endangered languages, the average ages of mother tongue speakers tend to approach the age range of seniors, from 50 to 60 years of age and over. Not only do viable languages have younger populations, the average age of these groups also rises more slowly than that of endangered languages.

Over the period 1981 to 2001, the average age of the Salish mother tongue population rose from 42 to 52 years; for Wakashan, from 40 to 56 years; and for Tshimshian, from 33 to 63 years. High rates of intergenerational transmission of Inuktitut, combined with Inuit fertility rates, contribute to only a slight shift in the average age of speakers, from 23 to 25 years over the past 20 years. On the other hand, the average age of Cree speakers is older and has increased from 26 years in 1981 to 33 by 2001. These trends in aging speakers reflect the long-term decline in the continuity of the Cree language.

The actual process and dynamics of sustaining language transmission and acquisition among children over the long-term are explored next within the context of families and communities—critical considerations in understanding transmission of Aboriginal languages to the next generation.

Intergenerational Transmission: Critical to Long-term Health and Vitality of Languages

Ensuring the transmission of a language as the mother tongue of the next generation is vital for both maintenance and revitalization of an Indigenous language. This is especially true, as Aboriginal languages cannot rely on immigration to sustain the population of speakers. Intergenerational transmission contributes to the maintenance of viable languages in communities where the Aboriginal language is the mother tongue as well as the main language of communication.

For endangered languages, in communities that are undergoing a shift to the dominant language, the capacity to transmit a language from one generation to the next must be restored. Increasing the number of second language speakers is part of the process of revitalization, and may go some way towards slowing down the rapid erosion of endangered languages. Nevertheless, it remains critical to increase the number of first language speakers, and to restore transmission of that language from one generation to the next.

Sustaining Intergenerational Transmission and Revitalization: Families and Communities

Both families and communities play critical roles and provide support in inter-generational transmission, maintenance, and revitalization of Aboriginal languages. Research shows that language acquisition in children, including the extent to which they acquire the Aboriginal mother tongue of their parent(s), is related to various family and community factors such as home and community use of languages, intermarriage/parenting, family patterns, and residence within an Aboriginal community or urban area. Over the life cycle, language loss and decline in home use, and hence transmission, is most likely to occur during the important 'family formation' years as youth leave home, enter the labour force, marry, start families or move to a larger urban environment. (Norris and Jantzen 2002, 2003; Norris 1998, 2003)

Transmission from Parent to Child: Mother Tongue, Home Language, Second Language

Children from two-parent families where only one parent has an Aboriginal mother tongue, (linguistically exogamous intermarried) are much less likely to acquire the Aboriginal mother tongue of their parent, than those children who have two parents that are first language speakers. An analysis of family data from the 1996 census (Norris and MacCon 2003) shows that among children aged 5–14, whose both parents have an Aboriginal mother tongue, nearly 70% have learned their parents' Aboriginal language as their mother tongue, and 40% use it as a major home language. In sharp contrast, when only one parent in a family has an Aboriginal mother tongue (exogamous parenting), only 11% of children have acquired an Aboriginal mother tongue, and just under 6% of children have an Aboriginal language as the major home language.

However, from the perspective of at least knowing an Aboriginal language, regardless of whether it is a first language or not, the vast majority, 83%, of these children with only one parent having an Aboriginal language, could converse in their parent's Aboriginal language, as could practically all of the children having both parents as first language speakers. Regardless of intermarriage/parenting patterns, among children who have at least one parent with an Aboriginal mother tongue, over 90% of children can converse in the Aboriginal language of their parent. However, only 47% of children had learned their parent's mother tongue, and only 38% of children speak an Aboriginal language at home.

Endangered Languages: Children Acquiring as a Second Language, Not as Mother Tongue

The pattern and the extent of parent/child transmission differs significantly between viable and endangered languages, especially when the prospects of linguistically exogamous parenting are much greater for endangered languages due to smaller numbers of first language speakers.[20] While viable languages such as Attikamek, Montagnais-Naskapi, and Inuktitut, tend to exhibit low rates of exogamous parenting, among a number of endangered languages, such as Haida, Tlingit, and Kutenai, nearly all children (90%) are in linguistically mixed Aboriginal and non-Aboriginal marriages. For most of the viable languages, at least 85% of children are able to speak their language, whereas among some of the endangered languages, only about half the children are able to speak the language. However, in the case of children with Salish or Tsimshian parents, higher proportions, about 70 and 90% respectively, are able to speak the language, compared to other endangered languages.

For endangered languages, there are sharp contrasts between the proportion of children who know an Aboriginal language, and the proportion that actually have an Aboriginal mother tongue, or home language. For example only about 10% of children with Salish and Tshimshian language parentage have an Aboriginal mother tongue, and even fewer (less than 2%) use them as major home languages. In general, endangered languages are increasingly likely to be learned as second languages rather than as mother tongues, especially with their diminishing use as major home languages (Norris and MacCon 2003). However, their transmission to children, even as second languages, may go towards preventing or at least slowing down the decline towards extinction of these languages that are no longer being transmitted as a mother tongue.

Children's Best Prospects: Both Parents First-language Speakers, in Aboriginal Community

Family and community together play critical roles in the transmission of language from parent to child. On their own, neither family capacity nor community support is sufficient to ensure the maintenance and transmission of an Aboriginal language from one generation to the next. The community can help to facilitate the transmission of language from parent to child within families by providing opportunities and settings that support the use of the language in day to day activities, and in schools with the help of other members of the community, such as elders and teachers (Norris 2004).

Communities Support the Transmission of an Aboriginal Mother Tongue

As the analysis demonstrates, children are most likely to acquire the Aboriginal language of their parent(s) in families where both parents have an Aboriginal mother tongue. However, the likelihood of such children acquiring an Aboriginal first language is significantly greater within, than outside, Aboriginal communities. In 1996, the highest proportions of children with an Aboriginal mother tongue occurred among children in families where both parents had an Aboriginal mother tongue, and where they were residing either on-reserve (68%), or in rural areas with Aboriginal communities (77%). In contrast, among children whose both parents had an Aboriginal mother tongue, but were residing in large cities, only 41% had an Aboriginal mother tongue. Similar effects are observed for lone parent families—in the case of female-headed families—corresponding proportions of children are 53% on-reserve, and 13% in large cities. It appears that the chances of children having Aboriginal mother tongue are almost nil, if one parent, especially the mother, has a non-Aboriginal mother tongue, and they reside in a large metropolitan area—fewer than 2% of these children have an Aboriginal first language.

Regardless of parenting patterns or residence, the vast majority of children who have at least one parent with an Aboriginal mother tongue have the ability to speak the Aboriginal language of their parent(s). However, what does differ by parenting patterns and residence is how children learn their Indigenous language. The index of second language acquisition shows that children living in large cities or those from linguistically exogamous families, compared to those from endogamous or lone-parent families within Aboriginal communities, are significantly more likely to learn their parent(s)' language as a second language (Norris 2003).

Future Prospects

For Aboriginal languages, both community and family are significant factors in the transmission from parent to child that can affect children's language outcomes. At the same time, while the research attests to the importance of communities as enclaves of language survival and maintenance, it also demonstrates that language conditions can differ significantly across communities, even among those with the same language. The state of languages in Aboriginal communities can range from flourishing large mother tongue populations to few or no first language speakers. In between these two extremes, many communities are undergoing a transition in learning their languages, moving from transmission as the mother tongue of the next generation to being learned as a second language. Other communities are experiencing declines in learning the language altogether, with few speakers remaining.

These findings suggest the best conditions for a child to learn an Aboriginal language as a mother tongue occur within Aboriginal communities, among families where the language has a strong presence in the home, when either both parents or a lone parent has an Aboriginal mother tongue, and ideally, in communities where languages are flourishing. Yet, the reality is that many Aboriginal children do not live in families and communities with such ideal learning conditions, let alone have a parent with an Aboriginal mother tongue, especially those living in urban areas, or whose languages are endangered.

The trends that underlie the current state of Aboriginal languages threaten the considerable diversity of the 50 or more Aboriginal languages that are spoken today in Canada, and in particular, the very survival of endangered languages. Nearly ten once flourishing languages have become extinct over the past 100 years or more. Many of the 50 Aboriginal languages spoken today are close to extinction or endangered, and only about a third of Aboriginal languages originally spoken in Canada have a good chance of survival. "Fewer than half of the remaining languages are likely to survive for another fifty years." (Kinkade 1991, 158, 163). In the face of these findings, many First Nations, Inuit, and Métis communities and organizations are committed to the preservation, revitalization, and promotion of their languages. The data attest to efforts of revitalization as younger speakers acquire these endangered languages by learning them as a second language. Also, while currently viable languages may also experience declines in transmission to younger generations, other viable languages are still showing strong signs of flourishing and continuing for at least the next generation to come.

And while it is true that children are increasingly likely over time to learn their Aboriginal language as a second rather than a first language, continued and increased efforts to learn one's language are also associated with developing and maintaining the links with identity, land, and traditional knowledge. The task force on Aboriginal languages and cultures reported from its consultations the import role of languages:

> ... Many stated that the ability to speak one's own language helps people to understand who they are in relation to themselves, their families, and their communities, and to Creation itself. They spoke of the connection between one's own language and spirituality, noting that focusing on language, spirituality, and ceremonies can increase personal self-esteem, familiarize people with their culture and bring about community healing. (Canadian Heritage 2005, iv)

From this viewpoint, emphasis on the revitalization and learning of Aboriginal languages cannot help but enhance the well-being of Aboriginal peoples, preserve and enrich their linguistic and cultural wealth, and increase the awareness of the importance of First Nations, Inuit, and Métis languages and cultures among all Canadians.

Endnotes

1   The author acknowledges the support of Canadian Heritage in the preparation of this work, with special thanks to: Stéphanie Leduc for excellent analytical and data support; John Clement for thoughtful discussion and feedback; Lorna Jantzen for her expertise, advice and long-standing contributions; and Norman Williams, Director Policy and Research, Aboriginal Affairs Branch for helpful editorial comments. The views expressed in the paper are those of the author and do not necessarily represent the views of either Canadian Heritage or Indian and Northern Affairs Canada.

2   Isolates are languages that cannot be related to any of the major families.

3   Michif, a language developed by the Métis, is also spoken in Canada. In the Canadian census data on Aboriginal languages, Michif is not separately classified, but is included in the category "Algonquian n.i.e." As a consequence data on Michif are not separately analysed in this paper.

4   Knowledge of languages refers to languages other than English or French in which the respondent can conduct a conversation. In the 2001 census guide respondents were instructed to report only those languages in which they can carry on a conversation of some length on various topics (Statistics Canada 2002).

5   Mother tongue is defined as the first language learned at home in childhood and still understood by the individual at the time of the census.

6   Home language is defined as language spoken most often at home by the individual at the time of the census. In the 2001 census a new section on languages spoken on a regular basis at home was added (Statistics Canada 2002). Here the analysis is restricted to language spoken most often.

7   Comparable counts adjusted for incomplete enumeration for 1996 and 2001 are 207,200 and 200,300 respectively, representing a 3.3% decrease.

8   Index of Continuity measures language continuity, or vitality, by comparing the number of those who speak a language at home to the number of those who learned that language as their mother tongue. A ratio less than 100 indicates some decline in the strength of the language (i.e., for every 100 people with an Aboriginal mother tongue, there are fewer than 100 in the overall population who use it at home). The lower the score is, the greater is the decline or erosion.

9   Index of Ability (KN/MT), or Second Language Acquisition, compares the number of people who report being able to speak the language with the number who have that Aboriginal language as a mother tongue. If for every 100 people with a specific Aboriginal mother tongue, more than 100 persons in the overall population are able to speak that language, then some learned it as a second language either in school or later in life. This may suggest some degree of language revival. Throughout this paper this index will be mostly referred to as the Index of "Second Language Acquisition."

10 Population reporting an Aboriginal Mother Tongue in 2001 = 203,300. Data for the Iroquoian family is not particularly representative due to the significant impact of incomplete enumeration of reserves for this language family. Other languages such as those in the Algonquian family may be affected to some extent by incomplete enumeration. For further discussion please see Section "Communities in Transition: A Continuum of Transmission, Acquisition, and Decline," "Category 9: Unknown: Communities with no Census data on state of their Language."

11 Generally, the level of detail in terms of individual languages increased over the censuses. However, some of the smaller languages coded separately in an earlier census had to be collapsed into broader groupings because of declining numbers. In 1991 several Aboriginal languages identified in 1986 (Kaska, Tahltan, Tutchone, and Yellowknife) were included in the category "Athapascan languages, n.i.e." It is interesting to note that Kinkade (1991) in his analysis of Aboriginal language survival classified Tahltan as being near extinction.

12 Aboriginal Communities are based on census subdivisions enumerated in the 2001 census, including reserves, settlements, northern communities etc. Not all of these communities have populations reporting an Aboriginal mother tongue. In the case of no Aboriginal MT popula-

tion, or incompletely enumerated communities, Aboriginal language was assigned from either previous 1996 census information where available, or from language information from Indian and Northern Affairs Canada (INAC).

13 This share is based on the number of individual languages classified in the census. Taking into account the smaller individual languages not coded separately by the census, British Columbia's share of Canada's Aboriginal languages would be greater than their census-based proportion.

14 Trends between 1996 and 2001 are based on single and multiple responses for mother tongue, home language, and knowledge variables. Also, comparisons between the two censuses incorporated adjustments for comparability. Four reserves in Manitoba had changes in reporting patterns for Cree, Oji-Cree and Ojibway between 1996 and 2001. Adjustments for these specific languages, along with adjustments for incomplete enumeration of reserves and settlements for all other languages concerned are incorporated.

15 Out of the 879 communities in this study, there are 445 communities reporting a minimum mother tongue population of 30 in 2001; of these, 390 were enumerated and shared the same CSD codes for both 1996 and 2001. Comparison of continuity and second language acquisition categories between 1996 and 2001 were based on these 390 comparable communities. Note that the extent of change among those communities shifting from one category to another is not the same: some shifts may be due to relatively minor changes in community index measures; others to notably larger changes.

16 Specific languages could not be assigned for 24 of the 90 enumerated communities without Aboriginal mother tongues. However, of the remaining 56 communities, well over half (38) were known to be Salish language communities, and most (33) of them from the smaller Salish (n.i.e.) language origins.

17 However, the interpretation of endangerment is not always necessarily appropriate for some communities because their languages of origin are not known. Also, in some cases, such as Métis communities, the traditional language may not necessarily correspond to an Aboriginal language specifically, but could be another, such as French.

18 In the case of the Iroquian language family, relatively little is known from the census since 1986 due to incomplete enumeration of practically all Iroquian reserves in the census.

19 For comparability over the period from 1981, continuity indexes are based on single responses to mother tongue and home language, and data were adjusted for changes in incomplete enumeration and language categories over the 1981 to 1996 censuses, and for changes in reporting, language variables and incomplete enumeration between 1996 and 2001 censuses. Note that long-term trends are not available for "Knowledge of Aboriginal language" since this variable was not introduced until the 1996 census; only short-terms trends in knowledge are available for the 1996–2001 period.

20 On the other hand, increased intermarriage could contribute to the growth of young second language speakers.

References

Canadian Heritage. (2005). "Towards a New Beginning: A Foundation Report for a Strategy to Revitalize First Nation, Inuit, and Métis Languages and Cultures." Report to the Minister of Canadian Heritage by The Task Force on Aboriginal Languages and Cultures, June, 2005. Ottawa. Cat. No. CH4-96/2005.

Kinkade, M.D. (1991). "The Decline of Native Languages in Canada" in *Endangered Languages*. Eds. Robert H. Robins and Eugenius M. Uhlenbeck. Published with the Authority of the Permanent International Committee of Linguists (CIPL). Canada: Berg Publishers Limited.

Norris, M.J. (1998). "Canada's Aboriginal Languages." *Canadian Social Trends.* 51 (Winter), Statistics Canada, Cat. No. 11-008.

Norris, M.J. and L. Jantzen. (2002a). Poster and Powerpoint Presentation "From Generation to Generation: Survival and Maintenance of Canada's Aboriginal Languages within Families, Communities, and Cities." INAC and Canadian Heritage.

Norris, M.J. and L. Jantzen. (2002b). Map "Aboriginal Languages in Canada, 1996." INAC and Canadian Heritage.

Norris, M.J. and L. Jantzen. (2003). "Aboriginal Languages in Canada's Urban Areas: Characteristics, Considerations and Implications." In *Not Strangers in These Parts: Urban Aboriginal Peoples*. Eds. David Newhouse and Evelyn Peters. Ottawa: Privy Council Office.

Norris, M.J. and K. MacCon. (2003). "Aboriginal Language, Transmission, and Maintenance in Families: Results of an Intergenerational and Gender-based Analysis for Canada, 1996." In *Aboriginal Conditions: Research as a Foundation for Public Policy*. Eds. J. White, P.Maxim and D. Beavon. Vancouver: UBC Press.

Norris, M.J. (2003). Paper "From Generation to Generation: Survival and Maintenance of Canada's Aboriginal Languages within Families, Communities, and Cities." Published in *Maintaining the Links: Language, Identity and the Lands, Proceedings of the Seventh Conference of The Foundation for Endangered Languages*. Presented at Broome, Western Australia, 22–24 September 2003.

Norris, M.J. (2004). "Status, Use, and Accessibility of Canada's Aboriginal Languages within Communities and Cities: Some Statistical Indicators." Poster Presented at Foundation for Endangered Languages, VIII International Conference in cooperation with UNESCO Chair on Languages and Education, Institut d'Estudis Catalans, On the Margins of Nations: Endangered Languages and Linguistic Rights, Barcelona, 29 September–4 October 2004.

Norris, M.J. (2005). "The Diversity and State of Aboriginal Languages in Canada." Published in: *Canadian and French Perspectives on Diversity, Conference Proceedings, October 6, 2003*. Canadian Heritage, Ottawa, Canada.

Report of the Royal Commission on Aboriginal Peoples. (1996). *Volume 3, Gathering Strength and Volume 4, Perspectives and Realities*, Minister of Supply and Services Canada.

Part Three:
International Research

12
Introduction to International Research

Internationalization

Introduction

The APRC 2006 had a much more international outreach, and examined many issues of comparative and international importance than previous conferences. During the APRC (2006) The Secretariat of the UN Permanent Forum on Indigenous Issues held a consultation on how best to develop well-being indicators that could be used across the many countries of the world. This consultation was part of a multi-continental set of consultations. Ms. Elsa Stamatopoulou, Chief of the Secretariat of the UN Permanent Forum on Indigenous Issues and Eric Guimond, acting director of the Strategic Research and Analysis Directorate, Indian Affairs Canada addressed a plenary of the conference on the issue of well-being indicators. The abridged versions of their speeches below provide a wonderful introduction to our international papers.

Part One

Address of Ms. Elsa Stamatopoulou, Chief, Secretariat of the UN Permanent Forum on Indigenous Issues, Division for Social Policy and Development, UN Department for Economic and Social Affairs

I would like, first of all, to recognize the Indigenous peoples of this land, the Ojibwe, for hosting us in these traditional territories.

Indicators are a difficult issue, they take long to develop and they are a so-called sensitive matter, at the UN and elsewhere. They raise the issue of the definition of no more and no less than what is happiness, or what Socrates called "the highest good."

Some years back, when I was working in OHCHR, I was very involved with our team in trying to integrate human rights in the UN system's development work and we had a really difficult time with indicators: our colleagues from the development agencies thought that our language was from another planet! Such conceptual differences are not unfamiliar to Indigenous peoples when they try to put forward their visions of their own development, and it is sure that one of the challenges is one of communication, of cultural translation between Indigenous development visions and non-Indigenous development visions.

One day, a seminar was organized in New York on good governance indicators by high-level experts of an important state: they said they had been working on good governance indicators for 13 years, with inconclusive results ... In our work during this conference, on Indigenous peoples and indicators of well-being I am thinking: the states can wait, the intergovernmental organizations can wait, but Indigenous peoples **cannot** wait.

1. The Work of the UNPFII

The development of data and indicators that capture the situation of Indigenous peoples based on their own perceptions and aspirations is a methodological priority of the UN Permanent Forum on Indigenous Issues. This priority is due to the overwhelming invisibility of Indigenous peoples in national censuses and other surveys which measure progress and inform policy initiatives in a large number of countries. We understand from certain global estimates that Indigenous peoples in most parts of the world are marginalized, and disproportionately constitute a significant number of the world's most impoverished people. We also know from statistical data that many Indigenous peoples in the developed world are living in conditions of the so called 'fourth world.' The Permanent Forum therefore believes that disaggregation of data is an essential strategy to bring more visibility to the disparities, and address the situation of Indigenous peoples. Without such data, or relevant indicators for measuring Indigenous peoples' well-being, mainstream models of development intervention are often thrust upon Indigenous peoples based on assumptions that they work, thereby resulting in inappropriate development policies, forcible assimilation, and dependency on certain welfare-oriented service delivery models.

In response to these issues, the Permanent Forum organized a workshop on data collection and disaggregation in January 2004. The workshop noted a number of important conclusions and recommendations which were consequently adopted by the Permanent Forum. Some of the key observations of the workshop included: that data collection and disaggregation should help "detect discrimination, inequality, and exclusion of indigenous peoples, both individually and as a group" and it should be "culturally specific" and relevant to the problems identified by Indigenous peoples.[1] The workshop also noted the necessity of qualitative and human rights indicators to assess the true social situation of Indigenous peoples.

Some of the key recommendations of the workshop included: the free, prior, and informed consent of Indigenous peoples in data collection; the involvement of Indigenous peoples themselves in data collection, analysis, and reporting; and the desirability of long-term standardized data based on multiple identification criteria developed with the full participation of local Indigenous peoples. The workshop also noted that data collection exercises should be conducted in local languages and employ local Indigenous interviewers.

Based on this work, last year, the Permanent Forum stated that "...poverty indicators based on Indigenous peoples' own perception of their situation and experiences should be developed jointly with Indigenous peoples."[2]

2. The Ottawa Conference in a Global Perspective

Let me explain how this conference, including the international expert meeting we conducted, fits within a global process and effort that will feed into the Permanent Forum and the international system.

In fact, during this year, in addition to the meeting in Ottawa which focused on Indigenous peoples in developed countries and indicators of well-being, we will hold three more regional meetings on participatory indicator-setting, in Latin America and the Caribbean, in Africa, and in Asia. Parallel to this effort, the Inter-agency Support Group on Indigenous Issues, which brings together 29 UN and other intergovernmental organizations, has prepared and submitted to the Forum's session this coming May, its own paper and survey of Indigenous-related indicators that already exist and also identifying the gaps. The results of all the regional meetings and the UN survey will then be synthesized, so that a number of core global and regional indicators can be proposed through the Permanent Forum, to the UN system and other intergovernmental organizations, including IFIs, governments, the private sector, and other civil society actors, such as conservationist organizations. They can also be used by Indigenous peoples themselves.

Dear friends, I am pleased that our international expert group meeting on Indigenous peoples and indicators of well-being—the first in the series we are planning—has come to a successful conclusion. And we are grateful to Indian and Northern Affairs Canada, and The University of Western Ontario and the NAFC, for co-sponsoring this workshop. The workshop brought in Indigenous experts from the Russian federation, the Arctic, the First Nations of Canada, Native America, Australia, and New Zealand to discuss work done on indicators of relevance to Indigenous peoples within their respective regions with the following objectives in mind:

- Identify gaps in existing indicators at the global, regional, and national levels that assess the situation of Indigenous peoples, and impact policy making, governance, and program development, including from a gender perspective.
- Examine work being done to improve indicators so that they take into account Indigenous peoples and their concerns, and assess them according to qualitative and quantitative criteria, including a gender perspective.
- Examine linkages between quantitative and qualitative indicators, particularly indicators that look at processes affecting Indigenous peoples.

- Propose the formulation of core global and regional indicators that address the specific concerns and situations of Indigenous peoples, including Indigenous women, and can also be used by international financial institutions, the UN system and other intergovernmental organizations, including regional ones.

3. The Main Results of the International Workshop on Indigenous Peoples and Indicators of Well-being

1. Our meeting highlighted the necessity and importance of indicators for understanding and measuring the quality of life of Indigenous peoples according to their own perceptions. In particular, the meeting addressed the question of measurement, i.e. what is being measured, and according to whose standards and visions—is it government or Indigenous peoples themselves? Existing international and national indicator frameworks developed by governments and international institutions in many parts of the world often do not capture the situation, or inadequately capture the situation of Indigenous peoples. For example, an indicator such as the proportion of the population below $1/day may not capture Indigenous peoples' perception of poverty. Indigenous peoples may perceive their own poverty in terms of lack of access to, and integrity of, their traditional lands and forests, scarcity and threats to traditional seeds, plant medicines, and food animals, or integrity of and access to sacred sites.

2. A second focus of the discussions was the gap in determinants of well-being amidst Indigenous peoples relative to the general population.

3. Thirdly, indicators were highlighted as a means for supporting data development, policy, and program responses. In many countries, collection techniques often overlook, or are unable to determine the quality of, life and well-being of Indigenous peoples. Inappropriate techniques or the lack of disaggregated data often place us in a quandary in terms of further data development in Indigenous communities. One method for breaking the cycle of data gaps is to develop indicators that are both statistically relevant and culturally appropriate as a means of capturing more precise and relevant information. When public policies are top-down, they result in improper and culturally irrelevant statistical information. And we all know that indicator and statistical frameworks inform debates and decision-making amongst Indigenous peoples themselves as much as government.

An important issue to capture in indicator-setting is the particular situation of Indigenous women—and gender more comprehensively—and also the situation of Indigenous peoples through the whole span of their life: children, youth, and elders.

We were encouraged to hear about some important efforts of Indigenous peoples themselves and others to capture culturally sensitive and relevant indicators of well-being, showing that good work is really possible if the will is there.

As one of our Maori participants from New Zealand repeatedly stressed, in doing this work on indicators and statistics "we need to continue to stay in a solution mode."

Participation as the Permeating Theme

The Permanent Forum strongly believes that indicators and disaggregated data are important, not just as a measure of the situation of Indigenous peoples, but as a vital strategy in improving their lives by capturing their aspirations and world views, promoting development with identity, protecting and promoting their cultures and integrity as Indigenous peoples, and empowering them to utilize such information to their benefit.

I am confident to state today that, what we heard with the most clarity in the discussions we held is that unless Indigenous peoples themselves participate fully and effectively in data collection and the establishment of indicators, efforts will likely be incomplete, baseless or irrelevant, and essentially provide too fragile a foundation for wise policies, including public resource allocations.

It is ironic and unacceptable that a number of mainstream discourses on poverty and development still continue to exclude and marginalize Indigenous peoples. It is only through the full and effective participation of Indigenous peoples in research, including in data collection and the setting of indicators, that we can go beyond the discourses to action that will improve Indigenous peoples' lives.

In the final analysis, indicators are about listening to Indigenous peoples, they are about a true dialogue between Indigenous peoples and the rest of society, they are about being open to Indigenous world views and respecting them.

Dear participants, the theme of the Second International Decade of the World's Indigenous People adopted by the General Assembly last December is "Partnership for Action and Dignity." The word "dignity" is linked to fundamental human rights and freedoms. And we all know, that there is no dignity without participation.

This is our major challenge. Let us respond to it.

Part Two

Address from Eric Guimond, Acting Director of the Strategic Research and Analysis Directorate, Indian Affairs and Northern Development Canada.

There are many angles by which we can discuss and reflect on the importance of indicators. One might be driven by pure scientific consideration and curiosity. Another might instead focus on indicators in relation to the flavour of the day, e.g., accountability. Planning could also be a legitimate way of approaching this topic of indicators and their importance. My intent here is not to make the case for any specific context in which indicators have their importance, but rather to reflect on three basic principles about indicators.

Principle One: Indicators and Research are a Key Part of Policy and Program Development

Let's have a quick survey of the audience: if you wear a watch, please lift your hand. So, almost everyone is wearing a watch today. What is the purpose of the watch? To indicate time, obviously. We measure time through this device and we keep track of it through observations. We monitor time. Time is important. Our lives are to some extent, sometimes too much for my own personal taste, regulated by time. We make decisions, and take actions, based on time.

What key elements have we touched on here through this simple example? (1) A device that provides data; (2) an observer; (3) monitoring; (4) transferring knowledge into decision-making.

While this may sounds a bit trivial and simplistic it is not. Let us take this four-part process apart, one key element at a time.

Scenario 1: Suppose we take away the data, we are left with a useless observer (might as well look for another job), no monitoring is possible as we have no way of monitoring changes, and finally any decisions made can only be in the absence of knowledge. In our own recent past in Canada, we never collected data on the movement between reserves (First Nations Communities) and cities. We assumed people were pouring from reserve to city. We made decisions based on this belief. When we finally began looking at the movement of people we found that First Nations people did indeed move from the reserves to the cities, and they also moved back. The churn migration actually meant that there has been a net positive inflow to reserves in the last few years. Lack of data is a recognized issue when its comes to policy and program development related to Aboriginal peoples and communities. There is an obvious need for more data. We'll come back to data collection in the second principle later on.

Scenario 2: Let's now eliminate the researcher from this process. What are we left with? A bunch of data, no monitoring, misinformed decision-making because knowledge transfer is disorganized and unstructured. Data and indicators do not have a life of their own. Indicators come to life through the work of the researcher. We have recently completed a study of community well-being. It has provided us with the capacity to assess the well-being of the many First Nations communities. Before we became the researchers and carried out this assessment we had no opportunity to make these observations and policy could only suffer.

Scenario 3: Let's remove the monitoring part. Now, we have data which is analyzed by the researcher, but this data is only collected once. The result is again misinformed decision-making because the knowledge is partial. Is it possible for anyone to figure out an entire movie with only one frame? So why is it that too often, our research presentations on issues of Aboriginal peoples and communities only focus on the latest census figures, e.g., the latest statistical snapshot of the population? Without this idea of monitoring, we are unable to assess progress, or lack thereof. Many of Canada's major commissions have pointed to the need for monitoring/tracking. My United Nations colleagues would attest to the fact that the collection of data over time allows us all to assess changes in the human development index for countries of the world. This comparison makes it possible to track improvements, and potentially isolate best practices.

Final scenario: Let's remove the knowledge transfer. In other words the researcher does not communicate his/her analysis. The end result is decisions made in the absence of knowledge. Researchers have a responsibility to communicate their work to Aboriginal leaders and communities, to policy and program analysts. Evidence-based policy and program development is dependent on this knowledge transfer.

Principle Two: It is Important to Distinguish Between Outcome and Output Indicators

In an area of accountability and performance measurement, the discourse around data and indicators has become increasingly confusing, probably even more so for Aboriginal data and indicators. One element contributing to this confusion is the obvious lack of distinction between two fundamentally different types of data/indicators: outcome versus output indicators. And most often, when the discourse points to the lack of data and, therefore, the need for increased data collection, efforts target both types of data indiscriminately. It is like mixing oil with water.

What is an outcome indicator? Simply put, an outcome indicator is an indicator that measures outcomes! So, for example, an outcome indicator in education could be the proportion of kids that graduate high school with a diploma. Kids go to school, and we all want to know if they are successful or not. With outcome indicators, we try to measure many basic fundamental questions (peoples' health, educational attainment, labour-force activity etc.)

With respect to programs and policy, these outcome indicators are measures of program and policy effectiveness.

Now, what is an output indicator? An output indicator is an indicator tied to program delivery, not to program effectiveness. In more simplistic terms, it is about how many people have been served by a program (remember the motto of a popular fast food chain of restaurants: one billion served). It is not about the actual outcome for the people of the program which might vary.

Principle Three: What is the Most Popular Research Product of Any Planning Activity? Demographic and Economic Forecasts.

Research about the past (e.g., trends in educational attainment) is extremely informative and essential to the work of policy and program designers. On the other hand, program and policy planners rely on research about the future, e.g., forecasts. Indicators about the past are useful. Indicators about future trends are equally useful.

Aboriginal research is largely, in fact to a disproportionate level in my own opinion, about the past, not enough about the future. For Aboriginal research to break out of its traditional limited role with respect to policy and programs, we need to invest in research about the future. Sound weird?

A little more than ten years ago, I was employed as a demographer by Hydro-Quebec, in a strategic planning and forecasting directorate. In this directorate, there were two units: one for electricity demand, one for the supply side. I worked on the demand side, and was responsible for developing the demographic forecast, e.g., population size, and number and size of households, for the entire province of Quebec. At the same time, another colleague, an economist, was in charge of producing the economic forecast of the province. The demographic and economic forecasts were the two pillars of the electricity demand forecast for the province of Quebec. The projected demand was then compared to the existing and projected supply of electricity. Thereafter, decisions were made on the necessity to curb the demand and/or increase the supply of electricity.

Now, the question that bears attention with respect to Aboriginal policy and program development and planning is: Do we have these two pillars of planning, e.g., demographic and economic forecasts?

With respect to demographic forecasts, current efforts are being made to fill a void at least as old as RCAP. With the exception of Indian Affairs and Northern Development Canada producing periodically registered Indian population projections, the last official set of Aboriginal population projections, e.g., Registered Indians, Non-Status Indians, Métis and Inuit, dates back to the Royal Commission (RCAP) in the mid-90s.

Developing indicators is an important task, for Canada and for all of us around the world. We have to base these indicators on sound research, careful assessment, and analysis. When we develop these indicators we have to use them in the process of understanding the realities facing peoples around the world and make worthwhile effective policy.

Endnotes

1 Report of the Workshop on Data Collection and Disaggregation for Indigenous Peoples to the Permanent Forum on Indigenous Issues, Third Session, E/C. 19/2004/2.

2 Paragraph 15, Report of the UN Permanent Forum on Indigenous Issues on its Fourth Session, E/C. 19/2005/9.

13

Natural Resource Management and Indigenous Well-being[1]

Brenda Dyack[2] and Romy Greiner[3]

Introduction

Natural resource management (NRM) has become a policy instrument and "slogan" for solutions in Australia in response to increasing evidence of environmental problems. Specific examples include water pollution from diffuse sources, soil salinization, and biodiversity decline. Debates about how resources are managed are supported by a growing body of biophysical research about how conditions are changing, and economic research into efficient policy approaches. Comparatively little attention is being paid to the question of whether people are better off under different management options, or who potential winners and losers might be. Equity issues such as these extend beyond individual impacts to stakeholders groups, and have inter-generational implications. One group that is afforded increasing significance—at least in principle—is the group of First Nations (FN), Traditional Owners (TO), or more generally, Indigenous peoples. While in many cases they may not have property rights over natural resources and/or have little market presence, they do derive benefits and/or bear costs from land-use changes and NRM responses.

In this paper, we acknowledge that NRM issues as they relate to Indigenous peoples, are of international significance. We review six research case studies in Australia, New Zealand, and Canada, which seek to quantify the benefits that Indigenous people derive from natural resources and/or NRM. While each project involves collaborative work among researchers, and Indigenous people and groups, they have taken different routes to providing evidence of the benefits that are generated by natural resources. The six approaches include the following: a well-being index approach used recently with the Australian Nywaigi people; a replacement value approach to valuing wild-resource harvests for the Wallis Lake area of northeastern New South Wales; a bio-economic approach to Indigenous/non-Indigenous fisheries management of the Great Lakes in Ontario; a stated preference approach used in New Zealand; a choice experiment in northern Saskatchewan and Alberta; and a goal programming/multi-criteria analysis with the Wik People from the York Peninsula in northeastern Australia.

This paper focuses on a review and critique of the methodological and analytical approaches used in the six studies surveyed. The objective is to demonstrate that a diversity of valuation methods exist that can support research, and that can, in turn, support evidence-based policy development. Our motive for taking this journey through the methodologies and how they have been applied is to develop better ways to describe the outcomes of NRM in support of society's goals, particularly for Indigenous people. Our hope is that by sharing this work with others, their own collaborations may be made easier. We are unable in this paper to explore broader economic and legal issues with resource use and property rights.

Background

Water Benefits, the Murray River Basin, and Indigenous People

Research into measuring the range of benefits that flow from different water uses and management practices was initiated by Australia's Commonwealth Scientific & Research Organization (CSIRO) under their "Water for a Healthy Country" research flagship for urban, coastal, and other areas, with the goal of supporting management changes for resources in general. Work is underway to study a range of options to measure, and understand how multiple forms of benefits could be increased for regional sectors, groups, and the environment. One group of interest is Indigenous peoples.

The project we are concerned with is based in the Murray River Basin of southeastern Australia. The Murray River is part of the Murray-Darling Basin, which is one of Australia's largest river systems extending across one seventh of the continent from Roma in Queensland to Goolwa in South Australia. The basin has a population of nearly two million people with another one million outside the region heavily dependent on its resources. The basin includes the three largest rivers in Australia—the Darling River (2,740 km), the Murray (2,530 km), and the Murrumbidgee (1,690 km). The basin has been highly developed over the past 200 years, and now generates about 40% of the national income derived from agriculture and grazing. It supports one quarter of the nation's cattle herd, half of the sheep flock, half of the cropland, and almost three quarters of the irrigated land. Water has been extracted from the Murray-Darling system for irrigation and other uses for over a century, but the volume extracted has risen dramatically since the mid-1950s. While this has brought many economic and social benefits, the health of the rivers and wetlands has suffered.[4]

Currently, wetlands are degrading, and the mouth of the system at the Coorong estuary in South Australia has been closed for most of the past two years. The Coorong is part of the lands traditionally owned by the Ngarrindjeri people, the group that is collaborating with CSIRO for this project. For the Coorong, the Murray mouth, and for the Murray River as a whole, there is widespread concern that the "cap," or official limit, on water diversions from the rivers has been exceeded, and that water is unavailable in the system to support a healthy river and floodplain environment throughout the system. Quiggin (2001) discussed these problems, noting that, given water scarcity relative to demand, the common pool characteristics of the basin water, and the institutions governing how water is taken from the rivers, there are inefficiencies that will not be resolved easily. The consequence is that the degradation has continued.

The Murray-Darling Basin Commission (MDBC) is responsible under a joint agreement between the states and the Commonwealth for managing the Murray River Basin water allocations in a sustainable way. Its actions have evolved over time, with more and more attention directed at the allocation of water to highest value uses and to the environment. This is because the cap is exceeded and the flow of the Murray River is over-allocated to urban and irrigation uses with detrimental impacts on environmental condition of floodplains, water levels, and water quality through increased salinity.

State and Commonwealth governments have been facing political pressure over the condition of the Murray-Darling Basin. The main policy now determining investments in renewal and management in general has been in place since November 2003 when the Murray-Darling Basin Ministerial Council (MDBMC) announced the Living Murray (TLM) "first step decision" towards its vision of a healthy Murray River system sustaining communities and preserving unique values (MDBMC 2004). The "first step decision" was made in support of the more general TLM initiative, which was announced earlier in 2002 by the MDBMC with the goal of taking collective action to return the Murray River to the status of a "healthy working river," thus addressing the degradation that has been evident in the decline in native fish populations, wetlands, and water quality (MDBMC 2002).

One of the key objectives of the intergovernmental agreement supporting TLM First Step includes a commitment to invest $500 million over five years in cost effective, permanent recovery of water to achieve environmental outcomes. In terms of volumes of water, up to an estimated average of 500 gallons per year of "new" water over a five year period is committed to what have become known as "environmental flows," with this water coming from "a matrix of options" including infrastructure improvements and rationalization, on-farm initiatives, efficiency gains, market based approaches, and purchase of water from willing sellers (MDBMC 2004). The focus of the environmental flows is on specific iconic sites along the Murray where there are significant ecological assets (SEAs), including sites of significance to bird breeding and feeding, and native vegetation. The Murray River channel is one of the six designated SEAs.

The Murray-Darling Basin Ministerial Council has also supported the development of the Murray-Darling Basin Indigenous Action Plan, which recognizes Indigenous interests. Determination of these interests, their measurement, evaluation, and prioritization in overall planning for the basin are as yet not well defined. However, there has been a commitment to appoint Indigenous officers to monitor and advise on the placement and construction of new engineering works in a sensitive manner so as to not disturb significant cultural heritage sites.

For the basin as a whole, the share of the population that is Indigenous is growing, and it is growing in the young age groups as well as through returns to country of older Indigenous people later in life. In 2001, the total estimated resident population of the basin[5] was just over 2 million and 3.4% were Indigenous people (approximately 70,000) with a share of 4.2% in non-urban centres. This compares with a share for all of Australia of 2.4%. What is significant is that the share has grown in the basin by 13% since 1996, with the share of population of non-Indigenous people falling. Indigenous population of the basin grew at five times the rate of non-Indigenous population. A major contributor to this shift is occurring with an out-migration of young non-Indigenous people that outweighs the losses of Indigenous young people. The Indigenous share of the population of the basin is predicted to continue to increase. Taylor and Biddle (2004) estimate that the Indigenous share of the population will grow by 44% from 2001 to 2016. This growth in the share of the population is an indicator of the need to better understand the needs and priorities of this group in resource management.

In terms of economic interest and control, the extent of the asset base of Indigenous people in the basin is not known clearly; however, the income figures do not indicate that there could be a very great saving and investment effort from the relatively low income levels. The income figures reported by Taylor and Biddle (2004) indicate that of the total $35 billion in gross personal income accruing to adult residents of the basin in 2001, only 1.6% went to Indigenous people despite the fact that they represented 2.9% of the adult population up to the age of 65, and only 1.2% of the total regional employment income went to the same group. This is because approximately 38% of total Indigenous income is attributable to "welfare" sources, such as the community development employment projects (CDEP), compared to only 19% for non-Indigenous income.

Benefits from Water for Murray Basin Indigenous People

The goal of the CSIRO collaboration between researchers and Indigenous people in the Murray Basin is to delineate benefits that derive from water for Indigenous people, in support of more informed water-resource management. Initially, this collaboration is being undertaken as a case study with the Ngarrindjeri people of the Coorong and Murray mouth. Benefits are assumed here to include the sum of values attached to resources and the outcomes deriving from them. Values are both for use and non-use. Values also derive from market and non-market returns from the resource. Hence, water is used directly in a market sense for drinking where the alternative is bottled water, and water supports fish, a further consumable with a market value. Water also supports non-monetary, non-use values attached to a sense of place, importance of living on "country" as ancestors had done, and a sense of well-being from being attached and responsible for country. Non-use values can incorporate non-monetary, bequeathed values to future generations as well. If the resource declines in value, through quality reductions or introduction of predator species or pollution, then the use and non-use values decline. To the extent that these changes in value are measurable and subject to management discretion, the value (or cost) of management decisions can be estimated. The methods described below take a number of perspectives on benefits and the values that determine them.

Measuring the Value of Resources

In this section a range of approaches for measuring the benefits that derive from resources are surveyed. Our main interest is in measuring benefits that flow from water resources, however, the review here draws upon research that covers a range of natural resources. Some take a comprehensive approach and measure changes in well-being while others measure values on a more restricted micro basis such as replacement value. The emphasis here is on examples of how the approaches have been used, and the advantages and disadvantages of the approaches. The final few examples provide alternatives to values measurement, taking the position that it is not possible to measure the benefits, and that the best management approach is one that takes into account that the benefits exist, although unquantified.

Well-Being Approach to Measuring the Value of Resources—The Nywaigi Traditional Owners, Northeastern Australia

The research by Greiner et al. (2005) seeks to identify the value of natural resources through use and non-use for one Traditional Owner group, the Nywaigi language group in northeastern Australia, through a well-being approach. "Well-being" is an inclusive concept, integrating aspects of human life such as economic opportunity (employment/income), health (mental/physical), country, and culture, among others. It offers an alternative perspective to the economic concepts of utility and welfare, which are typically applied in a narrow sense dealing with monetary measures and preferences.

This work was motivated by a perceived need on the part of natural resource managers in Queensland (Burdekin Dry Tropics NRM group), and the Nywaigi people that NRM policy development and implementation of measures would be improved by a better understanding of what mattered to people and how their well-being was affected by resource management. In particular, the approach taken pursues a number of purposes:

1. It is readily repeatable with other Traditional Owner groups, and can be employed to provide a comparative analysis of what things matter (most) to different groups. Similarities and differences can be established. Requirements for different Traditional Owner groups can be articulated and explained on the basis of systematic research and solutions developed for group-specific problems.

2. By providing understanding of issues, it delivers important clues for policy and service prioritization. The depth of information complements regional statistics, which typically include standard quantitative indicators of well-being, including age structures, employment, and house ownership.

Table 13.1: Comparison of Domains Contained in Various Human–Ecosystem Well-being Models

Human ecological model	Person/ Environment relationship	Concept of "liveability"	Millennium Assessment Framework	Australian Bureau of Statistics concept
(Shafer et all 2000)	(Mitchell 2000)	(van Kamp et al, 2003)	(MEA 2003)	(based on OECD, 1976)
Social equity	Community	Community	Material minimum	Family and community
Conviviality	Health	Health	Health	Health
Opportunity	Personal development	Personal development	Good social relations	Education and training
Accessibility	Goods and services	Economy	Security	Work
Liveability	Physical environment	Natural resources	Freedom of choice	Economic resources
Sustainability	Security	Built environment		Housing
		Services accessibility		Crime and justice
		Lifestyle		Culture and leisure
		Safety		
		Culture		

3. The quantitative aspect of the research, if repeated in intervals, can help measure changes in well-being over time, and assist with the evaluation of policies and programs.

4. By being part of the research, Traditional Owners and their representatives gain more understanding of themselves, have opportunity for self-reflection and articulation, and research collaborators gain methodological experience.

The conceptual approach is guided by a number of existing models that are useful for providing the principal connection between humans and the natural environment (**Table 13.1**). The person-environment model (Mitchell 2000) examines a combination of measurable spatial, physical, and social aspects of the environment, and a person's perception of these. The perception is not only related to the objective characteristics of the environment but also integrates personal and contextual aspects. The model is a "thinking model" and presents layers of concepts that are related to each other.

The concept of "liveability" (Pacione 2003) refers to the conditions of the environment in which people live (for example, air and water quality, state of housing) and the attributes of people themselves (such as health or educational achievement). Examples of various definitions of "liveability" are given in van Kamp et al. (2003). Veenhoven (1996, in van Kamp 2003) describes the concept of live-ability as quality of life of a nation, and the degree to which its provisions and requirements fit with the needs and capacities of its citizens. Newman (1999, in van Kamp 2003) notes that liveability is about the human requirement for social amenity, health, and well-being and includes both individual and community well-being.

The main differences between the various models relate to object, perspective, and time-frame (van Kamp et al. 2003). Some concepts are primarily related to the environment, (physical, built, social, economic, and cultural), while others are primarily related to the person. Some are normative while others are person-based/experiential. The time frame of the concepts of well-being, liveability, and quality of life tend to focus on the 'here and now' and are less concerned about long-term considerations associated with the notion of sustainability.

The empirical aspects of the research adopt a subjective experience approach to the concept of well-being. It reflects on how well one's life is going on balance, and a sense of the extent to which one feels life is enriching or rewarding. A person's assessment of well-being is based on his/her personal characteristics and circumstances. Well-being is determined by a suite of factors, which vary in the literature, but broadly encompass material sufficiency, health, social relations, security, and freedom of choice. The state of the natural environment and its ability to provide ecosystem services greatly influences the state of many of these factors.

The research method negotiated with the Nywaigi Traditional Owners was focus group discussions. The various insights developed by each focus group into what contributes to and detracts from well-being are consolidated into a model of Nywaigi well-being (**Figure 13.1**, page 246).

"Family and community" is the single most important domain of well-being, based on the close ties that exist among members of (extended) families, which sometimes manifest as large families living together in households. Health is iden-tified as a key contributor to well-being. Substance abuse and addiction, and the state of health services are key issues on the mind of Nywaigi people. "Country and culture" are identified as critical determinants of well-being that are seen as intrinsically linked to the identity of members of the Nywaigi community. There is a strong sense of loss and frustration at the extent to which traditional knowledge, stories, lore, and understanding of country have been lost. This is regarded as the root of many social problems that Nywaigi people are facing today.

Greiner et al. (2005) complement the qualitative approach given in **Figure 13.1** with a survey of workshop participants. The questionnaire is partially based on the Australian Unity Well-being Index (Cummins et al 2001; Cummins et al 2003; and Cummins et al 2004). The main reason for including a short questionnaire as a research tool at the end of the focus group discussions was to generate a quantita-tive data base that:

Figure 13.1: Model of Nywaigi Well-being

Note: The thickness of lines indicates the relative importance/contribution of the domain to well-being

1. Provides complementary quantitative information, which might enable triangulation of the qualitative information;

2. Assists the integration of data across all locations, and across all segments of the Nywaigi population; and

3. Makes it possible to compare aspects of Nywaigi life with other quality-of-life statistics compiled.

Respondents were asked to rate their satisfaction with a series of attributes relating to life in general, and to Nywaigi issues on a five-point scale from "not satisfied at all" to "highly satisfied." For analytical reasons, the answers are coded as ranging from -2 (not satisfied at all) to +2 (highly satisfied). **Figure 13.2** provides an overview of the survey results. It shows the mean values of scores obtained for each attribute. Research participants expressed their highest satisfaction rating for "feeling part of the Nywaigi community." They are also generally satisfied with life as a whole, their health (adult Nywaigi tend to be less satisfied), being part of Australian society, and being part of their town/city/island community. Respondents were least satisfied with their level of traditional knowledge (men are less satisfied than women), the extent of Nywaigi connection to country, and traditional cultural activities. Women tend to recognize the interest of young Nywaigi in culture and country.

The research outcomes have been readily accepted by the key stakeholders of the research who are: 1) the Burdekin Dry Tropics Board;[6] 2) official representa-

Figure 13.2: Mean Satisfaction with Attributes; Sorted by Mean Value

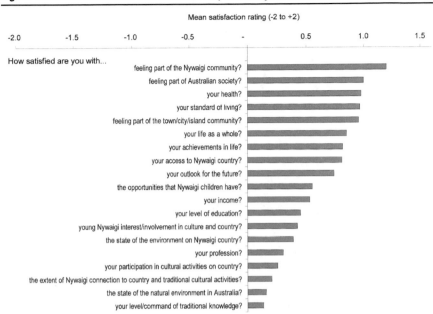

Mean satisfaction rating (-2 to +2)

tives of the Nywaigi Traditional Owners, specifically Girringun Aboriginal Corporation and Nywaigi Land Corporation. Research questions and methodology were developed in collaboration with both stakeholders, and the research team liaised with both on an ongoing basis and provided regular updates. The research has also received much interest from Queensland State Government departments, specifically the Department of Communities, and the Department of Aboriginal and Torres Strait Islander Policy. Multiple briefings and presentations were provided to bureaucrats at the levels of regional manager and senior policy advisor. The research results were influential in the "Girringun Round Table" discussions, which sought to establish a Federal/State co-funding model for the Girringun Aboriginal Corporation as a key service provider to Traditional Owners in northeastern Australia. However, these discussions have as yet, not been resolved, a major stumbling block being the issue of representation of traditional owners versus Indigenous people in general. A follow-up project has recently been established and has received funding; the project will provide an institutional analysis of Girringun Aboriginal Corporation, and seek to quantify the impact on Traditional Owner well-being generated by the services that Girringun provides.

This approach would be useful for the Murray River Basin because it is a comprehensive approach that could help identify values and priorities and provide a benchmark for future evaluation.[7] It would also provide a productive process for learning between researchers and Indigenous people in the basin. Running a parallel non-Indigenous valuation would be a novel addition that could build cross-cultural awareness as well. The challenge would be in applying the approach across language groups, Traditional Owner groups, and other Indigenous residents since there is no homogeneity expected across groups. One way of dealing with this challenge would be to identify groups that could self-identify as group members with preferences that could be aggregated for the purposes of producing the index. However, assigning group weights would still be challenging.

Replacement Cost Approach to Measuring the Value of Wild Resources—The Wallis Lake Catchment

A replacement cost approach includes a much narrower definition of values than the well-being approach discussed above. The replacement cost approach deals with one activity—wild harvests—and their substitute value in the market. One example, the motivation for the work, the methodology, and its usefulness are discussed below.

Jon Altman, Matthew Gray, and Natane Halasz of the Australian National University Centre for Aboriginal Economic Policy Research (ANU CAEPR) group were contracted by the NSW Department of Environment and Conservation to develop a cost-effective methodology for estimation of the value of wild resources to Indigenous communities, with a small pilot study. The task was to provide a methodology for measuring values of resources to Indigenous people in a way that would be accepted by the people, and also repeatable over time and across different groups. The goal was to provide an assessment of whether the use of wild resources by the Indigenous population is significant, and to provide an order of magnitude for their value. It was anticipated that the information provided in their report would be of value to the NSW Government's ongoing Comprehensive Coastal Assessment (CCA) process by quantifying one category of the economic value of natural resources in the CCA study area. The CCA process is primarily about collecting information on the value of different uses of coastal areas of NSW and developing decision-making tools and methods (Altman et al. 2004, 2005).

The study was also motivated by the fact that there is no reliable national information on use of wild resources by Indigenous Australians. The 1994 *National Aboriginal & Torres Strait Islander Survey* (ABS and CAEPR 1996) is the only nationally representative survey with any information on use of wild resources, but the use of wild resources is asked only as part of a question on voluntary work with the estimate of 6.3% of the Indigenous population being engaged in hunting, fishing, and gathering bush foods seeming implausibly low. The 2002 *National Aboriginal & Torres Strait Islander Social Survey* asked about use of wild resources in the previous three months only in remote areas with findings indicating that 52% participated in very remote areas, and 16% in remote areas. The Wallis Lake study was intended to provide better micro data that could be more useful in regional planning than these disparate estimates.

The study area was the part of the Great Lakes region of the mid-north coast of NSW covering 1440 square kilometres in either coastal plain and estuary, or ridges and valleys. The land use is 39% cleared for agriculture, mining, and infrastructure; 5% developed for urban and rural residential uses; and 9% managed by the NSW National Parks and Wildlife Service.

For the Indigenous people of Wallis Lake, the harvesting of wild resources is not seen as a recreational activity. They say that harvesting is done because it is a customary activity and part of being Indigenous, as well as a means of obtaining food. As noted by Gray these reasons are very different from the reasons given for fishing as reported by the Australian population as a whole. The reasons given for fishing in the general population are to relax and unwind (37%), for sport (18%), to be with friends (15%), to be outdoors (13%), and for food (8%) (National Recreational and Indigenous Fishing Survey 2000–01).

The Altman et al. study considered only economic benefits accruing from the direct use of wild resources through consumption of wild resources harvested, use of wild resources as an input into something that is sold (for example, a work of art), or employment resulting from connection with wild resources. Economic benefits were calculated using market prices to estimate the market replacement value of the wild resources harvested.

Information was collected about average amounts of each species harvested, number of people harvesting each species, market price of each type of wild resource, and costs of harvesting the wild resources. The method of collecting information was a retrospective questionnaire in an interview situation with information collected from 10 interviewees about amounts of each species harvested over the previous 12 months for 27 members of the Indigenous community. Interviews were conducted over four days in July 2004.

A wide range of wild resources is non-commercially harvested; terrestrial plants and wildlife have uses that are primarily symbolic and cultural, while the vast majority of plants and animals harvested are aquatic. It was decided that due to the scoping nature of the study and its small scale, only aquatic-based resources would be used in the economic valuation. This covered 33 species. The total value of resources to the whole community was estimated from the sample as the midpoint from the high catch harvesters versus the low catch harvesters in proportion to the sample population. Using this method, the estimate Altman et al. found was that harvesting of wild resources represented about 5% of total income for the community.

This approach provides a good first step in understanding the harvesting activities and ways of the people as well as a way to learn about what matters to the people. A replacement-cost approach does not, however, provide estimates of total value. Nor does this approach provide indications of the way values would differ under different management strategies. The stated preference methods described below provide opportunities to go beyond replacement value of currently extracted resources, and explore the way values change when site conditions change.

Optimal Resource Extraction in a Holistic Community Assessment—The Chippewas of Nawash First Nation, Great Lakes, Ontario, Canada

The work described in Chami et al. (1997) seeks to contribute to an understanding of how well the Nawash community is managing its resources, how well regional NRM of a shared fishery is supporting the wellness of the Nawash community, and how management could be improved. The approach taken focuses on the Nawash whitefish commercial fishery with an economic analysis, and then provides the results within the context of the importance of the economics as a basis of cultural, social, and economic well-being for the First Nation. The approach taken is characterized by three steps: 1) a direct estimate of economic values using a bio-economic model of the fishery that focuses on optimal resource extraction; 2) evaluation of this estimate within the context of the community and its culture and social structure as well as its control over its environment; and 3) sharing of this information with the wider community including provincial natural resource managers.

The Nawash people sought an opportunity to work collaboratively with a group of economists and with a fish biologist from the University of Guelph in 1996 in order to explore the opportunities to improve the management of their fishery. Although the basic expertise of the outside team was either economic or biophysical, it was clear that it would only be possible to evaluate the management of the fishery within the more general context of the culture of the people. However, the contributions of economic analysis were sought by the Nawash as a tool with which to communicate with provincial managers and other groups. Hence, the approach taken was to evaluate the economic implications of different management approaches, quantify these in market terms, and then to put this information within the context of the cultural and social values of the Nawash people.[8]

The Chippewas of Nawash First Nation is located at Cape Croker, Ontario approximately 64 kilometres north of Owen Sound, and an approximately four-hour drive westnorthwest of Toronto. The First Nation lands comprised 15,500 acres with three sides surrounded by the waters of Lake Huron and Georgian Bay, both part of the Canadian Great Lakes in central Canada. The key concerns about the value of the resource and how it affects community well-being include the following: Could the fishery be managed better so as to improve the long term sustainability of the fishery resource? Is there a better way to optimize the catch? Is there a better mix of boat and other capital stock than is currently used? Is Georgian Bay generally being managed to support sustainability of the commercial Nawash fishery?

Key characteristics of the fishery and the community:

- Given the nature of the reserve and its region, fishing is, and has always been, the main source of on-reserve employment that is not within the public service.

- The Nawash fishery is unique in Canada in that it is managed by the owners of the resource. This right was recognized by the courts in 1994 when it was established that the Nawash had operated a commercial fishery before first European contact.

- Other commercial and recreational fisheries in the Great Lakes are managed by some level of government.

- The Nawash fishery is characterized by a relatively small number of fishers and close contact among fishers. This provides a set of circumstances which is conducive to encouraging good resource stewardship with optimal extraction based on a whole-of-fishery impact assessment. Internalizing the impact of catch has the potential to avoid the open access problems typical in common property resources without intervention.

- A major concern is that the whitefish stock—the stock of the commercial catch of the Nawash fishery—is being depleted by habitat competition and predation by salmon. Salmon are not native. They are stocked by the sports fishing community which lives outside the Nawash community and typically is not permanently local.

- Salmon may not be caught commercially, they are strictly for recreational use, and they do not reproduce naturally in the Great Lakes.

Information has been gathered through interviews and sharing of memories. Based on the information gathered, a bio-economic model of the fishery was constructed, which indicated that through its effect on stock size and optimal harvest of whitefish salmon predation has a significant negative impact on the present value of the Nawash fishery, and it is likely that the fishery is over-capitalized. These general results would hold under a range of circumstances; however, better biological information on all fisheries and the rate of stocking of exotic species is required to derive specific management changes for the fishery.

The economic evaluation was assessed within the context of community well-being and the realities of the control the Nawash have over the joint use of the Great Lakes to support a number of fisheries. The main conclusions of the research were: 1) a lack of opportunities for investment off-reserve is potentially encouraging over-investment in the fishery; 2) due to the importance of the fishery to the community, the decline of the fishery would cause non-trivial community-wide impacts on the Nawash; and 3) predation and habitat competition by stocked exotic fish are detrimental to the Nawash commercial fishery under any set of parameters; however, there is no mechanism by which the Nawash could control this effect, which was modeled as pollution.

The outcome of the collaborative work was far-reaching. The results were shared widely with resource managers, and management strategies were modified. The success of the process has no doubt been due to the fact that the information was: 1) collaboratively generated; 2) freely shared; 3) provided in a way that managers could understand;[9] and 4) both quantitative and qualitative, which allowed a range of interested groups to understand and identify with the conclusions. This work has continued with improved biophysical information gathered, further analysis, and a more comprehensive and inclusive resource management approach being developed and adopted over the past decade (Chami et al 1997; Crawford 1996).[10]

Stated Preference Techniques

Stated preference techniques including contingent valuation and choice experiments provide the opportunity to ask respondents, through a survey or interview technique, how values change for them under altered conditions. They also allow for estimates of welfare change and investigation of preferences. Contingent valuation may have limited usefulness when it is applied to Indigenous communities. However, notwithstanding this limited utility, contingent valuation comes without a price tag for a number of reasons, including the smaller range of economic experiences and alternatives typical of this group, and a cultural approach that holds health of the country basic to all existence. Alternatively, as discussed below for one case study, the opportunities for choice experiments may be very promising.

Contingent Valuation Method (CVM)

Shaun Awatere (2005) used a CVM approach to estimate the values held for changes in the environment in New Zealand where the response was expected to be culturally influenced. He used cultural indicators to segment the respondents by their commitment and involvement in Maori cultural issues including language (Te Reo), Whakapapa (genealogy), Tikanga (Maori world view), and whanau (other Maori). The Maori worldview is holistic in nature because it embodies historical, environmental, and spiritual values as well as modern experiences.

The case study used was the "Improvements to the Road Surface and Roadside Survey," which was mailed out and designed to have equal explanatory power for both Maori and non-Maori respondents. Two sets of willingness-to-pay options were offered. One offered improved road services and the other offered improved native plantings for roadsides, thus improving scenery, biodiversity, and erosion control. For the first, the value would be reduced costs in the form of noise, fuel usage, and increased braking capacity. For the second, the costs would be higher for indigenous plantings. Also included were cultural knowledge questions for the Maori respondents. The results indicate that the willingness to pay was not dependent on cultural knowledge with all Maori willing to pay more for improved plantings and for environmental improvements in general.

Awatere interprets the results as indicating that to all Maori, it is not appropriate to ask the monetary value of the life-giving force of mauri (life force). This is not only because the question may not make sense, but also because there may be a perception that there is an intrinsic right to ownership that should not have to be paid for. This has been discussed widely elsewhere (Godden 1999; Adamowicz et al. 1998). In future studies, if CVM is pursued, Awatere recommends that alternative payment vehicles should be tested, including labour or knowledge contributions.

Choice Experiments (Choice Modeling—CM)

Two studies of the value of non-timber resources to Aboriginal people of the northern Saskatchewan and northern Alberta Boreal forest in Canada report on the usefulness of stated preference and revealed preference approaches (Haener et al. 2001; and Adamowicz et al. 2004). In the first study, a stated preference approach is used, and in the second, a combined stated and revealed preference approach is used with the stated preference information used to account for limitations of the revealed preference approach. The authors note that stated preference (or a choice experiment), is useful because the changes induced by management of forest resources, extraction, and development in general have changed the forest from any state familiar to current users and therefore revealed preference about response to these states in the past, is unavailable. Choice experiments allow the consideration of hypothetical cases that can allow respondents to imagine these altered states. The authors offer two further reasons for using a stated preference approach including: 1) the reality that traditional ways have dwindled with weakened connections to the land in consequence of migration, population pressures, and changing preferences thus revealed preference techniques may not give a good indication of future patterns of activity, and 2) stated preference technique can address choices without revealing private information. When sacred hunting or fishing sites are at issue, this is a valuable attribute of an approach. People can respond to the choices without revealing the secret information. This is in direct contrast to Altman et al. (2004), who also conducted interviews, but who asked for information that may have been considered to be private. In this situation, either the interviewer would need to be adept at extracting good information, or the information extracted may be incomplete. There are ethical considerations with the first and accuracy considerations with the second. Offering choices under the stated preference approach does not eliminate all problems since the choices must reflect real choices and these can only be determined with good, candid local input about the actual situations faced by those using wild resources.

Haener et al. (2001) discuss the importance of trust and reciprocity, or gift giving, during the interview process, as well as the importance placed on sharing results not only with the respondent group, but also with resource managers as users saw this as an important purpose for sharing with the researchers. Results indicated that the value estimated using replacement value of meat is similar to the value of the trip as a whole using choice experiments. However, the stated preference approach is preferred for the reasons discussed above and below.

Figure 13.3: Value of Resources to Indigenous Peoples: Six Research Study Locations

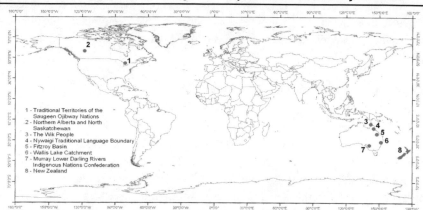

While the earlier study focuses on monetary welfare measures (Haener et al. 2001), the second (Adamowicz 2004) extends this by incorporating revealed preference data so as to develop spatially explicit models of resource use. Information was gathered on special sites, which is an important recognition of Indigenous ecological knowledge, and contributed to a supplementary "zonal" approach to resource management where special sites could be identified, mapped, and excluded from logging. The zonal approach is one way to incorporate Indigenous values directly into the management plan without having to estimate the dollar value of the sites. Revealed preference information about actual harvests was collected, as well as stated preference information for the identification of preference for attributes of wildlife harvesting sites where the preferences were influenced by values held for the total experience of hunting and gathering. Data were also gathered about forest characteristics from the forestry company.

The circumstances related to development and the emphasis on eliciting values so as to influence management in these Canadian studies are key similarities with the Murray River research being pursued by the CSIRO in collaboration with the Ngarrindjeri people. For the same reasons, it is likely that a stated preference approach may be a good process to use. As Haener et al. (2001) discuss, stated preference can address change in conditions as a "package" in a way that is more closely aligned with the Aboriginal approaches to holistic environmental well-being and their place in that environment. Replacement cost can only consider the value of a particular part of that environment—fish or moose harvest, which is limiting when a holistic approach makes more sense to the group being considered. However, there are challenges in estimating monetary values when it is difficult to estimate the opportunity cost of time for a group of people not fully active in the labour force. Resource compensation techniques may provide an alternative approach. Morrison and Hatton MacDonald (2006) suggest a budget reallocation approach for an alternative payment vehicle that could be pursued.

Use Value and Non-use Value

The approaches referred to above estimate use values. Rolfe and Windle (2003) address non-use values in a study that used a stated preference approach to estimate the value of cultural heritage in the Fitzroy Basin in Queensland, Australia. They found that the Indigenous group valued Indigenous cultural heritage more highly than the non-Indigenous groups when there were potential tradeoffs between protection of cultural heritage and development of water resources. The study raised issues about how valuations by different Indigenous groups, Traditional Owners, and other resident Indigenous people could be aggregated together, and aggregated with non-Indigenous groups to estimate total values. It was clear that preference sets are based on different foundations, and therefore, aggregation would be inappropriate. A further process for assigning relative weights for each group's values would be required for NRM decisions.

Goal Programming—The Wik People of Cape York Peninsula, Queensland, Australia

Venn and Quiggin (2005) suggest that price-based approaches to valuation, as discussed above, should be replaced or complemented by quantitative constraints that reflect the acknowledgment by planners that rights should not be violated. They suggest a multi-criteria analysis approach (MCA) in the form of goal programming, which is a continuous and quantity-based MCA technique. This approach was used with the Wik, Wik-Way, and Kugu people (Wik people) of Aurukun Shire on Cape York in Northern Queensland, northern Australia.[11] (**Figure 13.3**, Location 3) The goal with this research was finding a design for the commercial extraction of forestry resources that was compatible with the culture of the people. The Indigenous people were not involved in the model design, but they were involved in weighting a comprehensive set of feasible options. This was done in a culturally sensitive way during rest periods, and traditional and contemporary land management planning sessions (Venn 2004).

Venn interpreted the five goals for planning as: 1) maximize total employment generation; 2) maximize employment generation on country; 3) maximize income generation, measured in millions of dollars; 4) minimize forest area harvested south of the Archer River as protection for cultural heritage, environmental protection, and development of other economic ventures such as eco-tourism; and 5) minimize forest area harvested north of the Archer River and outside of mining leases.

Using this technique, shadow prices can be derived for the non-monetary goals. Although goal aspiration levels have not yet been identified, tradeoffs that implied weights could be identified in some cases. The Wik people have not yet come to a conclusion about a specific strategy, and are using the tool to continue to consider their options.

Given the wide variance of Indigenous People, including Traditional Owners, it is questionable if this approach would be appropriate on a basin-wide scale for the Murray; however, in a local region, as for the Ngarrindjeri case study, weighting of options could be incorporated into the overall evaluation of options and opportunities of value to the Ngarrindjeri. In addition, using stated and revealed preference as part of the information base of a goal programming/MCA could enrich the understanding of options, and perhaps encourage more clear choices and weighting for the Ngarrindjeri than was possible for the Wik people. This option could be explored collaboratively during the process of understanding what is important to the Ngarrindjeri people.

Venn and Quiggin (2005) caution against the use of stated preference approaches for a number of the same reasons discussed elsewhere in this paper. However, they emphasize that using a valuation approach may be an inappropriate strategy for policy analysis, in part because any values that are incomplete could compromise the Native land title claims made by traditional owner groups. This is an important point that needs to be heeded. However, it is not necessarily the case that partial information is bad information. If the information is gathered within a context that clearly defines it as partial, then there could be no claim that the partial value covers total value.

Venn and Quiggin recommend an iterative approach that does not involve economists "parachuting" into communities to elicit values using techniques that are incomprehensible to the people. We agree that this would be a costly option, both in monetary and non-monetary terms. It would not be useful. For this reason, we have worked over the past two years with the people in the Murray Basin to understand what can be done. This paper, and the work it summarizes for others, contributes to a sharing of information and inclusion of the people in a process of finding a workable solutions to understanding values, benefits, and acceptable management options.

Venn and Quiggin also recommend a quantity approach that is bounded by minimum acceptable protection levels for cultural heritage as constraints bounding the decision space. As an overall management planning tool this approach could circumvent the focus on values and benefits that derive from water in the same way that the MDBC used background information about biophysical and economic outcomes of various environmental flow options to decide to allocate 500 gallons under the Living Murray "first step decision" discussed above. However, for TLM, there was a great deal of valuation work done that underpinned this decision, and it is likely that any further decisions concerning cultural flows, for example, would need to be supported by a similar range of informative studies that address the values of the diversions, if not the exact total monetary value (For example: MDBC July 2004; Brennan 2004; Bennett 2002; CRCFE 2003).

Conclusions

As this review has illustrated, there is no one way to evaluate benefits that derive from resources when there is no simple set of market prices for valuing the outcomes. The challenges are greater than for activities such as agriculture where much of the value would be expected to be for market values. This is the research challenge. However, this is not the only challenge. The ultimate challenge is to adapt the tools we have to a situation that reflects the social welfare concepts that are relevant for Indigenous communities and individuals. The emphasis is on developing an approach that draws on established approaches, and is firmly based on a collaborative process that seeks to find a common language and common understanding of what it means to estimate the value of resources to specific groups or communities of Indigenous people.

Equally challenging is the need to express the information about values in a way that will induce management change. If cultural flows are to be allocated in the Murray Basin, it is likely that there will need to be evidence that benefits will increase if flows are diverted from profitable agricultural and urban uses. This evidence will need to be understandable to the river managers. The precedent has already been set in the Murray Basin with environment flow allocations. Although the value of the environmental flow was not estimated beforehand, it was assumed that a chosen level of environmental flow would be sufficient to attain positive outcomes. These positive outcomes reflect a change in condition that could be measured ex post to any augmented flows. Key here is that although the total value was not known beforehand, it was assumed and accepted that the value would be positive. The assumption was based on a great deal of supportive biophysical information about the relationship between flow and environmental benefit, which was available before TLM "first step" was taken. Hence, it is likely that before any cultural flows could be expected to be allocated, it would be necessary to provide at least some supportive evidence that positive benefits would be generated. The collaborative research with Indigenous people to delineate the benefits that flow from water could provide the evidence required to support the allocation of flows for cultural purposes. This is especially true when Murray flows are over-allocated to agricultural and urban uses, as they have been recently, and any diversion for cultural purposes could potentially result in direct declines in agricultural and other industrial output and value.

In conclusion, the review provided here suggests the following recommendations:

1. The process for communication could benefit from an approach such as that used by Greiner et al. for the well-being approach. From the first meetings onwards, the workshop approach in focus groups and the collective mental modelling could provide a good foundation for sharing information in a

group setting with Ngarrindjeri people from a range of age and interest groups, and with researchers. Hence, mental modelling towards development of a well-being index may be one approach that could not only provide a useful set of indicators, but could provide a format for sharing information, and understanding which other valuation methodologies are most appropriate.

2. As this overview has indicated, replacement value could provide a first step in the analysis of how resources are valued, but this approach does not allow for estimates of changes in value if future conditions were to change. For this, bio-economic modelling as for the Nawash fishery can provide estimates of the impact of management change on the value of resources. Stated preference methods such as CVM can provide further information about values as a willingness-to-pay estimate. Where CVM falls short in being able to value changes in intangibles such as cultural identity, choice experiments could indirectly elicit information about the cultural values attributed to different potential outcomes. In the limit, where values are not estimable, a goal programming approach that acknowledges a necessary amount of cultural flow may be a beneficial approach if it focuses on cultural flows as described by Morgan et al. (2004) in a way similar to environmental flows allocated under the MDBC Living Murray initiative.

These recommendations were offered for discussion with the research partners for the case study underway in the Murray Basin. Hopefully, this process of discovery can inform others in their collaborative research. With each of these approaches in turn, there can be an iterative accounting that addresses the determinants of social welfare, and therefore approaches a fuller picture of the value of the benefits that derive from water resources for Indigenous people of the Murray Basin. The body of knowledge built in support of identifying values of resources could provide evidence for supporting better resource management and policy development.

Acknowledgements

The authors would like to acknowledge the support of the social and economic integration initiative of CSIRO emerging science, the CSIRO "Water for a Healthy Country" research flagship. The Greiner research was funded by the Burdekin Dry Tropics NRM group and supported by the Girringun Aboriginal Corporation and Nywaigi Land Corporation.

Endnotes

1 Murray-Darling Basin Ministerial Council. (2003). Communiqué on the First Step Decision of The Living Murray, November, Canberra.

2 Economist and Policy Analyst, Social and Economic Integration—CSIRO Emerging Science & Policy and Economic Research Unit—CSIRO Land and Water.

3 Director & Ecological Economist, River Consulting.

4 Information is from the MDBC website: **www.mdbc.gov.au/river_murray/river_murray. htm**.

5 These shares refer to the whole of the Murray-Darling Basin of which the Murray Basin forms the southern portion. Figures for the Murray are not available independently at this time. All estimates are based on Taylor and Biddle (2004).

6 A regional natural resource management body in northeast Australia that provided financial sponsorship for the research. The Nywaigi people are one of 11 Traditional Owner groups in the region that the Board administers.

7 An extension could be the UN Human Development Index as used by Cooke et al. (2004) in Canada; however, the statistical base in Australia may be a limiting factor, and at its best this indicator is useful for whole-of-country comparisons rather than for evaluation of local conditions. Furthermore, the index uses three types of indicator: income, education and health whereas well-being goes beyond these three indicators as discussed in this section.

8 For the most part, this section draws directly from the report presented to the Nawash which is summarized in Chami et al. (1997).

9 This applies to the Nawash people, the state managers, the fish biologists, and the recreational fishers. Previously heated confrontations and intimidations reported in the press were defused by the objective analysis.

10 **www.uoguelph.ca/%7Escrawfor/research/research_greatlakes/research_greatlakes_ fisheries/research_greatlakes_fisheries_basins/research_greatlakes_fisheries_basins_ huron_commercial.shtml**.

11 They discuss the drawbacks of cost-benefit analysis that would use a price-based approach to including values.

References

Adamowicz, W., Beckley, T., Hatton MacDonald D., Just, L., Luckert, M., Murray, E., and Phillips, W. (1998). "In Search of Forest Resource Values of Indigenous Peoples: Are Non-market Techniques Applicable?" *Society and Natural Resources*, 11(1):51–66.

Adamowicz, W.L., Boxall, P.C., Haener, M.K., Zhang, Y., Dosman, D., and Marois, J. (2004). "An Assessment of the Impacts of Forest Management on Aboriginal Hunters: Evidence from Stated and Revealed Preference Data." *Forest Science.* 50(2): 139–52.

Adamowicz, W., Boxall, P., Louviere, J., Swait, J., and Williams, M. (1999). "Stated-Preference Methods for Valuing Environmental Amenities" In: Bateman, I.J. and Willis, K.G. (Editors) *Valuing Environmental Preferences: Theory and Practice of the Contingent Valuation Method in the US, EU and Developing Countries.* Oxford University Press, Oxford.

Altman, J., Gray, M., and Halasz, N. (2004). "Economic Value of Wild Resources to the Indigenous Community in Coastal New South Wales: The Wallis Lake Catchment Case." *Report to the New South Wales Government Department of Environment and Conservation.* Centre for Aboriginal Economic Policy Research, The Australian National University, Canberra.

Altman, J., Gray, M., and Halasz, N. (2005). "Economic Value of Wild Resources to the Indigenous Community of the Wallis Lake Catchment." *Centre for Aboriginal Economic Policy Research* Discussion Paper 272/2005, The Australian National University, Canberra.

Arrow, K., Cropper, M., Eads, G., Hahn, R., Lave, L., Noll, R., Portney, P., Russell, M., Schmalensee, R., Smith, K., and Stavins, R. (1996). "Is There a Role for Benefit-cost Analysis in Environmental, Health and Safety Regulations?" *Science* 272: 221–222.

Awatere, S. (2005). "Can Non-market Valuation Measure Indigenous Knowledge?" Paper presented to the 49th annual meetings of the Australian Agriculture and Resource Economics Society, Coffs Harbour, February, 2005.

Australian Bureau of Statistics and the Centre for Aboriginal Economic Policy Research. (1996). 1994 National Aboriginal & Torres Strait Islander Survey, Various Reports. Australian Bureau of Statistics, Canberra.

Bennett, J. (2002). Non-market Valuation Scoping Study, Report prepared for the Murray-Darling Basin Commission, *The Living Murray Project.* September 2002.

Boardman, A.E., Greenberg, D.H., Vining, A.R., and Weimer, D.L. (1996). *Cost-Benefit Analysis: Concepts and Practice*, Prentice-Hall Inc, New Jersey.

Brennan, D. (2004). Peer Review of MDBC Report, *Scoping of Economic Issues in the Living Murray, With an Emphasis on the Irrigation Sector, May 2004.*

Cooke, M., Beavon, D., and McHardy, M. (2004). "Measuring the Well-being of Aboriginal People: An Application of the United Nations Human Development Index to Registered Indians in Canada, 1981–2001." Paper prepared for the Strategic Research and Analysis Directorate, Indian and Northern Affairs Canada, October, 2004.

Chami, B., Dyack, B.J., Huennemeyer, A., Islam, T., Kanakaratnam, E., Nailor, M.G., Raymond, M., Syaukat, Y., and Rollings, K. (1997). "Aboriginal Self Management of a Commercial Fishery Resource: The Case of the Chippewas of Nawash First Nation," Paper co-authored and presented at the American Agricultural Economics Association Annual Meetings, Toronto, Ontario, July, 1997.

Crawford, S.S. (1996). A Biological Review and Evaluation of the OMNR Lake Huron Management Unit Commercial Fisheries Management Program: *A report prepared for the Chippewas of Nawash First Nation* pp. 217+appendices, R.R. #5 Wiarton, Ontario.

CRCFE (2003). Ecological Assessment of Environmental Flow Reference Points for the River Murray System: Interim Report prepared for the Scientific Reference Panel for the MDBC, *Living Murray Initiative, October 2003.*

Cummins, R.A., Eckersley, R., Lo, S.K., Okerstrom E., Woerner J., and Melanie D. (2004). "Australian Unity Well-being Index Survey 10." Australian Centre for Quality of Life, Deakin University, Melbourne, Report 10, April 2004.

Cummins, R.A., Eckersley, R., Pallant, J., van Vugt, J., and Misajon, R., (2003). "Developing a National Index of Subjective Well-being: The Australian Unity Well-being Index." *Social Indicators Research* 64: 159–190.

Cummins, R.A., Eckersley, R., Pallant, J., van Augt, J., Shelley, J., Pusey, M., and Misajon, R., (2001). "Australian Unity Well-being Index Survey 1: Report 1." Australian Centre on Quality of Life. Deakin University, Melbourne, June 2001.

Godden, D. (1999). "Attenuating Indigenous Property Rights: Land Policy after the Wik Decision." *Australian Journal of Agricultural Economics*, 43(1): 1–33.

Goodstein, E. (1999). *Economics and the Environment. 2nd ed.* John Wiley and Sons, Inc, New York.

Grafton, R., Adamowicz, W., Dupont, D., Nelson, H., Hill, R., and Renzetti, S. (2004). *The Economics of the Environment and Natural Resources.* Blackwell Publishing: Boston.

Greiner, R., Larson, S., Herr, A., and Bligh, V. (2005). Well-Being of Nywaigi Traditional Owners. Implications for Natural Resources Management. Report for the Burdekin Dry Tropics Board. CSIRO Sustainable Ecosystems, Townsville.

Haener, M.K., Dosman, D., Adamowicz, W.L., and Boxall, P.C. (2001). "Can Stated Preference Methods Be Used to Value Attributes of Subsistence Hunting by Aboriginal Peoples? A Case Study in Northern Saskatchewan." *American Journal of Agricultural Economics,* 83(5): 1334–40.

Hanley, N. and Splash, C.L. (1993). *Cost-Benefit Analysis and the Environment.* Edward Elgar Publishing Limited, UK.

Massam, B. (1988). "Multi-criteria Decision-making Techniques in Planning." Diamond, D. and McLoughlin, J. (Editors), *Progress in Planning,* Vol. 30, Part 1, Pergamon Press, Oxford.

MDBC (2003) "A Factsheet: Summary of Social Impact Assessment Studies in the Living Murray to November 2003." Murray-Darling Basin Commission, Canberra.

MEA (Millennium Ecosystem Assessment - authors: Alcamo, J. *et al.* (2003). *Ecosystems and human well-being: a framework for assessment.* Island Press, Washington, D.C.

Mitchell, G. (2000). "Indicators as Tools to Guide Progress on the Sustainable Development Pathway." In: Lawrence, R.J. (Editor) *Sustaining Human Settlement: A Challenge for the New Millennium.* Urban International Press, pp. 55–104.

Morgan, M., Strelein, L., and Weir, J. (2004). "Indigenous Rights to Water in the Murray Darling Basin" AIATSIS research discussion paper number 14 AIATSIS, Canberra.

Morrison, M. and Hatton MacDonald, D. (2006). "Valuing Biodiversity: A Comparison of Compensating Surplus and Compensating Tax Reallocation." Paper presented to the 50th Annual Meetings of the Australian Agricultural and Resource Economics Society, Manly, NSW, February 2006.

Murray-Darling Basin Commission, (2004). *Scoping of Economic Issues in the Living Murray, with an Emphasis on the Irrigation Sector.* July, Final Report.

Murray-Darling Basin Ministerial Council (2002). *The Living Murray.* July, Canberra.

OECD (Organisation for Economic Co-operation and Development) (1976). *Measuring Social Well-being: A Progress Report on the Development of Social Indicators.* OECD, Paris.

Pacione, M. (2003). "Urban Environmental Quality and Human Well-being—A Social Geographical Perspective." *Landscape and Urban Planning,* 65:19–30.

Quiggin, J. (2001). "Environmental Economics and the Murray-Darling River System." *Australian Journal of Agricultural and Resource Economics* 45(1):67–94.

Rolfe, J. and Windle, J. (2003). "Valuing the Protection of Aboriginal Cultural Heritage Sites." *The Economic Record,* 79 Special Issue:S85–S95.

Shafer, C.S., Koo Leea, B.K., and Turnerb, S. (2000). "A Tale of Three Greenway Trails: User Perceptions Related to Quality of Life." *Landscape and Urban Planning* 49:163–178.

Taylor, J. and Biddle, N. (2004). "Indigenous People in the Murray-Darling Basin: a Statistical Profile." Discussion Paper No 264/2004, Centre for Aboriginal Economic Policy Research.

Tecle, A. (1992). "Selecting a Multicriterion Decision Making Technique for Watershed Resources Management." *Water Resources Bulletin* 28(1):129–140.

Venn, T.J. (2004*). Socio-economic Evaluation of Forestry Development Opportunities for Wik People on Cape York Peninsula.* Unpublished PhD thesis, The University of Queensland, Brisbane.

Venn, T.J. and Quiggin, J. (2005). "Accommodating Cultural Heritage Values in Resource Assess-ment: Cape York Peninsula and the Murray-Darling Basin, Australia." Paper presented to the 49th annual meetings of the Australian Agriculture and Resource Economics Society, Coffs Harbour, February 2005.

Van Kamp, I., Leidelmeijer, K., Marsman, G., and de Hollander, A. (2003). "Urban Environmental Quality and Human Well-being. Towards a Conceptual Framework and Demarcation of Concepts; A Literature Study." *Landscape and Urban Planning*, 65:5–18.

14

Towards a Maori Statistics Framework

Whetu Wereta and Darin Bishop

Introduction

Work on a Maori statistics framework has progressed in fits and starts since 1995 when the Maori Statistics Forum set up a working party to formulate terms of reference for the development of a Maori Statistics Framework. The terms of reference made it clear that the framework had to be "centred on Maori people and their collective aspirations" and further, that it should be "linked to Maori development" (Statistics New Zealand May 1995). The developer took the view that the framework should not simply be linked to Maori development; rather, Maori development should be the subject of the framework, and this was subsequently agreed to by the forum (Minutes June 1996).

A number of principles were applied in the development of the framework that was proposed at the time, and these were also agreed to by the forum. These were:

- The framework should recognize the demographic, social, economic, and cultural diversity, and the different realities which characterize Maori society.
- Maori cultural institutions, and both traditional and modern resources, should be included among the units of measurement.
- Maori should be recognized as both consumers/users and producers/ providers of goods and services.
- The cultural attributes and socio-economic circumstances of an individual's household should be treated as standard analytical variables.
- Information should be collected and captured at the finest geographic level.
- As far as possible, standard definitions and classifications should be employed to ensure sectoral integration.
- The interconnectedness of Maori development, and the development of the nation as a whole, should be acknowledged by the establishment of linkages between the Maori statistical framework and the larger population, and social and economic databases.

Part 1—The Context

1. What Is the Official Statistical System—How Does it Work and for Whose Benefit?

Statistics New Zealand has a leadership role within the official statistical system. This means that as well as collecting many of the official statistics, it also develops, promotes, and monitors the use of agreed standards across the entire system. The use of standard definitions and classifications is a way of ensuring that the information produced is consistent across the different collections, and is comparable over time.

The main sources of official statistics are a government department's own administrative records and surveys (e.g., birth, death, and marriages registers, and school enrolments). The largest survey is the five-yearly population census, which covers the entire New Zealand population. Other surveys, which are called sample surveys, cover only a part of the population but are developed in such a way that the results can be said to apply for the whole population.

Official statistics are used by governments to inform debate, decision-making, and research within government. They are used in the same way by non-governmental institutions and groups such as private business, lobby groups, and service groups. Community groups and service providers also use official statistics, especially in making a case for funding approval. As official statistics "offer a window on the work and performance of government itself" they also provide the wider community with a means of observing the impact of official policies and assessing the overall performance of government.

Statistics New Zealand faces a number of challenges. The most important of these are maintaining trust in official statistics and protecting the privacy of people who respond to its surveys and to government surveys in general.

2. Official Statistics on Maori—What Are the Issues?

Successive governments have been collecting statistics on the Maori population since the late 1850s. For most of the period since then, these statistics have been collected for one purpose only—to assist government departments in formulating, monitoring, and assessing Maori policy. Maori researchers and commentators have been critical of the statistics for a number of years. Taking a post-colonial deconstruction approach to uncovering the precepts on which official Maori statistics are based and the perspectives that have shaped them and their presentation, Maori researchers and commentators have raised questions about the relevance to Maori themselves, of much of the existing official data on Maori.

In hindsight, having considered the issues that have been raised and having taken advice, Statistics New Zealand concedes that much of the criticism is warranted. Most Maori statistics were and still are being collected as a by-product of the information that is collected for the mainstream population, and very rarely were or are any of these statistics collected specifically to meet the needs of Maori.

What is to be measured and the standards (the definitions and classifications) by which the "what" is to be measured were decided on with little or no input from Maori. They cannot be expected therefore, to adequately reflect a Maori world view, or to fully accommodate Maori realities.

Over the same period, as treaty claims have been settled and Maori have taken progressively more control over their own development, the demand for statistical information from Maori authorities and community-based organizations has increased. Some of these needs have been met from existing information, and some by reproducing information from surveys in the form in which the users require it. Some cannot be met at all, either because the data does not exist or because there is the potential to breach confidentiality.

Part 2—Addressing Maori Statistical Needs

1. What Is Statistics New Zealand Doing about the Issues?

Statistics New Zealand recognizes that high quality information is as essential to good governance and efficient management at the community level as it is at the government level. It accepts that Maori are at a stage of development where they need good quality information to inform their own debates, decision-making, and research; to measure their own progress; and to monitor impact of government policies on their constituencies. In 2001, the department adopted a comprehensive strategy for addressing Maori statistical need.

The strategy is set out in its strategic plan, *Statistics New Zealand's Strategic Directions, 2002 and Beyond*. The key outcomes being sought are:

- Statistical information that is relevant to Maori;
- Enhanced knowledge and awareness of official statistics in Maori communities and extended usage at this level; and
- Enhanced statistical capability within Maori community-based organizations.

The Maori Statistics Framework project contributes to the first of the outcomes. It is critical to the development of a strategy for the long-term development, upgrading, and improvement of official statistics about and for Maori.

2. What Is a Statistical Framework and Why is it Important?

A statistical framework is a blueprint of a future statistical system or subsystem. It defines the scope of the system; lays out the structural elements of that system and organizes them in a coherent way; defines procedures for measurement of the different elements; and specifies in broad terms the data that is required. Very few of the current official statistical series are the product of planned development. Most have simply evolved as a result of government departments' ad hoc responses to changing statistical information needs. Statistical series that have evolved in this way tend to suffer from a lack of transparency, gaps in information, data overlaps, and all sorts of other inconsistencies. All of these deficiencies are apparent in the current Maori statistical series.

A sound statistical framework gives transparency to a statistical system by bringing to light the values that have gone into shaping it.

Part 3—Constructing the Maori Statistics Framework

The proposed Maori Statistics Framework marks the starting point for the planned development of a robust system of statistics for and about Maori. There were two stages to the process. The terms of reference directed that the framework should be focused on the collective aspirations of Maori, so the project team had to work out what these collective aspirations might be. Since collective aspirations or goals invariably entail more than one dimension, they are not directly measurable. Therefore, they had to be systematically unpacked and organized according to some theoretical understanding of the subject. The reason for unpacking is to clarify the dimensions, as it is the dimensions that are measured directly and not the aspirations or goals themselves.

1. What Are Maori Collective Aspirations?

As Maori, we all think we know what Maori aspirations are. The problem is one person's ideas about what they are will differ from another person's opinions. There is, in other words, no agreed definition as to what the term "Maori aspirations" means. If the statistics eventually produced are to measure what they are supposed to measure, nebulous or fuzzy concepts like "Maori aspirations" need to be defined so that it is clear what is and what is not in scope.

For guidance on what Maori mean when they talk about Maori aspirations, the project team turned to the proceedings of Maori development conferences that have been held since the early 1980s. Their search focused in particular, on finding points of agreement. Based on this review, the team concluded that what Maori aspire to, both as individuals and groups, is a sense of well-being. It also concluded that Maori development should be seen as a change process geared toward the realization of Maori well-being.

Stated more precisely, Maori well-being is the goal, and Maori development is the process.

2. How Was Maori Well-being Defined?

Well-being is another one of those fuzzy concepts requiring a tight definition. To assist in this exercise, the project team turned to New Zealand and overseas literature on monitoring and measuring quality of life and well-being at the societal level (e.g., social reporting). There is an abundance of literature on this subject, as social reporting is now used by most developed and many under-developed countries to monitor changes in social conditions and to measure social progress.

Several different approaches to defining well-being were evident in the literature. After examining the main ones, the project team settled for the one advocated by Amartya Sen. Amartya Sen won the Nobel Prize for economics in 1998, and his central argument is that development should be seen as a process of expanding people's freedom to choose and actually attain the kind of life they wish to live. People living in societies where there is illiteracy, poverty, ill-health, unemployment, and religious, racial, and/or cultural discrimination and repression, he argues, have little or no choice about the kind of life they live, regardless of how much they might aspire to something else. They are constrained from being what they want to be and doing what they want to do by circumstances that are outside their control. Development is the process of freeing people from such constraints, and putting in place the institutional arrangements, infrastructures, and other conditions necessary to widen the opportunities and choices open to them.

Consistent with Sen's approach, the project team decided that Maori well-being should be seen as a state in which Maori people are able to live whatever life they choose to live. There are a number of advantages to using this approach in the Maori Statistics Framework. Besides recognizing cultural diversity, it is consistent with Maori thinking in several other respects, including the following:

- Although it is conceived in terms of individual development, it can readily be adapted to development at the collective and societal levels (Sen readily acknowledges that individual and collective well-being are intertwined, and that the power of collective action is an essential driving force in the pursuit of development).

- Issues like freedom, security, and the empowerment and participation of people, often overlooked by other approaches, are key themes.

- It is rights-based rather than needs-based, although it does not discount the fact that in order for people to realize the kind of life they want to live, basic needs have to be satisfied.

- It recognizes the critical role that government plays, and the obligations of the rest of society and of the wider world, in enabling a people's development.

- It does not attempt to impose a single definition of the good life. It recognizes that conceptions of quality of life and well-being are shaped by culture.

- It can accommodate the fluidity, complexity, and diversity of Maori society, and it recognizes multiple realities.

3. What about Maori Development?

Following from the definition of Maori well-being, Maori development is seen as a process of enablement and empowerment, a process that seeks to extend people's scope for improving their own lives. As such, it is a process that involves notions of:

- Expanding opportunities;
- Enhanced choice;
- Better access (for example, to Maori knowledge and institutions, and to the knowledge and institutions of society in general);
- Increasing participation not just in Maori areas, but also in the larger economic, social, cultural, and political processes;
- Increasing command over goods and services; and,
- Increasing self-determination.

4. Unpacking the Dimensions of Maori Well-being and Development

The Dimensions of Well-being

As it has been approached above, the concept of Maori well-being is still ambiguous, and for purposes of measurement, it needs to be clarified by unpacking its various dimensions. It is important for the reader to understand that the process of identifying the dimensions of a concept involves the exercise of value judgement, and that one of the most important functions of a statistical framework is to make those judgments transparent.

In making its choices, the project team was guided by the theoretical perspective discussed above, and by the literature on Maori development. A number of conferences on this subject have been held over recent years, starting with the Hui Taumata in 1984 (Department of Maori Affairs, 1985). As well, many academic and policy papers have been written. The most helpful was Margaret Forster's paper to the 2000 DevNet Conference, which suggests that there are five main goals of Maori development (Forster, 2000). These are articulated as: cultural affirmation, social well-being, economic self-sufficiency, self-determination, and environmental sustainability. Although couched in different terms, all of these ideas had been identified in advance by the project team, who perceived them as aspects of life contributing to Maori being able to live according to their own values and preferences.

For the purposes of the list of dimensions for the framework, Forster's list was extended by adding human resource potential, which was assumed to be subsumed under either social well-being or economic self-sufficiency. The resulting list is as follows:

- Sustainability of Te Ao Maori (the Maori world)
- Social capability (since, capital is a word that Maori would not use in relation to people, and social relations and capability is more in keeping with the general approach being taken)
- Human resource potential (and not human capital)
- Economic self-sufficiency
- Environmental sustainability
- Empowerment and enablement

The dimensions as they now appear have been revised since the forum meeting in March. As well, the first attempt at structuring a framework proved to be less than fruitful, and the work done on it was eventually scrapped. As work on determining the proposed measures progressed, the boundaries between the different dimensions became more and more blurred. Measures of one dimension seemed to apply equally as well to others. For example, is proficiency in the Maori language a measure of cultural affirmation, social inclusion, human potential, or empowerment? Or is it an equally valid measure of all four? There is nothing in the literature that suggests the dimensions need to be treated as mutually exclusive categories. On the contrary, insofar as they acknowledge linkages among dimensions, all of the known approaches to well-being assessment also acknowledge a degree of overlap. In this instance, however, outputs were being repeated to such an extent that questions had to be asked about the robustness of the conceptual frame.

A review of the frame led to a reduction in the number of dimensions and a reversal of approach. Instead of subdividing the dimensions into domains or areas of concern as the project team had been doing, areas of concern became the context within which the dimensions were to be measured. Together, the reduction in the number of dimensions and the reversal of approach had the effect of lessening the amount of repetitiveness by a considerable margin.

Nevertheless, overlaps were still very much in evidence. Since one of the dimensions was concerned with culture (meaning a way of life), this is hardly surprising. A people's culture is all-pervasive. It penetrates and influences all aspects of life. Moreover, based on its work with indigenous people in other parts of the world, UNESCO has observed that cultural survival is both the reason for, and the ultimate end of, Indigenous people's development (Fukuda-Parr 2001). Cultural survival is no less critical for Maori. Indeed, the notion of cultural vitality is at the very heart of the concept of Maori well-being.

To reduce the extent to which the cultural dimension cut across the other dimensions of the framework, the focus was changed from cultural vitality, which now was seen as an integral component of Maori well-being, to cultural inheritance or taonga tuku iho, now termed Te Ao Maori. As far as the project team is concerned, there is still likely to be overlaps, but this will simply have to be lived with. Sen's views on the subject of ambiguity in this area of measurement are salutary. "Ambiguity," he says, "reflects the nature of human life" and where this condition is apparent, "the precise formulation of the idea should try to capture it." "In social investigation," he goes on to say, "it is undoubtedly more important to be vaguely right than to be precisely wrong" (Griffin & Knight 1990).

Defining Maori Development

Given the way in which Maori well-being has been defined, how should Maori development be viewed? In essence, Maori development is a process of enablement, a process that seeks to extend people's scope for improving their own lives.

The ultimate end of the process is a state of well-being, a state in which Maori have the capabilities and freedoms to live their life as they wish to. For the purposes of measurement, that desired state is defined by the variety of desirable outcomes that contribute to its achievement. In the context of the framework, these become the goal dimensions, that is, the dimensions of the ultimate end, well-being.

Thus, the thinking that went into the original conceptual framework remains largely intact (see Appendix 1). The changes that have been made have been to the specific elements that made up that framework, the way in which those elements were organized, and of course, the nomenclature.

Structure of the Draft Framework

The draft Maori framework is structured by areas of concern and the goal dimensions of well-being identified above. Measurement dimensions have been added as the first stage in the populating of the framework. The measurement dimensions establish the broad information requirements.

The framework is intended to measure the goal dimensions of well-being and hence, progress with Maori development, in the context of the areas which are of most concern to Maori. Thus, within each area of concern, one or more of the following dimensions will be identified and measured:

- Sustainability of Te Ao Maori or Te Ao Maori as the shortened version (which pertains to inheritance or taonga tuku iho)
- Social capability
- Human resource potential
- Economic self-sufficiency (which incorporates the notion of material well-being)
- Environmental sustainability
- Empowerment and enablement

Areas of concern are meant to correspond to important aspects of the quality of life or well-being. Their selection represents yet another judgement call by the project team. Again, it relied heavily on conference literature and the knowledge of the members for support. Comment on the appropriateness and the completeness of the selection would be welcomed.

By measuring the goal dimensions within an area of concern, linkages among the dimensions are easier to demonstrate. As already mentioned, the project team's first attempt at constructing and populating the framework took the reverse approach. Each of the goal dimensions were identified, and differentiated into areas of concern so that for example, Maori language was seen as a component of what was then the cultural vitality dimension (but is now called sustainability of the Te Ao Maori) rather than the other way around. This was the reason why repetitiveness became such a problem. With the area of concern approach, it is possible to see at a glance, what the linkages are within a particular area.

There is still a great deal of work to be done on populating the framework. The broad measurement categories derived from the goal dimensions within each area of concern mark only the beginning of the task. Work has already commenced on identifying outcomes for each area of concern, and on specifying the statistical outputs needed to measure them. Some attention has been given also, to the inputs. Value judgments are again involved in selecting the broad measurement areas. In making these judgments, the project team kept in mind, fundamental Maori values like manaaki, hau, whanaungatanga, and kaitiakitanga.

Now that the conceptual problems have been resolved and given competing priorities, it is expected that the identification of more specific information requirements will be completed by the end of the year.

Where to Go From Here

The shape and structure of the framework is based on a certain theoretical perspective. That perspective, which is explained in the body of the report, was chosen because it accommodates Maori ways of looking at the world. It was the project team's task to try and capture those world views, and recast them in a way that would render them measurable.

The framework's function, when it is finished, will be to help Statistics New Zealand to improve the relevance of the statistics it collects to those Maori individuals and organizations that need to plan, make decisions, and give advice. There are certain areas covered in the framework on which it would not be appropriate for a government department to be collecting information. The department is well aware of the need for discretion and care in this sensitive area. The department expects that iwi, hapu, or Maori organizations might want to collect, produce, and store some of this information themselves, and that where this is the case, Statistics New Zealand's role will change from provider to that of facilitating local collection through its statistical capability building program.

Structure of Draft Maori Statistics Framework

Area of Concern	Goal Dimensions	Measurement Dimension
Maori language	Te Ao Maori	Use of the Maori language
		Spoken proficiency
		Availability of Maori language speakers, services (e.g., television/radio hours) and products (e.g., literature, music, shows)
	Human resource potential	Acquisition of Maori language proficiency
		Recognition of proficiency
	Economic self-sufficiency	Purchase of, and expenditure on, Maori language-related products, services, and learning opportunities
	Empowerment and enablement	Opportunities to acquire/enhance proficiency (provision of formal and non-formal learning, including mentoring)
		Access to opportunities to acquire/enhance proficiency
		Government spending on provision of learning opportunities, resources, and services (e.g., television and radio)
		Maori spending on provision of learning opportunities, resources, and services (e.g., television and radio)
Maori knowledge	Te Ao Maori	Availability of expertise in specific areas of Maori knowledge, skills, and competencies
		Production and availability of material relating to specific areas of Maori knowledge, skills, and competencies including documents, sound-recordings, maps, and images
	Social capability	Reciprocal contributions (in lieu of money) by learners including labour, food, and care
		Barriers to accessing Maori knowledge, skills, and competencies
	Human resource potential	Acquisition of Maori knowledge, skills, and competencies including self-directed learning, mentoring, and coaching
		Recognition of competency (includes formal qualifications and/or hapu or iwi recognition)
	Economic self-sufficiency	Spending by Maori learners on learning-related activities
	Empowerment and enablement	Opportunities to acquire expertise in specific areas of Maori knowledge, skills, and competencies including: • One-on-one mentoring and coaching (the Maori method of transmitting and acquiring knowledge) • Non-formal and formal courses (provided by Maori and public education providers)

Area of Concern	Goal Dimensions	Measurement Dimension
Maori knowledge contd.	**Empowerment and enablement** contd.	Maori spending on preserving, protecting, and transmitting Maori knowledge, skills, and competencies
		Government expenditure on purchasing and provision of: • Maori advice to assist in decision-making • Learning opportunities • Protecting and preserving Maori knowledge
Marae	**Te Ao Maori**	Types of marae (ancestral and urban)
		Performance of rituals—paepae numbers, kaikaranga numbers, kaiwaiata numbers
	Social capability	Use of marae by households, frequency, and purpose
		Contributions by individuals or households of time, labour, money to building, maintenance, and operation of marae
		Role of individuals in respect of the marae
	Empowerment and enablement	Ownership of land and buildings by whanau, hapu, iwi, Maori organizations, and local government bodies
		Marae management and operations: • Hui held and type • Resources (human, physical, financial) • Status of the land
Wahi Taonga	**Te Ao Maori**	Availability of expertise and materials on cultural and historical significance of wahi taonga (includes experts, documents, sound-recordings, maps, and images)
		Customary use of wahi taonga by Maori individuals, households, and organizations, including permits issued
	Social capability	Relationships and working arrangements with mainstream environmental groups
		Contributions toward protection and preservation of wahi taonga by Maori individuals and households (includes time, labour, and money)
		Access to wahi taonga by individuals and households
	Environmental sustainability	Identification and recognition of sites by type, includes: • Sites recognized by hapu and iwi but not by authorities • Sites formally recognized by authorities (e.g. local bodies, government agencies)

Area of Concern	Goal Dimensions	Measurement Dimension
Wahi Taonga contd.	**Environmental sustainability (cont.).**	Quality of the resource obtained based on user observation of the resource site
		Depletion of natural resource stock (e.g. paua)
		Damage to, and destruction of, sites as result of local body management or operational procedures, consents for development
	Empowerment and enablement	Arrangements for hapu or iwi control over, or representation in, management, operation, protection, and preservation of wahi taonga
		Arrangements for representation in environmental management decision-making
		Number of hapu or iwi with environmental management plan (includes those that have and have not been incorporated in local district plan)
		Government and local body spending on protection and preservation of wahi taonga
Wahi Tapu	Much of the information requirement for wahi taonga will be repeated in this area	
Maori land	**Te Ao Maori**	Land held in Maori ownership by geographic location
	Economic self-sufficiency	Purposes for which it is used—productive or otherwise
		Maori land valuation
		Arrangements for retention and utilization of Maori land trusts and incorporations
	Empowerment and enablement	Claims before courts, tribunals involving land (include a basis of the claim—e.g. raupatu, public works act)
		Cases heard by Maori Land Court by land type, succession, and outcome
Population	**Social capability**	Maori and iwi population size, composition, and growth
		Geographic distribution of the Maori and iwi population
		Proportion of iwi living inside and outside iwi territory
Families and households	**Social capability**	Size and composition of Maori households
		Family size and type (including extended families)
		Characteristics of families/households: • With children in Maori-medium education • With children attending university or post-school training

Area of Concern	Goal Dimensions	Measurement Dimension
Families and households contd.	Social capability (cont.).	• With Maori language speakers • With members who contribute to care and support of whanau • That contribute to whanau, hapu, iwi affairs • With members who are self-employed • With members who have been hospitalized
Social connections and attachments	Te Ao Maori	Knowledge of iwi
		Knowledge of kinship ties and connections to others (within whanau, hapu, iwi, and across iwi)
		Numbers registered on iwi register (recognition)
	Social capability	Maintenance of relationship with kin living in community in which one/both parent(s) brought up
		Participation in organized community-based activities
		Culture-related leisure activities
		Contribution to and receipt of support from whanau including: • Material support (e.g. money, food, labour) • Advice/counselling • Direct care • Crisis support and management
		Contribution to maintenance and operation of hapu, iwi, and/or Maori organizations including time, labour, money, and other forms of donation
	Empowerment and enablement	Formal and informal arrangements for care and maintenance of whanau such as whanau hui and legal arrangements like whanau trusts
Modern knowledge, skills, competencies	Human resource potential	Distribution of knowledge, skills, competencies within Maori/iwi population
		Knowledge, skills, competencies used in paid or unpaid work for formal employer, hapu, iwi, and other Maori organizations
		Acquisition of knowledge, skills, competencies through formal structured, or non-formal education and training courses
		Knowledge, skills, competencies demanded by Maori and general market
	Economic self-sufficiency	Personal/household spending on acquiring knowledge, skills competencies
		Use of knowledge, skills, competencies in paid and unpaid work including leisure activities

Area of Concern	Goal Dimensions	Measurement Dimension
Modern knowledge, skills, competencies (cont.)	**Empowerment and enablement**	Opportunities to acquire generalized knowledge, skills, and competencies through provision by Maori and public providers of structured formal and non-formal education and training courses
		Maori providers of formal structured and non-formal education and training: • Types of courses • Resources (labour, physical, financial) • Students and their attainments
		Spending by Maori organizations on provision of structured formal and non-formal training programs
		Government spending on purchasing and provision of Maori-provided formal and non-formal structured training
Health	**Human resource potential**	Life expectancy
		Infant mortality
		Hospitalization rates
		Incidence and prevalence of diseases
	Social capability	Arrangements for care of elderly, sick, disabled whanau members
		Use of primary health services including Maori health services
		Accessibility of primary health services
	Empowerment and enablement	Maori providers of health services and programs including resources (human, physical, financial), users, and type of services or program
		Provision by health institutions for cultural needs of patients and whanau
		Spending by Maori organizations on provision of Maori health services and programs
		Government expenditure on purchasing and provision of Maori health services and programs
Housing	**Economic self-sufficiency**	Home ownership
		Quality of Maori housing stock
		Barriers to acquisition/improvement in housing including: • Finance • Location • Local body zoning • Status of land

Area of Concern	Goal Dimensions	Measurement Dimension
Housing (cont).	**Economic self-sufficiency** contd.	Opportunities to purchase/rent a home through iwi-operated schemes such as papakainga housing
		Housing-type preference
	Empowerment and enablement	Maori organization's (marae, iwi authorities, etc.) spending on housing provision and services
		Government expenditure on housing assistance and on purchase and provision of housing
Income and expenditure	**Economic self-sufficiency**	Level and source of personal and household income
		Household spending patterns
		Net worth, assets, and debts of Maori households
Work	**Economic self-sufficiency**	Labour force participation
		Employment and unemployment rate
		Hours of work
		Industry structure including Maori service provisions like: • Kohanga Reo • Maori-provided health services • Maori-provided training services
		Occupation structure including Maori occupations like: • Kaitiaki • Kaitakawaenga • Kaiako
		Job preferences
		Unpaid work by type and hours
	Human resource potential	Labour demand in locality
Social problems	**Social capability**	Maori voluntary community-based organizations like: • Type • Resources (human, physical, financial) • Membership
		Contributions to, and receipt of, support or assistance from Maori community-based organizations
	Human resource potential	Level of Maori juvenile and adult offending
		Level of truancy, suspensions, expulsions
		Children in care

Area of Concern	Goal Dimensions	Measurement Dimension
Social problems (cond).	**Human resource potential** contd.	Use of women's refuges
	Empowerment and enablement	Maori-provided social services including: • Types of service • Resources (human, physical, financial) • Clients
		Maori spending on provision of social services and social service programs
		Government spending on purchasing and provision of Maori-provided health services
Maori business development	**Economic self-sufficiency**	Number, distribution, structure, and characteristics of Maori businesses
		Net worth, assets, and debts
		Productivity and profitability
Participation in political decision-making processes	**Empowerment and enablement**	Participation in general and local government elections
		Arrangements for participation in decision-making by iwi/hapu members
		Participation in iwi, hapu, Maori organization elections, appointments, and other decision-making processes
		Representation in national and local decision-making organizations/bodies
		Partnerships with government agencies
		Funding/sponsorship of Maori institutions, individuals, events, activities
		Central and local government consultations
Rights	**Te Ao Maori**	Use of Maori institutions: for example—number of rahui imposed, and muru and tatau pounamu exercised, taiapure established
		Customary rights: Authorizations by Kaitiaki for customary fishing (may have this under Wahi Taonga)
	Empowerment and enablement	Claims/objections before local bodies, courts, and tribunals
		Successful claims, objections before local bodies, courts, tribunals
		Public agencies with responsiveness plans and procedures, Maori language capability
	Social capability	Access to justice: legal aid applications submitted/granted, applications to court

Appendix 1: Conceptual Framework for Maori Statistics

Definitions of Well-being & Development	Dimensions of Maori Well-beingp	Dimensions of Maori Development	Areas of Concern
Well-being is a function of the ability of people to make the choices that enable them to realize the kind of life they wish to live. Development is a process of expanding opportunities for people to realize the kind of life they wish to live.	A secure cultural identity and freedom of cultural expression	Revitalization of Maori language, knowledge, traditions, expressive arts, institutions	Cultural Vitality
	Strong connections and ties in the Maori community	Strengthening of Maori communities, social organizations, networks	Social Cohesion (Internal)
	Respect and goodwill of mainstream society	Strengthening of linkages with mainstream NGOs	Social Cohesion (Societal)
	Having the opportunity to live a long and healthy life	Increasing access to and command over the provision of health services	Human Capital
	Having the knowledge, skills, competencies to achieve the kind of live one chooses to live	Increasing access to, and command over, the provision of education and training services	Human Capital
	Having a level of income that enables one to achieve the kind of life one chooses to live	Increasing access to, and command over, the provision of employment, fostering the development of Maori enterprise	Standard Of Living/ living Conditions
	Being able to enjoy a clean and healthy natural environment	Protection of Maori food and medicine reserves, protection of sacred landmarks	Natural Capital
	Being able to exercise rights as Maori	Recognizing and giving effect to rights under the treat of Waitangi	Human Rights
		Recognizing international instruments and other legal doctrines	
		Recognizing Maori defined rights and institutions for Maori (tino rangatiratanga)	
		Recognizing and giving effect to rights fundamental to all human beings	

References

Australian Bureau of Statistics. (2000). *Measuring Well-Being*. Canberra.

Berger-Schmitt, R. & Noll, H. (2000). *Conceptual Framework and Structure of a European System of Social Indicators.* Euroreporting Working Paper No. 9.

Department of Maori Studies, Massey University. (1995). *Kia Pumau Tonu*. Proceedings of Maori Development Conference.

Department of Maori Studies, Massey University. (1998). *Te Oru Rangahau*. Proceeding of Maori Research & Development Conference.

Forster, Margaret. (2000). *Being Maori in the Context of Poverty, Prosperity and Progress.* Paper delivered at DevNet 2000 Conference.

Fukuda-Parr, S. (2001). *In Search of Indicators of Culture and Development: A Review of Progress and Proposals for Next Steps*. Article for World Culture Report. <**www.unesco.com**>

Maori Affairs Department. (1985). *Report on the Hui Taumata 1984.*

Maori Affairs Department. (*Hunn Report*). [AJHR 1961, G.10].

Sen, A. (1999). *Development as Freedom*. New York.

Sen, A. "Development as Capability Expansion." In Griffin, K and Knight, J. *Human Development and International Development Strategy for the 1990s.*

Statistics New Zealand. *Maori Statistics Forum Minutes*, May 1995.

Statistics New Zealand. *Maori Statistics Forum Minutes*, June 1996.

Statistics New Zealand. *Maori Statistics Forum Minutes*, November 2000.

Statistics New Zealand. *Maori Statistics Forum Minutes*, March 2002.

United Nations Development Programme. (2001). *Human Development Reports.*

15

The Impact of Australian Policy Regimes on Indigenous Population Movement: Evidence from the 2001 Census

John Taylor

Introduction

Policy questions regarding the relationship between mobility and the structural position of Indigenous Australians have gained prominence since the election of the conservative Howard government in 1996. With hindsight, it can be seen that 1996 marked a watershed in Indigenous affairs policy in Australia. The new conservative government articulated a view that there had been too much emphasis on "symbolic" reconciliation (Indigenous rights) at the expense of practical outcomes. As a consequence, it set about redressing this imbalance by giving greater emphasis to "practical" reconciliation, or closing the socio-economic gap in the key areas of health, housing, education, and employment.

In line with this approach, and looking ahead to imagine the course of mobility and migration into the future, the current signal from the government to Indigenous Australians, and especially those in remote areas, is a growing requirement to embrace the institutions of mainstream Australian life with potential implications for migration decision-making. The government sees the means to influencing such decisions as via the policy process, and key changes to have emerged over the past ten years with such implications include: the privatization of employment services; the introduction of the Indigenous Employment Strategy with an emphasis on private sector engagement and enhanced labour mobility; revised welfare reform provisions including the universal imposition of work activity tests; incentives to move workers off workfare schemes and into mainstream employment; attempts to shift from communal to privatized land tenure; the abolition of national and regional representative structures; and a shift towards more individualized (as opposed to community) articulation with government services.

The aim of this paper is to examine recent patterns and trends in Indigenous population movement against this background of policy shift to see if there are any discernable impacts on mobility behaviour, though it may be too soon to say. If so (or if not), what does this mean for the likely future distribution of the

Table 15.1: Indigenous and Non-Indigenous Population Distribution by Remoteness Category, 2001

	Non-Indigenous	Indigenous	Indigenous % of total
Major city	12,732,492	138,494	1.1
Inner regional	3,932,907	92,988	2.3
Outer regional	1,907,688	105,875	5.3
Remote	284,160	40,161	12.4
Very remote	97,473	81,002	45.4
Total	**18,954,720**	**458,520**	**2.4**

Source: Australian Bureau of Statistics (ABS) 2003, 22

Indigenous population? In short, has the new policy regime achieved a literal mobilization of the Indigenous population?

To examine this, it is fortunate that (for once) Australian statistical and political cycles coincide. Basically, the last change in government occurred just before the 1996 Census which means that 1996 data reflect the high-water mark of the previous centre-left Labor government's 15 years of Indigenous affairs policy, and while various types of policy lags no doubt exist, the last inter-censal period (1996–2001) can be interpreted as the policy domain (and emergent legacy) of the current centre-right government. Before commencing, it is helpful to obtain a sense of the spatial distribution of the Indigenous population compared to the Australian population generally.

Indigenous Population Distribution

Of all the transformations in the Australian Indigenous population since 1788, none has been more visible, nor more influential, than the geographic shift in distribution. From an original widespread occupation of the continent with numbers distributed in familial groupings at varying densities, residential arrangements are now focused mostly on the suburbs of towns and major cities. Over the long term, this reflects the impacts of colonization leading either to rural–urban migration, or to populations in situ being engulfed by expanding urban areas. Since 1971, it has also reflected a growing tendency for Indigenous people who were already urban-based to self-identify in census counts. Either way, the proportion of the Indigenous population resident in urban areas rose from 44% in 1971 to 74% in 2001. Almost one third of Indigenous Australians now reside in major cities (**Table 15.1**). While this number remains substantially less than that for the total population (67%), it nonetheless represents a marked increase from the figure of 15% recorded for major urban areas in 1971. As this process of rising Indigenous population counts in urban areas has unfolded, the rural share of the population has continued to decline—down from 56% in 1971 to almost one quarter in 2001.

A more structural interpretation of this shift would focus on the relative balance of remote/non-remote distribution. Reference to "remote" areas is long-standing

Figure 15.1: ASGC Remoteness Regions

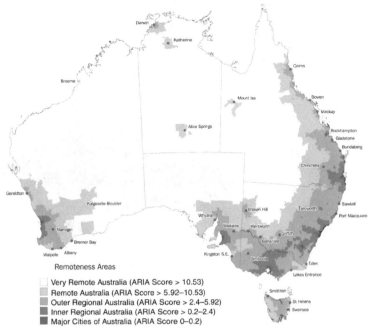

Remoteness Areas

☐ Very Remote Australia (ARIA Score > 10.53)
▨ Remote Australia (ARIA Score > 5.92–10.53)
▩ Outer Regional Australia (ARIA Score > 2.4–5.92)
▦ Inner Regional Australia (ARIA Score > 0.2–2.4)
▪ Major Cities of Australia (ARIA Score 0–0.2)

Source: Australian Bureau of Statistics

in Australian regional analysis, and essentially draws attention to a distinction in social and economic geography between closely settled areas and sparsely settled areas, with economic development and service provision severely impeded in the latter by force of relative locational disadvantage, low accessibility, and a specialization of economic activity. Since 1996, the Australian Standard Geographic Classification (ASGC) has attempted to capture this diversity by incorporating a continuum from those spatial units where geographic distance imposes minimal restriction on physical access to the widest range of goods, services, and opportunities for social interaction, to those where such restriction is maximized (**Figure 15.1**).

The salient point, then, from **Table 15.1**, is that Indigenous people remain far more likely than other Australians to reside away from cities, especially in remote areas covering the vast two thirds of the continent where economic development and access to goods and services are severely impeded by small numbers and long distances. Fully one quarter of the Indigenous population lives scattered across this landscape in places that are either close to, or on, lands over which they have owned via descent and other forms of kin-based succession for millennia. Overall, Indigenous people account for almost half (45%) of the resident population of very remote Australia. Although away from the main service and mining towns dotted across this vast area, they are by far the majority. As shown in **Figure 15.1**,

Figure 15.2: Indigenous Propensities to Move by Statistical Division, 1991–1996 and 1996–2001

1991–1996

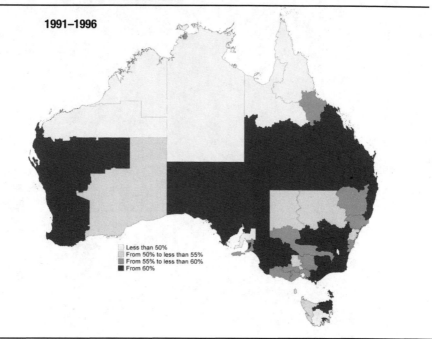

1996–2001

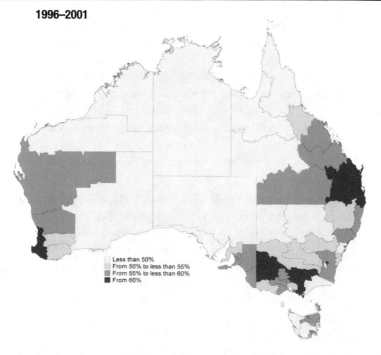

Source: Taylor 2006

this means that Indigenous people and their institutions predominate over the bulk of the continental land mass. This dispersal of the contemporary Indigenous population from the suburbs of global cities to the remotest parts of the continent produces an unusually diverse range of residential circumstances and opportunities for social and economic participation.

Propensity to Move

Successive census results since 1971 have indicated that Indigenous people change their usual place of residence at consistently higher rates than the rest of the population. However, this gap is mostly accounted for by the fact that the Indigenous population includes a higher proportion of people in younger, more mobile age groups. Consequently, Indigenous age-standardized rates are only slightly higher than non-Indigenous rates (Taylor 2006). In 2001, 51% of the Indigenous population reported a change of residence over the previous five-year period. Surprisingly though, given the proposed likely influence of recent policy changes on mobility, this represented a reduction in the overall level of movement down from 52% recorded at the previous census—or did it? The fact is, a major constraint on the analysis of Indigenous mobility change over time exists because demographic factors are not solely responsible for intercensal population change.

Between 1991 and 1996, for example, as much as half (51%) of the increase in the Indigenous count could not be accounted for by demographic factors, while the equivalent figure for the last inter-censal period was 31%, with the balance due to increased self-identification of Indigenous status in census counts. Thus, it is difficult to unequivocally ascribe higher (or lower) mobility in a time series to actual changes in the propensity to move among Indigenous people. In effect, successive census data capture the characteristics, including mobility, of different populations. All that can be said then, is that the mobility rate among those who identified as Indigenous in 2001 was somewhat lower than the rate observed for those recorded as Indigenous in 1996, though substantially higher than for those who identified as Indigenous in 1991. While there is some scope for estimating the compositional impact of new identifiers in the population using fixed population characteristics, such as age left school (Eschbach, Supple, and Snipp 1998), for characteristics that are variable over time, such as mobility status, this is simply not possible.

These issues aside, **Figure 15.2** shows that while the intensity of movement was considerably lower in many regions for the 2001 Census-identified population, the regional pattern remained essentially the same with relatively high movement propensities in the east and southwest, and generally low propensities in the remote areas of the interior and across the north. The picture it paints of persistently low Indigenous population movement in remote areas is true in the sense that remote Indigenous populations are not migrant, but it is grossly misleading in the sense that they are highly mobile, and engaged in circular mobility over the short-term (Taylor 1998; Taylor and Bell 2004; Peterson 2004; Memmott et al 2006).

Figure 15.3: Indigenous Age-specific Propensities to Move, 1991–1996 and 1996–2001

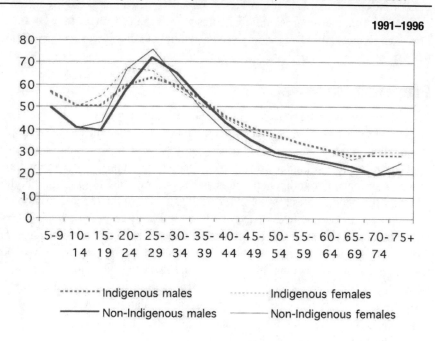

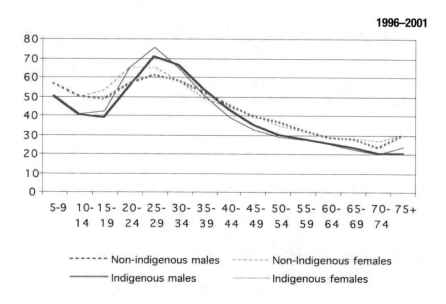

Source: Taylor 2006

Movement Propensities by Age and Sex

Overall, at the national level, the age profile of mobility for Indigenous people is very similar to that observed for all other Australians with movement rates peaking in the 20–29 age range followed by a sharp decline, but with a slight rise in retirement ages **(Figure 15.3)**. For the population in general, the peak in the age profile of migration in the young-adult age range has been firmly linked to the combined influence of life cycle events, including departure from the parental home, the start of tertiary education and training, entry into the labour force, and the establishment of independent living arrangements. While broad agreement in this patterning of migration by age suggests that similar influences also bear on the Indigenous young adult population, the much flatter profile of Indigenous mobility also indicates that such drivers are weaker. To the extent that migration rates reflect these socio-economic pressures it is again significant in the context of recent policy changes that the diagrams show no change at all in the rates by age between the first and second half of the 1990s.

This is consistent with other research, which shows that despite the government's focus on practical reconciliation, the gap between Indigenous and other Australians actually widened during the 1990s for important markers such as labour force participation, unemployment, education participation, private sector employment, home ownership, and individual income (Altman and Hunter 2003).

Mobility by Remoteness

At the broad regional scale, if the level of participation in mainstream institutions, such as tertiary education, labour markets, and housing markets, underpin the propensity to migrate, and if proximity to each of these is one factor that serves to facilitate or hinder such participation, then one would expect the age profile of mobility to vary according to remoteness. As indicated earlier, the capacity to explore mobility by a measure of remoteness is now provided for the first time by the inclusion of a remoteness index in the ASGC and **Figure 15.4** (page 288–90) shows a remarkably strong relationship between the age pattern of movement and remoteness.

Thus, in major cities, Indigenous people are more mobile than non-Indigenous people at all ages. However, as we progressively move away from major cities to very remote regions, the marked peaks among children and young adults in the age profile of Indigenous mobility are seen to progressively diminish to the point where age appears to have no effect at all on mobility in very remote areas, and the overall level is very low. In contrast, non-Indigenous mobility rates are largely unaffected by location, although especially high rates in the 20–34 age range are evident in remote and very remote areas mostly because of movement for employment.

Figure 15.4a: Age and Sex Profile of Indigenous and Non-Indigenous Mobility Rates by Remoteness Category, 1996–2001

Major Cities

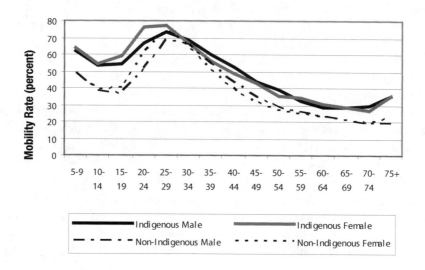

Inner regional

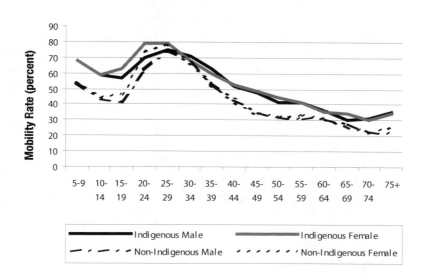

Source: Taylor 2006

Figure 15.4b: Age and Sex Profile of Indigenous and Non-Indigenous Mobility Rates by Remoteness Category, 1996–2001

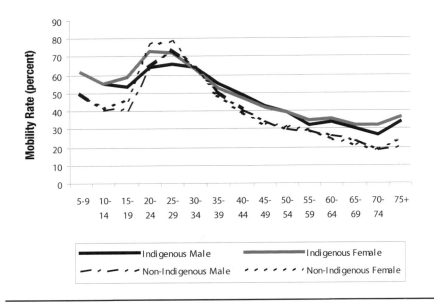

Outer regional

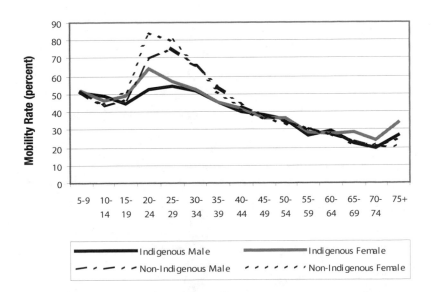

Remote

Source: Taylor 2006

Figure 15.4c: Age and Sex Profile of Indigenous and Non-Indigenous Mobility Rates by Remoteness Category, 1996–2001

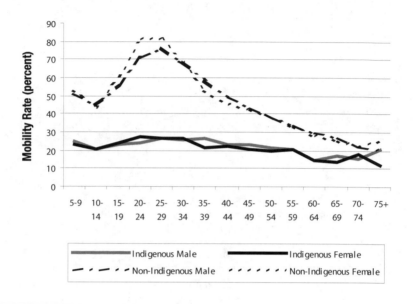

Very Remote

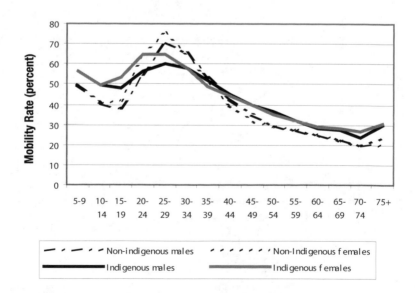

Total Australia

Source: Taylor 2006

Spatial Redistribution: Are Indigenous People Moving to More Accessible Regions?

Since these data suggest a steady decline in Indigenous social and economic mainstream participation away from major cities, a key question for policy is whether population redistribution is leading to more or less access to mainstream opportunity. Basically, what is the direction of net migration flows between regions according to their remoteness? Is net movement up or down the settlement hierarchy?

The first point of interest is the degree to which Indigenous people remain within or change their remoteness region of residence—in effect, to what extent do they move to a region with a different degree of relative access to goods, services, and labour markets? From **Table 15.2** (page 292) we can see that Indigenous residents of major cities in 2001 are more than twice as likely as non-Indigenous residents to have been in a different remoteness region in the previous five years. The Indigenous population in regional areas is also more likely to have shifted remoteness region. By contrast, in remote areas (especially in very remote areas), Indigenous people are far more likely to be non-movers.

The numbers of people involved in these inter-regional shifts, and the consequent net and gross migration rates are shown in **Tables 15.3 and 15.4** (page 292). In major cities and regional areas, relatively large numbers of Indigenous people are involved in migration between remoteness regions. In major cities for example, population turnover with other remoteness regions involves almost one third of the Indigenous population (325 per thousand).

This compares to only 141 per thousand among non-Indigenous major city residents. However, the net gain to major cities from this movement is much lower in both cases at just 14 per thousand for the Indigenous population and almost zero for the non-Indigenous population. By far the greatest net gains for both Indigenous and non-Indigenous populations are in the inner regional areas, although again the Indigenous gross migration rate associated with this is much higher. Outer regional areas provide an interesting contrast as these areas are net recipients of Indigenous population transfers from elsewhere, but net losers of non-Indigenous population. Finally, remote and very remote regions display net losses of both Indigenous and non-Indigenous population, although the rate of non-Indigenous loss is by far the greatest, as is the degree of non-Indigenous population turnover.

As for the direction of net migration flows, **Figure 15.5** (page 293) shows these to be broadly similar for Indigenous and non-Indigenous populations with a clear overall shift in residence up the settlement hierarchy. However, significant differences are apparent in the intensity of Indigenous and non-Indigenous flows. Thus, Indigenous net losses from remote and very remote areas are most prominent to relatively adjacent outer regional areas. In turn, outer regional areas lose Indigenous population mostly to inner regional areas. This is suggestive of a step-wise

Table 15.2: Percent of Indigenous and Non-Indigenous Populations who Changed Their Remoteness Region of Residence Between 1996 and 2001

	Indigenous (1)	Non-Indigenous (2)	Ratio (1/2)
Major Cities	16.3	7.1	2.29
Inner Regional	19.9	14.9	1.33
Outer Regional	19.4	17.3	1.12
Remote	22.2	25.7	0.86
Very Remote	8.2	33.9	0.24

Source: Taylor 2006

Table 15.3: Migration Rates[1] of Indigenous Population Movement Between Remoteness Zones 1996–2000

	Major Cities	Inner Regional	Outer Regional	Remote	Very Remote
Movers out	12,566	13,448	13,632	5,845	8,123
Movers in	13,747	16,111	14,666	4,704	4,386
Net	1,181	2,663	1,034	-1,141	-3,737
Net rates	14.6	35.8	14.2	-48.1	-48.9
Gross rate	325.0	397.1	388.7	444.8	163.8

Source: Taylor 2006
1.Per thousand of the mean of the 1996 and 2001 populations

Table 15.4: Migration Rates[1] of Non-Indigenous Population Movement Between Remoteness Zones 1996–2001

	Major Cities	Inner Regional	Outer Regional	Remote	Very Remote
Movers out	627,920	582,573	341,958	78,300	64,290
Movers in	628,251	685,262	283,742	53,948	43,838
Net	331	102,689	-58,216	-24,352	-20,452
Net rates	0.04	24.1	-32.2	-94.7	-128.6
Gross rate	141.2	297.6	345.7	514.4	679.7

Source: Taylor 2006
1.Per thousand of the mean of the 1996 and 2001 populations

Figure 15.5: Rates of Indigenous and Non-Indigenous Net Migration Loss by Remoteness Region, 1996–2001

Indigenous

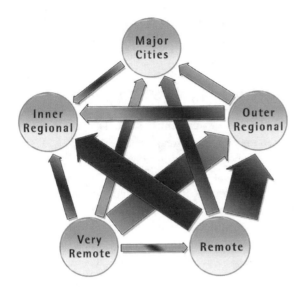

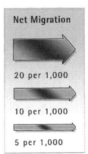

Non-Indigenous

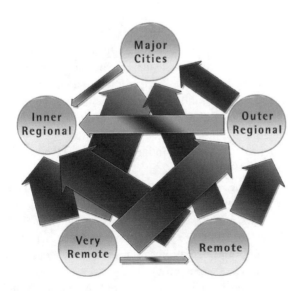

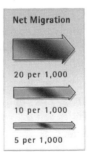

Source: Taylor 2006

migration similar to that reported in the past for Indigenous migration to major cities such as Adelaide (Gale and Wundersitz 1982). By contrast, non-Indigenous movement out of remote and very remote areas is substantial to all regions, often bypassing outer regional areas, with the largest single flows occurring directly into inner regional areas and major cities suggestive of employment and housing-led mobility. The considerable difference in the intensity of net migration loss between the Indigenous and non-Indigenous populations reveals the key demographic reason why the Indigenous share of total population in remote areas continues to rise.

But wouldn't such a gradual shift up the settlement hierarchy represent a positive step along the government's path to practical reconciliation? The answer depends largely on the stability of such a residential shift. The fact is, Indigenous population turnover rates in metropolitan areas are relatively high, at times involving half or more of a region's population (Taylor and Bell 1999). Furthermore, this high turnover is attributed largely to movement between cities and their hinterlands, as opposed to involving inter- or intra-metropolitan movement. For some cities, it has been suggested that this tends to undermine the notion of an "urban Aboriginal population" as distinct from any other, and that Indigenous people in the city are not just similar to those in surrounding country areas—to a large extent they are the same people spatially displaced at different stages of their lives (Gray 1989). The basis for Gray's assertion stemmed from his analysis of the age-specific pattern of net flows in and out of cities in the 1980s with two overlapping patterns of urbanization observed.

The first was evident in the large metropolitan centers of Sydney and Melbourne, and involved a cycle of young single people moving to the city then returning to the country maybe ten years later taking their new families with them. The second pattern was focused on the smaller cities of Adelaide and Perth and involved more permanent migration, possibly owing to the existence of more active Aboriginal housing programs in those cities. In all states, net in-migration to cities was concentrated in the 15–24 age group, highlighting an economic imperative in the context of education, training, and job search, while out-migration at older ages reflects difficulties in securing family housing. The common socio-economic determinant here was the much greater reliance of Indigenous people on access to housing via the public sector (Gray 1989, 2004).

If we consider the more recent age profiles of Indigenous net migration to metropolitan areas as shown in **Figure 15.6** (page 297–299), it appears that not much has changed since Gray's analysis 20 years ago. Overall, movement into cities tends to peak in the young adult age groups and tapers off thereafter. In Sydney, all but the 15–24 age group display net migration loss; Melbourne is somewhat similar in having clear net gains up to middle ages, and clear net losses at older ages; Adelaide and Perth also experience net gains of youth and young adults, but tend to experience net migration balance at all other ages while Brisbane is the only capital city to record consistent net gains for almost all age groups.

Reasons for Movement

Attempts to establish the proximate causes of population movement using census data have only recently been made (Kinfu 2005), while the 2002 National Aboriginal and Torres Strait Islander Social Survey (NATSISS) provided the first survey data on Indigenous migrant motivations (Taylor and Kinfu 2006). In both cases a mix of social and economic factors were identified, though with more importance attached to the former. Thus, from census analysis, family rather than labour-related characteristics were found to be the primary factors underpinning mobility with low socio-economic status producing a need for frequent residential adjustment (Kinfu 2005). Significantly, a strong association was found between the size and probability of positive migration flows, and the strength of social networks.

As for NATSISS data, the results from a logistic regression point to marginal labour force status as the biggest predictor of mobility. However, when asked directly to indicate the most important reasons for moving, respondents overwhelmingly identified family and housing factors with the single largest category being a desire to be close to family and friends. This is consistent with repeated findings from case studies of Indigenous mobility that stress the importance of kin location and general reliance on public rental housing in shaping the frequency and pattern of mobility (Gale and Wundersitz 1982; Young and Doohan 1989; Taylor and Bell 2004; Peterson 2004; Gray 2004; Memmott, Long, and Thomson 2006).

Conclusion

In summarizing the findings of a recent compendium of studies on population mobility and Indigenous peoples in the new world settings of Australasia and North America, Taylor and Bell (2004) argued the primacy of a political economy framework for understanding past and present Indigenous population movement. This is because in these particular settings, and especially (perhaps) in Australia, the movement and residential location of Indigenous peoples has been a key expression of colonial and post-colonial Indigenous-state relations reflecting the combined effects of government policy, and widespread and sustained social and economic marginalization. Although a significant shift in the Indigenous policy environment commenced in the mid-1990s, this appears not to have impacted on Indigenous mobility behaviour, at least not up until 2001. Thus, while the intent of government policy is to move towards a convergence in socio-demographic trends, there appears little evidence of this so far in Australia. This may all be in the timing of course, with a longer lead time necessary for policy impacts to take effect, and for this reason much interest will surround 2006 Census results.

At the same time, any rigorous assessment of inter-censal mobility change is made difficult by shifts in census identity, by the inability of fixed period census data to record mobility in remote areas, and by high population turnover in cities. At the same time, it is true that the 2001 Census-identified Indigenous population displays a lower propensity for residential shift while no difference is observed in age-specific movement rates compared to the 1996 Census-identified population. If convergence is evident at all it is found in the general pattern of net migration flow away from remote areas and up the settlement hierarchy towards areas of greater accessibility to services and labour markets. However, Indigenous net rates are much lower than non-Indigenous rates and this, combined with relatively high Indigenous fertility in remote areas, means that the only population growth across the vast expanse of the continent away from the settled urban and agricultural zone is Indigenous growth. As a consequence, Indigenous peoples constitute a growing share of the population in remote areas and the term "Indigenous domain" is increasingly applied here to signal the increasing prominence of Indigenous peoples and their institutions.

At one level, the lack of Indigenous responsiveness to market-led policy stimuli (notably in remote areas) can be seen as a measure of limited Indigenous integration with mainstream institutions; at another it can be seen as demonstrating an ongoing capacity and desire of Indigenous peoples to sustain difference. Accordingly, the idea of risk minimization as a strategy within highly segmented labour markets presents a realistic framework for understanding Indigenous population movement, as it highlights the distinctiveness of Indigenous economic participation (mostly in secondary labour markets), and lends prominence to the role of Indigenous social networks and social capital in both facilitating and constraining movement. Equally though, given the persistently low socio-economic status of Indigenous peoples across Australia, questions are increasingly raised regarding causality in the relationship between marginalization and mobility—does Indigenous mobility reflect socio-economic status, or does socio-economic status reflect mobility? As such, movement propensities and patterns of redistribution provide key indicators of social and economic transformation, marking individual and group responses to developmental and modernizing forces. They inform both social theory and policy debate.

Figure 15.6a: Age Profile of Indigenous Net Migration Rates in Australian Metropolitan Areas, 1996–2001

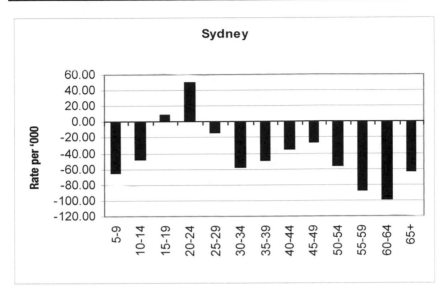

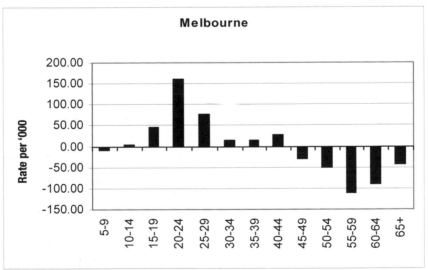

Source: Taylor 2006

Figure 15.6b: Age Profile of Indigenous Net Migration Rates in Australian Metropolitan Areas, 1996–2001

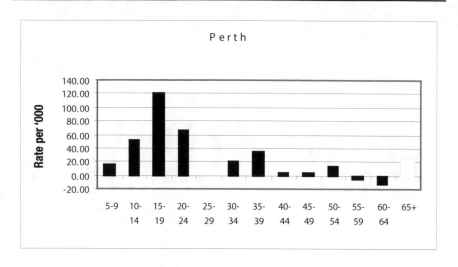

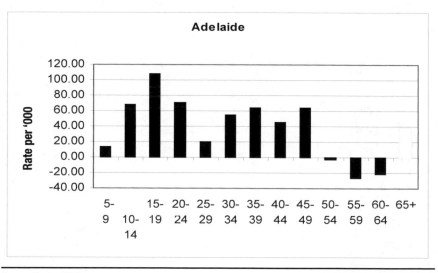

Source: Taylor 2006

Figure 15.6c: Age Profile of Indigenous Net Migration Rates in Australian Metropolitan Areas, 1996–2001

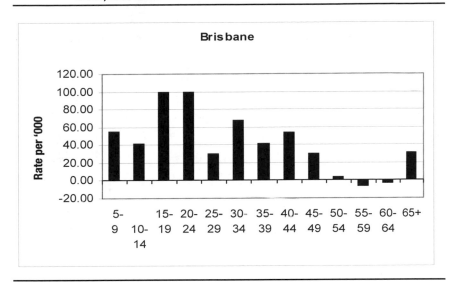

Source: Taylor 2006

References

Altman, J.C. and Hunter, B.H. (2003). "Monitoring 'Practical' Reconciliation: Evidence from the Reconciliation Decade, 1991–2001." *CAEPR Discussion Paper No. 254*. Centre for Aboriginal Economic Policy Research, The Australian National University: Canberra.

Australian Bureau of Statistics (ABS) (2003). *Population Characteristics Aboriginal and Torres Strait Islander Australians 2001*, ABS Cat. No. 4713.0, Canberra.

Eschbach, K., Supple, K., and Snipp, M.C. (1998). "Changes in Racial Identification and the Educational Attainment of American Indians, 1970–1990." *Demography*, 35. 1: 35–43.

Gray, A. (1989). "Aboriginal Migration to the Cities." *Journal of the Australian Population Association*, 6 (2): 122–44.

Gray, A. (2004). "The Formation of Contemporary Aboriginal Settlement Patterns in Australia: Government Policies and Programmes." in J. Taylor and M. Bell (eds) *Population Mobility and Indigenous Peoples in Australasia and North America*. Routledge: London and New York.

Gale, F. and Wundersitz, J. (1982). *Adelaide Aborigines: A Case Study of Urban Life 1966–1981*. Development Studies Centre, Australian National University: Canberra.

Kinfu, Y. (2005). "Spatial Mobility Among Indigenous Australians: Patterns and Determinants." *Working Paper in Demography No. 97*, Demography and Sociology Program, The Australian National University: Canberra.

Memmott, P., Long, S., and Thomson, L. (2006). *Indigenous Mobility in Rural and Remote Australia*. Australian Housing and Urban Research Institute, Queensland Research Centre: Brisbane.

Peterson, N. (2004). "Myth of the 'Walkabout': Movement in the Aboriginal Domain." in J. Taylor and M. Bell (eds) *Population Mobility and Indigenous Peoples in Australasia and North America*. Routledge: London and New York.

Taylor, J. (1998). "Measuring Short-term Population Mobility Among Indigenous Australians: Options and Implications." *Australian Geographer*, 29, 1: 125–37.

Taylor, J. (2006). in M. Bell, G. Hugo, and P. McDonald (eds), *Australians on the Move*. Melbourne University Press: Melbourne.

Taylor, J. and Bell, M. (1999). "Changing Places: Indigenous Population Movement in the 1990s." *CAEPR Discussion Paper No. 189*. Centre for Aboriginal Economic Policy Research, The Australian National University: Canberra.

Taylor J. and Bell, M. (2004). "Continuity and Change in Indigenous Australian Population Mobility." in J. Taylor and M. Bell (eds) *Population Mobility and Indigenous Peoples in Australasia and North America*. Routledge: London and New York.

Taylor, J. and Kinfu, Y. (2006). "Differentials and Determinants of Indigenous Population Mobility." in B. Hunter (ed) *Indigenous Socioeconomic Outcomes: Findings from the 2002 NATSISS*. ANU E Press: Canberra.

Young, E.A. and Doohan, K. (1989). *Mobility for Survival: A Process Analysis of Aboriginal Population Movement in Central Australia*. North Australia Research Unit, The Australian National University: Darwin.

16

Indigenous People of Northern Siberia: Human Capital, Labour Market Participation, and Living Standards

Zemfira Kalugina, Svetlana Soboleva, and Vera Tapilina

Introduction

This paper reports on the results of a pilot project, "Optimizing Social Policy in the Siberian Federal District (SFD)," conducted in partnership with the Department of Indian Affairs and Northern Development Canada, Carleton University (Joan De Bardeleben), and the Institute of Economics and Industrial Engineering, Siberian branch of the Russian Academy of Sciences (director professor Z.I. Kalugina). The objective of this project is to develop an effective mechanism to coordinate the activities of all levels of government in order to improve labour market participation and quality of life among Indigenous peoples of Siberia. The target region is Tomsk Oblast, or province, where an Indigenous people called the Selkup reside.

The study is based on data from the Russian state censuses and a sample of quantitative sociological studies. Pursuant to the available information, the authors attempted a macro-meso-micro analysis of the Russian Federation, Siberian federal district, Tomsk Oblast, and Yamalo-Nenets Okrug (a small local territory made up of compact communities where most of the Selkup live).

A Historical Overview

The Selkup are descendants of an ancient people who lived in western Siberia between the Ob and Yenisey rivers. The Selkup comprise two major groups: the southern Ob group who live in Tomsk Oblast on the Ob and its tributaries; and the northern Taz-Turukhan group who live in Tyumen Oblast on the Taz River and in Krasnoyarsk Krai on the Yenisey tributaries (**Figure 16.1**, page 302).

The Ob Selkup were hunters and fishermen. The Selkup borrowed deer-raising, which is common only in the northern area of the Selkup territory, from the Nenets and Ents. In the Taz-Tirukhan area, Selkup deer-raising is of a taiga type in which the size of herds and routes of seasonal movement are not large. The Selkup, unlike Nenets, did not use herdsmen's dogs. Deer pasturage was rarely used, even in winter.

Figure 16.1: The Area of Selkup Settlement in Russia

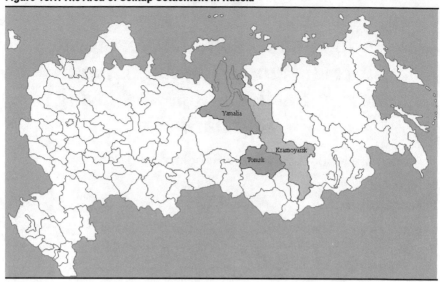

With Russian settlement in Siberia in the seventeenth to nineteenth centuries, Selkup–Russian economic and cultural bonds, as well as mixed-ethnicity marriages, increased. Under Russian influence, the Selkup began to settle in communities, take up animal breeding, and cultivate vegetables. Later on, most of the Selkup, like people of other ethnic groups in Tomsk Oblast, started to work in grain growing and animal breeding, which contributed to the loss of their traditional hunting and fishing skills. In the Soviet period, the creation of the Tym ethnic administrative unit, which brought immigrants from the basins of the Vasyugan, Chuzik, Parabel, Chan, and Keti rivers as well as the Tomsk part of the Ob area, brought the Selkup and Russians into even closer proximity. Given serious communication problems between the Selkup and new settlers, and among different groups of Selkup, Russian became the primary language used in everyday communications; it slowly replaced the Selkup dialects in the domestic sphere as well. After the liquidation of the Tym unit in 1950, Russian became the dominant language in the Selkup population of Tomsk Oblast.[1]

Contemporary Demographic Profile of Selkup

Age and Sex Structure of the Population

According to the 2002 population census, there are 4,056 Selkup people in Russia, 84.1% of whom live in rural areas (**Table 16.1**).

A portion of the Selkup population (45.8%) lives in Tyumen Oblast in which roughly equal numbers live in Yamalo-Nenets Autonomous Okrug, and Tomsk Oblast. Only 10.2% of the Selkup live outside of these areas. The population is

Table 16.1: Number of the Selkup by Area of Residence, 2002 (Persons, %)

Area	Total	Urban		Rural	
	persons	Persons	%	Persons	%
Total	4,056	645	15.9	3,411	84.1
Tyumen province	1,857	275	14.8	1,582	85.2
Tyumen province including the Yamalo-Nenets autonomous okrug	1,797	228	12.7	1,569	87.3
Tomsk province	1,787	312	17.5	1,475	82.5
Krasnoyarsk krai	412	312	14.1	354	85.9

Source: Itogi Vserossiiskoi perepisi naseleniia 2002 god. Korennye malochislennye narody Rossiiskoi Federatsii (The Results of the 2002 State Census of Population. Indigenous Peoples of the Russian Federation). Volume 13. M., 2005, p.9.

largely rural in Tomsk Oblast (82.5%). Over the period between the 1989 and 2002 censuses, the number of Selkups increased by 400 persons, but did not surpass the record number (4,300 Selkup) reported in the1959 census.

In rural places where there are high density Selkup communities the percentage of children and adolescents (29.3%) is higher than average and the percentage of people past retirement age (10.1%) is lower than average . These data suggest that the Selkup population is younger than the general Siberian population. Thus, the Selkup living in cities and rural areas are, on average, 2.3 and 5.3 years younger respectively than the population of the Siberian Federal District (SFD). The younger age structure, which is found among all Indigenous peoples in Siberia, is the consequence of their higher birth rate.

The percentage of the working-age persons is similar to the non-Selkup population but varies between rural (60.6%) and urban (70.2%). Among the population of working age, the percentage of young people aged 16–24 is relatively high. They make up 30.1% of the population in cities and 26.6% of the rural population. The 25–44 age group, who represent the bulk of working-age persons, account for 49.3% of the population in urban areas, and 52.6% in rural communities. For women aged 45–54 and men aged 45–59, who are considered to be the senior-working age population, the proportions are smaller. We find that this age group makes up 20.6% and 20.8% of the population in urban and rural communities respectively. Based on the present trends in Selkup demography, no intensive aging of the working population is anticipated, and the size of the retirement-age population will not surpass that of the working age. The relatively high labour potential of the Selkup, combined with a lower life expectancy, contributes to a lower than average dependency ratio, which refers to the proportion of dependent persons (who are younger or older than working age) relative to the working age population, compared to the general SFD population. We find that there are 651 dependent persons per 1,000 of working age in rural okrug communities versus 706 dependent persons per 1,000 of working age in rural communities of the general non-Selkup population.

Figure 16.2: Natural Movement of Selkup Population in Tomsk Oblast

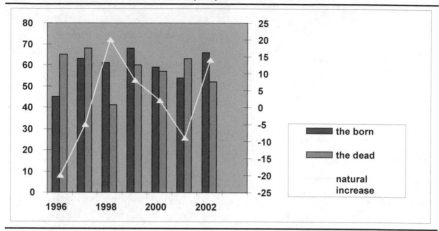

Source: Ekonomicheskoe i sotsialnoe razvitie korennykh malochislennykh narodov Severa (Economic and Social Development of the Indigenous Northern Peoples) 2002. M., 2003, pp. 13–15.

The population structure of the Selkup has been characterized by the prevalence of women of working age and, in particular, retired age. The latest data from the 2002 census, indicates this trend has continued, but with certain variations. While the male-female ratio among those under 40 is satisfactorily balanced (with a slightly larger number of women), among those over the age of 40 a significantly larger number of women relative to men is observed, which is mainly the result of extremely high death rates among men. Thus, in the 40–49 age group the percentage of men is 2.9 percentage points lower than women in urban communities and 4.9 percentage points lower in rural communities. In the post-working-age group, this difference is more pronounced. Thus, in city communities, there are twice as many women of retirement age compared to men, and in rural places, the difference is 4.5 percentage points. A higher death rate for Selkup men comparative to Selkup women is also demonstrated by the lower average age among men. The difference is 4 years in city communities and 3.2 years in rural communities

Birth Rate and Natural Increase

The high rate of marriage among the Selkup of Tomsk Oblast (74.6% of men, and 68.6% of women) provides a base for a significantly higher birth rate than the non-Selkup in the SFD. In 2002, the rate of marriage of the SFD population was 9.0 persons per 1,000, while for the Selkup it was 16.3 per 1,000.

A distinctive feature of Selkup families is the presence of a relatively large number of children. The average number of children per family by the end of the fertility period is 3.1, and a relatively high percentage of families have four children or more (11%+). This notwithstanding, if we compare the number of children per family in the cohort who have just completed the fertility period to those in the cohort whose fertility period was finished two decades ago, there is a reduction in the number of children born. For the Selkup of Tomsk Oblast, the number of children per woman in the senior generation was 3.3, while in the present generation it is 2.9.

Another feature of the Selkup birth rate is a long fertility period. For non-Selkup women in Russia, this period typically spans 10–12 years and the terminus age is 34–35 years of age. For Selkup women, it is 5–10 years longer, and the fourth and additional children are born to women 40 years of age and over.[2] However, the high birth rate among the Selkup is balanced by the high death rate. Since the second half of the 1990s, the natural increase among the Selkup has been negligible and, in certain years, there has even been a decline (**Figure 16.2**).

On the whole, the percentage of the Selkup population that was born between 1996 and 2002 was 1.4–2.2%, and the percent who died during these years was 1.9–3.0%. Therefore, we can see that there is a slow net decline in the Selkup population.

Social and Cultural Characteristics of the Selkup

Knowledge of Native Language

The Selkup of Tomsk province are classified as an endangered group of Aboriginal peoples. However, the knowledge of the native language, which is a major sign of ethnical identification, is consistently falling among the Selkup. According to the 1979 census, 16.8% of the Selkup reported that their native language was Selkup. By the 2002 state census, only 2.5% of the Selkup living in Tomsk Oblast had command of their native language. The result is a shrinkage in the ability to communicate in this native language. This decline is disturbing, because language, along with behavioural norms, morals, law, and folk and professional art, are the key elements of ethnic culture, and a crucial element of self-perception and self-identification of the ethnic community. If we examine **Figure 16.3** (page 306), we see some interesting comparisons.

The figure indicates that the Selkup of Tomsk Oblast are more assimilated into Russian culture than the northern Selkup living in Tyumen Oblast and Krasnoyarsk Krai. Northern Selkup have experienced intensive cultural and elevated intermarriage, and had more preservation of their ethnic individuality. In ethnically mixed areas in the North, both the Selkup language and Russian language are used in everyday communications. The retention of the native language is not due to its being taught in school. Over the 1996–2003 period, the proportion of Selkup who were taught their native language as a subject at the comprehensive school was only 4% in Tomsk Oblast, which is much lower than the 25% average across all Selkup territories.[3] In addition, there is not a single public library with literature in any of the languages used by northern Aboriginal peoples in Tomsk Oblast. In the region where these Indigenous peoples live, there are no schools close to the place of parents' places of work. We would argue that the differences in knowledge and

Figure 16.3: Knowledge of Native Language (%) in 2002

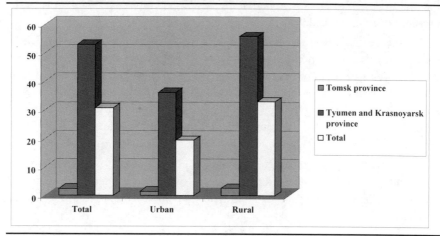

Source: Korennye i malochislennye narody Rossiiskoi Federatsii. Itogi Vserossiiskoi perepisi naselenia 2002 goda. Ofitsialnoye izdanie. (Indigenous peoples of the Russian Federation. The results of the 2002 State Census of the population. Official edition). Volume 13. M.:Federalnaya sluzhba gosudarstvennoi statistiki. 2005, p. 19.

everyday use of traditional languages is explained primarily through living condi-tions and extent of traditional work and activities still pursued by the different territorial groups of the Selkup.

The way of life of the northern Selkup (Yamalo-Nenets Autonomous Okrug) is more traditional than that of the southern Selkup (Tomsk Oblast). The majority of the northern Selkup population are employed in deer breeding, hunting, and fishing. According to many scholars, deer breeding remains the only sector of the traditional economy able to support the Selkup culture, including the use of native language, and all other traditional occupations.

Level of Education

The overwhelming majority of Selkup in Tomsk Oblast have undergone school and vocational training. Approximately 1% of the Selkup population over 15 years of age are illiterate. Almost half of Selkup in Tomsk Oblast (48.2%) have completed some post-secondary training, including post-graduate, graduate, undergraduate, middle special, and primary special (vocational schools based on general education) levels. But among those who have some kind of professional training, those with elementary vocational training dominate (44.4%). Specialists with graduate and undergraduate education make up 6.4% of urban Selkup and only 4.0% in rural areas, which is much lower than the corresponding percent-age for the general rural population of Tomsk Oblast, the SFD, and the national average (**Figures 16.4 & 16.5**).

Figure 16.4: Composition of Rural Population by General Education

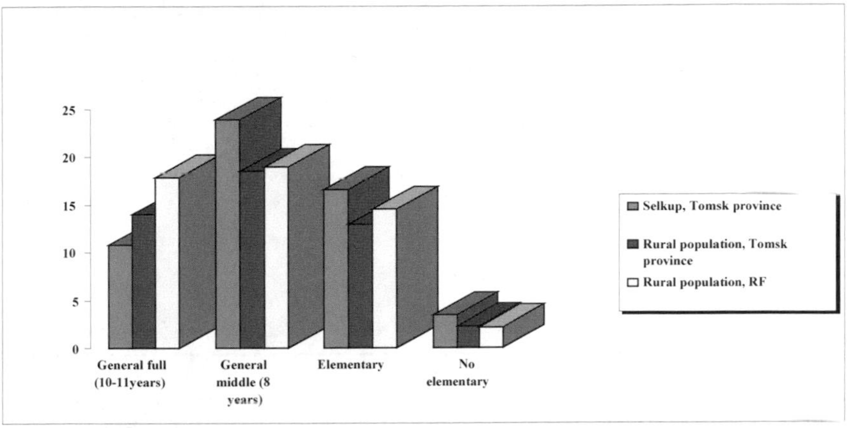

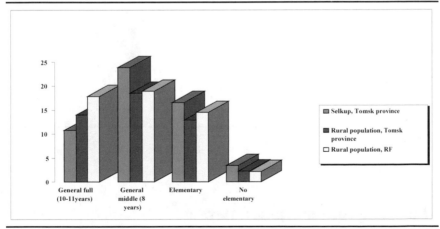

The Results of the 2002 State Census of the Population, %

Source: Korennye i malochislennye narody Rossiiskoi Federatsii. Itogi Vserossiiskoi perepisi naselenia 2002 goda. Ofitsialnoye izdanie. (Indigenous peoples of the Russian Federation. The results of the 2002 State Census of the population. Official edition). Volume 13. M.:Federalnaya sluzhba gosudarstvennoi statistiki. 2005, pp. 238–239.

Figure 16.5: Composition of Rural Population by Professional Education

The Results of the 2002 State Census of the Population, %

Source: Korennye i malochislennye narody Rossiiskoi Federatsii. Itogi Vserossiiskoi perepisi naselenia 2002 goda. Ofitsialnoye izdanie. (Indigenous peoples of the Russian Federation. The results of the 2002 State Census of the population. Official edition). Volume 13. M.:Federalnaya sluzhba gosudarstvennoi statistiki. 2005, pp. 238–239.

Table 16.2. Distribution of Selkup Aged 15–64 by Occupational Classification, %

Classification	Tomsk Oblast	The Yamalo-Nenets AO
Administrators	5.1	2.5
High skilled professionals	9.9	9.1
Middle skilled professionals	9.6	11.8
Office workers	2.5	1.3
Workers in trade, housing and utilities, attendants	12.1	12.2
Skilled agricultural workers	3.5	26.8
Skilled labour	34.1	15.4
Unskilled labour	21.0	17.
Unidentified	2.2	3.3

The Results of the 2002 State Census of the Population, %

Source: Korennye i malochislennye narody Rossiiskoi Federatsii. Itogi Vserossiiskoi perepisi naselenia 2002 goda. Ofitsialnoye izdanie. (Indigenous peoples of the Russian Federation. The results of the 2002 State Census of the population. Official edition). Volume 13. M.:FSGS. 2005, pp. 467–468.

Table 16.3. Distribution of Selkup by Sector

Sector	Tomsk Oblast	The Yamalo-Nenets AO
Agriculture, hunting, forestry	14.6	18.7
Fishing, fish breeding	1.9	19.5
Industry	9.0	5.3
Construction	5.7	3.5
Trade	5.7	1.7
Transportation and communications	13.1	2.1
Real estate business	10.5	4.4
Administration	9.9	5.8
Education	17.5	17.0
Public health	8.3	12.1
Housing and utilities	2.2	7.7

Results of the 2002 State Census of the Population

Source: Korennye i malochislennye narody Rossiiskoi Federatsii. Itogi Vserossiiskoi perepisi naselenia 2002 goda. Ofitsialnoye izdanie. (Indigenous peoples of the Russian Federation. The results of the 2002 State Census of the population. Official edition). Volume 13. M.:FSGS. 2005, pp. 418–419.

The Selkup in the Labour Market

If we examine the tables above we see some interesting patterns. The data indicate that the Selkup are generally employed in a range of occupations. A quarter are managers of different ranks, specialists in the top or middle categories; another quarter are in skilled occupations in different sectors of the economy and 21% are unskilled labourers (**Table 16.2**).

Figure 16.6: Distribution of Selkup Aged 15–64 by Participation in the Economy, the Results of the 2002 State Census of the Population, %

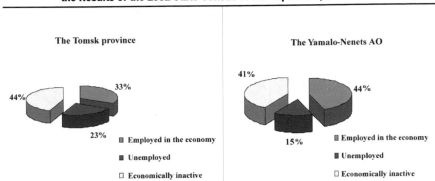

The Tomsk province

44% 33% 23%

The Yamalo-Nenets AO

41% 44% 15%

■ Employed in the economy
■ Unemployed
□ Economically inactive

Source: Korennye i malochislennye narody Rossiiskoi Federatsii. Itogi Vserossiiskoi perepisi naselenia 2002 goda. Ofitsialnoye izdanie. (Indigenous peoples of the Russian Federation. The results of the 2002 State Census of the population. Official edition). Volume 13. M.:FSGS. 2005, pp. 385

Those living in Tomsk Oblast have a higher concentration in the agrarian-industrial category. Besides agricultural production, the Aboriginal people of Tomsk Oblast are involved in the production of oil and electric power, wood carving, wood-related industries, and the conservation and preservation of fish and other sea life.

Those in Tomsk Oblast are involved in different kinds of manufacturing, construction, transport and communications, infrastructure-related services, and horticulture and animal breeding (mainly home production).

By employment status, 98% of the employed in the economy are wage workers and only 2% are self-employed, mostly without hired labour. However, the employment in the sphere of the official economy provides incomes to only one of four Indigenous persons.

Over 40% of the Selkup reported that home food production was their main source of income, while 23% received most of their income from pensions and over 7% from unemployment benefits. There were no notable differences in the income structure between urban and non-urban places, which, in our view, is caused by the tightness of the labour market in Tomsk Oblast, as well as high rates of unemployment (**Figure 16.6**).

The large proportion of the Indigenous population that does not participate in the labour market is noteworthy. According to the 2002 state census, the level of economic activity and employment among the Selkup was far below the national and the SFD average; in addition, unemployment among the Selkup appreciably exceeded these averages. Thus, the share of the Selkup in the economically active population was 55.8% in 2002, while the SFD average was 64.3% and the national average was 65.0%. The level of employment in this period was 33.0%,

Table 16.4. The Distribution of the Selkup Living in Rural Places, Source of Livelihood

Sources of Livelihood	The Selkup of Tomsk Oblast	The Selkup of the Yamalo-Nenets AO
Income from working activity	22.8	29.4
Home food production	47.5	5.8
Stipend	1.6	0.1
Pension (excepting disability pension)	23.1	10.1
Disability pension	3.9	3.7
Benefit (excepting unemployment benefit)	21.5	19.0
Unemployment benefit	8.1	3.0
Other kind of social security	0.1	11.0
Savings	0.2	0.6
Income from property lease	-	0.4
Live in dependence	38.3	43.8
Other source of subsistence	1.0	7.7
Number of reported sources:		
one source	38.1	66.2
two sources	55.9	30.9
three sources	5.8	2.1
four sources	0.2	0.1

% of the Population with these Sources of Livelihood

Source: Korennye i malochislennye narody Rossiiskoi Federatsii. Itogi Vserossiiskoi perepisi naselenia 2002 goda. Ofitsialnoye izdanie. (Indigenous peoples of the Russian Federation. The results of the 2002 State Census of the population. Official edition). Volume 13. M.: FSGS. 2005, pp. 418-419.

57.7%, and 61.2% respectively. The unemployment rate among the Selkup was 22.8% compared to 10.1% for the SFD, and the national average of 8.1%.[4]

In sum, we note that part of the Selkup population has adapted to contemporary economic conditions, occupy relatively high-status positions in the labour market, and are employed in both traditional and modern types of economic activity. However, a considerable proportion of the Indigenous population has insufficient social capital (general and professional education, health status, social networks, etc.) that would allow them to reach high-status positions in the contemporary labour market. A distinctive feature of this group is their low levels of involvement in independent business.

Quality of Life Among Indigenous People in Siberia

Sources and Levels of Income

The sources of income among the Selkup living in rural areas are presented in **Table 16.4**. The range of sources among the Selkup of Tomsk Oblast is broader than that of the northern Selkup. Particularly noteworthy is the relatively small amount of income from employment, compared to the amount from household production (vegetables, potatoes, milk, and butter for both commercial purposes

Figure 16.7: Average Size of Monthly Per Capita Monetary Income in the Indigenous Living Areas (rubles)

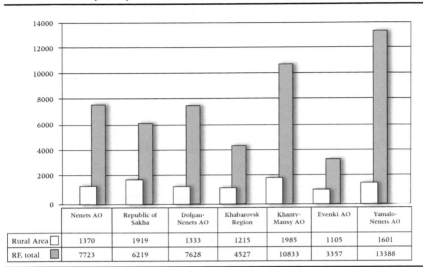

	Nenets AO	Republic of Sakha	Dolgan-Nenets AO	Khabarovsk Region	Khanty-Mansy AO	Evenki AO	Yamalo-Nenets AO
Rural Area ☐	1370	1919	1333	1215	1985	1105	1601
RF, total ▨	7723	6219	7628	4527	10833	3357	13388

Source: Ekonomisheskoye i sotsialnoye razvitiye korennykh malochislennykh narodov Severa. 2002 god (Economic and social development of Indigenous peoples of the North. 2002). M:Goskomstat of the RF, 2003, pp. 23-30.

and personal consumption) in Tomsk Oblast compared to the Selkup of the Yamalo-Nenets Autonomous Okrug. From this perspective, the Ob Selkup are not unlike the majority of rural inhabitants in Russia.

The data from our sampling of surveys on household budgets show that the difference between per capita monetary incomes of different Indigenous peoples in the north and their respective subjects in the Federation is from 12% to 33%, which is a large income gap **(Figure 16.7)**. At the same time, we should note that these figures indicate not only the difference in per capita income between Indigenous and non-Indigenous peoples, but the essential agricultural-industrial payment disparities. Thus, in 2002, the monthly nominal assigned wage in agriculture was 34.2% of that in industry.

A similar situation can be found in the level of income received by Selkup households in Tomsk province where most live in rural areas. Based on data from our sampling of surveys examining household budgets conducted at the state committee of statistics of the Russian Federation in Quarter II 2002, the per capita monetary income of the rural inhabitants of Tomsk Oblast was 1690 rubles, which is in the mid-interval of household incomes for Indigenous people on the whole.

The income distribution reveals very high inequality: Individuals in the 10% highest income group had incomes that were 16.8 times as high as the 10% lowest income group. Within the observed level of per capita monthly monetary income, 66.8% of rural inhabitants had incomes below the subsistence norm; that is, the level of indigence of the rural population was in fact 67%, while in the urban

Figure 16.8: Supply of Housing with Public Utilities in the Indigenous Area of Tomsk Oblast and Russian Federation, 2002, %

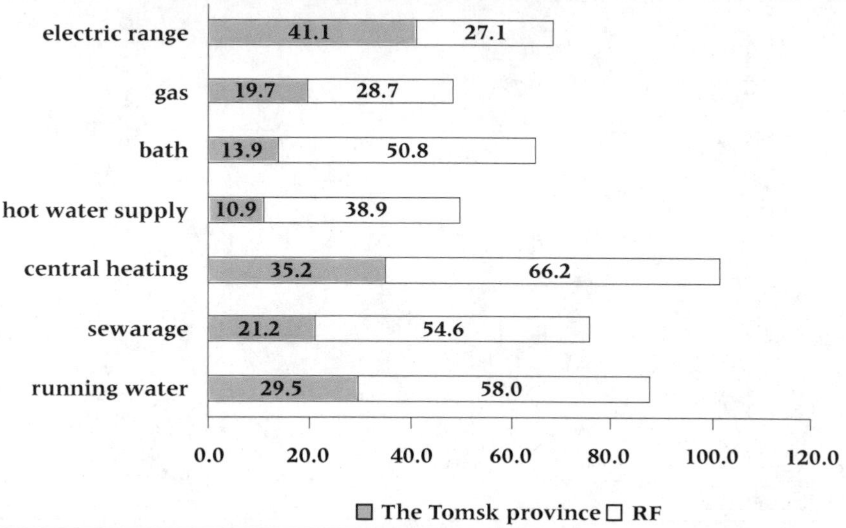

Source: Zhilishchnye usloviya naselenia. Itogi Vserossiiskoi perepisi naseleniya 2002 goda (Housing situation of the population. The results of the 2002 State Census of Population). Volume 11. M:FSGS, 2005, pp.33, 676-677..

population indigent inhabitants made up 42%. It should be noted that the poverty level in the rural population was, at the time, at the national rural average (the percent of the poor was 72.3%, the poverty deficit, 37%). This again confirms that the main source of poverty within the Indigenous population is among those living in rural areas; in particular, the Selkup of Tomsk Oblast experience high levels of poverty, not so much because of their status as Indigenous people, but rather their much lower level of paid employment, and lower per capita monetary income among rural inhabitants. The high concentration of poverty among the Selkup is also associated with their incumbency in lower positions in the occupational status hierarchy as a result of the Selkup generally being less competitive candidates compared to other groups in the population.

Housing Situation

According to the 2002 national census data, about 40% of housing in rural areas of Tomsk Oblast, the main area where the Selkup live, is very old (35 years and over) and dilapidated, as 89%–99% of residential houses of this age are made of wood. The rural housing stock also has few amenities. Only 11.5% of rural households live in buildings and apartments with comforts such as running water, sewage disposal, central heating and hot water, bath or shower, gas or electric ovens, and home telephones. Overall, less than half of the houses in the territory where the Indigenous people of Tomsk Oblast live have amenities commonly found in houses within the Federation **(Figure 16.8)**. A comparison of the housing stock according to rooms per occupant reveals a structural deficit; that is, there is an inconsistency between the number of rooms and household membership. Thus, about half of rural households with three or more members had fewer rooms than members, which means that rooms are shared.

Nutrition of Indigenous People

Nutrition is one of the important components of standard of living that influences rates of reproduction, and life expectancy, which, in turn, determine the supply of labour. The low level of incomes among Indigenous people limits the amount of money available for food expenditures. Food expenditures are structured so that the cheapest items, bread and bakery products such as sugar, confectionery, vegetable oil, and other fats, make up the largest part of dietary goods (20% to 35%). The diet of Indigenous people is characterized by low consumption, and even malnutrition. This trend is seen both in the amount of the foods consumed by food group and their caloric value, which is below the national average.[5] In the areas of the north where the Selkup live, 70% of calories consumed come from carbohydrates; whereas, according to medical-environmental studies, the climatic conditions of the northern areas of Siberia require a diet where 15–16% of calories come from protein, 40%–41% from fat, and 40–42% from carbohydrates. Therefore, the diet of Indigenous peoples in the north do not, in general, provide enough calories or the proper proportions of calories from each food group.

Health Status of the Indigenous Population

Health status is the one of the important characteristics of the pool of potential labour. Individuals must have the capacity to meet the physical and intellectual duties of their work in order to be competitive in the job market. Health, in its turn, is dependent on living conditions, such as income level, quality of nutrition, housing adequacy, personal safety, and social stability in society. These factors account for a great part of changes in health indicators, primarily the death rate. We have already cited data that shows that the proportion of retired age persons among the Selkup is 1.6 times below Tomsk Oblast average and 1.9 times below the average for the non-Indigenous population. The small portion of people living up to retirement age is evidence of the high rate of premature death among the Selkup.

At present, basic medical services that are needed to maintain the health of the population are inadequate to satisfy the demand in areas where the Selkup live. The lack of medical services is the result of the liquidation of medical-obstetric dispensaries, limited access to telephone services, and lack of transportation to centres where these services are available. These deficiencies have contributed to the high and, still rising, morbidity rate. The Selkup, more often than other inhabitants of Tomsk province, and also more often than the inhabitants of the SFD and the Russian Federation, are subject to diseases with "social" origins (e.g., active tuberculosis, alcohol addiction, and psychotic disorders as a result

Table 16.5. Morbidity Rates in Indigenous Area of Living, by Some Classes of Illness per 1,000 Population, Persons:

Class of illness	Tomsk province	Russia
Registered with initial diagnosis	1,032.2	618.3
Neoplasms	11.1	5.2
Mental disorders	12.5	7.3
Blood circulation diseases	23.9	18.4
Respiratory diseases	413.7	267.0
Digestive diseases	47.1	39.5
Bone-muscular diseases	70.4	32.1
Traumas, poisonings, suicide, etc.	88.8	58.4

Source: Ekonomisheskoye i sotsialnoye razvitiye korennykh malochislennykh narodov Severa. 2002 god (Economic and social development of Indigenous peoples of the North. 2002). M:Goskomstat of the RF, 2003, pp. 109–117.

of alcohol consumption) (**Table 16.5**,). Among Indigenous peoples, including the Selkup, 19% to 20% of the adult population meet the criteria for excessive alcohol consumption and/or addiction. It should be noted that the Selkup are ailing more often than both the non-Indigenous population and other Indigenous people in the North. As a rule, morbidity rates among Indigenous people in Tomsk Oblast are 1.5 times higher compared to other Indigenous peoples in all classes of disease.

Our analyses support the conclusion that the Selkup, who are one group of Indigenous people in Siberia, are not a kind of pariah or outcast in present day Russian society. Many problems related to the low quality of life among the Selkup are not the result of their ethnicity per se, but of social and territorial conditions specific to the rural communities in which they live. In addition, the Selkup, like other Indigenous people, face challenges related to poverty, unemployment, inadequate housing, poor health, as well as problems associated with their status and interaction with other cultural groups and changes in their environment. These problems include retention of the language and culture, rights to land and use of natural resources, political self-determination, and development of self-government.

The distinctive feature that characterizes the situation among the Selkup of Tomsk Oblast is that they have assimilated into Russian society, and have lost much of their native language and culture, but have retained their ethnic identity. So, it is not accidental that the Selkup were the first among the Indigenous people of Tomsk Oblast to take part in the formation and development of the social movement aimed at ethnic revival. In September 1989, the foundation congress was held with 87 members of the administrative units from the compact dwellings of the Selkup in attendance. In this congress, the ethnic society of the Tomsk Selkup—Kulta Kup—was established and its charter and program adopted. One of the basic tasks the society articulated at the congress was the creation of cultural, political, and economic structures in the compact dwellings of this group and formation of ethnic rural (village) communities. The ethnic community was seen as one of the main means through which to revive the culture of the Selkup people by restoring its ethno-cultural environment and native language. The authors of the paper "Concept of the Ethno-Political, Economic, and Cultural Development of Indigenous Peoples of the North of Tomsk province"[6] believe that the restoration of ethnic communities that have occupancy of hunting and fishing lands will make it possible to increase interest in these trades among Indigenous people. School curricula teaching trades, physical exercise, local history and geography, and other subjects will make it possible, in the authors' opinion, to transmit knowledge, and skills related to hunting and fishing, to future generations.

The time that elapsed after the Kolta Kup statement of these goals has shown that self-government is one of the most acute and unresolved problems, not only for the Indigenous people of the North, but for the whole population of Russia. The establishment and organization of Indigenous self-government has produced practical difficulties in the harmonization of interests of numerous parties (governments and administrations of different levels, non-Indigenous groups within the population, and various departments and organizations). Apart from this, there is no clarity as to whether this self-government will include all or selected spheres of activity, and cover the whole population or organize strictly according to ethnicity. The main difficulty with using foreign experience as a template is that, where self-government has been implemented in Alaska, Canada, and Greenland, Indigenous peoples make up the majority, while Indigenous people of Siberia, including the Selkup, comprise only a small part of the population in the respective administrative units. This makes it difficult to solve the problem of self-government. The solution seems to be not in searching for a universal approach, but in some non-conventional and non-standard solution. And, finally, it is especially important that the members of Indigenous areas are active participants throughout every step of this process, from the statement of goals, development of tasks, formation of programs, and their implementation in practice. This, however, presupposes that special surveys of the population would be conducted in an area where Indigenous peoples are concentrated to gather information about the matters discussed above. These surveys will yield reliable data about the perceptions of Indigenous inhabitants about the current situation and their views of possible solutions to problems, and possibilities around the creation of the rural ethnic communities, and economic structures in places where there is a concentration of Indigenous peoples.

Conclusions

1. The Selkup, who represent only one group of Indigenous peoples in Siberia, are not pariahs or outcasts in Russian society.
2. Low quality of life is not an issue that is limited to the Selkup popula-

tion; many other segments of Russian society also experience poor living conditions.

3. Many of the existing problems are determined by the specific conditions found in rural communities, which is where 82% of Selkup live, as opposed to by ethnicity itself.

4. Priorities for social policy are to raise employment levels and competitiveness in the labour market; reduce rural–urban disparities in employment income; and reduce unreasonable social regional disparities.

5. The mechanisms that have been used to improve quality of life for all people in Russia should be used to achieve the same goal with the Indigenous people in Siberia.

6. A distinctive feature of the Selkup population in Tomsk Oblast is that in spite of being highly assimilated and having lost their native language and culture, they have retained their ethnic identity.

7. Dealing with political-legal and ethnic-cultural problems requires special approaches and unique solutions.

Endnotes

1 Vassilev, V.I. and S.M. Malinovskaya. Kontseptsiya natsionalno-politicheskogo, ekonomi-cheskogo I kulturnogo razvitiya malochislennykh narodov Severa Tomskoi oblasti (Concept of ethnic-political, economic and cultural development of Indigenous people of the North of Tomsk Oblast). In Issledovania po prikladnoi i neotlozhnoi etnologii, No. 54.

2 Korennye i malochislennye narody Rossiiskoi Federatsii. Itogi Vserossiiskoi perepisi naselenia 2002 goda. Ofitsialnoye izdanie. (Indigenous peoples of the Russian Federation. The results of the 2002 State Census of the population. Official edition). Volume 13. M.:Federalnaya sluzhba gosudarstvennoi statistiki. 2005, 520–523.

3 Ekonomicheskoye i sotsialnoye razvitiye korennykh malochislennykh narodov Severa. 2002 (Economic and social development of Indigenous peoples of the North). M:Goskomstat of the RF, 2003, 46–47. * The SFD data are for the period of November 2003–August 2004

4 Regiony Rossii. Sotsialno-ekonomicheskiye pokazateli. Ofitsialnoye izdaniye (Regions of Russia. Social-economic indicators. Official edition). 2004. M:FSGS, pp. 102, 103, 84–87, 119–120; Obsledovaniye naseleniya po problemam zanyatosti. Avgust 2004 (Employment survey of the population. August 2004). M:FSGS, p. 77; Obsledovaniye naseleniya po problemam zanyatosti. fevral 2003 (Employment survey of the population. February 2003). M:Goskomstat, 318.4

5 Sotsialnoye polozheniye i uroven zhizni naseleniya Rossii (Social Situation and Standard of Living of Russia's Population) 2003. Statistical Volume. M:Goskomstate of the RF. 2003, 254–256.6

6 Vassilev, V.I. and S.M. Malinovskaya. Kontseptsiya natsionalno-politicheskogo, ekonomi-cheskogo I kulturnogo razvitiya malochislennykh narodov Severa Tomskoi oblasti (Concept of ethnic-political, economic and cultural development of Indigenous people of the North of Tomsk Oblast). In Issledovania po prikladnoi i neotlozhnoi etnologii, No. 54.

Notes on Contributors

Jessica Ball

Jessica Ball (MPH, PhD) is a professor in the School of Child and Youth Care at the University of Victoria. She is a third-generation Canadian of Irish and English ancestry, and the mother of a son and a daughter. Over the past decade, she has had the privilege of working in research and education partnerships with a large number of First Nations and urban Aboriginal community-based programs, focusing especially on early childhood development and fathers' involvement. Jessica has also worked extensively in southeast Asia in roles aimed at strengthening capacity to deliver early childhood, youth, and school-based services. Jessica's publications describe this work, particularly the applications of local and Indigenous knowledge in research, in community-based service development, and in professional education (visit **www.ecdip.org** and **www.fnpp.org**).

Dan Beavon

Daniel Beavon is the director of the Research and Analysis Directorate, Indian and Northern Affairs Canada. He has worked in policy research for twenty years and has dozens of publications to his credit. He manages an Aboriginal research program on a variety of issues, increasing the amount and quality of strategic information available to the policy process. Much of his work involves complex horizontal and sensitive issues requiring partnerships with other federal departments, academics, and First Nations organizations.

Darin Bishop

Darin Bishop is a senior researcher and leading expert on Maori Statistics for Statistics New Zealand (Tatauranga Aotearoa).

Robert Bone

Robert M. Bone is a Professor Emeritus at the University of Saskatchewan. His area of expertise is the development of the Canadian North. Dr. Bone is currently serving as Research Advisor to the Inuit Relations Secretariat of Indian and Northern Affairs Canada where he is constructing the 2001 Inuit Database. Professor Bone's other current activities include preparing the next editions of two textbooks—*Regional Geography of Canada* and *Geography of the Canadian North: Issues and Challenges*. He is also collaborating with Professor Robert Anderson to revise the book, *Natural Resources and Aboriginal People in Canada*. In July and August of 2006, Professor Bone taught a summer school class at the University of Saskatchewan.

Coryse Ciceri

Coryse Ciceri was a Research Associate with the Canadian Council on Social Development from July 2003 to March 2006. Coryse has over ten years of experience and expertise in both qualitative and quantitative research skills. Her work at the CCSD included the Council's Urban Poverty project (custom tabulations from census 2001), support and services for adults and children with disabilities (using PALS), and determinants of Aboriginal employment (using census 2001 PUMF).

Brenda Dyack

Brenda Dyack is an economist and policy analyst with CSIRO's Social and Economic Integration (SEI) group which is one of CSIRO's Emerging Science fields, and with the Policy and Economic Research Unit (PERU), which is part of CSIRO Land and Water. She has 20 years of experience as an applied economist and policy analyst. Brenda is involved in projects undertaken under the SEI Emerging Science area in CSIRO with particular interests in ethics, defining policy-relevant scientific research that is integrated with social and economic analysis, and defining protocols for including Indigenous Peoples' knowledge into CSIRO's Water for a Healthy Country Flagship research.

Anthony N. Ezeife

Dr. Anthony N. Ezeife (BSc, MA, MSc, PhD), is a Professor of Mathematics and Science Education in the Faculty of Education at the University of Windsor. A much-travelled educator, Dr. Ezeife has taught, and done extensive cross-cultural research, in several countries across the globe. His main research focus is on making math and science culturally relevant and meaningful to learners in general, and in particular, to students of Indigenous cultural backgrounds. To this end, he has targeted several math/science studies on Canadian Aboriginal students, Native populations in the USA, and some other at-risk learners in diverse cultures in many continents. These include students in West Africa, parts of Asia, and South America. His current study, the Math-Schema project, is based in Walpole Island, Ontario, where he is working with Anishnaabe-speaking First Nations students.

James Ford

Dr. James Ford is a SSHRC Postdoctoral fellow in the Department of Geography at McGill University. His research interests include how Inuit communities deal with environmental change in the context of social, economic, and political changes. He is currently working with the communities of Arctic Bay and Igloolik, NU, identifying characterizing climate-change vulnerabilities associated with sea-ice use and infrastructure. He is also working with youth in Nunavut to explore what climate change means for them. Dr Ford is a contributing author to the IPCC Fourth Assessment Report and has published widely in academic journals and the popular press.

Evlyn Fortier

Evlyn Fortier received her PhD in Philosophy at the University of Ottawa in 1999. She has taught courses in Critical Thinking, Logic, and Ethics at Carleton University, Saint Paul University, and the Dominican College in Ottawa. From 2003 to 2006, Evlyn was a Program Officer at the Institute on Governance. She worked in the knowledge areas Values, Ethics and Risk, Technology Governance, and Building Policy Capacity. Evlyn has conducted research and written reports for a variety of projects, including analysis of issues in Aboriginal governance, international oceans' governance, and health governance.

Ron George

Ron George, whose chief name is Tsaskiy, is a hereditary chief of the Wet'suwet'en Nation in BC. He graduated with distinction with a Bachelor of Social Work, First Nations Specialization degree and is now pursuing his Masters of Education, Leadership Studies degree at the University of Victoria. Tsaskiy has been involved in Aboriginal politics since 1969, serving as elected CEO in the United Native Nations in BC, and the Native Council of Canada in Ottawa, representing off-reserve Aboriginal interests for fourteen years until 1994. He is eight years into his healing journey from marijuana addiction and secondary trauma from residential school and colonialism. He is a single father to Allie (13) and Rowyn (10), to his adult daughters Heather, Vicki, and Rachel and a grandfather to Candice, Gordie, Veronica, and Vince. He is proud of working toward ending the cycle of dysfunction from colonialism within his family.

John Graham

Mr. Graham is a senior executive with over 35 years experience with the federal and Ontario governments, the private sector, the Bank of Canada, and a Royal Commission. He joined the Institute On Governance in 1996 as its Director on Aboriginal Governance. Since that time he has completed over 200 projects for a wide variety of clients and written numerous articles and papers. After receiving an Honours B.A. from Queen's University in mathematics and economics in 1967, Mr. Graham graduated from York University in 1969 with a Masters in Business Administration.

Romy Greiner

Dr. Romy Greiner is the Director and Ecological Economist for River Consulting in Townsville, Queensland, Australia. Dr. Greiner received a PhD from the University of Hohenheim in Stuttgart Germany and has authored and coauthored numerous publications on Aboriginal issues. Prior to working for River Consulting, Dr. Greiner was the Principal Research Scientist/Ecological Economist for CSIRO Sustainable Ecosystems in Canberra.

Éric Guimond

Éric Guimond is of Micmac and French descent and is a specialist in Aboriginal demography. His educational background includes demography, community health, physical education, and Aboriginal studies. He also possesses university research and teaching experience with expertise in projection models of population and Aboriginal groups. He is currently completing PhD studies at the University of Montreal on the topic of ethnic mobility of Aboriginal populations in Canada. Currently, Éric is engaged in projects related to First Nations Housing, Inuit social conditions, and the development of knowledge transfer mechanisms between research and policy. Éric is currently senior research manager at the Strategic Research and Analysis Directorate at Indian and Northern Affairs Canada.

Constantine Kapsalis

Constantine Kapsalis (PhD) is an economic consultant specializing in the areas of labour market analysis, training and education, and social policy. He grew up in Athens, Greece where he completed his undergraduate studies in Business and Economics. Constantine attended the University of Rochester, New York on a full scholarship and received his PhD in economics in 1975. He has worked at the Ontario Economic Council, the Economic Council of Canada, the Department of Regional Economic Development, the Bureau of Management Consulting, and the Canadian Labour Market and Productivity Centre. Since 1996 he has been working as a consultant.

Zemfira Kalugina

Dr. Kalugina is Head of the Department of Sociology at the Institute of Economics and Industrial Engineering at the Siberian Branch of the Russian Academy of Sciences. He is a teaching Professor of Sociology, the Novosibirsk State University. Dr Kalugina is Deputy Editor-in-Chief of the "Region: Economics and Sociology" journal and has authored over 20 monographs on a range of subjects related to development and Indigenous peoples.

Paul Maxim

Paul Maxim became Associate Vice President for Research at Wilfrid Laurier University in July 2006. Prior to that he was with the Department of Sociology at the University of Western Ontario. His primary research interests are in demographic processes and the socio-economic participation of Aboriginal people in Canadian society. He is the author of numerous articles and books including *Quantitative Research Methods in the Social Sciences* and his most recent book, released by UBC Press in September 2003, *Aboriginal Conditions: Research as a Foundation for Public Policy*, co-edited with Jerry White and Dan Beavon.

Sarah Morales

Sarah Morales graduated from the Indigenous Peoples Law and Policy program at the University of Arizona Rogers College of Law in the Spring of 2006.

Mary Jane Norris

Mary Jane Norris is a Senior Research Manager with the Strategic Research and Analysis Directorate of the Department of Indian and Northern Affairs Canada. She has specialized in Aboriginal studies and demography over the past 25 years, and has held previous research positions with the Demography Division of Statistics Canada and the Aboriginal Affairs Branch of Canadian Heritage. As part of her specialization in Aboriginal demography and demo-linguistics, her areas of research and publication include Aboriginal languages, migration, and population projections. She is of Aboriginal ancestry, with family roots in the Algonquins of Pikwàkanagán (Golden Lake), in the Ottawa Valley. Mary Jane holds a Masters in Sociology and a BA Honours in Sociology and Economics from Carleton University.

Katherine Scott

Katherine Scott is the Vice President of Research with the Canadian Council on Social Development in Ottawa. Her employment at the CCSD builds on past experience in government, in the university, and with other research organizations. She is the author of several publications, centering on issues of social and economic inclusion as they affect women, children, and families. More recently, Katherine has written about the profound funding challenges that non-profits currently face. She holds degrees in political science from Queen's University and York University.

Nicholas Spence

Nicholas Spence is a PhD candidate in the Department of Sociology at the University of Western Ontario. Nick will be defending his research and receiving his PhD in early 2007. At present, he is a member of the Aboriginal Policy Research Consortium (International), and after he receives his PhD he will take up the Post Doctoral Fellowship with that consortium. Nick has authored several articles on Aboriginal policy and was co-author on *Permission to Develop* also published by Thompson Educational Publishing.

Svetlana Soboleva

Svetlana Soboleva is a professor in the Department of Social Problems at the Institute of Economics and Industrial Engineering at the Siberian Branch of the Russian Academy of Sciences. Svetlana's research interests include the regional and interregional demographic analysis and population migration; foreign manpower on the Russian labour market; methodologies of regional demographic analysis and the demographic analysis of small national groups; and the demographic aspects of the examination of the ethnic stability of the small national groups of Siberia.

Elsa Stamatopoulou

Ms. Elsa Stamatopoulou, is Chief of the Secretariat of the UN Permanent Forum on Indigenous Issues, Division for Social Policy and Development, UN Department for Economic and Social Affairs. Ms Stamatopoulou has had a distinguished career at the United Nations, serving in the Centre for Human Rights, the Office of the Under-Secretary-General for Administration and Management, and from 1998-2003, in the Office of the High Commissioner for Human Rights. Ms Stamatopoulou is a lawyer by professional training and was born in Greece.

Vera Tapilina

Vera Tapilina is a Senior Researcher at the Institute of Economics and Industrial Engineering at the Siberian Branch of the Russian Academy of Sciences in Novosibirsk, Russia. Vera's research interests include income inequality, economic stratification, poverty, health, and social policy. In addition to working on 85 publications, Vera has lead numerous research projects and participated in a number of world and national congresses and conferences.

John Taylor

John Taylor is a Senior Fellow and Deputy Director at the Centre for Aboriginal Economic Policy Research at the Australian National University. From 1976 to 1986 he held various university research and teaching positions in Botswana and Nigeria before joining the ANU's North Australia Research Unit in Darwin. He was appointed to the Center for Aboriginal Economic Policy Research at the ANU in Canberra in 1991. In Australia, John's research interests have revolved around the measurement of demographic change among Indigenous peoples and assessment of their economic status at varying scales of analysis from the local to the regional and national. Increasingly, this also incorporates international comparisons with North America and New Zealand, particularly in terms of demographic analysis.

Johanna Wandel

Johanna Wandel is a post-doctoral research associate in the Global Environmental Change Group at the University of Guelph. Her research interests are focused on human-environment interaction, with particular emphasis on vulnerability and adaptation of communities in light of global-scale forces. Currently, she has research applications in the Canadian Arctic and dryland agriculture communities.

Whetu Wereta

Whetu Wereta is the General Manager of Maori Statistics for Statistics New Zealand (Tatauranga Aotearoa).

Jerry White

Jerry White was Chair of the Department of Sociology at the University of Western Ontario until June of 2006. He is currently Professor and Senior Adviser to the Vice President (Provost) at Western and the Director of the Aboriginal Policy Research Consortium (International). Jerry is the co-chair of the Aboriginal Policy Research Conference (with Dan Beavon and Peter Dinsdale) and a member of the Board of Governors for Western. He has written and co-written 11 books and numerous articles on health care, and Aboriginal policy, the most recent being *Aboriginal Conditions* (UBC Press) and *Permission to Develop* (TEP). He is co-editor of the 6 volume series on Aboriginal policy research of which this is one volume.

Susan Wingert

Susan Wingert is a PhD candidate in the Department of Sociology at the University of Western Ontario. She is also a Research Associate with the Aboriginal Policy Research Consortium. Her research interests include social inequality, race/ethnicity, culture, and mental health. Currently, her research examines social determinants of mental health in the off-reserve population.

DATE DUE	RETURNED

Canada
2008